WORD FREAK

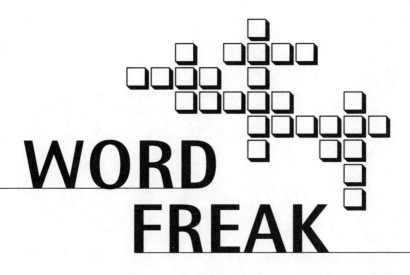

WORD
FREAK

Heartbreak, Triumph,
Genius, and Obsession
IN THE
World of Competitive *Scrabble* Players

Stefan Fatsis

HOUGHTON MIFFLIN COMPANY
Boston · New York

For Lampros, Cindy, and Michael

For information about permission to reproduce selections
from this book, write to Permissions, Houghton Mifflin Company,
215 Park Avenue South, New York, New York 10003.

Visit our Web site: www.houghtonmifflinbooks.com.

Library of Congress Cataloging-in-Publication Data
Fatsis, Stefan.
Word freak : heartbreak, triumph, genius, and obsession in
the world of competitive *Scrabble* players / Stefan Fatsis.
    p.   cm.
ISBN 0-618-01584-1
1. Scrabble (Game) — Tournaments. I. Title.
GV1507.S3 F38 2001
793.734 — dc21   2001016912

Printed in the United States of America

Book design by Robert Overholtzer
Board charts by Leslie Goldman, Cherrio, Ltd.

QUM 10 9 8 7 6

Excerpt from "pulled down shade" copyright © 1992 by Charles Bukowski. Reprinted
from *The Last Night of the Earth Poems* with the permission of Black Sparrow Press.

SCRABBLE® & © 2001 Hasbro, Inc., in the United States and Canada only.

For information on Scrabble® clubs, tournaments, publications, school programs, and
other activities, contact:

    National Scrabble® Association, c/o Williams & Company,
    P.O. Box 700, 408 Front Street, Greenport, New York 11944
    Phone: (631) 477-0033, www.scrabble-assoc.com

Contents

Author's Note

THE WORLD OF GAMES and the world of words are governed by their own sets of elaborate rules. This book is about one game, Scrabble, and the words used in playing that game. So it's only natural that it has a few rules of its own, too.

First, a little background: Organized, competitive, tournament Scrabble differs from the game played at home. A twenty-three-page rule book governs everything from how to select tiles properly (the bag containing them must be held at eye level or higher) to what to do when a player needs to go to the bathroom during a game (a situation that just happens to fall under Rule II P). I've tried to make clear the rules and conventions of tournament play as they arise in the course of the narrative. One, however, bears mentioning up front: Competitive Scrabble is a one-on-one game. Casual games sometimes are played two-on-two or two-on-one, but there are never more than two "sides."

The basic rules, however, are the same regardless of whether one is playing in a tournament or at the beach. The purpose is to make words. Players take turns making them. Points are totaled according to designations on the letters and on "premium" squares on the Scrabble board which double or triple the value of a letter or word. The back of the cover of the box from the first version manufactured in 1948 offers as good an explanation as any of the rules of the game. (If you already know how to play, feel free to skip the next page.)

- Each player draws seven tiles and places them on his rack.

- The first player combines two or more of his letters to form a word and places it on the board to read either across or down with one letter on the center square. Diagonal words are not permitted.

- A player completes a turn by counting and announcing the score for the turn. He then draws as many new letters as he has played, thus always keeping seven letters on his rack.

- The second player, and then each in turn, adds one or more letters to those already played so as to form new words. All letters played in any one turn must be placed in one row across or down the board. They must form one complete word and if, at the same time, they touch other letters in adjacent rows, they must form complete words, crossword fashion, with all such letters. The player gets credit for all words formed or modified by his play.

- New words may be formed by:

  a. Adding one or more letters to a word or letters already on the board.

  b. Placing a word at right angles to a word already on the board. The new word must use one of the letters already on the board or must add a letter to it.

  c. Placing a complete word parallel to a word already played so that adjoining letters also form complete words.

- The score for each turn is the sum of the score values of all the letters in each word formed or modified in the play plus the premium values resulting from placing letters on premium squares.

- When two or more words are formed in the same play, each is scored. The common letter is counted (with full premium values, if any) in the score for each word.

- Any player who plays all seven of his tiles in a single turn scores a premium of 50 points in addition to his regular score for the play.

- Play continues until all tiles have been drawn and one of the players has used all of the letters in his rack or until all possible plays have been made.

The Scrabble board is a fifteen-by-fifteen grid. There are one hundred tiles in a set, ninety-eight letters and two blanks. For reference, the following tables denote the frequency of each tile in the set and their point values.

A-9	D-4	G-3	J-1	M-2	P-2	S-4	V-2	Y-2
B-2	E-12	H-2	K-1	N-6	Q-1	T-6	W-2	Z-1
C-2	F-2	I-9	L-4	O-8	R-6	U-4	X-1	Blanks-2

0 points: Blanks
1 point: A, E, I, L, N, O, R, S, T, U
2 points: D, G
3 points: B, C, M, P
4 points: F, H, V, W, Y
5 points: K
8 points: J, X
10 points: Q, Z

While it isn't necessary to memorize the tile frequencies and point values in order to read this book — or to know anything at all about Scrabble, for that matter — there are a few important notes about the text itself:

• Letters, groups of letters, and words referred to in the context of the game are written in capital letters.

• Blanks are denoted by a question mark.

• Groups of letters are listed in alphabetical order, and the blank or blanks always go last. For instance, a rack containing the letters E, A, M, O, N, D, and a blank would be written as ADEMNO?.

• When a word includes a blank, the letter represented by the blank is written in lowercase. The tiles in the above example can be used to form eight seven-letter words, which would be written as AbDOMEN, ADENOMa (or aDENOMA, depending on whether the blank is designated as the first or last letter), AMiDONE, DAEMONs, MADrONE, MAsONED, MONADEs, and wOMANED.

I occasionally use diagrams to illustrate board positions. The four abbreviations on a diagram represent the premium squares. The abbreviations are DLS (double-letter score), DWS (double-word score), TLS (triple-letter score), and TWS (triple-word score). The center square, a star on the board, is a DWS. Here's an example:

As in chess, Scrabble has a system for indicating the square on which a play starts, and sometimes I'll refer to plays made according to that system. Here's how it works. The position of a play is designated by the location of the first letter of the word. If the word is played horizontally, the designation starts with the number of the square on which the first letter falls. If the word is played vertically, the designation starts with the letter of the square. The notation for the two words in the diagram above are MADrONE 8D and MAYBE D8.

Finally, three symbols often mark words in the text: *, $, and #. The asterisk appears the most frequently. It indicates that a word is a "phony," or unacceptable in Scrabble, like EMAIL* or LONGSHOT*. The other two symbols are used to differentiate between the separate word sources that govern Scrabble in North America and Great Britain. The dollar sign denotes a word acceptable only under North American rules, like MM$ or DREAMLIKE$, while the pound sign refers to a word acceptable only under British rules, like ZO# or DREAMBOAT#.

However, I use the pound and dollar signs *only* when writing about international play, which combines the North American and British word sources. Otherwise, I follow the rules of North American play. For instance, the word QI is acceptable in Britain but not in North America. If that word were to appear in a discussion of a game played under North American rules, it would be written as QI*. But in sections of the book about international competition, it would be QI#.

Accordingly, I wrote *Word Freak* using the two North American word sources as my official references. The main book is the *Official Tournament and Club Word List*, which contains in list form without definitions or parts of speech all acceptable two- through nine-letter words plus their inflected forms. For base words longer than nine letters, the source is *Merriam-Webster's Collegiate Dictionary, Tenth Edition*. (The British word list is *Official Scrabble Words*, which is based on *The Chambers Dictionary*.)

Except for words that are capitalized, hyphenated, contracted, foreign, or part of a multiple-word phrase — the standards for the game — the words in this book between two and fifteen letters long are acceptable in Scrabble. A few, however, are not found in either reference source. For fun, I've listed them in an appendix at the end of the book.

"Virtually everyone suffers from the deeply ingrained habit of considering language as a medium of communication."

— DMITRI BORGMANN, *Language on Vacation*

"Without effort, he had learned English, French, Portuguese, Latin. I suspect, nevertheless, that he was not very capable of thought. To think is to forget a difference, to generalize, to abstract. In the overly replete world of Funes there were nothing but details, almost contiguous details."

— JORGE LUIS BORGES, "Funes, the Memorious"

"Words, words, words. I'm so sick of words."

— ELIZA DOOLITTLE, *My Fair Lady*

1

The Park

THE COPS ARRIVE, as they always do, their Aegean blue NYPD cruiser bumping onto the sidewalk and into the northwest corner of Washington Square Park. There are no sirens or flashing lights, but the late-model Buick does emit a staccato *bwip-bwip* to signal to the public that business is at hand. The drug dealers usually shuffle away, perpetuating the cat-and-mouse game that occurs hourly in this six-acre plot of concrete, grass, dirt, and action in Greenwich Village. The druggies whisper, "Sense, smoke, sense, smoke," as they have for twenty or thirty years, seemingly in tacit agreement with the cops to ply their trade as long as they do it quietly. But now, instead of allowing the dealers to scatter as they normally do, officers in short-sleeved summer uniforms, chests bulging from flak jackets, actually step out of the cruiser, grab a man, and slap on cuffs.

"What's going on?" someone asks.

"They're arresting a drug dealer."

I don't look up.

It is a hot, humid, windless Sunday afternoon in August 1997 in New York City, an asphalt-and-concrete circle of hell. The blacktop is thick with urban detritus — broken glass, bits of yellowed newspaper pages, stained paper coffee cups, dozens upon dozens of cigarette butts. In the southwest corner of the park, hustlers occupying the dozen or so stone tables attempt to lure the unsuspecting. "You *need* to play chess," one of them announces. Tens and twenties are exchanged and surreptitiously pocketed with a glance over the shoulder. Not that the hustlers need worry; on the scale of petty crimes, board-game gambling ranks even below selling $10 bags of marijuana to New York University students. Around the fountain in the center of the park, hundreds gather to watch the street performer of the moment — the juggler, the magician, the guy with the trained monkey that jumps on the arm of a rube. On the south side, the dog people take refuge in their fenced-in, gravel-covered enclosure, where humans and animals eye one another cautiously before succumbing to the bond of their shared interests, dogs and other dogs, respectively. There is hair of all colors and styles, piercings and tattoos that would make Dennis Rodman blush, bikers and skaters and readers and sleepers and sunbathers, homeless and Hare Krishna, the constant murmur of crowd noise floating in the thick air.

None of it matters.

I've already squandered points with consecutive low-scoring plays intended to ditch a few tiles in hopes of picking up better companions for the Q that fortunately, I think, has appeared on my rack. And I got them: a U, two E's, an R, and an S. But the chess clock to my right taunts me like a grade school bully as it winds down from twenty-five minutes toward zero. I have these great letters, but no place to score a lot of points with them. It's only the second time that I've played in Washington Square Park and, frankly, I'm intimidated.

My opponent is Diane Firstman, a fact I know only because she has handwritten and taped her name to the back of each of the standard-issue wooden racks that hold the game's tiles. She is a six-foot-plus, physically awkward woman with short hair and glasses. She carries a clipboard with her personal scorecard — "Diane's Score," it is titled — which contains boxed areas to record her point totals and those of her opponent, each of the words they create, and all one hundred tiles. She marks off the letters as they are laid out in word combinations so she can keep track of what's left in the plaid sack sitting next to the board.

Diane is an up-and-coming player at the Manhattan Scrabble Club, which meets Thursday nights at an old residence hotel in midtown. On her right wrist she wears a watch featuring the trademarked Scrabble logo. On her head is a crumpled San Diego Padres baseball cap, circa 1985. Without knowing, I imagine that excelling at Scrabble is a way for this thirty-something woman to shed whatever insecurities she might have. During a game, shed them she does. I have watched her play another novice, Chris, who chats during play. Among the Scrabble elite this habit might be a highly scorned mind-game tactic known as "coffeehousing," but in this case it's just friendly banter. Worse, Chris *thinks* out loud, and when her brain momentarily short-circuits and she questions Diane's play of the word LEAFS, the retort comes quickly: "Duh! As in leafs through a book!" When Diane makes a particularly satisfying or high-scoring play, she struggles to stifle a smile, rocks her head from side to side, proudly (and loudly) announces her score, and smacks the chess clock with too much élan.

I have made sure that Diane and the others who gather daily at the three picnic tables in this corner of the park know that I'm a newbie. When asked, I say that I'm just learning to play the game. Which in the strictest sense isn't true. Everyone knows how to play Scrabble. Along with Monopoly, Candy Land, and a few other chestnuts, Scrabble is among the best-selling and most enduring games in the two-hundred-year history of the American toy industry. Hasbro Inc., which owns the rights to Scrabble in North America, sells well over a million sets a year. Around a hundred million sets have been sold worldwide since the game was first mass-produced in 1948. In some households, Scrabble is extricated from closets around the holidays as a way for families to kill time; in others, it's a kitchen-table mainstay. Regardless, say the word "Scrabble" and everyone knows what you're talking about: the game in which you make words.

But it's much more than that. Before I discovered Washington Square Park, I was aware of the game's wider cultural significance. Scrabble is one of those one-size-fits-all totems that pops up in movies, books, and the news. I once wrote an article that mentioned the Scrabble tournament that Michael Milken had organized in the white-collar prison where he did time for securities fraud. There's the scene in the movie *Foul Play* in which one little old lady plays the word MOTHER and another extends it with FUCKERS. *Mad* magazine has regularly made fun of the game. (A 1973 feature on "magazines for neglected sports" included *Scrabble Happenings*: "My Wife

Made XEROXED on a Triple . . . So I Shot Her!") Scrabble has appeared in *The Simpsons* and *Seinfeld,* the Robert Altman films *3 Women* and *Cookie's Fortune,* the Cary Grant snoozer *The Grass Is Greener,* and the seventies comedy *Freebie and the Bean.* In *Rosemary's Baby,* Mia Farrow uses Scrabble tiles to figure out that the name of her friendly neighbor Roman Castevet anagrams to that of a witch named Steven Marcato.

Rosie O'Donnell regularly talks about her Scrabble addiction. Higher brows love it, too. In a bit about mythical Florida tourist traps, Garrison Keillor lists the International Scrabble Hall of Fame. Charles Bukowski's poem "pulled down shade" ends with the lines: "this fucking/Scotch is/great./let's play/Scrabble." Vladimir Nabokov, in his novel *Ada,* describes an old Russian game said to be a forerunner of Scrabble. The game is a cultural Zelig: a mockable emblem of Eisenhower-era family values, a stand-in for geekiness, a pastime so decidedly unhip that it's hip. In places like the park, I'm learning, it also embodies the narcotic allure of strategic games and the beauty of the English language.

I have been dabbling in Scrabble since I was a teenager. There is a summer-vacation photo of my two older brothers playing with two older cousins; barred from their game, I — somewhat pathetically but what choice do I have, really? — am relegated to keeping score. Like many childhood snubs, this one haunts me into adulthood. In the last years of high school, I play late-night games with a friend on the next block, a couple of decent suburban kids listening to seventies rock and killing time before the next sports event or night of bar- and diner-hopping.

Around the same time, my brother Lampros gets hooked on the game. He is eight years my senior and mathematically inclined; he scored a perfect 800 on his SAT and taught me square roots when I was in the second grade. It's the middle of the lost decade of his twenties, and Lamp is on a long-term plan to graduate from M.I.T. He's got plenty of time on his hands, so when he and his journalism-student roommate pick up the game, he becomes obsessed. He masters the two- and three-letter words. He stays up all night reading the newly published Scrabble dictionary. The two play marathon sessions, and keep a running dime-a-point tally of their scores, which they apply against utility bills. I think them weird. And cool.

But I'm never much intrigued until a girlfriend and I christen our blooming love with a travel set. We tote it to the Canadian Rockies and the Grand Tetons, to Greece and Turkey, to a ranch in Colorado and an adobe in Santa Fe, to Vermont ski chalets and Hamptons beach motels, where we play constantly, recording the date and place of each encounter. She presents me with a copy of the *OSPD* — *The Official Scrabble Players Dictionary* (first edition) — with the following inscription: "For consultation only. NO memorizing!" And though I abide her request regarding the dictionary, I win too often. "Why do you even want to play with me?" she asks after one especially lopsided contest, and my heart sinks as I realize that this refuge in what has become an otherwise imperfect life together is forever gone. When the time comes to divide our belongings, book and board are mine.

Panicking, I lay down the obvious QUEERS, aware somehow that I am doomed.

A good living room player. That's what John D. Williams, Jr., had dubbed me, and if it sounds like a backhanded compliment, that's because it is. From a storefront office on the eastern shore of Long Island, Williams runs the National Scrabble Association, the governing body of the game. Many top players, I learn, resent his authority, but he's also partly responsible for the wild growth of tournament play in recent years. The NSA, which is independent of but funded predominantly by Hasbro, publishes a Scrabble newsletter received by about 10,000 people, keeps track of the ratings of some 2,300 active tournament players, sanctions 200 clubs, and oversees 150 tournaments a year, twice as many as a decade earlier. The national championship the previous summer had attracted 400 players. In a few months, Williams tells me, Hasbro and the NSA will host the world championships, with players from thirty countries, some of whom barely speak English.

I had proposed a game against Williams as a starting point for the quest I had hatched with friends on New Year's Day: to become a competitive Scrabble player. Why? I couldn't say exactly. I had read a recent *Sports Illustrated* story about the eccentric, apparently cutthroat world of competitive Scrabble and thought, I've played this game, I can do that. My newlywed friends Jonathan and Lynn Hock had been squaring off daily and would call to brag about seven-letter words and high-scoring contests. I joined them for occasional three-handed games, hoping that engaging in a cherished pastime from my old relationship would help me mourn its demise. In the aftermath of the breakup, I conveniently blew out a knee playing soccer and spent most of my nights in obsessive postsurgical rehab. But physical therapy was winding down. I needed something to do. I needed, horrors, a hobby.

En route to Jon and Lynn's Upper West Side apartment to ring in the new year with a few games, I stopped in a Barnes & Noble and bought every Scrabble-related book on the shelf, including (a mistake, I later learned) the third edition of the *OSPD*. To record the first step of my journey, we photographed the board. Weeks later, I called John Williams to propose a friendly game. My goal: to lose, and lose badly. After all, this was supposed to be a journey. Odysseus wandered around for ten years. Columbus's crew nearly mutinied before he happened upon land. The Donner party starved in the mountains.

"You just might win," Williams says as we sit down to play in his midtown hotel room.

"Yeah, right," I reply, clinging to my script.

Williams plays CARED to open the game, scoring 22 points. I draw a bingo — a play using all seven of one's tiles, worth an extra 50 points — on my first turn: LEAPING, which I place below the last two letters of CARED, forming EL and DE. "There you go," Williams says, before pointing out that PEALING would have been worth more. But I am unaware that PE, which I could have made by placing the P above the E in CARED, is an acceptable word (it's a Hebrew letter). After a few low-scoring turns for each of us, I lay down SQUIRE, and suddenly I'm ahead, 139–44. A few plays later, I throw down another bingo, RESIDUE, for 77, and my lead grows to 233–116.

"I will say you're getting great tiles," Williams remarks. It's true, I already have pulled both blank tiles, three of the four precious S's, the lone Q accompanied by a U, and a bunch of E's and R's. Still, I think, he could be a little more generous. But then Williams says, "Not only are you getting great tiles, you know what to do with them," and I feel a touch guilty for my ungracious thought.

I play LOGE for 13. He plays DICE for 27. I play ZEST for 41. Score: 287–140.

"I'm surprised you didn't have a Y for ZESTY and a double-word score," Williams cracks, gibing me for my good fortune. He passes his turn, trading in an I, O, R, and two U's. Okay, so maybe I am getting good tiles. I play WIDTH on a triple-word score for 36. I play TAX on a triple-word score for 30. I finally do get that Y, and play YAM for 21: 391–202. FIT for 30, NO for 17. When it's over, I have beaten the executive director of the National Scrabble Association, 457–277.

"Holy shit," I remark, trying not to gloat.

"You're not kidding," Williams replies. "This may be the worst I've ever lost. I couldn't manage my rack. It wasn't happening."

"By the way, that was my highest score ever."

"Glad I could help."

I ask Williams to assess my current ability, and my potential.

"You're probably like an eleven hundred player," he says. Player ratings in Scrabble are based on the Elo system for rating chess tournaments and range from 500 at the bottom to over 2000 at the top. "You could be a twelve hundred player. It's hard to tell after one game. Your strategy is sound. Clearly, you're a good living room player."

Humph. Surely, I think, I'm better than that.

A few weeks later, we stage a rematch. I lose, 502–291.

By the time of my first game against Diane, I have been watching the parkies for three weeks. During my first visit, I sit on a concrete wall behind the forest green picnic tables where the parkies play and I observe. During my second visit, I wait for an invitation to a game, and when I get one, I lose, but just barely, to a regular named Herb. My third summer weekend in Washington Square, the parkies begin to recognize me, asking my name again and how much I play. "Just learning the game," I demur, tossing off the deliberately self-effacing line that is becoming my mantra. I ask how often there is a game. "Weekends," says Herb. "For those who have day jobs, that is. Those who don't . . ." His voice trails off. "They're here every day."

Always, the same faces are huddled over the banged-up rotating boards, and everyone smokes. There's a well-built African-American guy with doe eyes and salt-and-pepper hair named Alan Williams, a general contractor who takes long drags and ponders his moves for long stretches. A regular opponent of his is Aldo Cardia, who is always dressed in black slacks and a white shirt because he runs a local restaurant. Aldo rides over on a three-speed bicycle, Scrabble board, clock, and dictionary stowed in a front basket. An excellent bridge player, Aldo spent a full winter studying words before getting behind a board in the park and now is a top player here. I meet Joe Simpson, a curmudgeonly African-American World War II veteran usually dressed in a beret and army fatigues. There's a woman with blue nail polish who's loudly kibitzing other people's games. There's Steve Pfeiffer, whose name I learn because it is spelled out in Scrabble tiles glued to the back of a double-long rack. Pfeiffer is a New York Scrabble legend who played in the first sanctioned tournaments back in the mid-1970s. He's topless, with a blue windbreaker covering his legs. Pfeiffer is playing another expert-level player, Matthew Laufer, who also has doffed his shirt in the heat, exposing an ample gut and underwear protruding from the rear of his pants. Matthew seems to have a predilection toward random proclamations about Scrabble, language, or virtually any other subject. Matthew tells me he is a poet.

"You know, you're better off with one E than two E's," he says. "And you're better off with one S than two S's."

I make a list of some of the words laid out on the boards: LEZ, GOBO, VOGIE, TAOS, FOVEAL, GUID, MOKE, JEREED, LEVANTER, ZAYIN, GLAIVES, SHELTIE, DOVENED, CAVIE. They all are alien to me. And as for my beloved Q, I learn that it is a Trojan horse. Sure, it and the Z are the only tiles worth 10 points, but clinging to the Q for too long in hopes of a big score, as I did against Diane, prevents you from drawing letters that offer a fresh chance for a bingo. A lingering Q is like an unwanted houseguest, gnawing on your nerves, consuming your attentions, refusing to take the hint and get lost. I've let the visitor raid the refrigerator, plop his feet on the coffee table, and channel-surf.

Even the least accomplished competitive players memorize all of the acceptable Q words that don't require a U (there are ten, plus their plurals), with QAT the most frequently played. But, novice that I am, I pass up QAT as too skimpy for my precious high-scoring letter, hoping instead that randomly plucking tiles from the bag will lead to the kind of play that would move Diane to whack the clock and announce her score with smug self-satisfaction. QUEERS isn't it. It is worth too few points to have justified inaction for so long. (In competitive Scrabble, each player has twenty-five minutes to complete a game; "go over" on time and you are penalized 10 points per minute.) It is the result of ineptitude, and of desperation. Desperate Scrabble players normally lose.

And I do. The Q play unnerves me. Diane turns a tight game in which we trade bingos on our second turns (she KINDLING, me RESOUNDS) into a rout. For good measure, she ends the game with another bingo, REDIRECTS. "Eighty-six," she chirps. *Whack.* Final score: 429–291.

Oh, well, I think, I'm just learning the game.

On my subway rides back and forth to the park, I study a list of the ninety-seven two-letter words and nearly one thousand three-letter words which John Williams had given me. I see a license plate and wonder whether KEW is a word. (It isn't.) I see the Yankees pitcher Graeme Lloyd's name on the TV screen and anagram it: MEAGER DOLLY. I learn the U-less Q words. I lose to Diane three more times in the park. I make notes: "1. Need to learn my threes. Some doubts on twos during game. 2. Clock — over on all three games. 3. Feel pressure when game close. 4. Diane not so obnoxious."

And after a few weeks in the park, I realize I have made a small impression. Matthew, the poet, says while I play Diane, "This guy could be dangerous." I'm not sure if it's praise or sarcasm, whether I'm viewed as fresh meat or a potential *player.* But I'll take it. Diane and the others invite me to the Thursday-night games at the midtown hotel.

The beginners, someone notes, gather at 5:30.

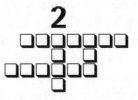

2

The Best

M ATT GRAHAM is popping pills.
It's unclear which ones he's downing at precisely this moment, but the possibilities seem endless. Plastic containers are scattered on the end tables, on the desk, next to the television, inside drawers. Zinc. Caffeine. Glucose. Glycine. L-phenylalanine. Pyroglutanic acid. Taurine. Tyrosine. Next to the sink, atop the toilet tank, spread across the bed. On a five-by-seven index card, Graham has written in one column the names of twenty pills to be taken in the morning on an empty stomach; in another column, he has listed seventeen more to be downed with breakfast. NADH. Glutamine. Herb for Men. Mega Mind. Gotu kola. Potassium.

Graham squeezes a few drops of DMAE-H3 into a glass of cranberry-orange-flavored Blast Off II, a powdered amino-acid concoction containing twenty-one vitamins and minerals — and, more to the point, eighty milligrams of caffeine — per serving. The label reads: "Excessive consumption of tyrosine or phenylalanine may cause symptoms of excessive stimulation such as tremors, rapid heartbeat, irritability, or insomnia."

"This stuff," Graham announces, "turned me around more than anything else."

We are in Washington, D.C., in Room 611 of the gilt- and marble-adorned Mayflower Hotel, where every president since Herbert Hoover has held an inauguration party. It's 7:55 A.M. on a cold Monday in late November 1997, and the tyrosine is kicking in. In precisely sixty-five minutes Graham will play a best-of-five-games match against Joel Sherman to determine the world Scrabble champion. Six feet tall, with a buzz cut on a long, narrow head that is dominated by wide, energetic eyes, Graham is a thirty-two-year-old standup comedian who wears unbuttoned flannel shirts over old T-shirts; droopy, tattered jeans; and high-top Nike basketball sneakers. He talks rapidly, his mind racing ahead of his thoughts. He refuses to see an orthopedist about a damaged knee that sometimes leaves him hobbling in pain. He doesn't sleep much, doesn't eat much, and doesn't relax much, certainly not on this morning. The pills, of course, have something to do with it; if they drug-tested in Scrabble, Matt Graham would be banned for life.

The hotel room reflects the man. Housekeeping has left a voice-mail message apologizing for not making the bed or cleaning the bathroom, but the maid was afraid to touch anything. There are copies of *Sports Illustrated* and *Playboy's Nudes*. Myriad cassette tapes are scattered across the bed: Indigo Girls. Bad Religion. R.E.M. The Proclaimers. Super Hits of the '70s, Volume 10. There's a fading photograph of Graham's grandmother, a computer mouse pad in the shape of a Shar-Pei ("It's a lucky charm," he says), a red and white stocking cap, and pens with smiley faces on one end. More bottles: Ginseng. Lipoic acid. Ashwagandha. Healthy Greens. Coenzyme Q. Pygeum, a prostate drug promising "Natural Health Care for Men Over 50." Suphedrine. Herbal Formula for Men. ("The reason I take this is it's got ma huang, which is ephedrine, which is a stimulant," Graham says, as if there were any doubt.)

There are index cards plastered with obscure words. A Cookie Monster doll. A copy of the December 1993 issue of a Scrabble newsletter called *Medleys* which includes an article about that year's world championships titled "On Crowns and Clowns." The piece takes a potshot at Graham, who was then just emerging on the Scrabble scene but qualified for the event in New York nonetheless. "We sent a few of our best — and a few comedians," the article notes. "I brought it for inspiration," Graham says. "A lot of petty fuckers in this game." And there are the stuffed animals: the bear, the gorilla, the lucky manatee. Graham won't play without the lucky manatee.

All of it — the junk, the souvenirs, the "smart drugs" he ingests like a bird pecking from a feeder — has one purpose: to help Matt Graham win, to beat not only Joel Sherman but everyone who resents the fact that he doesn't study as obsessively as they do, that he is an outsider in an insider's game, that he doesn't join in the rabid on-line discussion groups or perform in the annual talent show at the Atlantic City tournament or show up for the Thursday-night sessions at the Manhattan club.

"Different breed of cat," says Marlon Hill, one of Graham's few friends on the competitive Scrabble circuit, an African-American guy from inner-city Baltimore and an expert himself, who is helping Graham prepare for the championship match. "Fucking alien."

Might as well be a UFO convention. The Scrabble tournament scene, it turns out — and I'm shocked, *shocked* — isn't the most highly functional subculture around. "We're dealing with some borderline pathology here," Charlie Southwell, a former highly ranked player who is directing the World Scrabble Championship, says as he surveys the hotel ballroom where eighty top players are competing.

My limited exposure in Washington Square Park has prepared me well. I arrive on the third day of the four-day tournament and, as a journalist, am given free roaming rights on the playing-room floor. Southwell and John Williams, who has invited me to attend, point out the exotic mammals in their natural habitats. There's Adam Logan, a red-bearded, mathematics doctoral student at Harvard, padding around in short pants and holey socks, his hands pulled inside his shirtsleeves like a shy schoolgirl. There's Bob Felt, a former national champion, notorious for his rambling monologues about long-forgotten games and his slovenly appearance; at this moment his fly is open. There's Joel Sherman, who calls himself a professional Scrabble player. He lives in the Bronx with his brother and father and hasn't worked in years, ostensibly because of a *Merck Manual*'s worth of physical disorders; his most notorious is a volcanic gut that has earned him the nickname G.I. Joel, as in gastrointestinal. There's Joe Edley, who in addition to being a two-time national champion is associate director of the National Scrabble Association and perceived as arrogant by his peers. When I first encounter Edley, he is lecturing Felt for messing up the score of their game, a fact that went uncorrected and has affected the pairings for the next round of play. Overhearing the exchange, an expert-level American woman not participating in the event mutters about Edley, "Busy, busy, busy. He plays. He administrates. Prick."

Graham started the tournament with a 2–4 record, but by the time I arrive he has reeled off ten straight wins, a feat unmatched in the history of the Worlds, and one of the greatest pressure-packed streaks ever. When I first glimpse Matt, he is wearing a Walkman, inhaling nose spray, and swallowing a handful of unidentified pills. Then he sits down to play Joel, who extracts a piece of pita bread from a mug of water and eats it. Matt whips him by a score of 576–327 to improve to 13–4. "He might run the table," says Marlon Hill, who seems to be president of the Matt Graham Fan Club. "It's like DiMaggio's fifty-six."

Joel has a different perspective. "Matt just got every fucking thing in the world," he says. "That game probably cost me twenty-five thousand. Somehow it always goes this way. I always get blown out in the key game. He just played EGOTISE# in the last game on the second play. This time he did it for twenty points more." Joel belches. It's his stomach talking. He can't control it.

Matt wins his next game, and the one after that. Thirteen straight wins. Two to go. The top two finishers will play in the finals. Matt, Joel, and Edley are in the strongest position to advance. First prize is $25,000. Second prize is $10,000. It's not the World Series of Poker, where the winner takes home $1 million, but to these players it's not small change, either. "I owe my mom ten thousand or she's going to throw me out of my apartment," Matt says. "I'm maxed on one of her credit cards for twenty thousand." Standup comedy, which Matt does part-time when he isn't studying words or playing games, is not a lucrative vocation, and neither is Scrabble.

In the hallway between rounds, the players and spectators — which include a number of top American experts who didn't qualify for the event — gather to pore over the results and swap stories about great plays or tricky board positions. I listen attentively, struggling to understand the Scrabble argot. Even more than I was in the park, I'm amazed by the words I'm seeing played, and there's a reason: British Scrabble has a more expansive word source than does Scrabble in North America, an additional thirty thousand or so two- through eight-letter words above the one hundred thousand in the *OSPD*. At the Worlds, words found in both the *OSPD* and the British word source, *Official Scrabble Words,* or *OSW,* are acceptable. (Play using both word sources is known as SOWPODS, a pronounceable combination of *OSPD* and *OSW.*) "Ours or theirs?" is a commonly asked question, meaning, Is that word in our (the North American) or their (the British) dictionary?

I came looking for a story, and I found one. I came wondering whether this world was interesting enough to write about, and I wasn't disappointed. But I didn't expect to get so absorbed so quickly. I'm blown away by the plays — HAFTAROT$, NITCHIE$, OXTERING#, RATICIDE$, ANGIOMAS. I'm drawn to the intense concentration and complex banter. After losing to Matt, Joel, a balding, sunken-eyed thirty-five-year-old, is kneeling on his chair hovering over the board. "Oh, shit. OUTEDGES# is good," he says. "I could have bingoed instead of playing UDO. I could have been in the game, darn it. I could have bingoed right through the G." "Oh, Jesus Christ," he says a bit later. "I missed FILARIID$. That's bad. That's disgraceful. There's no reason I shouldn't have spotted that. I was just making incredibly stupid plays." He's suffering, I think, he's really suffering.

By the time I observe my third game in the room, I'm running scores to a woman who is posting the results on a Web site. I'm hanging on the results. The park felt casual, an intellectual challenge more than a competitive one. But this — the money, the tension, the pressure, the egos, the pride, the prestige. This isn't just about playing a board game. This is about skill and achievement and self-worth.

Standing at the front of the playing room, rapt with wonder, I think: I want to be able to do what they do. I want to be one of these people.

Matt Graham has never beaten Joe Edley in a tournament, and now he faces him in the twentieth game of the twenty-one-game event. If Matt wins, Edley is out of contention for the finals.

"He get to eliminate you," the Fila-wearing, trash-talking Marlon Hill says to Edley.

"No, actually I have a good record against Matt," Edley replies.

"That mean he due," Marlon says.

But he don't. Joe beats Matt, but not without controversy: Matt accuses Joe of coffeehousing. "I opened with QUINOA, and he says,

'That's a good sign — for me,'" Matt relates after the game. "Then on the second play, I play ZINCKES*, and he says, 'Well, that looks like a good sign — for you.'" Matt says Joe made the remark before Matt had hit his clock, ending his turn. And once he did, Joe challenged the word, which was indeed a "phony," costing Matt his turn. "Just to screw with me. It's an absolute absurdity that it continues. He makes the rules. And he violates all the principles of etiquette. He doesn't shut his mouth."

"Yeah, he's outrageous," Bob Felt concurs.

"I don't think it disrupted my play a lot, but it made me more conservative," Matt says. "It upset me. I'm concerned about getting into the finals. It's weird. Other people's coffeehousing doesn't bother me that much. But him, because of his position . . ."

Matt stalks off, donning his Walkman and heading to his room between games. He has a 15–5 record and has to play Edley, who is 14–6, again in the next round. Edley still can advance to the finals, but he needs to win by 138 or more points to do so. (Ties between players with the same record are broken based on "spread," the difference between the total number of points scored by a player during an entire tournament and the total number of points allowed. Joe needs to score 138 points more than Matt in order for his spread to exceed Matt's.) Joel Sherman, who rebounded from two losses to Matt, can clinch a spot with a win over a teenager from Bahrain. Matt won't let the previous game go. "I'm just so outraged. And he knows I'm an emotional player."

Edley is a master of calm who meditates and practices tai chi chuan before games. His unflappable behavior is easily perceived as arrogant detachment, or, as by Matt, psychological arson. Matt is so tightly wound that Edley's mere presence seems to unnerve him. Now Edley is staring at the table, breathing deeply, barely even blinking. He takes a quick lead, but Matt stays close. I don't know most of the words they are playing: ELOINERS, REZ#, NONSOLAR. I check on G.I. Joel's game.

"Any idea what's going on there?" Jan Dixon, one of the top American women players, who is spectating, asks me.

"Joel's kicking ass," I report.

"Good," Jan says. "Because I think Edley could pull this one out and still not make it."

Edley wins by 99. Not enough. The players shake hands, all slights momentarily forgotten in a display of sportsmanship. Matt will play G.I. Joel in the finals the next morning.

I meet Joel in his room late that night. My Scrabble-playing friend Jon is shooting film for a possible documentary, and Joel is a willing subject. He's been down this road before, posing in *Sports Illustrated* on the edge of a bathtub in his BVDs, reading a word-list book. Joel apparently likes flaunting his idiosyncrasies. And I don't get the sense he's acting. For our encounter, he's wearing mismatched striped flannel pajamas — a red, white, and blue top with a gray, white, and maroon bottom. He rips down the bedcovers and stuffs a blanket in the closet, then climbs in bed and reads a dictionary while Jon stands on the mattress to get an overhead shot. An inhaler rests on an end table, asthma being one of Joel's ailments.

Joel tells us about his life. How he mostly just plays Scrabble, having opted out of the working world because he was physically unable to sustain his job. How he sleeps but four hours a night. How he figures he's going to win.

"This is definitely the biggest deal he's ever had in Scrabble," Joel says of Matt. "Although we've expected him to reach this level. But I can't imagine he's going to win five in a row from me. I don't know anybody who's capable of beating me five in a row head to head."

Joel has another thought, about being awarded the first-place trophy, a silver cup. "I hope I can lift it," he says. "I'm kind of a weakling."

For his prefinals dinner, Joel wore a suit and tie, tucking his napkin into his collar, and splurged on lamb chops in the hotel dining room. Matt had one and a half beers and a bag of chips. He's skipping breakfast but will have a couple of MET-Rx energy performance bars. And, of course, the regimen of pills.

"I can be a little haphazard as my own pharmacist once in a while," Matt tells me as he prepares on the morning of the finale. "But I try not to take anything that would contraindicate.

"I used to be heavy into protein, but now I find that carbs are better. While they won't make me super sharp in the first game, they'll help in the fifth game."

Because he snores, Marlon slept on the floor of the hotel-room closet so as not to disturb Matt. They fight like a codependent couple, but Matt considers Marlon a lucky roommate.

Matt sits on the edge of the bed eating a peanut butter MET-Rx bar. "I think I might need some Claritin," he says.

Marlon had unnerved Matt by saying that another player was giving Matt a funny look after one of the games against Edley. Matt suddenly remembers his anger, and launches in on Marlon. "I need to know who gave me a funny look," he says. "No one," Marlon replies, knowing it's no time to freak out his nervous friend even more. "Then shut up, asshole," Matt says.

Marlon lets it drop. Before we head downstairs, Marlon helps Matt conduct a final inventory.

"What do I need when I play?" Matt asks rhetorically.

"You got your cow?"

Matt nods and races off down the hall, hauling his bag of supplies — manatee, stress ball, smart-drug concoction, distilled water, lucky pencil, clipboard.

"He just said, 'Shut up, asshole,'" Marlon says to me. "Crush him like a fucking bug. Most high-strung guy. I stay friends with him because I don't have many friends. We share this in common."

The finals are staged in a small room outfitted with camera equipment so the games can be televised on closed circuit to the rest of the players, who gather in the main playing room. It's an elaborate production: a camera suspended over the board, others trained on Matt and Joel, others on their racks. In the hallway before play starts, Matt proposes to Joel that they split the prize money — $20,000 to the winner, $15,000 to the loser. Joel refuses. He combs his hair, puts on a gray sweatshirt that says G.I. JOEL on it, and stretches in a corner. He kicks his left leg up toward an outstretched hand, stumbles, then kicks the right one. He stretches his arms overhead. He burps. He pulls one leg back.

"Suddenly he's Joe Edley," Matt cracks.

Matt goes first and plays FUSTIAN, a cotton fabric. Joel plays DJIN. Matt plays MiSTHrOW$, using both blanks. Joel plays TORNADIC. In the playing hall, England's Mark Nyman, a former world champion who is doing play-by-play commentary, notes the possibility of extending FUSTIAN to RUMFUSTIAN#, a drink containing port or sherry mixed with hot water and spices. These guys are scary.

As the game progresses, the tight board prevents Joel from making a comeback. "Apparently there's a blockage problem," Nyman says. "Usually when there's a blockage problem it refers to G.I. Joel."

Matt wins the first game. He bounces out to a lead in the second, and his spokesman, Marlon, is shouting, "World champ." But Matt misses a play the other experts spot — BOWNED# — and Joel ekes out a win. He does the same in the third game, and the crowd boos when Matt misses a big score with the common word BERTH and plays HERB instead. "I just missed it," he says afterward. "Maybe I need more coffee."

Before the fourth game, Joel suddenly tears down the hallway.

"He does that all the time," John Williams tells me when I express concern. "Bathroom."

Upon returning, Joel announces, "I just want to warn everyone in the room during the next game that the reason I'm called G.I. Joel will become evident."

Matt ingests more caffeine. Joel belches.

Joel jumps out to a 304–218 lead — a respectable final total in most living room games — and Matt needs to score big before Joel shuts down the board, that is, closes off the places where Matt can bingo. So he takes a risk on an iffy word, laying down FLEXERS for 101 points.

"I want to check," Joel says, challenging the play. (Under the so-called "free challenge" rule used in international competition, a player who challenges a word that turns out to be acceptable isn't penalized with a loss of turn, as under North American rules.)

"I hope it's good," Matt says. "There's an understatement."

It's not, and Joel plays defense. After a few more turns, it's clear that Matt doesn't have a chance, especially when he draws a rack consisting of the letters DLPRSTV.

Joel looks as if he would topple in a light breeze.

He gets a standing ovation from his peers. He manages to hoist the small, silver cup over his head and accepts a giant cardboard check for $25,000. Joel delivers a five-minute acceptance speech, thanking dozens of people, a list so long that other players are laughing and hooting for him to stop. Finally, he does.

"I want to thank the late Alfred Butts for creating this game," Joel finishes. "Without it I don't know where I'd be."

I ride the elevator with Joel back to his room. He literally bounces off one of the walls. "Whooooo!"

"I know I'm not the brightest guy out there. There are a lot of geniuses in the room," Joel says. "Here's something that even a lazy, good-for-nothing bum can accomplish if he's got a little common sense."

Joel jams his crumpled clothing and his word books and his medicines into a hard-paneled suitcase. He had packed several ties in case he won, as the champion would get billeted at a fancy Manhattan hotel that night and appear on *Good Morning America* the following day.

"It's the only thing I've ever put a lot of hard work into," Joel says. "When I can prove that my approach to the game is just as good as their approach — my concentration on strategy as opposed to their concentration on rote dictionary memorization — it elevates my self-esteem. It's the one thing I'm really good at, and if I can't accomplish something in this field, it's unlikely I'll accomplish something in any other field.

"So this basically validates my existence." He pauses. "I'm not kidding."

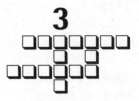

3

Unrated

THE ALLERTON HOTEL FOR WOMEN opened in the 1920s at the corner of East 57th Street and Lexington Avenue as a single-room-occupancy residential hotel for young ladies of proper breeding embarking on careers in postwar New York. For decades it boasted a lobby adorned with a white marble staircase, a grand piano, and elevator maids in white gloves. When I first visit, the lobby is dingy, the paint peeling, the elevators slow or broken. Not a white glove in the place.

This is where the Manhattan Scrabble Club meets, on the second floor, in space rented from the old-line Beverly Bridge Club. Inside the Scrabble room on this Sunday afternoon, Susi Tiekert is playing solitaire on a computer between cigarette breaks. Along with her husband, Ron, who is one of the game's all-time greats, Susi runs Scrabble Club No. 56, and I've decided to join a one-day, six-game tournament (entry fee: $25) that they are staging the following weekend. The park games have ended with the colder weather, and I've been playing alone on a Turkish rug on the living room floor of my one-bedroom Brooklyn apartment late at night after work. I don't feel ready to play in a tournament; I still haven't memorized the three-letter words. Susi is a big confidence-booster.

"Even if you study you could lose every game," she says. Susi has a gravelly Noo Yawk voice she wields like a blunt object. "Or it could happen immediately. You get lucky with the tiles and have an idiot opponent." She recalls the story of one such woman who started off with an expert-level rating. "We've seen her play for many, many years, and she stinks."

Susi explains that I'll enter the tournament with no rating and compete in the novice division, where the ratings cutoff is 1200. From 1200 to 1700, she says, is the intermediate division. (The unofficial designation of "expert" is 1600, but division breaks at tournaments vary according to the number of players and the director's discretion.) Above 1700 is the expert division. Susi says it took her three frustrating years to climb out of novice and eight more to get out of intermediate. "You get the hell out of that division and move to a better board," Susi says of the beginner group. "These people have no respect for the board whatsoever. I can't tell you the dumb things they do that bring tears to your eyes. They can fuck up the board and it's terrible. It's like Kafka."

Call me Franz. A week later, as nervous as a kindergartener on the first day of school, I make a mockery of the board. I know that I don't know the three-letter words, which are crucial to scoring well, but I think everyone else does; when I guess and play EXO*, my opponent immediately challenges it off. I lose the first three games but salvage the final three, including a small-consolation-department victory over a junior high school kid. Yippee.

Still, I'm exhilarated. I love the prematch suspense and the clocks and the rattling tiles and the in-game tension. In the park, the judgments are harsher but less final. Here, a loss matters for reasons beyond credibility and acceptance in the park clique. In the end I will be judged on paper, with a rating, which will be entered into a computer and listed with thousands of others for all to see. That rating will define me.

I do learn one lesson that day. Walking to the subway with Matt Graham, who won four out of six games, I complain about one loss in which my opponent drew all eleven power tiles — the two blanks, the four S's, and J, K, Q, X, and Z. "Don't *ever* let me hear you whine about not getting tiles," Matt says. Luck, if it exists at all, is part of the game; sometimes you get it, sometimes you don't. Worrying about it won't make you a better player. And complaining about it won't make you a more serious player.

This journey is going to take time. A few weeks later, my inaugural rating arrives in the mail from the National Scrabble Association. A cross-table lists every player in the tournament, ranked by division and order of finish. I flip over the sheet of paper to find the results of Division 3. I scan the first column until I find my name. There it is, in sixteenth place, out of twenty-eight. Under the header "Old Rating," there's a zero. Then come the game-by-game results. Then the total number of wins. Finally, in the far-right column: "New Rating." I run my finger across the page and see it: 761.

Scrabble isn't like any of the other thinking-person's board games, for one reason: Someone owns it. Chess and backgammon, which have been played and studied for centuries, are nonproprietary. Anyone can make a copy. As such, there's a sort of theoretical purity about them, as if they were handed down from the gods for humankind's analysis and bemusement.

There are more than two dozen legends associated with the invention of chess, from patricide to war to diversion from war to intellectual struggle to *mater dolorosa,* or the grieving mother. In many stories, chess is linked with backgammon, which was invented earlier, probably as an outgrowth of the ancient Indian game pachisi. In the battle between intellect (chess) and chance (backgammon), chess won out among the ancient elite. According to one Muslim scholar, backgammon was all about fate. "The player," he wrote, "when the chances are favorable, secures what he wants; but the ready and prudent man cannot succeed in gain what a happy chance has given to the other." After its invention, chess supplanted backgammon as the kings' game of choice because "in this game skill always succeeds against ignorance."

Scrabble hardly has a romantic or mythic history. The game was invented by an unemployed, young New York architect named Alfred Mosher Butts during the Depression. The timing was right. A new game, one of skill and chance, Butts figured, would be a welcome diversion for down-on-their-luck Americans like the inventor himself. He tinkered with the game for years, but never was able to generate interest from the game companies. Eventually, Butts cut a deal with an aspiring businessman named James Brunot. Brunot made the sets in a small factory in rural Connecticut, but when Scrabble took off in the early 1950s, he handed over production and marketing to Selchow & Righter Co. That company acquired the game outright when Brunot decided to retire about twenty years later. Scrabble was passed on to Coleco Industries Inc. in the mid-1980s, when Selchow & Righter went out of business. Hasbro acquired it out of bankruptcy court when Coleco went belly up a few years later.

No medieval intrigue or philosophical heft there. Just a twentieth-century American business story. But Scrabble isn't Battleship or Monopoly, either. The National Scrabble Association's player ratings list contains the names of about seven thousand current or former tournament players, twenty-three hundred of whom have played in a tournament in the past year. That may not sound like a lot, particularly compared to the United States Chess Federation, which claims eighty thousand members, and I quickly meet devoted Scrabble players who insist that with more money, better organization, or a dictionary that didn't include so many strange or obsolete words, the ranks of the initiated would be far fatter. Regardless, it's more people than gather formally to play any other packaged board game, by far, and more than any other mind game besides poker, bridge, and chess.

I have never been a serious games player — never attended a club, played on a school chess team, or read a strategy book — but I dabbled in the classics. Along with millions of other Americans, I watched the Bobby Fischer–Boris Spassky chess match on public television in 1972. I can still visualize the giant cardboard pieces that the commentator Shelby Lyman would affix to the giant chessboard after each move in this match between two eccentrics representing capitalism and Communism. Lampros and I would record the moves on the chessboard in our living room, and for a time we would play. I was nine, he was seventeen. I never won a game. The problem was that I never learned to "see" the board, to visualize the next series of moves and aggregate the spatial relationship among the pieces. Backgammon, though, I could play. Summers on the Greek island of Chios, where my father was born, passed with endless sessions of the game in three variant forms — standard backgammon, *plakoto* (Greek backgammon), and *moultezimi* (Turkish backgammon). I recall sitting in the coffee shop in the central square of the ancestral village eating sweets and beating local men sixty years my senior. I never analyzed the mathematics or probabilities. I just grasped the game intuitively. I played, and won.

Observing the parkies and the Worlds, and now playing in a tournament, I was learning that Scrabble offered some of the best of both games. Chess has a catalogue of hundreds of standard sequences that have to be memorized; Scrabble has the words. Chess has its 64 alternating black-and-white squares; Scrabble has its 225 multicolored squares. Backgammon has the roll of the dice; Scrabble has the drawing of new tiles. All of them share a critical aspect of game theory: battling for control of a board in an effort to subjugate an opponent.

I don't have a clue, though, about how intricate the battle can be. I play and play at the Beverly, and lose and lose. To get the hell out of that division and move to a better board, as Susi so delicately advised, would take work. I would have to study thousands of words, learn fundamental techniques like rack balancing (maintaining a healthy balance between vowels and consonants) and rack management (knowing which letters to dump and which to keep), and understand board-game strategy. In short, I'd have to take the game seriously. And while I've always been competent at most skill-based pursuits — from playing soccer and the clarinet to completing *New York Times* crossword puzzles — I've never been exceptional at, or exceptionally dedicated to, anything. I've lacked inner drive and the killer instinct; while I love competition, I usually expect to lose.

Still, what was missing as a child in chess and other pursuits surely, I think, can be manufactured as an adult. The skill component of the game, learning the words, should be a snap, I figure, because I already love language; and the chance component, the hope of drawing seven magical tiles from the bag, is inherently seductive. In Scrabble, like poker, you can bluff, a maneuver for which I also discover an affinity. I sneak SPENDFUL* past another novice at the club one Sunday afternoon and correctly guess that TRIAGED is a real word. "Nice find. That was added with the last dictionary update," Ron Tiekert, who won the national championship in 1985, tells me. And in Scrabble you can get lucky: I nearly beat Ron in that game, and the same day nearly beat another former national champion, Rita Norr, who won in 1987.

There is one more attraction: That 761 makes me about two thousandth of the twenty-three hundred active players. Surely I can do better than that.

In a bland hotel meeting room just off Interstate 84 in Danbury, Connecticut, shortly after midnight, G.I. Joel is showing Marlon Hill a stack of snapshots from his recent trip to Bangkok, where he won first place and $5,000 (in local currency) in a major international Scrabble tournament. Scrabble is popular in Southeast Asia, even among people for whom English is a second language, after Thai or Tagalog, and the prize money is more generous there than in the States, so Joel travels. After his recent world championship, Joel is on a roll. These last three months have been the most esteem-building of his life, and for all of his frumpy sadness, Joel is reveling in his success. Here's Joel with the tournament director in Thailand. Here he is with a woman who played a zitherlike instrument at a reception. Here he is at the royal palace. Here he is lying on his Bangkok hotel bed after the awards ceremony, a pile of baht scattered around him. As Joel shows Marlon the pictures, I notice that he's wearing his nametag from the Thai tournament, which bears the logo of a sponsor, a chicken company named Brand's.

Marlon politely looks at the photos, then the talk turns to the tournament at hand, the Eastern Championships, which start the next day. "I'm a knock your ass out in the morning," Marlon says. He plays Joel first thing. Someone makes fun of Marlon's speech. "What?" Marlon says, dropping the T. "We all speaking the Queen's English?"

It's my first big tournament. Four divisions. One hundred fifteen players. Four days and twenty games of Scrabble. Players greet one another like long-lost friends as they stumble around the hotel lobby toting too much luggage for a three-day trip. They carefully inspect the goody bags the local tourist board has prepared. They confusedly look for their rooms. They make silly demands of the hotel staff. They are, in short, typical American hotel guests, yet they also bear custom Scrabble boards — heavy wooden ones, ultralight plastic ones on lazy Susans, boards adorned with drawings or names or sports team logos, some stashed in expensive cymbal cases to protect against wear and tear — and $150 digital clocks and multicolored plastic Protiles and magnetized tile picker-uppers to clear the board and mesh bags straight out of Martha Stewart into which to dump a boardful of letters.

Players wear nametags crafted from wooden Scrabble letters, and T-shirts with slogans like SCRABBLE PLAYERS DO IT ON THE TILES. A tall thin player in electric blue drawstring pants hiked up past his navel and a tie-dyed tank top zips into the playing room carrying a fancy wooden board as a waiter would, with two sets of tiles arranged on the squares. I secretly hope he trips, just to see what two hundred flying tiles looks like.

My rating is now 779. A month earlier, I played in a one-day event at a cheap motel hard by Exit 48 of the Long Island Expressway. In the lowest division, I posted a 4–3 record, including a loss to a fourteen-year-old whose doting parents hovered over him between games as if he were a child actor at an audition. At the Beverly, I can't win a game unless it's against a newer newbie than I. I drop six in a row to Diane from the park. I see a player pick her ears with her finger and wipe it on her pants. An apparent narcoleptic falls asleep while we play; I kick him under the table when it's his turn. I watch G.I. Joel and Ron play in what seems a foreign language, when I discover that it sort of is — SOWPODS, the combined North American–British dictionary.

The club and the one-day tourneys feel like spring training. Danbury is Opening Day. I'm in Division 4, which seems to consist of newcomers like me and blue-haired ladies who have been shuffling tiles since the Truman administration. There is little in Scrabble more humiliating than losing to a blue-hair.

I drove from New York with Matt Graham (whose rating is 1942). Matt consumed most of the two-hour drive with a convoluted story about a bartender at the Greenwich Village college bar he frequents whom he dated and continued to obsess about after the relationship ended. It was hard to follow; Matt can ramble, pausing only for affirmation. But the defensiveness and insecurity apparent in the story made me wonder.

Matt was raised in Indianapolis. His mother is a lawyer, his father an actor who used to program computers. They divorced when Matt was in the seventh grade, sharing custody. Matt wasn't into sports or schoolwork. He had a couple of close friends, but was mostly introverted and antisocial. He was, however, interested in the high school quiz bowl. "I loved recall and trivia," he says, adding, "I got completely screwed." As Matt tells it, he made the quiz-bowl team in the ninth grade (and dominated), but the matches were televised and the coach told him he was too immature to appear on TV. "I think that was the beginning of the real bitterness," Matt says. The next year he made the team again, but was declared academically ineligible. By then he pretty much had stopped attending classes. "When I realized I didn't have to go to school, I just didn't." Matt slept in, ate junk food, watched television.

He did like comedy; at age four, he was mimicking a Woody Allen routine about a moose. After he was expelled from high school, he began doing standup. Soon after, he moved to Boston, where he attended open-mike nights and played Scrabble with his girlfriend, also a comic. Though he'd never been much interested in the game growing up, now, in his midtwenties, he found himself searching the *OSPD* for the two-letter words. After about a year of playing at home, Matt tracked down a local club, and a month later, in the spring of 1991, he entered a tournament in the Boston suburb of Waltham. It happened to be one of the key tournaments on the Scrabble circuit, featuring a special "premier" division of top players. Matt, playing in the novice division, wandered over to the premier section in the rear of the hotel ballroom.

"Their boards looked different from the [novice] boards, which were all congested, tiles moving down to the corner in blocks," he says. "Theirs would have these spider shapes, shooting out to the ends. Someone played ANTEFIXA to an A, and the other guy bingos back with ATROPINE. It blew me away. That was the turning point. I said, 'I want to be really good at this game.'"

Matt began dedicating himself. He played against an electronic Scrabble game called Master Monty. He fell asleep reading the dictionary. "Nothing magic," he says.

But something clicked. In six months, his rating soared from 1170 to over 1700, and six months after that, at the 1992 Waltham event, he finished fourth in the expert division, right below premier. At the Nationals in Atlanta the following summer, Matt went 12–15, 114th out of 176 players, but his point spread was an astonishing +891, *fif-teenth*-best in the field. In one game, he defeated the defending world champion by 350 points.

For an underachieving high school dropout like Matt, Scrabble was a way to show up the perceived geniuses. "I always feel they look down on me and a lot of these guys think they're so much smarter than me," Matt told me over lunch shortly after the Worlds. "I look at Joel and I look at Adam [Logan, the Harvard Ph.D. candidate and 1996 national champion], and on the surface they're much more people's idea of brainiacs. I do worry about it. I don't get respect from them, but I try to control myself with that thought."

By 1994, Matt was winning tournaments regularly, and his rating was among the top fifty in the game. He slumped at the Nationals that year and failed to qualify for the 1995 Worlds. But he won a couple of big tournaments in 1996 and finished respectably at the Nationals in Dallas. Then came his second-place finish at the Worlds. Matt won $13,000 playing Scrabble in 1997. No one could dispute that he was now one of the best.

"Comedy is so subjective," Matt says. "Two people can look at the same thing, and one person can say, 'That's great. That guy's a genius. That is terrific.' And the other person can say, 'That sucks.' That was a big appeal with Scrabble in the beginning, that it doesn't matter what people think, that if you're really good at this that's all that matters."

"What's TRANSMEDIA plus a V?"

Matt, Marlon, and I are sitting on barstools at a small, round laminated table in a cheap Mexican restaurant in Danbury. It's Saturday night, and the second day of play in the tournament has just ended. I'm ecstatic: I'm among the novice division leaders with an 8–2 record. After one of the losses, I overhear the winner whisper to another player, "I beat Fatsis!" as if this is the 1972 Winter Olympics and I'm the Russian ice hockey team. Larry Sherman, G.I. Joel's older brother and himself an expert, stops to congratulate me in the hallway. Marlon holds up his fist to knock with mine. "Mr. Eight and Two," he says. "Kicking ass."

And I should be 9–1, having blown a game by attempting a silly phony, FUTZIeR*, for 94, to open the game, rather than playing FRITZ for 54 (which I didn't see until later — two years later, as I typed this paragraph), or even FUTZ for 32 (which I did see). But my game isn't so advanced that I beat myself up over missed opportunities, mostly because I usually don't realize when I miss opportunities. I don't play fast or confidently enough yet to keep track of the tiles played. And I don't write down my racks — that is, all seven tiles from every turn, a practice that allows players to review their games and see what they "missed" — just the words that my opponent and I play. In a seating area outside the playing room, for the first time I see players — two young guys in their early twenties, one a short engineer with shoulder-length slacker-style hair named Dominic Grillo, the other a tall and thin African-American schoolteacher with dreadlocks named Martin Smith — energetically re-creating each sequence from their games on a full-page, photocopied grid of a Scrabble board. Dominic records the date of each game, his opponent, the score, and a few comments. There is so much I don't know.

"What's TRANSMEDIA plus a V?" Matt repeats. We've been making fun of Marlon's Transmedia credit card, a discount card not accepted by the restaurant, nor by a bunch of other restaurants that Marlon insisted on calling before we left the hotel that night. Marlon quickly says MAIDSERVANT. Then Matt quickly notes another, ANIMADVERTS.

It is my initiation into anagrams. Technically, an anagram is a word or phrase that is formed by transposing the letters of another word or phrase. But Anagrams is also the name of a game, popular in the United States in the early twentieth century — Alfred Butts, the inventor of Scrabble, played it with his brothers — in which words are formed from a pool of letters written on cards or tiles and then new words are created by adding letters to the existing ones. Colloquially, Scrabble players tend to describe anagramming as the process of forming words from random tiles. Using that loose definition, anagramming is the essence of the game.

It's not new. The thirteenth-century Jewish mystics known as cabalists believed that the letters in the Hebrew alphabet had magical properties; assigning numerical values to each letter, they would rearrange the letters in sacred Jewish writings to reveal other truths. In Hebrew, the letters in the name "Noah" formed "grace," while "Messiah" became "he shall rejoice." Anagramming has been used to flatter kings and queens, or to reveal hidden secrets in a person's name. In his poem "Cassandra," about the siege of Troy, the ancient Greek writer Lycophron, who purportedly invented the anagram, revealed two sycophantic anagrams, one of the name of the king at the time Lycophron lived, Ptolemy Philadelphus, and the other of his queen, Arsinoe. He anagrammed PTOLEMAIOS to APO MELITOS, or "made of honey," and ARSINOE to ERAS ION, or "Juno's violet." In the Book of John, Pontius Pilate asks Jesus, *"Quid est veritas?"* ("What is truth?"). His answer is an anagram: *"Est vir qui adest"* ("It is the man who is before you"). The word *anagrams* itself anagrams to the Latin *ars magna,* or great art.

For the logophile, anagramming can be about turning words into apposite phrases. In his groundbreaking 1965 book *Language on Vacation* (a copy of which Matt gives me), Dmitri Borgmann, the father of modern wordplay, offers anagrams for VILLAINOUSNESS ("an evil soul's sin"), CONVERSATION ("voices rant on"), and DESPERATION ("a rope ends it"). He also lists antigrams — words and phrases with opposite meanings — such as "evil's agents" for EVANGELISTS and "I limit arms" for MILITARISM. The name of pop star Britney Spears anagrams to PRESBYTERIANS, which in turn anagrams to "best in prayers." Eric Clapton is NARCOLEPTIC. "President Clinton of the USA" turns into "to copulate, he finds interns."

But for Scrabble players, single words are the goal, and with Matt and Marlon the longer the words and the more unlikely the letters, the better.

"A-D-D . . . R . . . S-S-S . . . T-U-Y," Matt says. He has announced the letters of the word in alphabetical order, an arrangement known to Scrabble players as an alphagram.† Before Marlon (or I, but get real) can solve the first alphagram, Matt announces a second: ABHILNRTY.

"DRYASDUSTS," Matt says when Marlon doesn't get the first one within a few seconds.

"I've got one for you," Marlon says. "PITTANCE with an R."

"CREPITANT?" Matt says.

---

† The term has another, older meaning that appears in *Webster's Third New International Dictionary of the English Language:* a puzzle consisting of a phrase, with another phrase made up of rhyming words that corresponds to the first phrase. A "male doll" is a "boy toy." An amusing rabbit is a "funny bunny." On *Jeopardy!,* alphagrams are played in a category called "Rhyme Time."

"It's LABYRINTH," Marlon says, meaning Matt's other alpha-gram.

"All right," Matt says. "A-A-B . . . L-M-M . . . N-N . . . O-S-T-U." He's doing this off the top of his head. He thinks of a word, mentally rearranges the letters in alphabetical order, and rattles them off faster than it would take most people simply to spell the word. So far I haven't managed as much as a guess. I've been scribbling down the alphagrams in my notebook — a crutch Matt and Marlon don't need.

A minute goes by. Marlon's still thinking.

"SOMNAMBULANT."

That's me talking.

High-fives all around. "That's a good find," Marlon says, using the phrase denoting a creative, difficult, or elusive play, and then laughing his deep-throated, Fat Albert laugh. "That's a major-*league* find."

It's starting to feel like an initiation rite. Matt says he's going to give me two long words with no repeating letters, known in the wordplay world as "isograms."† The term was coined by Borgmann in *Language on Vacation*. Matt alphagrams the first isogram: ABDEILMORSTUXY. Fourteen letters.

Within ten seconds, I say it: "AMBIDEXTROUSLY."

Matt gives me the second, a fifteen-letter isogram. ABCEGHI-LNOPRTUY. I scribble and struggle and cross out letters and scribble and struggle some more. Matt and Marlon advise me to look for common prefixes and suffixes. I write down UN and ABLE and solve it: UNCOPYRIGHTABLE.

It's the longest isogram in *Merriam-Webster's Collegiate Dictionary, Tenth Edition,* the source used in Scrabble for long words. Borgmann, who searched the dictionary manually in his quest to manipulate the language, coined UNCOPYRIGHTABLE by placing the prefix UN before the dictionary-sanctioned COPYRIGHTABLE.

On we go through dinner. BDEEIRSUW. There's a bottle of it on the table. BUDWEISER, Marlon announces. CDEINORSTUY. They stay quiet while I labor. I ask for the first letter. C. Minutes go by. I finally blurt it out: COUNTRYSIDE. Another: ADEFGILRU. I see LIFE, and find it: LIFEGUARD. "It took you longer than it should have," Marlon says.

† Like *alphagram,* the word *isogram* also has a dictionary definition: a line on a map or chart along which there is a constant value, like temperature or elevation.

ADEEFGHIRU, lovely for its EFGHI string.

"FIGUREHEAD!" I shout.

"I'm telling you," Marlon says. "He got talent."

Matt says, "GUACAMOLE plus F."

I ask them why they're so good at this.

"It's called A.D.D.," Matt says. "You need something that seems like a life project but you can resolve in five seconds."

A straight answer will have to wait, and it might not come from them. I ask Matt for the first letter of GUACAMOLE plus F.

"No, you're not riding on that bus anymore," he says.

And like a schoolchild who completes a task only when it becomes evident that help is not forthcoming, I get the answer a second later. "Oh, CAMOUFLAGE."

"TRANSMEDIA with an M!" Matt blurts, and then offers another combination. "If you take away the A, it's MASTERMIND!"

Marlon solves it. DISARMAMENT.

"You sure picked the right credit card," Matt says.

By midday Sunday, I'm 11–3 and in first place of the thirty-one players in the division. My spread is +918. I'm cockier than a first-round draft pick in the NBA. My next opponent has halitosis, but I have confidence. I'm about to wrap up a win when, with my clock under one minute, I see two spots for my valuable Y. One of them creates the word YE in two directions for 20 points. The other is worth 24 points, creating YER. I choose the latter, which is unfortunate because YER* is a phony that my opponent spots instantly, leaping from his chair and shouting, "Challenge!" I lose by 15 points. I lose the next game by 34. And the one after that by 22. Nailbiters all. The day ends, and I'm no longer in first, but still in the top three.

Dinner is another anagram fest. Matt, Marlon, and I are joined by Dominic and Martin, the Scrabble hipsters, and Eric Chaikin, who has just quit the Wall Street computer-software company founded by his father to take time off, largely to study words. Eric has been a wordie since he was a kid growing up in New York City, a *Games* magazine acolyte who read the dictionary for fun and subscribes to *Word Ways: The Journal of Recreational Linguistics,* which was founded by Dmitri Borgmann. Eric, who studied cognitive science at Brown, also seems to have an outer life, composing and recording music at a house he is renting in the Catskills. But he certainly has the anagramming skill, keeping up with Matt and Marlon.

AACCNORSST.

SACROSANCT.

CGIILNNNSUU.

Matt gets this in two seconds. CUNNILINGUS.

Eric tosses out some "pair isograms," words in which every letter appears twice. AACCEEHHNNPP: HAPPENCHANCE. EEIINNSSTT: INTESTINES.

HISTRIONICS? TRICHINOSIS. Eric throws out a fifteen-letter word that he says has an anagram, MEGACHIROPTERAN.

Everyone oohs and aahs, asking questions. Eric says it's a common word. Marlon solves it in a few seconds — CINEMATOGRAPHER — and we whoop and high-five.

"This is my favorite anagram of all," Eric says, and he makes me write this down in my notebook: $11 + 2 = 12 + 1$.

Then he instructs me to spell it out: ELEVEN + TWO = TWELVE + ONE.

"God put that there," Eric says. "There is no other explanation."

Returning to the hotel, we join the late-night games that are ritual at weekend tournaments. People are playing Scrabble and Boggle and cards. Experts are shouting out words in two-on-two games. Matt wanders by my game. "Play DILATORS," he instructs on the fly. Later, looking over the shoulder of a doubles game I'm playing with Dominic, who is a quickly rising intermediate, Marlon spots an impossibly low-probability word. "BUSHPIG," he says, as if we were morons for not seeing it. "Play BUSHPIG!"

"So, Stefan," G.I. Joel says. "It's ten minutes to one. Are you here for research purposes on the after-hours Scrabble life? Or are you hooked?"

I stare at Joel for a second. Sure, I'm toting my reporter's notebook, jotting down conversations overheard, like dozens of writers before who happened upon the quirky Scrabble subculture. But one can only take so much anagramming and so many games without caring.

"I'm hooked," I say.

Joel pauses. A smile creases his sad-sack face. He nods slowly and

deliberately, the self-appointed chief justice of Scrabble about to pronounce a verdict on my entry into his tight, little world.

"Cool."

At 1:40 A.M., I can't sleep, too nervous. I lie in bed. In the hallway I hear two players returning from the game room. "He tried
REPUNT*," one says. "To punt again." I look up words. I review my
games. I watch Olympic ice hockey from Nagano, Japan. The Rus-
sians win.

The tournament is over. I'm standing in front of a large oak tag
scoreboard taped to the wall in the anteroom where the late-night
games were held. The poster is divided into thirty-one rows, an alphabetical listing of the names of each player in my division, and
twenty columns, one for each game. A player's cumulative point
spread is recorded in the appropriate box. Win the game, and the
spread is written in black Magic Marker. Lose, it's in red. Ties are in
green.

I run my eyes along the row bearing my name, seeing a line of
black interrupted only three times by red. The line, however, ends at
Game 14, where a black +918 decorates the box. Then a river of red
ink begins: +903, +869, +847, +677, +364, +227. The six straight
losses mark a collapse of titanic proportions, one I didn't imagine
possible in a game so larded with probability and luck, especially in
the weakest division, where everyone's word knowledge is slim and
strategy suspect. I gave up in my last two games, demoralized, dejected, humiliated; in fact, I scored an embarrassing total of 179
points in the finale, having exceeded my twenty-five-minute time
limit by more than six minutes, earning a penalty of 70 points.

Dragging my sorry ass away from the evidence of my own ineptitude, I bump into Joe Edley in the hallway. Edley won the expert division. Marlon finished second and Matt third.

I tell him that I lost my last six games. That I'm a pathetic choker, a
Bill Buckner with tiles, that I will never amount to anything in a
game that a few days ago I didn't care nearly as deeply about, didn't
care about as a sport anyway. But now I've experienced the head-
inflating rush of competitive success and the hide-under-the-covers
agony of defeat — they should substitute footage of me playing YER*
in Game 15 for that Yugoslav skier tumbling ass over teakettle on

ABC's Wide World of Sports. Now I want to win, win, win, I want to understand what you and Joel and Matt and Marlon and the other pros understand, I want to succeed in a way I've never wanted to before.

I really just tell him that I lost my last six games.

"You have to get out of the won-lost syndrome," Edley says. "Did you care about losing?" he asks.

"Yes," I reply, because isn't that what it's all about?

"Well, if you put too much stress on winning and losing you won't last," Edley says. "You'll burn out. You can only make the best play you can make at any time. That's all you can control."

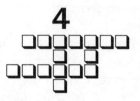

4

1005

ESPITE A SWOON worthy of a silent film star, my rating after Danbury actually increases more than 200 points. Long tournaments are graded in two chunks. My 8–2 opening half sent my rating rocketing to 1069. But my 3–7 second half sent it down to 1005. Even so, the big jump seems odd; surely expert ratings don't swing like the Dow. But Joe Edley explains that players receive something called "acceleration points" during the first fifty games of their Scrabble careers. In other words, my best chance to make a big rating jump is now.

I've already burned thirty-three games of the fifty. Logic would dictate that now would be the time to prepare before playing in another event — that is, if one were concerned with earning a higher rating fast. I wanted to start my journey at the bottom in order to have a benchmark: Knowing virtually nothing save the two-letter words, and not feeling entirely comfortable with those, what sort of a Scrabble player was I? The answer was clear: not a very good one, as my six straight losses in Danbury indicated.

But the Horatio Alger thing already seems hackneyed, and embarrassing. My new friends all seem to have been prodigies. Marlon played with his relatives for years before being dragged to a tournament, where he emerged with a rating over 1700. G.I. Joel was close to 1800 after a few events. Dominic Grillo tells me he went undefeated in his first event and after less than a year is closing in on 1600.

Their numbers seem stratospheric, and mine feels pathetic, even when I fall back on my convenient "I'm just a journalist" excuse.

Scrabble tournaments are naturally hierarchical. In the playing room, you can't just sit wherever you fancy. The top-division tables typically are farthest from the main doors. And Table 1 of Division 1 — where the players with the best records meet in the latter stages of most tournaments — is usually in the farthest corner. The quality of play descends to the weakest novices in the room's opposite corner. And there isn't much interdivisional mingling. Experts have no interest in novice boards, and novices, who could benefit from learning new words or watching experts analyze positions, appear afraid to cross class boundaries.

But there's attitude everywhere. In my very first game at Danbury, my opponent, whose 1160 rating seemed so impressive, attributed my victory to luck. How else could she have lost to someone playing in just his third tournament? My opponent in Game 3 didn't wait until it was over. He bitched with every pull. "Look at this!" he exclaimed after one draw, showing his tiles to his neighbor. Their snarkiness is telling. Matt already gave me the no-whining lecture about tiles. And I know that in any game of chance, people will complain about their misfortune. But as Herbert O. Yardley lectured wisely in his classic *The Education of a Poker Player,* "I do not believe in luck, only in the immutable law of averages." Better players tend to accept bad draws as part of the game and deal with them.

That seems an important distinction between the Scrabble pro and the hobbyist. The pro, with his board vision and word knowledge, understands that the act of selecting tiles randomly from a bag is a crapshoot. I've already heard that the odds of drawing a bingo out of the bag to start the game are 12.63 percent. So if I know all of the seven-letter bingos, I should bingo one out of eight times when drawing first. Which means that seven out of eight times I *shouldn't* bingo. Sometimes you get the bear, sometimes the bear gets you. Luck is considered responsible for 15 to 30 percent of the game. "You can't control the tiles," Joe Edley tells me.

This given doesn't stop pros from whinging, but it also doesn't stop them from treating each rack, even the lousy ones, as a life-or-death riddle. You can measure skill and desire, I've decided, in how long players linger over a board after a game. The experts rehash games for as long as it takes to find a satisfactory solution. Was there a better strategic move here? If I had done this, then what would you have done? Experts home in on postmortems in progress like pigeons to a statue. If an acceptable solution is not forthcoming, a computer is consulted. The hobbyists, me included, quickly clear away all evidence of a game as if it were a bloody glove at O.J.'s house.

Of course, we novices can't see many possibilities in a Scrabble play because we don't know the words or strategies. When I lose a tournament game by 2 points, Marlon happens to pass by. He examines the board, inspecting both my and my opponent's final racks.

"CRONE is your best play," he says definitively. "CRONE wins you the game."

"I don't know CRONE," I reply. (Later, when I think about it, I realize that I do know CRONE, a withered old woman.)

"CONGER also look like it wins," he says.

"CONGER? Don't know that, either." (It's a kind of marine eel.)

Since I don't see these words, Marlon's assessment of how I could have won is like asking what if Butch and Sundance were backed by a battalion of heavily armed troops. Like a lot of *ex post facto* Scrabble analysis, it is purely theoretical, given my limited word knowledge. Of course, if I hadn't asked Marlon to help analyze the game, I wouldn't have seen or learned CRONE or CONGER.

I *could* learn those words by studying. But five- and six-letter words are a long way off. I'm following the study plan advised for all novices. First, I devour the cheat sheet. The National Scrabble Association publishes a beginner's list that includes the two- and three-letter words; short words containing J, Q, X, and Z; and the ten U-less Q words (QAT, QAID, QOPH, FAQIR, QANAT, TRANQ, QINDAR, QINTAR, QWERTY, and SHEQEL). It also has a list of "vowel dumps," that is, four-letter words with two I's, two U's, or three vowels, and five-letter words with four vowels. All of it is on one piece of paper, which I tote around until it's stained and torn.

The "twos" were an afternoon's work, back before my first tournament, absorbed simply by reading them and then writing them down in sequence, starting with AA (a type of Hawaiian lava) and ending with YO (as in, "Yo, Adrian!"). But even after a few months, I discover the twos still are not second nature. Is BO good or is it OB? (BO, as in beau, is acceptable.) Is it HM or SH that plays? (Both.)

The 972 "threes" are more challenging. I read down the columns on the cheat sheet and cross out those already familiar. About 70 percent go on the first pass. I try to assimilate the rest through repetition. No one has suggested a better method; the threes, I'm told, you just have to learn cold. So on a separate piece of paper, I write down the 300 or so unfamiliar words. AAL, ABA, ABO, ABY, AFF . . . I read each word over and over, staring at it in hopes the image will imprint on my brain. When I'm confident it has, I place a check mark next to the word. Then I write up a new list: 180 words this time. I place a dot next to a word when it feels secure, a dash when it doesn't.

What I don't do is write down the definitions, which could help, and might be interesting. But definitions, for the limited purpose of playing Scrabble, don't matter. One could even argue that the words really aren't words at all. They are strings of letters, dancing across the board, an array of lines and arcs and circles. The strings usually represent language, but the letters that comprise them really are nothing more than, as G.I. Joel Sherman crudely puts it, "scoring tools," which must be juxtaposed in a fashion deemed acceptable by a source or else rejected from the playing field. They could be random shapes or colors or buttons or widgets that must be placed in a regulated order. They just happen to be "letters" forming "words."

That's a formalistic view but a useful one for now. Over time, I will come to discover the beauty of words like FLOKATI and GANTLOPE and SEADROME and PANTOFLE and PERDU and OUGUIYA and SNAFUED and SIEROZEM and OQUASSA. I will fall in love with seven-letter words that take an eighth letter in front of them: LEVATOR-ELEVATOR, LEADERS-PLEADERS, ESTIVAL-AESTIVAL-FESTIVAL, INCITES-ZINCITES, ONETIME-ZONETIME. And I'll even look up their meanings and be better for it.

For now, though, I understand only that while definitions can be interesting, they're not necessary. It's just about impossible to play high-level (or even low-level) competitive Scrabble if you're hung up on the game's use of odd words. The two most common refrains of living room players are the incredulous "That's a word?" and the indignant "That can't be a word!" Because how can something be a word if I've never seen it before? The answer, I decide early on, is that there are lots and lots of words (hundreds of thousands, actually) that even the most highly educated person doesn't know.

To play competitive Scrabble, one has to get over the conceit of refusing to acknowledge certain words as real and accept that the game requires learning words that may not have any outside utility. In the living room, Scrabble is about who has a better working vocabulary. It's a sort of crossword puzzle in reverse. But in the tournament room, Scrabble has nothing to do with vocabulary. If it did, I — an Ivy League–educated professional journalist, for crying out loud — would rule. But I can only dream of competing with the champions. No, Scrabble isn't about words. It's about mastering the rules of the game, and the words are the rules.

Some players — like Matthew, the poet from Washington Square Park, or Ron Tiekert — seem to know the meanings of almost every word they play. They are curious word lovers who accept, if not agree with, the oddities and contradictions of the language. Some players, usually not the better ones, dumb down the game to their level. Words are weird — until *they* learn them. Then they aren't. On the e-mail Scrabble discussion forum Crossword Games-Pro, or CGP, which I join, one player sums up the contradiction nicely. The issue "appears not to be the number of words, nor the strangeness of words, but the realization that one's opponent gets to use the strange words he/she knows, but you don't get to use the ones you know." I save the post. In Danbury, playing "new" words like QUOIN, QANAT, and OUTVIES is almost as satisfying as winning.

"Each dictionary," Dmitri Borgmann writes, "no matter how comprehensive, no matter how 'unabridged,' has selected a comparatively small number of words from the enormously large mass of words that make up the language." Lexicographers get to decide what goes into dictionaries, and then people decide which dictionaries to use as sources. Another wordplay giant, Ross Eckler, writes that "each person must draw his own line between words and nonwords and, once having done so, communicate carefully to others what stockpile of words he is using. There is no right answer."

The Scrabble world decided that *The Official Scrabble Players Dictionary,* first published in 1978, would, for the purposes of the game, answer the question: What is a word? The latest edition (the third, or *OSPD3*) includes words found in at least one of ten editions of five major U.S. college dictionaries. The Scrabble world was riven by a decision by Hasbro in 1994 to delete about 200 "offensive" words from the *OSPD*. As part of a compromise, the company agreed to have Merriam-Webster publish a book for use in sanctioned play which lists every word, dirty ones included, but without definitions or parts of speech. Just the words. The new book, which is published as I'm beginning my Scrabble career, is called the *Official Tournament and Club Word List,* and is known as the *OWL*.

Generally speaking, if a word is among the 120,302 two- through nine-letter words (plus inflected forms) listed in the *OWL*, it's good. If not, it isn't. Scrabble players argue about whether certain words should be deleted or others added; the NSA has a dictionary committee that is supposed to discuss such matters. While I'm quickly learning that the book isn't without its inconsistencies, I decide that there's no point worrying about it. I'm no lexicographer.

In addition to eschewing definitions, I also don't write down which of the three-letter words can be pluralized and which can't. That can come later. The magnitude of even this relatively short list feels overwhelming enough. A couple of mnemonic tricks, though, help. All of the letters in the phrase BETSY'S FEET, someone tells me, can be appended to the two-letter word KA (the spiritual form of a human being in Egyptian religion) to make a three-letter word (KAB, KAE, KAT, KAS, KAY, KAF), while all of the consonants in the phrase KNIGHT SWAM can be placed before AE (Scottish for "one").

I buy some study aids, including a Franklin, a handheld electronic device the size of a credit card and the thickness of a cigarette case — and as addictive as either. It's loaded with the now out-of-date *OSPD2*. Made in the early 1990s by Franklin Electronic Publishers, the gizmo apparently is available only in the Scrabble underground; I pay $43.25 to a guy in San Francisco who has bought much of the leftover inventory. He's a black marketeer, but it's worth it. Type in a word, press ENTER, and the Franklin tells you if the word is acceptable (and if so gives a definition) or not (in which case it suggests corrections). Type in a rack of letters, and the Franklin lists every acceptable word in the rack. Type in four question marks and the Franklin lists every four-letter word, in alphabetical order. Seven question marks followed by a rack of letters yields all of the bingos in the rack.

At tournaments, players whip out their Franklins as soon as games end to see what they missed. In one game, I have AEEEST? on my rack and there is an open H on the board. I play EH to unburden myself of an E. Afterward, I wonder whether I could have bingoed, and the Franklin mocks me with cyborg efficiency: AESTHETE. When I don't know what to do with the promising-looking rack of ADENOPR, the Franklin points out my shortcomings in quadruplicate: APRONED, OPERAND, PADRONE, PANDORE.

For $20, I buy *The Complete Wordbook* and *The Complete Blankbook,* two oversized, multi-hundred-page tomes filled with words categorized in ways I have not yet seen. The psychedelic blue *Wordbook* is a classic, cocreated by Mike Baron, an expert player who was instrumental in the evolution of word lists for Scrabble study: Words with 70 percent vowels. Eight-letter words containing five vowels. Words of fewer than seven letters containing J, Q, X, or Z. Seven-letter words arranged according to the most probable six-letter combinations plus a seventh letter. The same for eights. Four-letter words made from three-letter ones. Fives made from fours. *Every* three-, four-, five-, six-, seven-, and eight-letter word arranged alphabetically by alphagram. The *Blankbook* is even more bizarre: nothing more than two lists in alphagram order — words formed from six letters plus a blank and words formed from seven letters plus a blank.

The books are a blurry mass of capital letters that neatly categorize the language, but also make it seem impossible to digest. Column after column after column of words. No definitions or embellishments. Just the words. But when I open the books and began riffling the pages, I feel a pulse. It feels as if I have found the secret to Scrabble success.

Mike Baron's bingo blueprint starts on page 24 of the *Wordbook,* but it actually began long before the days of clubs and tournaments, when competitive Scrabble was played mostly in game rooms ruled by chess hustlers. The most famous was the Chess & Checker Club of New York, better known as the Flea House. Scrabble had been played there since the fifties, when the game first took the country by storm.

Players learned words mostly by over-the-board osmosis, assisted by *Funk & Wagnalls Standard College Dictionary,* a liberal volume of 150,000 entries that was the Flea House word source (because a Funk & Wagnalls editor played there regularly). Sometime in the late 1960s, though, one of the players determined that the six letters in the word SATIRE offered enormous opportunities to make bingos. Poring through the dictionary, he determined that eighteen of the twenty-six letters in the alphabet combined with SATIRE to form sixty-seven seven-letter words.

In those days, there were no cheat sheets or computer programs that spit out words. No one practiced anagramming in the way Matt and Marlon do, barking out words in rapid succession. At the Flea House, the Scrabble players would swap anagrams, and spend hours or even days trying to solve them, "stuff that most intermediate players would just swat away these days," Lester Schonbrun, the best New York player in the 1960s, and still one of the game's best, tells me.

In the early 1970s, Selchow & Righter formed a national players organization and began publishing a newsletter. SATIRE was introduced in the second issue of the *Scrabble Players Newsletter.* The third issue posed another productive six-letter group: AENRST, dubbed SANTER*. More "stems" followed: SETTER, ENTERS, RETINA, SALTER, and, finally, TISANE, which combined with twenty-three letters forming fifty-nine words. (Both SATIRE and TISANE, a.k.a. SATINE*, now make more words thanks to additions to the Scrabble dictionary.) From seven-letter words, the quest moved on to eights.

The word searchers applied mathematical logic to the game. They knew that prefixes and suffixes were a key to making bingos. So it followed that letters like A, E, I, N, R, S, and T were good potential combiners. D, G, L, N, and O also seemed to show up a lot. The players' intuition was backed up by history and linguistic research. In the 1890 edition of his wordplay book *Gleanings for the Curious from the Harvest Fields of Literature,* Charles Carroll Bombaugh published a chart listing the proportional frequency of the letters of the alphabet, which "have been pretty accurately determined." In order, the first twelve were ETAOINSHRDLU, the sequence on which the standard Linotype keyboard was based. (The two left-hand columns of the keyboard produce the sequences ETAOIN and SHRDLU.) Academic studies of letter frequency in published American English confirmed the order. In Scrabble, it wasn't surprising to find the G tossed in, because of the common occurrence of words ending in -ING. The H and U could be tossed out because there are only two H's in a set and because the U is the clunkiest of the vowels.

The early lists, which were compiled by hand, weren't always reliable. Almost every time one appeared in the newsletter, players wrote in with corrections, a sign of how the word-obsessed community was growing: "John Turner missed GANTRIES and PANTRIES in his RETAINS list. Make that at least 62 eight-letter bingos." "Joe Cortese's Crazee Eights anagrams need some help. ACONITES — CANOEIST and SONICATE. ASTERISM — MISRATES and SMARTIES. PSILOTIC — POLITICS and COLPITIS."

The publication of the 662-page *OSPD* made it easier for players to search for words, but they still had to do it manually. One of the most prolific word searchers was David Shulman. A cryptanalyst of Japanese codes in the army during World War II and contributor to the *Oxford English Dictionary* supplement, Shulman took the study of bingo words to its first computational level. In 1979, he assigned a rating to the "top" fourteen six-letter stems by adding the number of letters in the alphabet with which the stem combined and the number of bingos that were formed; SATIRE was first with a rating of 85 (18 letters plus 67 bingos), followed by SATINE with an 82 (23 letters, 59 bingos).

It was as if sex or chocolate had just been discovered; the players couldn't get enough. By 1980, the newsletter was dominated by lists; tournament results and club news were secondary. It was all about mastering the game, pulling the sword from the stone that was the *OSPD.*

Serious players learned that the word game was really a math game, as the pages of the renamed *Scrabble Players Newspaper* reinforced. In the February 1980 issue, an expert named Albert Weissman, a Connecticut psychologist, conducted the game's first computerized mathematical experiments. Weissman calculated the probability of drawing certain racks to start play. The least likely combination of letters was BBJKQXZ, where the B could be replaced by any tile of which there are two in the bag (B, C, F, H, M, P, V, W, Y, and the blanks); the probability of drawing such a rack was about 1 in 16 billion. The single most probable rack, he found, was

AEINORT, with an expected frequency of 1 in about 9,530 draws from a fresh bag.

But there was no acceptable seven-letter word in AEINORT (there still isn't), so Weissman figured out the most and least probable bingo-producing draws. The former was (and still is) AEEINRT, which made RETINAE and TRAINEE (ARENITE, a kind of rock, was added to the second edition of the *OSPD*), with a probability of 1 in about 13,870 opening draws. A word like ERRATIC would come up 1 in 91,743 opening pulls. POACHES, 1 in 588,235. MUZJIKS, 1 in 55,555,555. Finally, MUUMUU?, where the blank is an S, could be expected to appear once every 8 *billion* opening turns, making it the least probable opening bingo.

The point was probability. As a game progresses, the number of letters from the finite pool of one hundred tiles is reduced toward zero, increasing or decreasing the odds of certain mathematical occurrences: drawing an S or a blank, playing a bingo, getting stuck with the Q, pulling a letter that would form a bingo with SATINE. If you could determine the letters most likely to be extracted from the bag, you could figure out which words were best to learn.

Weissman published the 125 most-probable seven-letter racks, 220 words in all. He concluded that players should study words based on the probability that they will show up during a game. Not everyone agreed; after all, 220 wasn't many words. And the stems could be "built" deliberately during a game through expeditious play. The newsletter didn't take sides. It just transmitted the information received. Next came a refinement of Shulman's research. Rather than how many different letters of the alphabet combined with a six-letter stem to form a bingo, what mattered, it was decided, was how many of the ninety-four tiles that remained in the bag after drawing the stem could be used to make a bingo.

So the word searchers examined all 21,734 seven-letter words in the *OSPD*. One of them, a reclusive dictionary lover named Joseph Leonard, identified some two hundred worthwhile six-letter stems. The searchers combined the number of tiles in the bag which can be used to form bingos with the total number of bingos formed. SATINE took over the top spot, with a "Bonus Power Rating" of 150: Ninety of the remaining ninety-four tiles in the bag (every letter except J, Q, and Y) could be added to SATINE to make sixty different words. SATIRE was second at 142 (67 words plus 75 usable tiles), followed by SANTER and CLEARS.

It was a deluge. And, for players, manna from heaven.

Mike Baron gave them even more. In the early 1980s, Baron was a psychologist at the University of New Mexico. His father and brother played in an early Scrabble tournament on Long Island, in 1973, and Mike and a few friends took up the game. He formed a club in Albuquerque, and as a result was invited to play in a qualifying tournament for the 1980 Nationals, the second of its kind.

Mike was seeded sixty-fourth in the field — dead last. He went 0–5 on the first day but thought, I can play this game. I just need to learn some words. On his flight home Mike started to circle every four-letter word in the *OSPD* containing K. After a few pages, though, he decided to tease out all of the short JQXZ words as well. Then he culled all the threes, and with the twos created the first cheat sheet, which he distributed to club members. Then he generated a list of "two-to-make-threes" — three-letter words formed by placing a letter in front or behind two-letter words — and then three-to-make-fours and four-to-make-fives.

His lists were a revelation: With all the emphasis in the newsletter on flashy bingos with their 50-point bonus, short words hadn't gotten their due, and no one had determined their relative importance to play. "I was aware of certain parameters of the game," Baron tells me. "The J, Q, X, and Z prevent you from bingoing, and you need to play two- to five-letter words to score. It was obvious to me, but there hadn't been anything in the *Scrabble News* about it."

With oversized glasses and a head of straight silvery hair parted far to the right, Baron looks a little like Andy Warhol circa the Factory. A trace of Brooklyn still infects his speech, he has a big smile and a goofy, overeager laugh, and he sometimes breaks into a Three Stooges nyuk-nyuk-nyuk voice. When we meet, he is wearing a T-shirt that asks DOES ANAL RETENTIVE HAVE A HYPHEN? He's never been a champion player himself, but Baron brought precise, clerical thinking to the game.

After completing his short-word lists, Baron moved Scrabble into analysis, examining sixteen games reprinted in the newsletter. The conclusion: While the twos, threes, and fours comprised just 5 percent of the dictionary, they accounted for 75 percent of all the words formed and nearly half of the total score. Bingos accounted for 6 percent of words formed and 28 percent of the total score. Or, twelve and a half short words appeared for every bingo played. "That was amazing," Baron says. "That five percent of the dictionary would account for seventy-five percent of the words on the board only emphasized all the more the importance of learning the short words."

In the games Mike analyzed, the winner outscored the loser by 414.5 to 338.5. The winner drew 4.3 more tiles than the loser. The winner went first more often than the loser. The winner played more of the eleven power tiles than the loser. And, most important, the winner outbingoed the loser two to one on average, with nearly 90 percent of the scoring differential attributable to bingos. "This was a breakthrough in sensitizing players to learn the short words," Baron says, "but you've got to know your bingos."

He felt his discoveries were just too good not to share: a loaf of bread and a fish that would feed the Scrabble multitudes. Baron soon discovered flaws in how players were being advised to learn bingos. The high-probability lists published in the newsletter offered only a few hundred words. And the bingo stems weren't logical; for instance, it didn't make sense to learn the bingos that could be formed from the letters in CLEARS — one of the top stems — because drawing the C was already a low-probability occurrence, and drawing it with, say, a V, was even less likely. You needed to learn the words that showed up a lot, not CARVELS or CLAVERS. And the way to do that was to learn the bingos that contained the most frequent tiles, those worth one or two points. Mike dubbed those letters — A, D, E, G, I, L, N, O, R, S, T, and U — "three percenters" because there are at least three of each of them among the hundred tiles. And they made about four thousand bingos.

But the "three-percent list" had no built-in mnemonic aids, the way the stems did, and it would take two years for Baron to compile it. In the meantime, he applied probability thinking to the stems. There was a basic flaw in determining which stems were most fruitful: The system didn't consider the probability of the stem itself.

For instance, the six letters in PAPERS and the six in AINERS* had nearly identical Bonus Power Ratings; you could make twenty-three bingos with seventy-eight usable tiles from the former and thirty-eight bingos with sixty-one usable tiles from the latter. But a player was *fifty-four times* more likely to draw AINERS out of a full bag than PAPERS.

So Baron created the Modified Power Rating, obtained by multiplying the probability of a stem by the number of tiles left in the bag that combined with it. (He assigned the SATINE stem a probability of 1.0 and adjusted accordingly based on the frequency of the letters in a stem.) It worked. RETINA, which was number eleven on the old list, rose to the top of the new list. SATINE came second and SATIRE third. CLEARS, which was fourth on the old list because it yielded so many bingos, plummeted because the probability of drawing the C was low.

Baron tinkered some more with his formula, because he realized that the letter S deserved greater weight since players hung onto it in order to develop bingo racks. In the summer of 1986, in a centerfold pullout as sexy to Scrabble players as any Playboy Playmate, *Scrabble Players News* published Baron's "Top 100" bonus word stems, about twenty-five hundred seven-letter bingos in all. For good measure, the same issue contained four other Baron lists: JQXZ nonbingos, words consisting of 70 percent or more vowels, six-letter words containing four vowels, and words with multiple I's or U's.

All of those lists were generated by hand by Baron and Joseph Leonard. I asked Mike how he knew which letter combinations to inspect. "Once you know that SATINE is good," he says, "let's change the S to a D or an R. Let's change RATINE to RADINE. Let's change it to an L, RALINE or NAILER. Let's change R-A-L-I-N-E to R-O-L-I-N-E. I generated the top hundred by hand. Of the fifty-five thousand potential six-letter stems, I missed four of the top hundred."

Baron created separate lists of high-probability words that weren't covered by the stems, like AGATOID and EROTICA. All of it, plus the five thousand eight-letter words that could be formed from the Top 100 stems, were published in the newsletter in 1987 under the headline "Seriously Folks, My Final Bingo Lists." Baron put all of his lists together and published them in book form one year later.

* * *

On page 24, the bingos start.

1 **SATINE**
A ENTASIA
  TAENIAS
B BANTIES
  BASINET
C ACETINS
  CINEAST
D DESTAIN
  DETAINS
  INSTEAD
  SAINTED
  STAINED
E ETESIAN
F FAINEST

All one hundred stems, from SATINE to OUTENS, are contained on four pages, eight columns to a page. Just four pages. It seems manageable, especially when I photocopy and stick them in my brief-case. Memorizing them is a different story. Starting with SATINE (pronounced sat-TEEN or sat-TINE), I tackle them as I did the threes: by staring at them. The threes, though, are short, simple letter strings. Words like DUI or VAV seem less like words than like groups of symbols that can be identified easily by their shape or pattern. The bingos are real words, long words, that need deeper context. I have to remember them, not just recognize them.

I cover up the additional letter in the stem, and can tell by the line spacing how many anagrams await. SATINE plus L. I count. Seven lines. I talk aloud, or just move my lips if I'm in public. "ELASTIN, ENTAILS." Pause. "NAILSET." Longer pause. I know there are three starting with S. "SALIENT, SALTINE, SLAINTE." And one more. "TENAILS." Got 'em. Sometimes I singsong the answers, which ties the words together. "INSTATE-SATINET." They are forever linked. Oh, those ZANIEST ZEATINS. Whatever it takes.

What it takes is weeks. I move from reading to writing. I record the stem, then every letter it takes, and how many words for each letter. And then I try to fill in the blanks. I show off for friends who feign interest in my new obsession.

"Quiz me. Look at the second list, the one that starts with SATIRE. Now give me a letter."

"Okay. R."

"ARTSIER, TARRIES, TARSIER." I sound like a snotty eight-year-old who can recite the names of the U.S. presidents in order.

"Wow. That's great. That's so interesting. I've got to get back to work now."

It takes months before the words seem embedded, which only reinforces the feeling of hopelessness. There's just too much to learn. SATINE and SATIRE are the C-major scale to a musician, the first block of stone in the Pyramids. I can't conceive of making it to REGINA (No. 28) or STORED (No. 58) or AMINES (No. 95). Absorbing thousands of words seems like a fool's errand. I have difficulty remembering names, images from my past, plots of novels, what I did last weekend. How can I, closing in on age thirty-five, start learning words? Where in my brain will I put them?

I tote my new study aids to a weekend tournament in the resort town of Port Jefferson, on Long Island. I have my photocopied lists, my Franklin, and a stack of index cards on which I have written three-, four-, and five-letter words containing J, Q, X, and Z and some mnemonic aids. For JOTA, a Spanish dance, I write "JO + TA," which are acceptable two-letter words. For JIMP, I write "JUMP IMP." For ZARF, I underline ARF. Sitting on the john in the inn where the tournament is being staged, reading my cards, I say aloud, "JAPAN is good," using proper Scrabble lingo. I'm learning! And I'm in the third division of four! I'm moving up!

I casually win five of the first six games. It feels like Danbury all over again — especially when I lose five of the next six. It must go beyond knowing words, because my opponents can't know many more than I do (except for an older gentleman with a 1330 rating who plays SEISING, which I challenge, en route to a rout; I'm psyched out by his rating). Maybe it's my lack of tournament experience. Maybe it's the typical novice inability to score when your tiles betray you — the inclination to take 5 or 10 points rather than exchange bad letters — or even when they don't, playing off one or two tiles for a few points when larger "turnover" is called for. Maybe it's not knowing which tiles to keep. Maybe the words aren't sticking; in one game I can't remember SATIRE plus an A (ARISTAE, ASTERIA, ATRESIA).

Maybe it's physical. During my slump, Joe Edley, who has jumped out to a 10–2 record, asks if I'm tired. Well, I admit, I was up late hanging out with Marlon and playing some after-hours games, and up early because I was nervous.

"Your body needs rest," he says. Scrabble is a game of physical as well as mental stamina. Edley doesn't play after-hours games, doesn't partake of late-night beers (in fact, he's never touched a drop of alcohol in his life). He is there to win and nothing more. Edley tries not to be rude; in every tournament he plays, he also functions as a de facto NSA representative. But the social niceties can wait. If his opponents don't understand, tough.

Edley wins the expert division with a 12–3 mark. I take two of the last three games for an 8–7 finish, sixth place out of sixteen. I had been seeded fifteenth in the division, though. Because I'm still receiving acceleration points, and because ratings are calculated based on the strength of your opponents — the tougher the field, the more your rating increases, and vice versa — mine rises to 1155, a healthy 150-point jump.

My Deluxe Scrabble board and new white-on-navy plastic Protiles, which I ordered for $25, have a permanent spot on the living room floor, books and Franklin beside them. I play every night after work. (Alone.) With the Franklin, I check racks and record lists of new words and find obscure plays. SIGNIORS, SORBENT, LATHERER, and PINIONED. CERVINE, COOTIE, and DOYLIES. RANI, ARECA, AERIED, EQUID, HYOID, LITAI. TABANID, WAUR, EQUITES, TOGAE, BETH, LAURA.

When I let the Scrabble lovers on CGP, the e-mail forum, know that a reporter-player is lurking, one of them welcomes me by posting a quiz: Find all of the bingos in STEFAN? and FATSIS? I reply privately that I'm flattered and rattle off the few bingos I do see (I'm at work; the Franklin is at home): FASTENs, FAScIST, FAiNEST (SATINE plus F). He sends back the rest: FANjETS, FATNESs, FATtENS, SATISFy, FIeSTAS, FISSATe. A week later, playing solitaire, I draw AEFNST?, and play rEFASTEN.

I bag my first expert at the club, Joel's brother, Larry. The same day, I score a record (for me) 522 points in a game. In my notebook, I scribble "Turning Point" because I'm proud that I've played some

Scrabble words, including the vowel dumps TAENIAE, AECIA, and AWEE.

I map out a schedule. Three weeks after Port Jefferson is the Seventeenth Boston Area Scrabble Tournament, the one with the premier division, in Waltham. Three weeks after that, a weekender in the Catskills. A week after that — and every month! — another one-day event at the motel by Exit 48 of the Long Island Expressway.

I'm planning my life around Scrabble.

"I've seen this before," John Williams says when I tell him about my schedule. "We have a twelve-step program. When your personal hygiene starts to take a beating, we'll really know."

Something changes in Waltham. I give away the first two games with panicky strategic misplays. I learn a lesson about the importance of high-probability racks when I try SALINED* where SNAILED is the correct move, and with a chance to bingo out and win I play OUTRISE* instead of STOURIE, which is the only word in that rack (and means "dusty"). I lose a game on time. I lose to two blue-hairs. I play scads of phonies. How low I sink: During my last, losing game, the woman at the next table, seeing CUPID on the board, says, "Oh, that's a cute word."

In Danbury, I was upset because of the losses. Other than YER*, though, I didn't analyze, game by game, why I lost. In Waltham, the specific mistakes, the tactical errors, linger. For the first time, I make a list of my flubs: "Didn't block X spot up by 42." "Opened a double-word score for a Q play for 44 in end." "Played a phony when down 30 with good rack midgame." "Opened a triple late. Should have passed."

In Danbury, I exited disappointed and embarrassed. In Waltham, with a 5–7 record, I leave angry. I can't even say I had fun. For the first time, my rating falls, to 1078.

The pretense of attending tournaments for reportorial purposes is gone. I have stopped asking opponents their age and occupation — just in case, I had told them, I wanted to include them in whatever I would write. Now, I want good company at events, and settle on my Scrabble homeys: Matt and Marlon; Dominic and Martin, the twenty-somethings who were replaying their games at Danbury; Eric

Chaikin, the word-obsessed Brown graduate and former Wall Street computer guy.

Eric is abandoning his Manhattan apartment and retreating full-time to his Catskills rental in the town of Margaretville. The house isn't too far from the tournament that Joe Edley is directing at a resort in Rosendale, a mini-Woodstock, that artifact of sixties white counterculture, where natural-foods stores and vegan menus predominate. It's a lovely, summer camp–like setting amid the woods on a glassine lake. In springtime, the place is virtually empty but for us Scrabblers. It's shirtsleeves weather, there's a light wind, birds are chirping. I stayed here once before and fell in love by the lake; I can't believe I'm here again to play Scrabble.

Eric invites Matt, Marlon, and me to save the hotel costs by sleeping at his house, which turns out to be almost an hour away on the country roads. By the time the first night's games have ended (I'm 3–0), we don't make it back until after midnight. Anagrams pass the time. Matt dishes out TROUTMANIA*, which has two: MATURATION, NATATORIUM. "Someone give me one," he commands, almost whiningly. "SHIRTSLEEVE," Marlon offers. "THEIRSELVES," Matt responds.

For Marlon, it's like a Fresh Air Fund weekend. "I'm a city boy," he says as he emerges from the car after the long climb up the dirt driveway. He gazes at the night sky crowded with stars. "Never seen stars like this. Can't show me sky like that. *Damn.*" The next morning, Matt picks up the theme. "There's a waterfall for you to see, Marlon," he says. "Why I need to see that?" Marlon replies. "Part of our community service," Matt says.

Matt forgets his tracking sheets. Marlon forgets his shorts. Matt sports his uniform of jeans, plaid flannel shirt, and basketball sneakers, and he sort of ambles, hopping from one leg to the other, favoring his bad knee. Marlon looks like a fireplug with legs, dressed in an electric blue nylon tracksuit plastered with silver logos for a NASCAR racing team. When he walks, Marlon makes a whooshing sound. Eric and I laugh at the sight of the two Scrabble geniuses scampering back into the house.

In the car, Eric rehashes a particularly painful loss from the previous night when Matt suddenly interrupts. "I've got one," he says.

"A-C-E-I-O-P-R-R-S-T-T." Marlon says he has the answer: TETRA-SPORIC. Everyone hoots derisively. "TETRASPORIC is good!" Marlon insists. "TETRASPORIC is good!"

At the day's end, I'm 7–3. Unfortunately, I'm one of the highest-rated players in the third and bottom division, so, statistically, I'm expected to perform well. Nonetheless, I'm feeling pretty Zen about my efforts, choosing to focus on my overall record and not my 4–3 performance of the day. With Edley around, I'm hyperconscious of my mental state. Joe encourages me to relax, to breathe deeply, stay positive, and not worry about winning or losing. It seems to be working, but thanks to the travel time to Eric's I'm extra-tired. As we head back that night, I try to convince myself that the six hours of sleep I'll be getting will be preparation enough to win the five remaining games, and the tournament, on Sunday morning.

As I doze in the passenger seat, the background anagramming an effective soporific, periodically I hear Eric say that he's not sure what road we're on and that we don't have much gas but should make it home. Deer flash in our headlights, and when we almost hit one Matt notes that the near collision was planned with the deer in advance for Marlon's benefit. It's cold. The car begins sputtering. We finally conk out on a desolate two-lane highway in deepest Delaware County.

Matt hums the theme from *Deliverance*. We wait for a car to pass, and Eric finally flags down a guy in a Trans Am who takes him to a gas station a half mile away. I open my eyes to see Marlon bathed in the car's flashing emergency lights, a round mound of nylon facing the windshield, looking in his shiny outfit like Neil Armstrong on the moon. I can hear Matt riffing on the scene, imagining a local mistaking Marlon for an alien from a UFO. "He was in a blue space suit and his face was blacker than night. He came out of a flashing craft. . . ." I laugh and try to fall asleep. Matt and Marlon do some more anagrams to pass the time. Eric returns with a canister of gas. This is *not*, I think, a situation that Edley would find himself in at a tournament.

We ran out of fuel a mile from home. We get there at 2:30.

Five hours later I hear Matt talking to Eric in the kitchen. "A-A-B-D. . . ." Predictably, we're running late, and it's doubtful we'll make it to the hotel in time for the first game, which in all likelihood means our opponents will be instructed to start our clocks and we'll have to play a shortened game or, if we show up twenty-five or more minutes late, forfeit. Eric is speeding and, naturally, a cop emerges from nowhere to pull us over.

Eric explains with a straight face that we're late in getting to a Scrabble tournament.

"These two guys are two of the top players in the world," he adds, pointing at Matt and Marlon.

"A Scrabble tournament?" the cop says.

Eric shows him a score sheet.

Compelling, but not enough. He writes a ticket anyway.

As we drive away, I ask Eric whether he got the score sheet back. (He did.)

"Son, what's this FINI*?" Matt says, impersonating the cop. Eric's opponent had challenged FINI* off the board the day before. "What were you thinking here? Haven't you ever heard of defense?"

"Didn't you see AGUEWEED on this rack?" Eric adds. "I'm going to have to write you up for that play."

Marlon blurts out, "TETRASPORIC is TRICERATOPS."

"What's nice is ATOP," Matt says. He means that if the word ATOP were on the board, you could wrap letters around it to make TRICERATOPS.

"Oh, shit," Marlon says. "And I nearly played ATOP thinking it would close the board."

We all laugh. The odds against someone playing TRICER in front of ATOP and an S behind it are astronomical.

"Talk about risks. And Eric nearly passed someone on a curve doing sixty," Matt says.

We make it on time. I win four out of five, but the loss is a final-game showdown for first place. I lose by just two points, 347–345, blowing the endgame. In the wake of Waltham, I'm content with the second-place 11–4, +806 finish, even if it was in a weak field. (Matt takes the first division with a 10–5 mark; Marlon wins just seven. Eric does the same in division two.)

I collect my first winnings from a Scrabble tournament — $150 — and I smile for the disposable camera that Edley's wife, Laura Klein, uses to photograph the winners. Maybe it's the setting, maybe the absurdity of running out of gas and the speeding ticket and Marlon's space suit, but I accept my mistakes, as Edley has advised, and I move on.

Back in Brooklyn that night, the phone rings at 10:30. It's Marlon. He's just gotten home to Baltimore.

"I'm calling all of y'all," he says. "TETRASPORIC is *goooood.*" Marlon looked it up in his *Merriam-Webster's.* "I just called Matt and told him I don't know how he win any tournaments. Motherfucker doubting me. *Daaaaaamn.*"

The median rating of the people who have played in a Scrabble tournament in the past year is about 1150. After the one-day Long Island event a week after Rosendale, my rating increases from 1118 to 1165. This jump leads to two conclusions: There must be a lot of people who play in one tournament and never come back, and there must be a lot of people who just enjoy playing in tournaments for fun, because there is no way that I'm as good as half of the people playing competitive Scrabble.

The definition of a good player is relative. Armed with the two- and (most of the) three-letter words, I can now beat casual players handily. I even sweep my brother, the onetime word-list maker, when we play a few games. But if I'm suddenly rated as highly as half of the active competitive Scrabblers, what does it take to become an expert, not to mention an Expert? And who is one, anyway? To a 2000 player like Edley or G.I. Joel, a 1600 player — technically an expert — is a patzer, a fly on an elephant's back. To me, a 1600 player is a demigod, while Edley and G.I. and the other 2000s are full-fledged Scrabble gods. I said I wanted to be like them. But how?

The words are a start. By now, I even have a pretty good idea of which ones to learn and in what order, and I have accepted that it will take harder work than I've put in so far. But I also realize that it's the psychological, not logological, blunders that torment me. And as I'm pondering this fact, Joe Edley weighs in on CGP with his recipe for becoming a champion:

1. The ability to DESIRE to be the best. Or, DESIRE to WIN whatever championship is important to you.
2. Unshakable honesty within oneself to answer the questions about your own strengths and weaknesses.

3. Controlling your breath.
4. Finding a way to control your emotional states.
5. The X factor. I don't know what it is. It's just the seemingly extraordinary state that any given champion has during the winning tournament.

It's time to learn from the master.

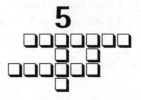

5

Edley

"THE BEST PLAYERS," Joe Edley tells me, "are focused on the goal of winning. Because all else becomes less important. Every other behavior is extraneous. Every behavior you display while you play should be the focus of winning. Otherwise, why are you there?

"Well," he says, answering his own rhetorical question, "a lot of other people are there for other reasons. And that's why they don't win."

If Scrabble had "majors," as in tennis and golf, the Big Four in North America would be the Nationals, the Eastern Championships in Danbury, the Boston Area Scrabble Tournament in Waltham, and the Western Championships in Reno, Nevada. The Nationals, Danbury, Waltham, Reno. It's not about the money. The Nationals pays $25,000 to the champion, but first prize in Waltham is only a few hundred. The glory and prestige of winning a major is what really matters.

When Joe Edley captured the expert division in Danbury (while I was choking on the other side of the room), he became the only player to win the sport's equivalent of a career grand slam. The Nationals? Twice, the only player to have done that. Waltham? Twice. Reno? Five times, including four in a row in the early 1990s. And now Danbury. Edley had won other biggies, too. The big winter event at the Holiday Inn in Atlantic City? Five times. The popular spring tourney in Gatlinburg, Tennessee, near Dollywood? Twice. The old

Grand Canyon tournament, which attracted the best from both coasts? Twice again. On an unofficial list of career Scrabble earnings, Edley stood second with more than $60,000, and that didn't include earnings in tourneys where first prize was less than $1,000. (David Gibson, who won $50,000 in one event, the 1995 Superstars, was first.)

Yet, less than two months after his Danbury win, I wander to the rear of the ballroom at the DoubleTree Guest Suites Hotel in Waltham, where thirteen of the game's best are slugging it out in the premier division. Edley is 0–10. In twenty years of tournament Scrabble, Edley had never lost more than *five* games in a row in a tournament. Even more remarkably, Edley says he is playing well, that all his games have been close ones. "I'm having fun," he says.

So are Edley's opponents.

"I'm trying not to give you a hard time because of what's going on here," one expert says.

G.I. Joel chuckles a bit too loudly. If schadenfreude were a liquid, it would be oozing from his shrunken being. Joel looks like Mr. Burns, the evil nuclear power plant owner on *The Simpsons*.

"This is fine," Edley says. "Really."

Really? *Really?* Fine to lose every game you play? Fine to know that other players secretly hope you'll lose the rest of your games, so that you, one of the most successful players in the history of the game, Scrabble's Jack Nicklaus, can suffer one of the most humiliating performances ever by a top player, one that will live in infamy in the Scrabble world? This is fine?

To Joe Edley, it is. Just as it is fine that one expert writes FIRE EDLEY on the $18 check renewing his membership in the National Scrabble Association every year. Fine for the warm, sweet, gentlemanly Lester Schonbrun to say of Edley: "He has zero noblesse oblige." And fine for Edley to be dubbed (as a result of a misquotation, it turns out) "the Darth Vader of Scrabble." Edley has been called arrogant, aloof, insensitive, rude, conniving, and worse, most of it behind his back. He doesn't care, because he doesn't worry much about what other people think. In the New Age story of Joe Edley, it's mind over everything.

An only child, Edley was born in 1947 and grew up in Detroit.

His father was a dental technician until he was accepted as a violinist in the Detroit Symphony at the age of forty-six. His mother worked as a bookkeeper. Edley was on the chess team in high school, and for fun he played a word game called Jotto, in which one person has to deduce a five-letter word thought of by another person. He studied math and philosophy at Wayne State University, and twice won the university chess championship. His father gave him a gold ring with a chess knight in the center and Joe's initials on either side, which he still wears on his right middle finger, though it looks as if it's choking his circulation now. Edley liked the strategic component of games. But he hated the performance aspect of competition.

"In chess, I got to the expert level, but I couldn't understand why I would win and lose," he says. We're sitting in the sparsely decorated Long Island town house where he lives with his wife and their four-year-old daughter, Amber. "Sometimes I performed my best and sometimes I didn't. It was a mystery to me."

After graduation, in 1969, Edley moved to San Francisco. He wasn't chasing the Summer of Love; Edley didn't drink, smoke, or do drugs. But everybody he knew did. "It was very exciting from my sheltered middle-class existence to come across all these people. And to be one of them but at the same time so totally alien. I would become like a chameleon. I'd be like them. They'd get high, I'd act high. It wasn't a puton. It was just fun to do that."

He got married one April Fool's Day and divorced the next Thanksgiving. He didn't have sex for two years. He hitchhiked home with $10 in his pocket. He drove a cab. He lived in a residence club called the Monroe, where everyone worked fourteen hours a week in exchange for room and board. But mostly he meditated, played pool and Risk and table tennis and Monopoly, some backgammon for money, and stood in the bookstore on Polk between California and Pine reading about human potential.

There Edley began to figure out whom he would be. He read *I Am That: The Science of Hamsa from Tha Vijnana Bhairava,* a guide to achieving inner peace by Swami Muktananda. He read Isaac Asimov and Robert Silverberg and Jack Chalker. But he was influenced most by Jane Roberts, a New Age philosopher who claimed that a "non-physical teacher" named Seth spoke through her while she was in a trance. Roberts's message was that human beings could manifest their own reality. As Seth said through Jane, "in a manner of speaking you are given the gifts of the gods. Your beliefs become reality. What you believe is, and becomes real in your experience. There is no area in your life to which this does not apply." So Edley asked himself, "What beliefs do I have? What are my attitudes? What kind of reality do I want to create?"

In the end, he decided that he was good at games, playing them and creating them, so that's what he would do with his life. He read about the first national championship in Scrabble, and about the publication of the first Scrabble dictionary. While he didn't play the game growing up or with his friends at the Monroe, something called him to it nonetheless. Edley decided that he *could* become a top Scrabble player; therefore he *would*. "I felt there was a destiny there," he says. To manifest his destiny, Edley decided he would learn the *OSPD*. All of it. He took a night watchman's job. "I would stay up all night studying Scrabble," he says. "I punched in every half-hour just to make sure I was awake."

On his girlfriend's business cards, Edley wrote alphagrams on one side with the answers on the other. Once a week, he and a friend who had moved with him to San Francisco, Jerry Lerman, would play six- or eight-game sessions. He reminded himself where he wanted to be: in a place where he could anagram all of the bingos in the *OSPD* instantly, first without a blank and then with one. "I felt that I could win the national championship, and said, That's what I want to manifest. Let me prove to myself I can do that."

Why that, I ask Edley, as opposed to — well, as opposed to just about anything else?

"That can't be explained," he says. "That cannot be explained. All I can say is that my life up until that point had been leading up to the fact that I was a games player, that I just needed the attitude, I needed the drive, and I needed the game. Everything I had been doing in my life was leading up to this moment."

After seven tournaments, and accumulating frustration, I need a tutor. Edley, of course, has the playing résumé; even his detractors concede that he is among the all-time greats. But that's not why I seek out his counsel. Most 1800 players could teach me the finer points I need to climb the ratings ladder. It is Edley's blanket calm and unswaying belief in an inner game of Scrabble that make him the ideal Scrabble swami.

When I call, though, I'm not after a deep skull session. I don't feel as though I've played enough games or know enough words to benefit from a heavy lecture on topics like opening moves, board control, and rack management — the strategic aspects of the game explored on CGP, over the board, and in cultish newsletters and how-to books. I've osmosed some of the basics, but I think it takes thousands and thousands of draws from the bag to appreciate the difference between moving tiles, which is what novice and intermediate players do, and playing a complete game of Scrabble, which is what the high experts do. It's finger painting versus Picasso, and I'm just a finger painter.

Edley senses this, and doesn't push a strategy lecture. Instead, we sit down at his kitchen table and, between installments of the Joe Edley Story, we talk about the fundamentals, and the metaphysics, of the game.

I open with a confession. "I feel overwhelmed by the words," I say. "All the lists and sublists and potential lists. There's just too much, so I don't do much at all."

Joe calmly reminds me that, in this matter, there is no choice. "You know what to do. Learn the words."

It's not overwhelming, he says. You can train your brain to do it, to anagram and retain learned words. "It's a process of asking yourself questions, forcing your brain to ask yourself questions constantly and answer yourself constantly in a search," Joe says. "Rather than just searching aimlessly. Forcing your brain to talk to yourself is one thing you'll see in every top player."

"Is it memory?" I ask. "Because I don't think I have a good memory."

"It's not memory. You're not remembering anything. You're going in the direction you need to go in and you didn't know which direction it was. All of a sudden some light or some image or some feeling says, 'Go there,' and that's where you go. It's like a lock. I don't know what letter combinations to try anymore. I've looked at every combination. And then I ask for help. And then all of a sudden the door opens and I know what to try. It comes to me. Sometimes I'll sit there, and I'll say, 'Help me,' and all of a sudden I'll see a bingo. And I won't know where it came from."

The human-potential movement, with its ashrams and est and cult-of-personality gurus and other Me Decade silliness, spawned a man for whom the meaning of life was Scrabble. Jane had channeled Seth, who told Joe *to play a board game.*

For the two years leading up to the 1980 Nationals, Edley told himself that he would win the tournament. He had no idea why or how; in fact, he barely had faced other top players in tournament competition. In the western qualifier for the event, Edley finished sixth; only five players from the region made the field of thirty-two, but Edley was invited as a wild card. "Fate," he says. "Fate was guiding me."

Needing to train against the legendary New York players, Edley headed east. He set up a session at one of the games parlors against Ron Tiekert. Tiekert won the first six games. "I realized there's something going on. It's not just luck," Edley says. "There's another level I have to learn. It was apparent as we were playing all these games and I was losing every one that I was all nerves and making lots of mistakes, helping me to lose. Finally, I put it all together in the seventh game. And I won it by controlling my breathing. That was the key. Understanding how to control my breath was nearly the last thing I needed to do."

Edley had studied yoga and tai chi chuan, in which breathing is a component of discipline and concentration. But he hadn't linked it to Scrabble. The idea was to control your breath: take a full breath. Push energy into the center of your head. Move feelings from your stomach to your head. Push air farther or faster to generate more heat when you need it the most.

"I wound up leaving ecstatic," Edley says. "When I went home I knew I had learned what I needed to learn."

Edley was virtually unknown among the experts at the Miramar-Sheraton Hotel in Santa Monica, California, where the 1980 Nationals were staged. The favorites were players like Tiekert, the king of the New York scene, and Lester Schonbrun, the former king of the New York scene, who was now living in Berkeley; there was David Prinz of San Francisco, who had won the first Nationals, and Jim Neuberger, a New York lawyer whose father founded a prominent Wall Street firm. Edley couldn't sleep from nervousness: two hours the first night of the tournament, two the second. He lay awake in bed doing his deep-breathing exercises and learning his "last lesson," the last component of the psychological matrix that would make him one with the board.

"I was repeating in my consciousness a phrase that would stay with me the rest of my Scrabble career," he says. "Please guide me," Edley would beseech a higher force. "You can do it."

Edley repeated it over and over, hundreds of time. The effect, he tells me, was to take his ego out of the process. Edley wasn't doing anything; something else had taken over. Regardless of what the reality was — because we create our own reality, no? — regardless of what others would say, Edley believed he was doing nothing. That something was guiding him to think the thoughts he was thinking, to make the plays he was making, to push himself. He went 6–1 on the first day of the three-day, seventeen-game tournament, good enough for second place. He was 7–3 at lunchtime on day two, physically exhausted from lack of sleep. He took a long shower and did more breathing exercises and kept up his mental mantra. *Please guide me. You can do it.*

Edley would play his last seven games against the top seven Scrabblers in the country. He won his last four that day, 11–3 and still in second to Jim Neuberger. He won Games 15 and 16, the latter when Prinz mistracked the score in the endgame and blew a sure win. He was one-half game behind Neuberger, who tied Tiekert in Game 16 when a win would have all but assured him the championship. In the decisive Game 17, Edley drew better tiles than Neuberger and won. "Night Watchman Is North American Champ," the *Scrabble Players Newspaper* declared. For Edley, age thirty-two, the championship had justified his life during his twenties, his psychological apprenticeship to Seth and Jane and Eastern disciplines, his deliberately crafted New Age mind-control system. But it was also a colossal letdown.

"I felt I hadn't done anything. I felt it was fated to happen for two years prior. I was just doing whatever the universe told me to do."

As we talk, Joe suggests setting up a board and playing a consultation game. I make a move, and Joe critiques it, recommending better moves, ones that he might have made based on his superior word knowledge, but also ones within the confines of my limited Scrabble vocabulary. The plays are fairly pedestrian — three- and four-letter dumps to "clean up a rack" while preserving potential bingo tiles. Joe is steering me toward understanding which letter combinations are better than others, and how to maintain them without sacrificing points.

Then, with the G on the board, and the letters BDIONRS on my rack, I shuffle and shuffle and shuffle. I look for words ending in ING. I look for words ending in S. Then I see BIRD. I lay down BIRDSONG. "No, but close. Try it again."

Whoops. SONGBIRD. (Actually, BIRDSONG had just been added to the *OSPD*. Edley had simply forgotten.)

What I just did, Edley says, is what I should remember.

"There's always something more going on in your head or on the board," he says. "It's just that the act of finding a word in a jumble of letters, that act is fun. That's the essential act of Scrabble. You don't need probabilities, you don't need to win, you don't need to care about anything else other than finding plays. It doesn't matter. It's just finding the plays."

Winning becomes a byproduct, I conclude on my own. Find the right play, and the winning follows. I think of Michael Milken, the junk bond Pied Piper, whom I covered as a reporter. Milken liked to say that money is a byproduct. Make the right deal, and the money will follow. Edley, I decide, is more Mike Milken than Darth Vader: tireless, single-minded, preachy, pensive, persuasive, unflappable, intellectually abstract, a bit of a charlatan.

"In chess," Edley continues, "you have standard positions that appear over and over and over again. In Scrabble, the only position you see over and over again is the opening. The second position is always different. The thinking is different, too. In chess, you're always looking for the theoretically best play. You can do that by looking ahead and seeing possibilities. In Scrabble, you never really know what the best play is. You can come close, but you're never really sure. It's hard to tell."

Joe is describing one of the core facts about Scrabble: It is a game of imperfect information. Chess is a game of perfect information. Both players have access to all of the information about the game. All of the pieces are on the board. Both players can conduct the same evaluation. In Scrabble, not only are your opponents' pieces — the tiles — hidden, but there is an unseen pool of pieces yet to be drawn — the bag. That randomness means there is an element of luck, and when luck plays a role, even the better player sometimes will lose.

"You play so many games," Joe says, "that you have to be prepared to lose and overcome your own negative thinking. Negative thinking has a much bigger impact than in chess. Because you can win in Scrabble when you're way down. That's not true in chess. If you're a championship player, if you get a pawn or two pawns down, the game's virtually over.

"That's one of the beauties of [Scrabble]. Your negative thinking, if you get down — or even if you're up and your opponent has a bingo or a blank and you could be in trouble — has a much bigger impact. The very best players are the ones that are the most optimistic."

I'm not very optimistic over the board, I tell Joe. I worry about dangers ahead. About missing bingos. About the poor tiles I have in front of me. About my opponent's plays.

"You should never whine," Edley reminds me. "Take responsibility for your wins and losses. For your letters, even."

"Your letters?" I say. "Letters are pure chance."

"How do we know? How do we know that?" Edley mimes reaching into the bag and whispers that he will pick the blank. "How do we know that's not going to happen? We don't. That's the answer. How did Matt draw so well to win thirteen games in a row [at the 1997 Worlds]? I don't think it was just luck. I think there was something else going on."

"What else could be going on?" I say.

"I don't know. I don't know the inner workings of Matt. But I know there was something going on. Why did I have the feeling I was going to win in 1980 and have an incredible number of miracles to happen that allowed me to win?"

"Chance isn't a good enough explanation?"

"No, it's not. Not for me. I don't know what it is. If I could bottle it, I could win every tournament."

Edley spent some of his $5,000 winnings from the 1980 Nationals on seminars in neurolinguistic programming, another human-potential movement developed in California in the 1970s, this one designed to help individuals change their behavior by changing their language, movements, and thoughts. (Edley chose it over psychic healing.) For two years, he studied NLP, ran seminars, and "trained" clients he found by placing ads in counterculture newspapers. But Edley became dissatisfied. "I wasn't altruistic enough to deal with people who didn't really want to change. I realized I wanted to help people in the game world, through games. Promoting my own ideas about manifesting your own reality through Scrabble — that became my next goal."

How, exactly, wasn't yet clear. In 1983, just as he was deciding to get out of the field, the Nationals were held in Chicago. Edley was just coming off of a two-month fruit-only diet that sent his weight plummeting to 120 pounds (Edley is five feet ten) from an already scrawny 142. His speech was slow or stuttering, and he had difficulty coordinating his movements. At the same time, Edley was adopting the breathing technique qi gong, taught to him by a wrinkly, octogenarian Chinese master in San Francisco. And he was exhausted from teaching one of his last NLP seminars. He told himself that second or third place would be fine — not exactly the positive manifestation of success as in 1980.

With an 8–2 record and in a virtual first-place tie with Joel Wapnick, a music professor from Montreal, Edley was practicing his new breathing when the left side of his body went numb. "I'm not in control anymore because I'm fearful. I threw three games away because I was scared." Still, Edley managed to win enough to force a deciding finale against Wapnick. But he lost, and finished third overall, just as he had prophesied. "Because of my physical problem, I couldn't manifest what I needed to manifest," he says.

Edley next manifested himself on a six-month cross-country Scrabble and backgammon odyssey, staying with friends, playing in eleven Scrabble tournaments (four firsts, four seconds), and netting $500. When he returned to San Francisco, he had one last piece of personal growth to attend to: living outdoors. Edley stashed his belongings at the apartment of an old girlfriend, donned an army jacket, slept under a bush outside the arboretum in Golden Gate Park, and showered at a park near Fisherman's Wharf. At age thirty-seven. "I wanted to feel comfortable being a citizen of the world."

After five months, Edley decided to live indoors again. And he hatched a plan: He would start a Scrabble newsletter. About two hundred players subscribed to Edley's twelve-page type- and hand-written *Tile Rack,* which contained game boards, anagrams, and other puzzles. At the same time, he worked as a bicycle messenger on the steep hills of San Francisco and drove an airport shuttle bus. And he was hired by the Scrabble association's new public-relations man, John Williams, to proofread the *SPN*. He helped organize an alternate Nationals in Las Vegas in 1987, held when Coleco, which then owned the game, backed out of its sponsorship amid financial problems. In February 1988, a decade after deciding to memorize the *OSPD* and win the national championship, Edley finished manifesting his reality: Williams hired him as the Scrabble Association's in-house expert.

By the time I met Joe Edley, he had, by all accounts, mellowed. He won his second Nationals in 1992 and a year later married Laura, a social worker whom he had met before leaving San Francisco for Long Island, where the Scrabble Association was based. ("I manifested Laura in my life," Edley says. "After having studied NLP and gone through the Scrabble thing, I realized I could do the same thing with a woman. So I visualized who I wanted in my life." Good with people, intellectual, sexy, and "charmingly ditzy, Lucy Ricardo. I constantly visualized that. When I met Laura I recognized she had all those parts.")

Still, the mere mention of Edley's name sends some Scrabble players into apoplexy. Matt Graham launches into unprompted diatribes about Edley's behavior as if they were part of a giant morality play. At almost every tournament I attend, some expert gripes, whether about Edley's table manners or his dual role as player and NSA official or his alleged favoritism in controlling the content of *Scrabble News*. There was the time Edley supposedly dissed the perennial star Brian Cappelletto in the pages of the newsletter, calling him "a little rusty" after a year off. There was the perceived slight when Edley wrote that Jan Dixon "played the best Scrabble of her career to finish fourth" in the big Superstars tournament in Las Vegas. There was the accusation (denied) that Edley deleted all references to Cappelletto and Charles Goldstein, who had vilified Edley for years, from a story about that event in the Scrabble newsletter.

All of those allegations — and more — are contained in "The Trial," a twelve-chapter, ten-thousand-word screed posted to CGP in 1996 by Edley's onetime friend Mike Baron. Written as a mock trial, with "J" the defendant and "M" the plaintiff, it's a chronicle of slights, aspersions, grievances, and misunderstandings. Baron rehashes his falling-out with Edley, which stemmed from his having accused Edley of acting out of "self-interest" regarding the structure of the Worlds. He recalls how Edley took a year and a half to review *The Wordbook* in *Scrabble News*. He reprises snide remarks that Edley is alleged to have made to players and reprints a flaming e-mail by Edley questioning Baron's business ethics. He revives complaints that the Scrabble Association — which offered him Edley's job first — neither acknowledged nor compensated him for appropriating many of his word lists.

Baron had long felt his contributions to Scrabble had been slighted, and clearly his play in twelve acts had as much to do with him as with Joe. But still:

> Lawyer for the People: It's July 30, 1988, 3 P.M. Where are you J?
>
> J: I don't know, New York?
>
> LP: No, basking poolside at the Sands Regent [Baron changed the names of some companies, places, and people] in Reno at the 1988 Nationals, just six months after assuming the throne . . .
>
> Lawyer for J: Objection!
>
> Judge: Sustained.
>
> LP: . . . after assuming your current position. The 1988 Nationals. Memory returning?
>
> J: Yeah.

LP: And what are you doing poolside?

J: Sunbathing?

LP: Yeah. But just before that, you saw there was a shipment of many boxes of books, all addressed to M c/o the Sands Regent sales office. M was very much looking forward to not only unveiling his seven-years-in-the-making project, but eyeing the very first copy from the manufacturers, a finished product he had yet to see. But there you were, poolside, having ripped open the first box yourself, having taken the first copy, and begun reading *The Wordbook*. Did you *really* have the chutzpah to do such a thing?

J: Yes, but . . .

LP: Eh, eh, eh. Did you or did you not do this?

J: I did.

LP: First to read the book and last to review it, when, a year and a half later, it finally makes the *News*. Can you anagram AEIPSSV AEEGGIRSSV? I have no further questions at this time. . . .

LP: Can you imagine: The final game of the WSC, you're paired against, oh, say, hmm, Brian Cappelletto. Let's see, oh, here it is. You said "Brian knows I love him" (8/4/96, CGP). Okay, so you're down 423–322, you've gotten seven power tiles, and you stick Brian with the Q, while bingoing out with rETAiNS, with both blanks, scoring 82 points, catch 20 for his Q, and win 424–423. You're the "World Champion!" Headlines read (goes to a blackboard, takes chalk in hand, and loudly pounds out with big block letters) "J WINS!" But, you know, there's one little peculiarity. It *really* reads (he inserts four large loud periods) "J W.I.N.S.!" And everyone saying this comes to know it stands for "J Who Is Never Sorry!"

LJ: Objection! Objection!

Judge: Sustained. Mr. LP, let this serve as a warning. No further outbursts and remain on point.

LP: I am sorry your honor. . . . I do have two small questions left for the witness.

Ju: Proceed.

LP: Earlier, J, did you get the anagram for AEIPSSV AEEGGIRSSV?

J: Passive aggressive.

LP: And what is the anagram of IM ORRSY?

J: I'M YORRS.

LP: Try again.

J: I'M RROSY.

LP: I have no further questions, your honor.

Edley barely blanched. He didn't hire a lawyer. He didn't bitch to John Williams. He defended himself in a few relatively short, occasionally sarcastic, responses. "I couldn't have made a better case against Mike if I tried," he wrote on CGP. "He could probably get Mother Teresa hung for murder with his technique: 'You mean all those people died while in your care? Very suspicious!' Quote out of context, then slant to perfection. That's the recipe." And then he let it go. He just decided he and Baron couldn't be friends. Four years later, Baron was still making awkward attempts at reconciliation, which Edley ignored.

To Edley, "The Trial" was just one more example of how his behavior is misunderstood. But his response makes me wonder: Is he so self-aware that it truly didn't bother him or so *un*-self-aware that he couldn't or wouldn't recognize the behavior that prompted such bile?

Either way, the reality that Edley has manifested is one that sometimes makes him appear — over a Scrabble board or in a tournament room or at dinner — oblivious to others. But then Edley *can* be oblivious. He sits in his tiny office at the NSA on the hottest days and doesn't open a window. He brushes off interlopers after a lousy day's Scrabble. He explains away poor performances in ways that make other players smirk. ("I don't have my energy back. It's not coming up. It's blocked down here," he tells me at one tournament, pointing to his stomach. At another, he says, "I think it was just a lapse in endorphins. It was a loss of focus. And I was breathing.")

But don't misunderstand, Edley will say, it's not arrogance and it's not personal. It's just who I am, how I prepare, how I focus, *why* I win. Noblesse oblige is beside the point.

"It has nothing to do with the other person," he says. "I'm engaging with myself. It's a battle, trying to manifest my best. Off the Scrabble board, I want to help everybody give their best. I recognize that my competitive self is not my social self."

Edley does have friends in Scrabble, people who understand that disconnect; he's not universally hated. "It's the life well examined that Joe is living," says expert Jerry Lerman, who's known Edley since they were teenagers in Detroit and was best man at his wedding to Laura. "But it's internal, not external. He hasn't necessarily become a master of dealing with others. But it doesn't cast him in the villain's role that others have put him in."

I see beyond the disconnect. I admire his ability to detach when he plays and the passion he brings to teaching the game. That's why I turn to Edley.

As I'm preparing to drive home to Brooklyn, Edley asks when I'm next playing in a tournament. I hem and haw. I tell him how I've played in four tournaments in seven weeks and feel as if all my performances were mediocre. The 8–7 on Long Island, then 5–7 at Waltham, 11–4 in the Catskills in the weak field, and 4–5 on Long Island. A 27–24 record. I don't tell him this, but I'm beginning to feel burned out. The game is too stressful, the prospect of improving too daunting. There's a seven-game tournament the following Saturday on Long Island, but I roll out a list of excuses not to play — it's a holiday weekend, there will be a lot of traffic, the weather's too nice.

Edley cuts me off. "If you were really dedicated," he says, "you'd be playing."

At 8:15 A.M. the following Saturday, a glorious one at that, I'm in my battered red Volkswagen Jetta, groggy after staying out until 1:30 that morning — un-Edleylike behavior — but breathing deeply and ready to play.

"I'm going to run the table. Seven and oh," I say aloud while driving. "Make the best play. Winning is a byproduct." *Make the best play. Winning is a byproduct. Make the best play. Winning is a byproduct. Make the best play . . .*

That would be my mantra. Asking some higher force for help, Edley-style, wouldn't seem genuine; I tend to place greater faith in mo — as in momentum — than om. I'm not yet ready to surrender responsibility for my play to a higher being.

It's a big crowd this Saturday, sixty-four players in the windowless basement conference room at the Comfort Inn. The tournament director shouts her usual Pollyannaish "Bingos to all!" — a Scrabble equivalent of "Gentlemen, start your engines." I think, Screw that, bingos to *me* — and we're drawing tiles. I concentrate on breathing. I try to focus. The first two games, against the sixth and eighth seeds in our group of eight (I'm seventh) are cakewalks. The first is particularly gratifying, an autopilot game against the guy who wouldn't stop complaining about his tiles in Danbury, marred only by my insistence on trying two phony bingos. The tile gods are kind in the following game; I jump out to a 142–32 lead when I start with MARINATE and RELINED, and cinch it by playing HOGTIES a few moves later.

Then hopelessness and panic set in, and no mantra can stop them. My next opponent is Marie, a forty-something woman with a gum-chewing, Pinky Tuscadero toughness that's accented by a look of perpetual disgust. When she drops down SAUSAGE and then UNGREEDY, which I challenge, losing a turn, she's up 205–67 and I'm psyched out. I have drawn three S's at once and used two of them on low-scoring plays. Now I have to pass. She plays AGITATER,* which I don't challenge. I'm on the short end of 277–67.

I sink lower in my chair, resignation washing over me. I can't remember a thing Edley told me — about playing every rack, about the beauty in just finding the plays, about being optimistic. I have the letters EILSTTV on my rack, and if ever there was a time to ask for help, it's now. I see VITTLES. Or is it VITTELS? I inexplicably choose VITTELS*. It's challenged off the board, and I sink lower. I play another phony bingo, in a futile attempt to cut the deficit, only to see it widen, 348–79. Then I play a phony three, KEV*, one of the five threes just excised from the dictionary (it's an acronym for kilowatt electron volt): 366–79. For good measure, Marie then picks up the J, X, and Z, and I eat the Q. Final score: 591–228.

In almost every Scrabble tournament, you face an unwinnable game. Even the Edleys of the world do. Usually, however, it isn't a 363-point drubbing, because better players know how to stanch the bleeding. This defeat may be the worst I'll ever suffer, and the right thing to do is forget about it. Immediately. It has no bearing on the next seven tiles I will pull from the bag. As Edley said, you have to be prepared to lose, and know how to overcome negative thinking.

But the rout takes root, and I just move tiles the rest of the afternoon. Lose, win, lose, win. I attribute the victories to my opponents' incompetence (one spelled REPELLED with one L, another tried RESTONED*), the losses to my own ample failings.

The 4–3 record isn't terrible; I finish fourth in the group, and my rating will increase. But that feels secondary. I'm ready to dismiss Edley's message — the breathing, the mantras, the power of positive thinking — as New Age doublespeak that can't work for me. But after one tournament, why should it work? Why should I expect to win when I won't devote the time required to improve my chances of winning? Why should I be satisfied, anyway?

"You can always come away from tournaments thinking you could have played better," Edley had said.

"Even you?"

"Of course me. I'm always saying that. If I didn't feel like I could play better, what would be the point of continuing?"

6

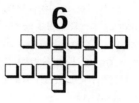

1191

N A BALLROOM big enough for the Reverend Sun Myung Moon to hold a mass wedding, on pink carpeting below five crystal chandeliers, the Scrabble masses have gathered. The high church of Scrabble is the ritzy Fairmont Hotel in downtown Chicago, where I am one of 535 people who will be married to the game for the next week. It's the Nationals, the every-other-year event for which players of all ratings take vacation, spend thousands of dollars on airfare and hotel rooms, and gather with the similarly afflicted for a marathon of their favorite game. The 1998 event is the biggest and longest to date — the most players, up from four hundred two years earlier, and the most games, thirty-one. It is also the most money, nearly $500,000, that Scrabble's corporate owner, Hasbro, will spend on a single event promoting its product.

The opening-night reception is part family reunion, part carnival sideshow. Everyone gets a Scrabble tote bag, complete with a T-shirt, which some players don immediately, and a special fiftieth-anniversary-edition board. (No one likes it; too tall, too brown, too ugly, too glary.) A guy spinning a giant flower on his finger walks by. A woman in a tight red dress and high heels leads her husband by a leash attached to a collar around his neck. G.I. Joel, in a powder blue suit, totes the trophy that he won in Thailand. A heavy, bearded guy in a wheelchair and a Cat in the Hat stocking cap whizzes by.

I greet Lester Schonbrun, the veteran of New York Scrabble in the 1960s, an erudite, easygoing avowed Communist, and his partner,

Joan Mocine. They sell me a copy of their Scrabble humor 'zine, *The Daily Astonisher.* (One piece reports that Joe Edley has switched from tai chi to Irish clog dancing. "It really loosens up the old biceps and triceps," he says.) I see Marlon Hill, who has been boasting in recent months, "Chicago is mine. They can write me out a check with four zeros on it. I'm ready. I'm fucking ready. I'm ready to win." Marlon and Matt Graham took Amtrak to Chicago together; they're both afraid to fly. I see the Washington Square parkie Richie Lund, who less than two months earlier had quintuple-bypass surgery. Richie celebrated by getting a tattoo of Bruce Lee on his upper right arm. Lee is in a fighting pose, wrapped in dragons with three bloody gashes across his face and chest, in a scene from his film *Enter the Dragon.* It's Richie's first Nationals since 1992.

"I'm dazed and confused," he says.

The first North American Scrabble championship was held in 1978 in New York. There were sixty-four invitees. Selchow & Righter paid a $1,500 first prize to David Prinz, who was one of the main compilers of the *OSPD,* which was published later in the year. The next two Nationals — won by Joe Edley in 1980 and Joel Wapnick in 1983 — were limited to thirty-two qualifiers, and from then on, a basic principle applied: As goes the company that owns Scrabble, so go the Nationals.

Flush with cash thanks to the unexpected and unprecedented popularity of Trivial Pursuit, Selchow in 1985 made the Nationals an open event. More than three hundred players competed for $52,000 in prize money. Selchow fed the players a sit-down hot lunch every day, held two cocktail receptions, and hired a guy dressed in a town crier costume who delivered a "Hear ye! Hear ye!" proclamation to open the event. Ron Tiekert won the biggest-ever first prize of $10,000 with a remarkable 20–2 record. Edley took fifteen of his last sixteen games to finish second. Lund, then an unknown, shocked the field by finishing third.

A year later, Scrabble's fortunes reversed. Selchow & Righter, unable to manage the growth caused by Trivial Pursuit, sold itself to Coleco, a brash company known for its boom-and-bust cycles which was trying to buy respectability in the form of other toy and game manufacturers. Coleco didn't care about the competitive side of

Scrabble; it dropped ownership of the Scrabble Association and canceled the 1987 Nationals in San Francisco. John Williams, who had taken over stewardship of the Association, already had booked a hotel, ordered coffee mugs as gifts for the players, and printed a special edition of the *OSPD*. Coleco promised to hold the event the following year.

"We are confident that this timing will ultimately contribute to the advancement of the Scrabble brand name, and that someday [the Nationals] can be elevated to a *Wide World of Sports* type profile, with our two best word experts battling it out for prize money before a national audience," the company announced.

The players revolted. Edley and a Californian named Johnny Nevarez organized an alternate nationals in Las Vegas. Some 320 players attended, and Coleco was shamed into donating $5,000 for first-prize money. The event was won by Rita Norr, a Brooklyn mother of three and a student, the first and only woman ever to win the Nationals. To the players, the message was clear: The game transcended its corporate owner.

Coleco did keep its promise. Though the company teetered on the brink of collapse, it held a 1988 national championships in Reno anyway. Two weeks afterward, Coleco filed for Chapter 11 bankruptcy-court protection. Coleco was still in bankruptcy court a year later, but John Williams, who had gone into debt himself to keep the players association afloat, scheduled another Nationals anyway. It was a bare-bones affair held in a grimy hotel across the street from Madison Square Garden in New York. There wasn't even enough money for a reception. "We had no funding," Williams recalls. "I remember going out and buying potato chips and the hotel not allowing us to bring them in." Some 220 diehards turned out.

But there was reason for optimism. Hasbro had just agreed to acquire most of Coleco's assets, including Scrabble. Under Coleco, the game had languished. Coleco sold just over three hundred thousand sets of basic Scrabble in its last year of control, the fewest since 1952. Distribution channels had dried up. Advertising was nil. It took Hasbro three years to rebuild sales to the one-million-a-year level, but it happened. Over the objection of some senior Hasbro executives, who didn't understand why Scrabble needed an outside association when other board games didn't, Williams received a commitment for financial support from Hasbro's Milton Bradley division. The Nationals stabilized and grew.

Players expected a lavish and well-organized affair, and they got it, even if they weren't always happy. The Nationals became the forum for a "town meeting" that Williams began holding so players could air their gripes. Once the tournament was even the site of a demonstration, in 1994, after Hasbro agreed to expurgate the so-called offensive words from the *OSPD*. Given its burgeoning size and the growing ranks of top-level experts, the Nationals also became the place where legends were made: Wapnick won seventeen straight games in 1992 only to drop his final three, and the tournament, to Edley, who won his second title; the quiet, self-effacing David Gibson won the 1994 event and then shared some of his prize money with fellow players; twenty-one-year-old Adam Logan became the youngest champion, in 1996, with Marlon Hill behind him as the highest-finishing African American.

In 1998, the oddsmakers — okay, the oddsmaker, Jim Geary, a young, poker-playing expert from Phoenix who operates a book on the tournament — have cofavorites: Logan and another former whiz kid, Brian Cappelletto, an options trader in Chicago, with odds of 5 to 2. G.I. Joel is 3 to 1 and Edley is 7 to 2. Matt Graham is 10 to 1, Marlon 25 to 1.

There is no betting on the third division of four, which is where I'm situated. I'm seeded 117th of the 133 players, which means there are but sixteen players in the division with ratings below my 1191. That's because I am "playing up"; the division technically is for those rated between 1200 and 1500, but players can play up a full division. I could have stayed in the bottom division, whomped the blue-hairs and newbies, and maybe even been national novice champion. Or I could play to what I think is my true skill level and give my rating a chance to spike higher. The choice was easy.

One problem: I am not prepared. I have spent much of the summer in France covering the World Cup soccer tournament. I toted my Franklin, *OSPD*, and word lists to the Continent but didn't study at all, which surely must be to my credit as a human being, if not as a Scrabble player. Upon my return, burdened by work, I didn't visit the club or the park. I reviewed the threes, began the three-to-make-fours, and studied a few more stems from Mike Baron's Top 100 list — AINERS, SENIOR, TONIES. When Marlon stops by my hotel room, I page through one of his notebooks, which contains every *six*-letter word — the last thing most players learn, if they even bother — and the gap between me and the top players once again becomes frighteningly evident.

But the gap between my peers and me doesn't feel so great. Despite the rating disparity that places me at the bottom of my field, and despite my lack of preparation, my expectations remain high. In a game in which luck is a factor, in which logic and intelligence play a role, I'm finding it hard to accept that there are other, larger, empirical reasons for failure. I still want to overlook the seminal rule of Scrabble: There is no substitute for word knowledge. I have very little but still believe that can be overcome, that I am somehow different — smarter — than the other assorted blue-hairs, hobbyists, and expert wanna-bes in my division.

Inside the ballroom, official boards and tiles (red and blue, alternating in color from board to board so that players don't inadvertently reach into neighboring bags and grab the same color tiles), supplied by Hasbro, are arrayed on the evenly spaced and numbered tables. There is a bank of computers for entering results, a big 1998 National Scrabble Championship banner, and a giant Scrabble board that reads DAY ONE: STOP BY FOR A SPELL.

From a podium, John Williams thanks us for making this tournament the biggest Scrabble event ever. He then announces the death of two prominent Scrabblers: Joel Skolnick, "one of the founding fathers if not the founding father of the tournament scene" — Skolnick organized the first big New York tournaments in the early 1970s — and Mike Wise, "the founding father of Scrabble in Canada." John's voice cracks. It's a touching scene, a reminder of how important this game is in people's lives. After a moment of silence, G.I. Joel races up and announces a prize in honor of the men: $20 for the highest-scoring word containing JOEL or WISE. "JOWLIEST would qualify for both, yes," Joel says.

As if to prove I'm better than my rating, I start 6–3. But on day two of the tournament (AS GOOD AS YOUR WORD, the giant board says), I botch three endgames, and fall to 7–7. At 10–8 on day three (THE WORD IS OUT. WE ARE SPELLBOUND.), I hold a lead but can't find

ETESIAN — SATINE plus an E, one of the most basic Scrabble racks. I lose three turns passing and searching for a bingo, and finally lose the game. Two games later, I get and play ETESIAN, but lose anyway. I lose four in a row. I win four in a row. I lose four in a row.

As I lumber through the event, nothing makes sense. I play phonies almost every game, an addiction that seems to be worsening; guessing is generally a bad strategy, but I can't seem to help myself. I challenge acceptable words. I lose two games by exceeding my time. I'm confused as to what letters to keep and what to trade, often opting mistakenly to hang on to more vowels than I should. After three days, my record is 10–11, somewhere in the middle of the pack.

Ah, but the nightlife is fun. Dozens of players while away the evenings doing what they just spent all day doing, playing Scrabble, as if thirty-one games aren't enough. For the first time, I see big money changing hands over a board; there are $100 doubles matches involving a few of the best players. Matt and Marlon are their usual opinionated, codependent selves. (And, as usual, they're both broke; I agree to cover the hotel room they are sharing.) Eric Chaikin shows up midtournament, straight from his overseas travels. One night, Dominic Grillo and Martin Smith throw a party in their hotel room. The one socialized under-thirty woman in the tournament shows up, so it's not all men. We order pizzas and play Scrabble and Anagrams. I find JAILBIRD and CAUSEWAY, and shout out WATERLILY, for which Matt praises me, even though it turns out not to be acceptable (it's two words).

In Division 1, Matt and Marlon are as out of contention as I am. Brian Cappelletto is proving the oddsmaker correct. He's 17–4 and threatening a runaway.

If the rules of Scrabble are the hundred thousand words, then Brian Cappelletto learned the rules faster than anyone.

At age thirteen, in 1983, Brian began playing against a neighbor, a tournament player, but it took two years to get him to the local club in Phoenix. After his first visit, not realizing there was a printed cheat sheet, Brian culled from the *OSPD* all of the two-letter words and all of the three-letter words they formed. "Somebody gave me SATIRE and RETINA and that crap," Brian says, and then an early book of seven- and eight-letter bingos. Within a few months, between sessions in front of his favorite video arcade game, Centipede, Brian was memorizing the fives, which he transcribed from the dictionary.

Brian's father, an aerospace engineer, died of cancer when Brian was three years old. His mother is an architect. Brian wasn't especially bookish. He was just attracted to the words.

"It was a hundred twenty degrees outside," Brian tells me. "There was nothing to do out there. I'd go swimming and then it would be, 'Let's do some Scrabble.'" Brian would turn on the radio and compile lists for a couple of hours, sometimes twice a day if he hit a particularly interesting stretch of words. It came easily. "I could memorize stuff pretty well," he says. "We'd go over something in class and I'd go over it once before the quiz and that was all I needed to do."

We're sitting on a bench in a park in downtown Chicago adjacent to Lake Michigan. It's a cool summer evening. A breeze is blowing. Brian is cruising through the tournament. "Stop it and give it to him," Marlon said earlier in the day. "Give him his check." Brian is modest but honest. "I feel like I've been in the zone for most of these games."

Brian doesn't have the outer quirks that distinguish so many top players. He dresses neatly and boringly: khaki shorts, tucked-in golf shirts, and New Balance cross-trainers. He wears his thick black hair short. Brian could be any clean-cut suburbanite or member of the preppy frat house. He is twenty-eight years old, but talks younger. He can be shy, a low-energy foot shuffler who turns red easily, makes eye contact reluctantly, and seems nervous and un-self-assured in conversation, answering questions in short bursts and not articulating thoughts in depth.

But Brian also works in the frenzied options pits in Chicago, where fellow traders place bets on whether he can solve anagrams in five seconds or less. When he's comfortable, he's loose, and even funny. Brian does dead-on impersonations of fellow Scrabble players. And he is relentless over the board. Brian just sees more words, more possibilities in his racks, and more places to put them than others. Says Lester Schonbrun: "He's from Mars."

Brian's first rating was an expert-level 1812. Within months, he was beating top experts, playing words like KOUMISS, PINNULAE, POLONIUM, and INTROMIT. When one opponent opened with ENTASIS, Brian calmly laid down REALISE atop it, forming seven two-letter words. As a party trick, he would tell people where on a page of the *OSPD* a particular word could be found. At sixteen, under the headline "Prodigious Start for Cappelletto," Mike Baron profiled him on the front of the *Scrabble Players News*. At seventeen, his rating hit 2000, the youngest player ever to crack that plateau, and he finished fifth in the Nationals. He went to UCLA, and kept studying, flashcarding every seven-letter word in the *OSPD* and then every eight-letter word.

A few years later, Jim Geary, who had just begun playing, met Brian at a tournament in Phoenix. The two were discussing particular plays when Geary asked incredulously, "You know all the UN words? You know all the OUT words?"

"I know *all* the words," Brian replied.

They went to Brian's car, from which he removed a Ziploc bag of sample flash cards. Geary remembers seeing BLUEFISH and FUNGIBLE — common words. Brian had indeed recorded every bingo in alphabetical order, not just those unfamiliar to him.

"I thought I could become the best there was at this game, that was part of it," he says. "And then everything would follow. I just had these crazy ideas of what the game could become." Sponsors. Television. Big money. Brian imagined being a celebrity. Or at least imagined that telling people he was one of the best Scrabble players in the world would elicit more than a shrug and a mention of how much their grandmothers loved to play.

It wasn't until the early 1990s, long after he had passed 2000 and peaked at 2122, one of the highest ratings of all time, that Brian felt he had the game nailed. He knew the dictionary, but he also understood the importance of strategic thinking — of word placement, tile turnover, rack management, and defense, how to vary the style of play at different junctures in a game, how to make good decisions. He rarely made mistakes. He won tournament after tournament, but never the big ones. Brian bombed out at the 1989 Nationals in New York, where he arrived as the top seed, and finished second at the 1991 Worlds in London and third at the 1992 Nationals in Atlanta.

Then he had had it. He couldn't take the unfairness anymore. You play and you play and you play. And for what? No glory. Not much money. And even worse, from a Scrabble player's perspective, no equity. "What's the fucking point?" Brian thought. "You go to a tournament. You're better than anybody else in the room. You should win, right? But you don't always. It's just tough to reconcile."

At the peak of his game, Brian quit. He was tired of struggling to maintain his lofty rating by beating up on inferior players. When you cross over to the other side, to the place where the game *is* interesting because you and a few others *do* know all the words, anything else seems pointless.

"Unfortunately," Brian wrote in a retirement announcement published in the short-lived Scrabble newsletter *Medleys,*

> the main premise of tournament play is exploiting 1800 and 1900 players' weaknesses. 2050 players are lucky to face one another in one fifth of the rounds in any given tournament. The vast majority of the time they are playing opponents against whom they have very little to gain and a lot to lose. There is little satisfaction in beating someone whom one should beat regularly. Winning is expected. Period.
>
> Given this environment, one must play phonies, use baiting tactics, and find other ways to steal games that are seemingly out of reach. I find this part of the game unenjoyable. Against 2050 players, such games are sure losses. Against 1800 and 1900 players, such games can be wins, and hollow ones at that. How much fun is it to exploit their weaknesses? "Only I know this word doesn't take an S." Or, "Watch me steal this game."
>
> I'm sorry, but that's not what the game should be about, and as long as that element is a big part of the game, I don't want to be a part of it. Life is too short to keep trying to win 85 percent of the time against 1800 and 1900 players. Few would ever admit to this, but take it from me, it's definitely true. Is it really a sin to put in the work and then desire to play opponents who also put in the work?

Brian was suffering from a problem few have the chance to experience: He was too good, and consequently bored. He wasn't in Scrabble, like some 1900-plus players, for the social scene. It wasn't a hobby. It was a challenge, and he couldn't stand not being challenged. He'd rather not play at all. So he finished school at Arizona State with a degree in finance, found a job as a night clerk with a trading firm in Chicago, and began moving up until he was trading on the Chicago Board Options Exchange.

But like Michael Jordan shagging flies or Sugar Ray Leonard do-

ing color commentary, Brian found that being merely adequate at
something else — like golf, in which he shoots in the eighties — isn't
enough. The best usually can't stay away. He decided to return — but
only for the majors. He played the Waltham premier event in 1995.
Then Hasbro announced that it was holding the Superstars Showdown in Las Vegas with a $50,000 first prize. "Now we're talking,"
Brian remembers thinking. "I just got this job that doesn't pay much.
What else am I going to do? Here's a chance to get out of this little
shoebox I'm living in."

He studied for months, played Reno, finishing fourth, then started
out 8–6 in Vegas, and wondered, "Why did I come back and start
playing this fucking game again? This is so stupid. I'm eight and six
and don't have a prayer. Somehow I won nine out of my last ten
games and finished second and won twenty thousand bucks. It was
so bizarre."

But rewarding again. Brian was maturing, so he got over the fact
that the rest of the world would never appreciate his talents, and he
accepted that competitive Scrabble would never be a blockbuster
sport, and even that he sometimes had to face inferior players. He
still didn't win a Nationals or a Worlds, but he knew it was inevitable.

Through day four (BE TRUE TO YOUR WORD), I have played a
woman confined to a wheelchair, a heavy-breathing fat guy wearing a
T-shirt that says PAY ME, an older woman who complained after
every draw in a sixty-grit sandpaper voice that could raise the dead, a
woman who complained even more *and* smelled like an ashtray *and*
tried to quit before my 200-point win was done, and a prim, middle-
aged woman who played CUNT for 37 points. (It's a fact of Scrabble
that the novice and intermediate ranks are heavy, literally and figura-
tively, with middle-aged women; twenty-five of my thirty-one opponents will be of the opposite sex, maybe one under age thirty.) My
record is 14–14. But my spread — the difference between the points
I score and those my opponents score — is +510. That indicates two
things. I've won a few blowouts and lost a lot of close games. Indeed,
eleven of my fourteen losses have been decided by fewer than 70
points. Less than the typical bingo.

None of my opponents dazzles me. The oddest play I see is RAD-
DLING, meaning "to weave together"; I challenge it. But I know too

that lack of confidence in the words is devastating; I miss several "common" Scrabble words other than ETESIAN, like XYSTI, important because it starts with X and there aren't many of those, and JINN, a supernatural being in Muslim mythology, which I should know because it evolves from JIN. (As do DJIN, DJINS, DJINNI, DJINNY, JINNI, and JINNEE, I later learn.)

It's clear I haven't absorbed Edley's lessons, and I realize that knowing more words compensates for a lot of other games-playing deficiencies, particularly at this level. I'm not Brian, with a gifted memory and a powerful Scrabble work ethic and whatever missing piece makes a fifteen-year-old kid memorize words a couple of hours a day while listening to classic rock radio. I'm not naturally attracted to the unfathomable possibilities of word formation or preternaturally skilled at finding words in strings of letters. I'm not especially intrigued by the history of language or the mathematical ramifications of the game. I'm discovering, though, that I do like the rational mindset required to assimilate the huge amounts of random information presented. And that I love to play. I love the adrenaline rush of competition, even if some little old lady is sitting across the table. I like the Christmas-morning sensation of not knowing what comes next: that the next rack might be the one in which some harmonic convergence produces ZYzzYVA, or, as in one of Matt Graham's dream plays, AVGOLEMONO manifests itself through an opening play of GOLEM.

In Scrabble, the thrill of victory is restrained. It's an intellectual game, after all. Brian doesn't spike a tile on the board or taunt his latest victim. Even after a championship game in a big tournament, the two contestants will linger over the board in analysis, as if the exercise is more important than the outcome. But don't be mistaken: Everyone hates losing. Brian overcomes that by doing everything to ensure he wins. He knows he has worked hard enough to develop the tools that will allow him to do so; plus, he doesn't worry about it. It just happens, because the plays are intuitive, almost automatic. Brian had told me with a shrug about a game he won by calculating the odds of drawing an N out of the bag in the endgame. He had AAGIINS on his rack, and saw that if he could play off one of the I's and draw an N he could win. "I was fishing for the last N for ANGINAS," he says. "It was a twelve to one shot."

The one-on-one challenge doesn't seem to be some endorphin release for Brian. For me, it's all about nervous energy, the caveman thrill of killing the beast and eating it for dinner. But if I want to experience that feeling more frequently — if I want to win, to have a high rating, to be an expert — something has to change. I have to listen to Edley — that winning is secondary to making every play. But I also have to emulate Brian. With his "who wouldn't have seen that play?" bemusement, Brian supplies a distinct lesson: To win, you need the ability to win. You have to develop your mind to the point at which seeing the plays, considering the best options over the board, becomes possible.

Right now, it's all I can do to play within the twenty-five-minute time allotment. Probabilities, though their importance has been explained to me, remain a mystery. Tracking tiles accurately and with purpose is beyond me. And I only rarely record my racks for later review. As with the words, I feel overwhelmed by the *process* of playing. The more I watch the pros, the more complicated the game feels.

The day after we talk, Brian wins all seven games to run his record to 24–4. He is four games ahead of his nearest challenger with just three games left to play. Brian has clinched his first national championship.

"So here's the winning board," Jim Geary says. "Kind of pedestrian. But he'll take it." On the board are DYNEL, DELFT, ELUATES, JUBA, KELPY, and ANORETIC. All new to me.

"It is kind of pedestrian," Brian admits.

Marlon comes over. "'Chicago's Own,' that should be the headline," he says by way of congratulations.

"OWN is the anagram of WON," says Mike Baron, Brian's biggest booster. "'Chicago's Own Won.'"

"Now," the champion says.

They all high-five and laugh. Almost no one begrudges Brian his victory. His prodigious talent, his years of hard work, his unflagging sportsmanship — all of it is universally respected. And his inoffensive personality makes respecting him easy. Brian may not be exactly likable, but he certainly isn't unlikable. In fact, he may be the exception to a rule articulated by John Williams, half in defense, I think, of his constituents. "Scratch the surface of any champion in any individual sport," John said, "and you're often going to find an obsessed misfit who's deficient in many parts of his life because he devotes eight hours a day to it." Brian isn't the only nice guy with a steady job and a reasonable grasp on reality among the elite players, but he is by far the best of the nice.

"I dreamed he'd win the tournament," Richie Lund says. "That's awesome."

"Way to go, kid," G.I. Joel offers. "It couldn't have happened to a more appropriate person."

Brian wins two of the three meaningless games the next morning (day five: YOUR WORDS AGAINST MINE) to finish with a record of 26–5. For the tournament, he averages 433 points per game against 358 for his opponents, with a high game of 590. (By comparison, I average 360 points per game, a full bingo less, against 354 for my opponents, with a high game of 490.) Brian's rating will climb to a mind-blowing 2109, by far the best in the game, and more impressive because of substantial ratings deflation in recent years. When John Williams introduces the new champion, he says, "It certainly has been a long time coming."

In the back of the ballroom, sitting on the floor with his duffel bags and two bottles of Afrin, Matt Graham pretends to be interviewed. "Thank you for allowing me to come here and have the shittiest week ever in Scrabble," he says.

Matt, Marlon, and I all finish with records of 15–16. Marlon blames a woman on the Scrabble scene with whom he had become infatuated. "When you're Samson and you get your hair cut off you get distracted," he says. "The only thing that can distract me is pussy." But Samson also blames himself. "I screwed up at nine and four. I thought my opponent had six tiles on his rack but had seven and bingoed out with REInVITE through a V. You miss a bus, it change your life. REINVITE. Fuck. Reinvite me to Chicago." Marlon had counted on winning a few thousand dollars. "I got to get a job next week," he says. "Next week."

With a nervous smile on his face, a red-faced Brian bounces to the podium to a standing ovation from his peers and collects the photo-op-ready giant check signed by Alfred Butts. "I just don't know what to say. I can't describe what it means," Brian tells the crowd of players in his awkward, aw-shucks way. "It's really something. I don't know what else to say."

"Another electrifying personality," Matt Graham cracks, "wins the National Scrabble Championship."

Maybe not electrifying, but for a moment profound. I watch Brian talk to a television interviewer. "There's always more to learn about this game," he says. "Always more to know. If only we had a little more time to solve the nuances."

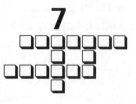

7

Alfred

T HERE COMES A TIME in any obsession when you have to learn more. It doesn't much matter whether the object of an obsession is a person, a sports car, a football team, or a board game. You just do. You need to see the shrinking world into which you are being sucked as a fully formed whole. Before I throw myself deeper into the abyss that Scrabble appears to be, hijacking my nights, weekends, and idle thoughts — I've started dreaming about the game — I need to understand where it came from, and how it became an institution unlike any other in the two-hundred-year history of the American toy industry. To do that, I need to answer one question: Who was Alfred Butts?

In lore, Butts is the unemployed architect who invented Scrabble as a none-too-bright get-rich-quick scheme during the Depression. I don't know how embellished the myth is, but I need more than facts. I want to know if Butts sensed he was inventing the most sophisticated board game of modern times, a worthy companion to chess and backgammon, which had centuries-old pedigrees. I want to know if he consulted dictionaries, if he marveled at the geometric forms of juxtaposed letters, if he loved words.

I want to know, in short, if he was one of us.

The two-story white colonial on Cold Spring Road in the rural hamlet of Stanfordville, New York, population three thousand, has changed little since Alfred Butts bought it in 1954 with royalties from his overnight game sensation. Yellowing floral wallpaper, creaky metal kitchen cabinets, dim-bulbed lamps — all seems untouched from when Butts bought the old house. Built in 1811 by his great-great-grandfather, but out of the family for decades, it would be a summer-and-weekend place; Butts and his wife, Nina, were ensconced in Jackson Heights, a middle-class neighborhood in the New York City borough of Queens. They had lived there for twenty years, and the steady, handsome income from Scrabble wasn't going to change the lives of the quiet, modest couple. If there was to be an extravagance in Butts's life, this would be it: the rolling grassland up Shelley Hill Road, the drafty windows, the alcove study for Alfred's books.

After Alfred died almost forty years later, his nephew, Robert Butts, a reserved, sandy-haired, owl-eyed lawyer who helped an aging Alfred manage his affairs, bought the Stanfordville house. With it came his great uncle's furniture and some of his possessions. Among them are what I dub the Scrabble Archives. Visiting the Archives, which I first do on a glorious early summer's day, becomes a personal hadj: Mecca, the Louvre, and Cooperstown rolled into one. I imagine the place as a shrine with framed boards decorating the walls, old tiles in spotlit display cases like Egyptian antiquities, an original set of rules under glass like the Declaration of Independence.

Bob Butts, though, doesn't display any memorabilia. Even a handful of documents framed by the National Scrabble Association for a recent celebration — a 1933 rejection letter from Milton Bradley; a bill for $40 from the Dover Inlay Manufacturing Company ("Marqueterie of Distinction") for cutting one hundred sets of wooden tiles; the scorecard from a 1956 game in which Nina scored 284 points by playing QUIXOTIC across two triple-word scores — remain wrapped in brown paper and sealed with masking tape. Bob doesn't play Scrabble very often. The game, it turns out, isn't much more than a family curiosity for him.

Bob extracts three boxes of artifacts. "This is the stuff," he tells me. One contains the framed items; another holds original boards, tiles, and blueprints; the third contains Alfred's personal papers. A presidential library it isn't, but for me this discovery is more than historical research. It's like being allowed to touch Edison's first drawings of the lightbulb or Frank Lloyd Wright's sketches for Fallingwater. So when I see the bankers' boxes piled on a sideboard, it seems a little sad: Alfred Butts created an enduring piece of American popular culture, and here it is reduced to a few boxes in an aging house in the country.

But it also seems to fit. Bob describes his great-uncle as humble and self-effacing, a thin gentleman no more than five feet six who was proud of his invention but never boastful, a regular guy who happened upon something that wound up amusing the millions. Alfred himself displayed but one plaque commemorating his invention, and he talked about Scrabble only when asked. When the game attracted a cultish following and adherents began deconstructing the language to play it better, Alfred more than anything was bemused. "He never envisioned it," Bob tells me. "He thought he was inventing a game people would play around a card table, like bridge or something like that. He didn't quite get the point of memorizing word lists."

Alfred Mosher Butts was born in 1899 in Poughkeepsie, the youngest of five boys of Allison Butts, a prominent local attorney, and the former Arrie Mosher. After graduating from the University of Pennsylvania in 1924 with a degree in architecture, Alfred joined a New York firm, Holden McLaughlin and Associates, and took an apartment on the Upper East Side with his new wife, Nina. He worked on suburban homes in Westchester and Fairfield counties and a boys' club housing project in Madison Square. In 1931, as the Depression deepened, the firm cut salaries by 20 percent, and later laid off some employees. Butts was among them. He was thirty-two years old.

Butts tried to put his dilettantish interests in writing, painting, and illustrating to the test. He created a dozen prints of New York scenes, using India ink on architect's linen, which he ran through a blueprint machine. Butts called them "Vandyke prints" because he used brown tones. He made 150, and sold a few at $3 apiece. (A local dentist gave three to the Metropolitan Museum of Art, which bought three more. They're still in the Met's permanent collection.) Butts painted watercolors. He wrote essays and plays, which garnered rejection notices. Nothing generated much income. Even after landing a job as a statistician with a federal welfare agency, he had plenty of time and not enough money.

Games, he thought. People need distractions during hard times. He studied three types: "men on a board" games, numbers games that used dice or cards, and letter games. "These are all of ancient lineage," Butts wrote in his three-page "Study of Games," which continued, "The origin of board games is unknown, but in the seventh century in India we find the highly developed game of chess. The simplest number games are played with dice, forms of which have been found with the remains of the earliest civilized people. The playing cards of today, combining numbers and symbols, still bear their medieval designs. Alphabet games were known to the Greeks and Romans."

Chess is a game of pure skill, Butts wrote. Backgammon combines luck and skill, providing "a much more satisfactory and enduring amusement." Contract bridge was sweeping the nation, but was too intricate for the masses. Butts noted that those three games are of his first two schools: moving pieces on a board and numbers. "It is curious," he wrote, "that while two of the three bases of table games have yielded such interesting developments, the third has produced nothing better than Anagrams." Not that there was anything wrong with Anagrams. Butts and his brothers played the boxed game growing up. But it was not as popular as chess or bridge. It needed tweaking.

In the study in Stanfordville, Bob Butts pulls down Alfred's 1904 edition of *The Works of Edgar Allan Poe*. Marked with a deposit ticket from the Stissing National Bank in Pine Plains, New York, is the first page of the short story "The Gold Bug," in which the character Legrand solves a cipher about a hidden treasure by comparing its symbols to letters in the alphabet. "Now, in English," Poe wrote, "the letter which most frequently occurs is *e*. Afterwards, the succession runs thus: *a o i d h n r s t u y c f g l m w b k p q x z*." (Poe wasn't even close.) "*E*, however, predominates so remarkably that an individual sentence of any length is rarely seen, in which it is not the prevailing character."

Poe inspired in Butts a eureka moment.

"It follows that word games should be played not with a jumble of letters," he wrote, "but with a mixture so proportioned that the individual letters will occur in the same frequency as they do in normal word formation."

That would solve one problem with Anagrams. It would be easier to make words if letters appeared proportionately to their use in the language. Another problem, he wrote, was that the game was too slow. Rather than draw one tile at a time, Butts suggested giving players a handful of letters that they would rearrange into words by drawing and discarding. The result would be a word game with "a proper speed and snap; an excellent balance between the skill of the players and the luck of the draw."

He went on: "It is neither childish nor complex, yet may be played and enjoyed both by children and the deepest of students . . . The true worth of a game depends, of course, on its entertainment value, but, if in addition its players gain an increased vocabulary, a further knowledge of word structure and of spelling, it possesses something of which no card or board game can boast . . . LEXIKO (Greek *lexikos,* of words) is that game."

Alfred Butts was a linguistic layman. Other than Poe's fictional musings, he had no secondary source to tell him the frequency of letter usage in the English language. Butts hadn't been much interested in words before deciding to invent a word game. But he was suited to it: In everything he did, Butts was meticulous. On graph paper, in block capital letters, he recorded the precise time of departure and arrival and distance traveled, to the tenth of a mile, of automobile excursions. A postcard collection was indexed according to a personal classification system (amphitheaters, 3E4; balloons, 4E2; Catskills, 2E3; servants' quarters, 3F1; stockyards, 6C). Even as he disdained games playing as a serious avocation, Butts had the organized, mathematical mind of a games player.

Butts pulled out his architect's supplies and got to work. His files are thick with spreadsheets containing twenty-six rows, one for each letter, and slash marks in groups of five denoting their appearance in one publication or another. The popular story is that Butts figured out the breakdown of the letters in Scrabble by counting letters from the front page of *The New York Times*. Actually, he used several sources, including the *Times,* the *New York Herald Tribune,* and *The Saturday Evening Post.*

On October 5, 1933, Butts underlined in green and brown ink all of the words of nine letters or more on page 21 of the *Herald Tribune,* the obituary page; the notice of the death of Earl Cadogan, the British representative to the International Olympic Committee, included *landowner, hereditary, succeeded, assisting, lieutenant, commandant, secondary,* and *viscountcy.* There were 125 nine-letter words in all, and Butts wrote them down in long columns in block caps on the left side of a page, then tallied up the frequency of their letters in a column on the right:

A-71, B-5, C-50, D-55, E-157, F-13, G-36, H-18, I-107, J-2, K-4, L-33, M-27, N-105, O-98, P-34, Q-2, R-92, S-76, T-97, U-36, V-12, W-10, X-5, Y-16, Z-1

He increased the number of words and broke down letter frequency by percentage: He created a list of one thousand words of four letters or longer and recorded the percentage by word length. He compared letter frequency of varying word lengths on a page of the dictionary versus a page of *The Saturday Evening Post,* sampling a total of 12,082 letters and 2,412 words. He combined samples from different sources; one study of 18,165 letters included 6,083 letters from the *Times.*

Page after page after page of tattered, fraying paper with the notations of a bean counter spill from the Archives. I imagine tiny Alfred, who looks so meek in photographs, balding and bespectacled, like an expressionless Don Knotts, hunched over some newspaper or magazine in the fifth-floor walkup in Queens, counting letters. It wouldn't have mattered to the success or marketability of his game whether there were ten or eleven or fifteen E's. But Butts's perfectionist mind insisted that he figure it out. That the game be *right* was paramount.

Based on his calculations, Butts decided that Lexiko should contain one hundred tiles. To start the game, each player selected a letter; closest to A went first (just as in Scrabble). Everyone then drew nine letters. The first player would draw another letter, add it to his rack, and try to make a nine- or ten-letter word. (Good luck.) If he couldn't, he would discard a letter, placing it face up in the center of the table. The next player could take a letter from the pool or draw a face-down letter. Play continued until someone made a nine- or ten-letter word, at which point the other players would form the best single word possible from their racks and tally their scores.

A four-letter word was worth one point, and each letter used thereafter was worth an additional point. Letters of which there were two each were "minor honors" and marked with a blue square below the letter, and worth an extra point. "Major honors," those of which there were just one, were marked with a red square and doubled the entire score of the word.

Butts manufactured the game in his living room, cutting and shellacking the square, plywood tiles and long racks made from baseboard molding. He printed the letters in India ink on architect's linen, as with his Vandyke prints, and glued them to the plywood.

He gave a few sets to friends to test out and then began selling them from home for $1.50. He sold two in October 1933, four in November, and nineteen in December. On the telephone, he spoke to a Mr. Carpenter from the Adult Game Company. His notes reveal a rude welcome to the business world: "would not be interested in manufacturing — selling is his line . . . take a year to do anything . . . need capital — sell in department stores . . . game business very tricky — never can tell — might take and might not . . . two big game companies — Parker and Milton Bradley — if you go to them first they'll say they have one like it — if they take your game on royalty they won't give any guarantee — then they'll just put it on the shelf because they have their own games to push."

Milton Bradley, Parker Brothers, and the publisher Simon & Schuster all rejected Lexiko. By August 1934, Butts had sold eighty-four sets. Receipts: $127.03. Expenses: $147.46.

But he persevered. He made sets whenever orders came in — and they did, entirely by word of mouth, from London, Louisiana, Washington State, Mississippi, from P.S. 26 in Albany, from a convent in Rochester. In 1935, he couldn't meet a rush of Christmas orders and the next spring began turning down requests. By now, he had his government job and part-time work for an architect. He told inquirers he would be happy to have someone else manufacture the game and pay him a small royalty. In 1938, he told a would-be customer, "I do not make the Lexiko sets any more as I am now working on a game which I believe will be an improvement over Lexiko. I expect to have this new game ready in a few weeks and will let you know the details and price as soon as I am ready to take orders."

Butts had been tinkering. When Lexiko didn't find a manufacturer, he decided that the fault lay in the game itself. It needed a board. Butts made blueprints of various designs and pasted them onto a checkerboard. It needed better scoring. Butts assigned the letters specific values that corresponded with their frequency; the more frequently the letter appeared, the less it was worth. He reduced the number of tiles on a player's rack from nine to seven, which was easier to manage and, based on his word-length studies, offered more chances to use all of one's letters. To enliven scoring and strategy, he decided that placing letters on certain squares on his board would result in doubling or tripling the value of the letter or word.

And Butts kept toying with letter distribution, his primary passion. One sheet of paper in his files includes four charts describing various letter distributions. One has eleven A's, nine E's, and four I's; another ten E's, nine A's, eight I's; a third twelve E's, ten I's, nine A's. He varied the number of E's from ten to fifteen, and the total number of tiles from 100 to 110. He added a blank that could be designated as any letter. He fiddled with the ratio of vowels to consonants.

With every change, the Buttses would play. "I was the guinea pig," Nina told a reporter. "It began as a simple game and got more complicated. He'd come home at night and say, 'I have a new idea.' Then we'd try it out and he'd incorporate it or discard it." And as they had done with Lexiko, the couple invited friends to their Jackson Heights apartment, or reserved the social room at the United Community Methodist Church, and on Sunday nights they would test the game and ask for feedback.

Rehired by his architectural firm in 1938, Butts regained financial security, but he still wanted to market his game. He couldn't come up with a good name, though. For a while he called his creation "it," until finally settling on "Criss-Cross Words." He was convinced that this time his game was a winner. But while Butts may have solved the mysteries of letter distribution, he still didn't have a clue about product distribution.

He hired a patent lawyer who told him that a patent already existed for a word-formation game using a grid-like board and letters that "almost completely anticipates your game." The lawyer told Butts the basic principles were so similar that any manufacturer would have to pay royalties to the holder of the other patent, someone named Beckwith. "In view of this situation, it appears to me that the possibilities of realizing any profits from your invention are very small and do not warrant that you should incur further expenses in connection with this matter," the lawyer wrote.

My jaw drops. Was Scrabble a ripoff? I had come to admire little Alfred for his ingenuity and stick-to-itiveness. Butts was no architectural wunderkind, his artwork was unrefined, his writing was pedestrian, he wasn't financially ambitious or savvy. But he showed a surprising single-mindedness when it came to developing his games. Untrained in linguistics or mathematics, he used logic to determine the best way to manipulate the alphabet to offer the best chances of creating a multiplicity of words. And he obsessed over it. He may not have gotten it later in life — it being the lengths to which his game was carried — but I have decided that Alfred Butts really was one of us. Counting letters was no different from memorizing words.

But a cheater? I feel on the brink of unmasking a fraud, of rewriting games history. In the 1926 volume of musty U.S. Patent Office indexes, I find the Beckwith patent. It's four pages long, including two pages of diagrams. Reuben P. Beckwith of San Francisco invented a game, and it was a word game, and it used two to four boards. Each board was divided into sixteen squares. Players were dealt sixteen letters and tried to make as many words as they could in their grids. They discarded and selected letters one at a time. First player to make four words won.

It wasn't Scrabble, and I can't find any evidence that it was ever manufactured, or that Butts ever heard of it. But it did pose a problem. Beckwith claimed a patent on a game "combining with a player-board divided into rows of squares, or the like, each square being provided with a scoring number, a plurality of player-pieces, some of said pieces being provided with letters, and others of said pieces being blanks, said lettered pieces being adapted to be placed upon the numbered squares to form complete words, either horizontally or vertically." The Patent Office twice rejected applications from Butts.

Still, he kept tinkering. He tried a fourteen-by-fourteen grid, a fifteen-by-fifteen, a sixteen-by-sixteen, a seventeen-by-seventeen. He placed the "star" — the starting point for the game — in the upper left-hand corner. He placed it in the center. He placed it five columns in and five rows down. He put a quadruple-word-score square in the lower right-hand corner. He tried four triple-word-score squares. He tried six. He increased and decreased the number of double- and triple-letter-score squares. He changed the colors of these squares. He tweaked the letter distribution. He included a blank. He tried two.

Perfection isn't arrived at overnight, and the more I play, the more Alfred's game seems perfect. I think he was like Alexander Cartwright's Knickerbocker Base Ball Club laying the bases ninety feet apart or James Naismith setting the height of his peach baskets at ten feet. The distances and location of the premium squares are just right. The game is a carefully choreographed pas de deux, a delicate balance between risk and reward.

The first player is rewarded for making a five-letter word, since the value of the first or last letter is doubled; but five-letter words are pretty difficult to find when you have just seven letters on your rack. The first player also benefits from a free double-word score, the star; but laying a tile on the star means the second player can reach a triple-word score, which is seven squares away. Butts wanted scoring to increase as the game progressed away from the center, with the most lucrative plays on the fringes. On the board's second interior row or column, a five-letter word can hit a triple-letter-score square and a double-word-score square simultaneously, one of the juiciest spots on the board; use it, however, and you are likely to give your opponent access to a triple-word score. On the board's perimeter, a word can start on a double-letter square and reach a double-word; but that creates a lane for the game's holy grail, hitting two triple-word scores at once, a triple triple.

"The arrangement of the premium squares took a long time," Butts said years later. "It's not hit or miss. It's carefully worked out."

When I think of Butts, I imagine the ancients in India deciding that the knight should move two squares over and one up or one up and two over. I think of the Greeks or Egyptians determining what to do when a black backgammon chip landed on a space occupied by a white one. Because Butts lived in the twentieth century, his game had to be protected legally; it couldn't just exist. Just as war begat chess, the advancing state of communications in America all but mandated creation of a language-based strategy game. Butts invented a game that filled a void in the hierarchy of games, and in the culture.

Butts started selling Criss-Cross Words as before: filling word-of-mouth orders from his living room, waiting for someone who could help to notice. For $2 a set and 25 cents for shipping, Butts satisfied customers in Washington, D.C.; Bryn Mawr, Pennsylvania; Hagerstown, Indiana; Louisville, Kentucky; Oshkosh, Wisconsin; and Oneida, New York. He mailed about a hundred sets in all, and complained. "I have found it practically impossible to get a patent on any game," he told one buyer. "The commercial houses do not want games unless they have been proven successful, but if a game is successful there is no protection for the idea."

He was tired of making the pieces, hunting for boxes in five-and-dimes, mimeographing the rules. So he just gave up. If an interested partner approached him, fine. In 1947, someone did. He was James Brunot, who worked for a New York State welfare agency and had served as executive director of the President's War Relief Control Board in Washington. Brunot was living in Newtown, Connecticut, not far from Danbury, and getting tired of his two-hour commute to New York City. He wanted to start a small business that could keep him at home, where he and his wife, Helen, raised Dorset sheep.

Brunot later said he was given a copy of Criss-Cross Words by a New York social worker who was one of Butts's guinea pigs, and he played the game with his wife when they lived in Washington. When Brunot returned to New York, he learned that no one was manufacturing it. He contacted Butts, who figured he had nothing to lose. No one else wanted his game. Why not let this guy have a shot?

Brunot hired a lawyer who said they could manufacture the game without infringing on any patent. Brunot played down the potential of the business. "It seems apparent that . . . there is no marketable proprietary interest" in Criss-Cross Words, he wrote Butts. But "we do consider that it would be reasonable and fair in view of all the circumstances to have at least an informal understanding." He offered Butts a small royalty on sales, which Butts accepted.

Brunot made two significant changes to the board, turning the center star into a double-word-score square and eliminating four double-letter-score squares near it. He also made some minor cosmetic changes, altering the colors and design of the premium squares, which became pastel pink (double-word), baby blue (double-letter), indigo (triple-letter), and bright red (triple-word); the starburst-ridged sides came later. Brunot also conceived the 50-point bonus for using all seven tiles.

And he changed the name. Brunot later said he never could remember where the word "Scrabble" came from, or whether he or his wife thought of it. "We made up a list of names we liked and we sent them to our lawyers in Washington, and when they wrote back that nobody had ever used Scrabble as a trademark, we used that," Brunot said. The name wasn't chosen so much for its sense as its sound. It means "to scrawl or scribble, or to scratch or grope around clumsily or frantically," which can describe the act of searching for words on a rack, or grabbing tiles in the bag, but the aural link to *scramble* was what Brunot was after.

In 1948, Brunot trademarked the name and obtained a copyright on the board design. Production started that summer. Brunot bought a supply of birch plywood that had been advertised as scrap lumber in *The New York Times*. He hired a few local woodworkers who sawed into tiles the long strips of wood onto which letters and point values had been silk-screened. Brunot wasn't equipped to make boards, so he ordered a few hundred from Selchow & Righter. After assembling the component parts in his kitchen, Brunot sent copies to Alfred's former customers, including an order form in each set.

Alfred had little to do with the game. "Thank you for the set of 'Scrabble,'" he wrote to Brunot in December 1948. "It looks pretty good to me, though I haven't had time to do much more than glance at it. We are having a terrible rush of work, working nights until January 1. I would like to get two more sets to use as Christmas presents. Not knowing whether I can get it wholesale, I will wait until you let me know how big a check I should send you." Brunot sent along the two sets, presumably at no charge.

The newly christened game didn't set the toy industry on fire. In 1949, Brunot sold 2,413 sets of Scrabble. Butts earned royalties of $149.27. In 1950, sales fell to 1,632 sets, and while Butts received royalties of $101.23, Scrabble lost $450. The next year was only marginally better: 4,853 sets and royalties of $135.43 for Butts. Brunot was still losing money.

Brunot had named his venture Production & Marketing Company. At least the first part was appropriate. Unlike Butts, Brunot had the wherewithal, and capital, to produce the game in bulk; like Butts, though, he relied mostly on word of mouth to sell it. Promotion was limited to a few small ads in *Saturday Review* and in college publications like the *Smith College Alumnae Quarterly*.

Nonetheless, by the summer of 1952, sales had increased to about two hundred sets a week. Customers wrote asking for replacement tiles and complaining that their dogs were attracted to a chemical coating on the wood. But still Brunot considered folding the business if it didn't do better soon. Then he and his wife went on vacation to Kentucky in search of a breeding ram for their sheep farm, expecting another two hundred orders on their return. Instead, they found orders for twenty-five hundred sets. The next week, they received another three thousand orders. And more the week after that.

What happened? One theory, suggested by *Life* magazine in a lengthy profile of Brunot and the game, held that distribution had reached a critical mass by that summer and hit a tipping point among the smart set, who came home from their vacations and tried to purchase the game in stores. A more plausible story was that Macy's chairman Jack Straus played Scrabble during his vacation on Long Island and was irate when he returned to New York to discover that the store didn't stock it. Macy's placed a big order, which triggered orders from other retailers.

For whatever reason, sales shot up to more than five hundred sets a week in the third quarter of 1952 and two thousand a week in the fourth quarter. Brunot recruited his wife and friends to assemble the sets, which spilled out of the kitchen and into the living room.

Brunot bought more machinery, began ordering tiles from a factory in Germany (which made them of Bavarian maple from the Black Forest), and rented an old schoolhouse. Orders kept increasing, and Brunot had to move into a converted woodworking shop, a small white building in the Connecticut hills next to a stream filled with trout and surrounded by woods and cornfields.

By early 1953, Brunot had thirty-five employees working in two shifts producing six thousand sets a week. Which was terrific, except that orders were arriving by the tens of thousands, so fast that "they couldn't even add them up, much less fill them," *The New Yorker* magazine reported. Brunot licensed a cheaper version of the game, with cardboard letters and a board that was part of the box, to be made by Cadaco-Ellis Co. in Chicago and renamed "Skip-a-Cross"; it sold for $2. Finally, in March, he licensed the production and marketing to Selchow & Righter. And he converted the machinery in his Connecticut factory to manufacture the first deluxe version of Scrabble, a $10 item in a red imitation-leather case with white plastic tiles and plastic racks that included a built-in scoring device.

In 1953, nearly eight hundred thousand standard sets, three hundred thousand cardboard ones, and thirty thousand deluxe versions of Scrabble were sold. In the span of two years, sales had increased more than two hundred times. In the history of the toy industry, no game had ever taken off so rapidly and unexpectedly. And it didn't slow down.

As I pore through Butts's papers, the story of the game as a game — not as an obsessive, strategic, mathematical exercise — begins to make cultural sense. The country's shimmering, suburban, stay-at-home, postwar prosperity was fertile soil for the sudden rise of Scrabble. What better way to demonstrate the American know-how and ingenuity that had just saved the world than with a game that tested one's knowledge and creativity? What better way to luxuriate in the greatest prosperity the nation had ever known than by relaxing over a board game that, unlike Monopoly (Depression-era wealth fantasies) or Life (turn-of-the-century moralism), had no intentional social overtones? Leisure time was a concept just taking root, and what could be more leisurely, if not decadent, than Scrabble? It was a game of the mind that often took hours to play. America finally could devote itself to trivial pastimes. The country was infused with prosperity and suddenly enamored of education. Scrabble fit.

Saturday Review said "the new word game has practically routed canasta among the upper I.Q.'s of the nation." *Time* reported that Scrabble clubs "have convened all over the country" and that "hostesses serve a Scrabble board with the after-dinner coffee, and shiny markers with A_1 and Z_{10} inscribed are popping up on rural porches and in transcontinental trains." The *Life* article said that "in intellectual circles the game is played in French or Latin; in Hollywood, games of dirty-word Scrabble are in constant progress; in New York, the Guys-and-Dolls set has converted Scrabble into the hottest gambling game since gin rummy." The composer Igor Stravinsky and his wife, Vera, were photographed for *The New York Times Magazine* playing Scrabble at their Hollywood home.

A newspaper ad for summer clothing at the Lord & Taylor department store showed three girls lounging around a Scrabble board with tiles floating around the page: "Some girls have more fun than anybody!" The queen mother apparently was one of them. While shopping in New York, she bought a Betty Crocker baking set from F.A.O. Schwarz, bejeweled sweaters from Saks Fifth Avenue, and bar gadgets and a Scrabble set on a revolving table from Hammacher Schlemmer. "I am just learning to play Scrabble," she told the salesgirl. "Before 1953 departs," the *Herald Tribune* wrote in an article summarizing the passing year, "it can point to any number of notable events, from the inauguration of a Republican president to the growth of Scrabble."

Shortages were epidemic. "Buying a Scrabble set in New York today is something akin to nabbing a prime rib roast at ceiling price during World War II," the *World-Telegram* reported. Some customers placed their names on waiting lists, while others simply stood for hours inside stores until the next shipment arrived. A toy store on Manhattan's Third Avenue posted a sign in its window: WE HAVE SCRABBLES. A *New Yorker* cartoon showed wedding guests rushing out of a church, leaving the bride to explain to the priest, "Somebody made an announcement that the store next door has Scrabble!" There were a half-dozen or more knockoffs, with names like Score-a-Word, Jaymar Crosswords, and Cabu, sending Brunot's lawyers into action and prompting Selchow & Righter to take out ads urging customers to wait for the real thing.

Devotees sheared off the tops of lazy Susans to make the board revolve, argued over what was and wasn't a word, and discovered that surreptitiously feeling the tiles could yield the blanks (a form of cheating that came to be known as "brailling"). Brunot was flooded with proposals for innovations, to which he responded with a form letter. "If your idea relates to a turntable, a timing device, a box or bag to hold the letter tiles, or a device for turning the tiles over, we wish to discourage you from submitting it because such devices already have been submitted by a considerable number of persons."

Time, Look, Business Week, Cue, Pageant, Reader's Digest, Family Weekly. When major media called, Brunot fielded the calls and was profiled. And Butts achieved minor celebrity as the quirky out-of-work architect who invented the game as a way to scrape together a few bucks during the Depression. He appeared on NBC's *The Today Show,* on WOR radio, on the Faye Emerson and Skitch Henderson TV talk show on NBC. When he was included in *Current Biography* for 1954, Butts was so delighted that he ordered twelve copies.

Brunot didn't appreciate, or understand, the depth or the passion Scrabble was inspiring. Disputes arose early over the use of words like MA and PA, and the musical notes RE, MI, FA, LA, and TI. "Brunot's feeling is that if players want to use such words, they can," *Life* wrote. "He personally does not give a damn." Asked about players frustrated by the slow nature of the game, Brunot said, "Let them go out and buy an egg timer. It doesn't have to have 'Scrabble' printed on it." Approached by publishers to endorse one dictionary or another, Brunot was miffed that Scrabble was being taken so seriously. "It's only a game," he said. "It's something you're supposed to enjoy."

If Butts was hurt by Brunot's dismissive comments, he didn't show it. He simply answered every question he received — about where to purchase sets and whether colloquial words were acceptable and what to do if an opponent is stuck with the Q and can't make a play. And he counted his money.

An astounding 3,798,555 units of Scrabble were sold in 1954, one of the greatest performances in toy industry history. That included more than 2.5 million of the standard sets, 1 million cardboard ones, 82,000 deluxe, and, for the first time, 100,000 in foreign languages. Production of a braille edition began.

Scrabble was the nation's leading board game. Once the publicity abated, Butts had little to do with the game but sit back and await his royalty checks, which he tracked meticulously, in pencil, on block graph paper and yellow legal pads, in his neat architect's handwriting. "The worst feature of all this is the tough time I have trying to convince people I am not a millionaire," Butts wrote to an old college friend. "However, I will admit it is a pleasant change to stop worrying about income and begin worrying about income tax."

On each set of the standard game, which accounted for roughly three-quarters of all unit sales, Brunot received about 12 cents per set to 2.5 cents for Butts. Butts received no compensation from any other products using the Scrabble license. As bargains go, Brunot and Selchow got a great one. But Butts never complained, at least not publicly. "I never heard him speak ill of Brunot," Bob Butts tells me during one of several pilgrimages I make to the Archives. "I kind of got the impression that it was his decision to go forward with the deal with Brunot and it was okay with him and that he just didn't want to play hardball."

Alfred wasn't a businessman. He was an unassuming and competent architect, content to live peaceably with his wife in his rental apartment and his ancestor's house in the country and pass the time with his modest-man's hobbies like collecting postcards and crafting wooden jigsaw puzzles. He and Nina had no children. He designed and helped start a local library. He organized his Poughkeepsie High School Class of 1917 reunions. The Scrabble royalties were more than enough for the couple to live the quiet, comfortable life they desired.

It wasn't chump change. Alfred's royalties peaked at $81,376.37 in 1955. "I didn't expect anything as big as that," he told Brunot. "Scrabble should improve the vocabulary and I can claim I have played Scrabble longer than anyone else, but now I am running out of words. What comes after 'fantastic'?"

Much to everyone's astonishment, the game's popularity held strong. As expected, after the boom, sales did drop, to 2.3 million in 1955 and to just over 1 million the next year. In one of their infrequent meetings, Brunot told Butts that he figured sales would level off at about 300,000, and that "S&R believes same." But it wouldn't happen during Selchow & Righter's stewardship. The company introduced magnetic travel sets, nonmagnetic travel sets, junior sets, "Waffle-Grid Revolving Board" sets. Sales ranged between 1.1 million and 1.6 million a year through 1970, and Butts's royalties kept rolling in.

In the late sixties, Brunot wanted to retire and have Selchow & Righter buy out his business. Butts balked, but eventually agreed. In his papers is a manila envelope, on it written in the shaky handwriting of a seventy-year-old man the words FINAL SCRABBLE AGREEMENT. Butts would receive $75,000 on January 1, 1971, and $38,000 a year for the next five years. A total of $265,000, plus interest. Brunot would get about five times that amount, or $1.325 million.

Their business relationship over, the two men responsible for Scrabble dropped out of contact. They were never really friends; for the first five years of their relationship, they referred to each other as Mr. Butts and Mr. Brunot. When Butts once was asked to pass on regards to Brunot, he replied, "I have not seen or heard from Jim Brunot in a long, long time. After his wife died and he sold out all the rights to Scrabble, I believe he moved to North Carolina. But now I don't even know whether he is still living." A month later, in October 1984, James Brunot would die at the age of eighty-two.

As I read the papers, I want to fight for Alfred. It was his game, his brilliant, enduring game, of which more than twenty-six million sets were sold by Production & Marketing and Selchow & Righter in the twenty-two years he was involved. Certainly that was worth more than $265,000. Not even *all* the money Alfred received over the years seems just. (And he calculated it to the penny: $848,046.28 through 1971, plus the remaining buyout and interest, for a grand total of $1,066,500.) Alfred may have been content, but I see him as another exploited inventor.

I think of the hundred million or so Scrabble sets sold worldwide over the last half century, and the hundreds of millions of dollars reaped by the game's three big corporate owners, Selchow, Coleco, and Hasbro. And I think that no marketplace can adequately compensate genius, and this one certainly didn't.

*   *   *

Nina Butts died of cancer in 1979, leaving Alfred alone in the Stanfordville house, where the couple had moved a year earlier after thirty-five years in Queens. To pass the time, Butts, in fine health at age eighty, once again started designing games, usually involving letters and numbers, which he would share with family members. "They were usually pretty tedious," Bob Butts says.

He sent one, though, to Selchow & Righter with a note. "The *Scrabble Players Handbook* shows my name as the inventor in the story 'as American as apple pie,'" Butts wrote. "I have always been grateful for that recognition. However, I have never met anyone at Selchow & Righter since all of my dealings were with James Brunot and the Production and Marketing Co."

Indeed, Alfred had vanished into games history; some company executives didn't even recognize his name. But they invited him down to New York, and learned that 1981 was the fiftieth anniversary of his conception of Lexiko, and the company trotted Alfred around the country on a media tour. Alfred got a kick out of it (and a $350 per diem), preparing for radio and television appearances with copious handwritten notes summarizing his life and his game. He liked the attention, particularly from young, female publicists who accompanied him on his rounds. When Selchow manufactured his new word game — which it named, oddly, Alfred's Other Game — for the box cover photograph it posed the octogenarian in a tuxedo and seated him in a leather chair next to a buxom model in a black cocktail dress. He made guest appearances at a few Scrabble tournaments.

Butts appreciated the long-overdue recognition. On his first tour of Selchow & Righter's factory on Long Island, Butts saw four assembly lines cranking out Trivial Pursuit and one producing Scrabble. The company president, Richard Selchow, turned to him, and said, "Trivial Pursuit is a fad. When Trivial Pursuit is long gone we'll still be turning out Scrabble."

In the fall of 1987, with the leaves still on the trees, a storm dumped a foot of wet snow on the Hudson Valley. The weight toppled power lines. Without electricity, Butts decided to drive over to his niece's house in Poughkeepsie. Crossing the Taconic Parkway, his car was struck by another car heading in the opposite direction. Butts wasn't wearing a seat belt, and his head rammed the windshield. He survived, but spent a month in the hospital, where he suffered bouts of delusion, at times thinking Nina was still alive. He had a small stroke, became depressed, and was eventually transferred to a nursing home. Alfred died on April 4, 1993.

As he began to suffer dementia, Butts some days couldn't remember the names of the people who visited him, including his nephew Bob. One day Bob suggested that they play a game of Scrabble. Bob stuck the rack to a table with window caulk, because Alfred's hands would shake. Butts would recall that his wife was the better player; she had made QUIXOTIC for 284 points, he would say. He, on the other hand, was an indifferent speller.

"Some days we'd play three turns. Some days we'd play a full game," Bob Butts tells me. "Some days he'd put down four consonants and it would be complete gibberish. Some days he'd play OX and XI on a triple letter. When you become senile, you hang onto the things that are closest to you."

8

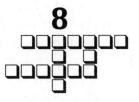

G.I. Joel

Y OU GET the big bed."
  Well, I am the marginally bigger man, I think, as I drop my bags. It's 12:30 A.M. and I have just played the first three games of another weekend tournament in the Catskills. This time, Eric Chaikin has moved to Los Angeles to pursue an acting career, Matt Graham is out of town, and Marlon Hill couldn't afford the trip from Baltimore. So I'm rooming with G.I. Joel Sherman.

Joel has discovered an ant in a plastic bag containing a half-eaten box of Archway oatmeal cookies that he toted up from the Bronx. Joel spotted some ants in the room after checking in, secured the cookies in the plastic bag with a twist tie, locked them in his suitcase, and went to play Scrabble. An ant managed to infiltrate the bag, however, and Joel is worried that fellow ants have penetrated other key territories. He dumps out a box of Mike & Ike jelly beans onto a towel.

"How do you find out if there are holes in a plastic bag?" he says. I suggest placing the cookies in the hallway or in my car, but Joel will have none of that. He's determined to identify the source of the invasion.

"Now I'm going to have to go through my suitcase to see if there are ants," he says. "And turn down the bedding." Which he does.

Joel runs water through the plastic bag. "This bag has integrity," he announces. He has changed from his customary G.I. Joel sweatshirt into his red-white-and-blue-striped flannel pajamas. "This is how my life goes every day," he says. "Encountering idiotic obstacles and trying to find a way around them."

He returns the cookies to the bag, again trying to choke off any possible intruders with the twist tie. "Okay, damn ants! You just try it!" He repeats the process with the jelly beans. "Die, mo-fos!"

Joel's snacks should survive the night. I'm less confident about my own prospects. Joel arranges a 6:45 A.M. wake-up call. This is earlier than I'd planned, as the tournament doesn't resume until 9:00 A.M. I want to sleep as late as possible and grab a quick breakfast. Joel doesn't need nearly as much sleep. At home, he often stays up all night playing Scrabble on the computer or writing e-mails or watching television, and sleeps a few hours during the day. It's no wonder he often seems groggy. But that could have to do with his eating habits, lack of exercise, or infrequent encounters with anyone other than his father and brother.

"So do you want to sleep or do you want a lesson?" Joel asks.

I want to sleep so that I can focus the next morning as I try again to raise my somnolent rating. But I also want to listen to Joel declaim about Scrabble. After all, he's great at it — playing and declaiming. It's his purpose on the planet, and as his roommate I see myself as an enabler. "A lesson," I say.

For the next hour, Joel proffers a blow-by-blow of that night's games. In two of them, he scored 603 and 601 points, so he's pumped. His voice leaps octaves, his arms flail about, he is virtually bouncing on his mattress as he recounts his conquests, reading off the plays from his score sheet. I love his strategic analysis and his arcane word plays, his acid commentary about opponent ineptitude, and even his goofy, obsessive, uncensored wonder at the most mundane happenings, like an ant crawling into a box of cookies. His body is a Superfund site, but that hasn't stopped G.I. Joel from getting back at the world with his mind, through this game.

Joel breathlessly explains how he worked his way through a troubling opening rack in the 603-point game, why he kept the three vowels IIO to go with a blank, how he saw that he would be able to turn the word BICES into IBICES (the plural of IBEX), how he drew the second blank and was able to play vICHIeS for 100 points. Now he's on a roll.

"I play SERIFED, the anagram of DEFIERS, I get eighty-two for that, and she challenges. I get a forty-point BOZOS, ENTAILER for seventy-seven, AXE for fifty-eight, JIGS for sixty, MANNITE for seventy-three. The total bingo count was actually only four, and not a triple-triple among them."

I steal a glance at the digital clock next to my bed: 1:15. But Joel isn't through. Now comes the lesson part. "The trick is if you have good word knowledge like I do, you're not afraid of any letter," he says. "You know which are generally bad letters. The W you would be concerned with. U's you would be concerned with. J's and Q's, obviously. But just about anything else you don't have to be afraid of."

And when you don't have a world champion's word knowledge? I ask.

"Anytime you're on equal or superior footing to your opponent in word knowledge you don't have to worry about closing the board. The main reason people in your division stay in that division for years is they don't understand that there's no reason to play scared. Making the best of your opportunities, even with much poorer word knowledge than I have, there are better ways of solving the rack problems and controlling the board than to just play three-letter ladders."

Joel's referring to the common pattern in lower-division games in which players take turns overlapping or underlapping three-letter words, staircasing down from the center, usually to the bottom left corner. Expert boards, by contrast, can be freeform and rambling, quickly stretching from top to bottom and side to side.

Of course, prodigious word knowledge allows for more adventuresome playing, but Joel's point is less about tactics than style. Experts become experts not only because they study words, but because they are open to danger and are able to weigh risks versus consequences. Away from the game, they may not be skydivers or day traders, but their willingness to stare down a problem, fearlessly, before the knowing gaze of others is one of the things I admire about Joel and the other experts. They may be mild-mannered geeks or underachieving layabouts, but behind a rack, for fifty minutes, they are stone-faced killers. So what if I put a naked E in the triple-word column? Let's see you do something about it.

As with most games, this one says something about how we choose to live our lives. Scrabble players, even career hobbyists who don't study words or crave expert status, are gamblers; not without reason are Atlantic City, Reno, and Las Vegas frequent tournament venues. Players are drawn to the long odds, and to the idea of risk. For the best players, the board is a place to lay it all on the line, to test one's confidence, knowledge, and emotional mettle. As in poker, bluffing is part of Scrabble, playing a word you know to be unacceptable and seeing if your opponent bites. But you have to know when and against whom to bluff. Otherwise you will be exposed as a fraud. In Scrabble, the least self-conscious are those who win the most. They aren't afraid of the consequences. They can hide their fraudulence.

"Do you have allergies?" Joel asks.

"That was a yawn," I reply.

"Your yawn sounded like my mucus."

Rooming with Joel provides my first exposure to a portable expectoration cup, which he keeps bedside for his frequent mucoid needs. And to bug paranoia. That there are ants in a subluxury hotel in the woods in late spring should not be surprising, and neither should the discovery of a spider in the bathroom. But that serves as my wake-up call: Joel, in a Scrabble T-shirt and gray slacks held up by red suspenders, describing the scene.

My late-night lessons from Joel notwithstanding, I once again play mediocre Scrabble. I don't make three-letter-word ladders, but I violate cardinal rules: In one game, despite a comfortable lead, I burn a blank for 28 points early on so that I can play off a dreaded Q when I should exchange. In another game, I play four phonies, all of them challenged off the board. With a 78-point lead and the bag empty, I fail to close the only bingo lane, a triple-word column beginning with B, and, having failed to track the remaining tiles accurately, watch my opponent lay down BUNDLING for 80-something points and the win.

It's all the more frustrating because I *am* learning. I'm writing down racks with more frequency. I've begun studying all of the four-letter words, and they're taking hold. Words like YEUK, GINK,

TWAE, and DEIL all find a path from my brain to the board, as do OIDIA, ZAIRE, and OBEAH. I find OVERFISH for 101 points and BLATTER and MORGAN and FAKIR. But I seem to have an aversion to winning, as if I'm afraid of the very thing I say I want. I'll amass a big lead and let it slip away. I'll guess that some absurd arrangement of letters is good, or that my opponent will be too intimidated to challenge. Of course, she won't be afraid, it won't be good, and I will get mad, stalking out of the tournament room damning my name.

After a three-win, four-loss day, I stroll to the lake that abuts the hotel to clear the anger from my head. The sun is bright, there's a light breeze, birds are chirping, and I plop down on the grass and greet another player seated nearby.

"How's it going?" she asks.

"Badly," I say. "I'm five and five."

"Try oh and ten!" she replies. "I've lost every game!"

She introduces herself as Roz Grossman. Roz is seventy-two years old, and she tells me she was one of the original tournament players in New York in the 1970s. After her children left home, she and her husband moved to Israel, where she plays in the Jerusalem club, which boasts that it's the biggest in the world, attracting forty or fifty devotees a week. During the Gulf War, club members donned gas masks and played between air-raid sirens.

Roz reminisces about using an old Merriam-Webster's dictionary long before there were tournaments, about the early New York scene, when she was one of the top players, about how she once wrote a paean to Scrabble that was published in *Games* magazine. I ask her to recite it, and, with a little prodding, she does:

> I hate to play Scrabble with people who babble.
> My psyche gets balky when they become talky.
> I hate to play Scrabble with people who dabble
> In encyclopedias.
> I think they are tedious.
> I hate to play Scrabble with people who wabble
> All over the board until they have scored.
> But I love to play Scrabble with my kind of rabble.

We're not erudite but we keep our mouth quite
Shut.
We keep the game moving.
Hell, what are we proving?

"It's very Ogden Nash-y," Roz says with a laugh. It's the nicest moment of the weekend, and it relaxes me enough to win four of the last five games for a 9–6 record, sixth place out of sixteen. My rating inches higher, to 1268, and when Joe Edley, who directed the tournament, posts the results to CGP the next day, he writes next to my name: "Going up a little; goal to be expert by the time the book is finished. Can he do it? If he stops playing phonies!"

For a moment I wonder, like Roz, what my obsession is proving. Maybe nothing. Maybe more than I care to admit. With the board and tiles and word books splayed across my living room, and my regular circuit of tournaments, and leaving work early on Thursdays to get to the club on time, I have managed to reorder my life so that I can play a board game. This doesn't seem healthy, especially because I still suck. But it doesn't seem avoidable, either. I entered this world because it was a curiosity, a good story. Then it became an infatuation. I'm having trouble typing these words, but right now Scrabble is the most important thing in my life.

"My asthma started in my early twenties. I pretty much had allergies as a kid. I've always had a runny nose or a sneeze. It's mainly dust and animal hair. I don't remember historically having that much reaction to pollen." G.I. Joel belches, raises some mucus in his throat, and parts with it.

We're walking along busy Pelham Parkway in the Pelham Bay section of the Bronx, taking a *This Is Your Life* guided tour of Joel's neighborhood and his maladies. As usual, he's wearing his G.I. Joel sweatshirt, and his big, sad-sack eyes peer out from under his G.I. Joel cap. Joel is in black Reebok exer-sneakers, his gray slacks, and a New York Rangers windbreaker. He carries a Scrabble tote bag.

Joel points out the Jewish center where he studied Hebrew, the synagogue on the other side of the housing projects, his dentist's office. "My dentist is probably the main reason I am not a rich man today," he says. "I have had so much dental work over the years." But his real problems are farther south. The cold air, Joel is explaining, "creates pressure against my pants and that starts an asthma attack or it starts a gas attack. Or it starts something else."

There's the lactose intolerance, which Joel traces to grade school, when his daily milk intake was "three eight-ounce, seven-cent cartons and then another glass when I got home." There are the food allergies, which seemed to emerge in his twenties. "I'm allergic to almost anything I put in my mouth in one way or another. Citrus fruits cause very thick, viscous mucus. Starches give me gas. So does lactose. Beyond gas, beer or wine causes very bad acid. Tomatoes also do the acid trick. Fried food does the acid. It doubles up back through my esophagus, through my throat, and it has to be spit out once it reaches here. And when it comes up this far, it's got so much acid that it literally burns the tissue of my esophagus." That was diagnosed as gastroesophageal reflux disease. Then there's the postnasal drip, which requires frequent expectoration. For a while Joel suffered from the thyroid condition Graves' disease, which caused him to lose 15 pounds in six months from his 130-pound norm.

"At one point I was seeing this idiotic doctor who was a specialist in psychomedications. He diagnosed me as having anxiety that was responsible for my swallowing air," Joel says. "He might have been right except that I never perceived it as anxiety. It was just somehow an involuntary physical response to nothing in particular. The medication did seem to help for a little while. Eventually I went off medication and I didn't feel I was doing this involuntary gulping that made me go see that doctor. This was maybe four or five years ago."

I've seen Joel do the gulping.

"The thing that bothered me about it was the idea that it could be mental."

"The building we're standing in front of is a very important building historically in my life."

"A women's clothing store, Joel?" I ask, smiling. It's a mustard-colored shop at 2150 White Plains Road, under the Number 2 elevated subway line that bisects the commercial thoroughfare. Frishman's.

"It used to be the Washington Heights Federal Savings and Loan, where I worked for five years as a teller and head teller, which was before it was bought by a company from Florida called Ensign Bank, which actually owned the Carnival cruise lines. And then they got bought by Chemical Bank. When Chemical Bank bought Ensign, this office was closed because there's an office of Chemical on the next block. And then, of course, Chemical was bought by Chase and Manufacturers Hanover together. And now it's just Chase." Joel is nothing if not precise.

Joel was an undistinguished student, first at the prestigious Bronx High School of Science and then at Queens College, which he quit after two years of mostly playing pinball. But he wasn't incompetent. At the bank, where he started at age nineteen, Joel eventually was in charge of eight employees. He showed up early to open the vault, distributed cash to the tellers, and made sure they balanced their accounts. "The more aptitude I showed, the more I was asked to learn, which I didn't mind. But once I learned everything, the more I was expected to help others. The more work got piled on me that eventually I was doing so much work of other people I wasn't finishing my own. That became stressful to me."

The stress, Joel says, triggered his illnesses. He quit that bank to be treated for Graves' disease, then took another bank job in midtown Manhattan, which he held for five more years. When his stomach distress became unbearable, Joel finally "retired." He was twenty-nine. "I'd love to be able to work. All the problems I have are so debilitating that it's ridiculous to even consider trying to stay on a job nine to five."

Joel points out the Off-Track Betting parlor where he misspent some of his youth. We buy knishes, fruit, and cannoli — all seemingly gastric no-nos, but then Joel seems to eat most everything despite his problems — and Joel bolts into a supermarket in search of calf's brain. No luck. Then we're off to the Rite Aid, where Joel buys fruit drinks. He checks the citrus content and settles on a blue kiwi concoction and Juicy Juice punch plus a bottle of water, which is for me. Water gives Joel mucus.

The Sherman house is a brick two-family on Laconia Avenue, with a pink awning, a chain-link fence, and a decrepit yew tree out front. A sign on the door says, MISSIONARIES AND OTHER SALESPEOPLE PLEASE USE ENTRANCE IN NEW JERSEY. Joel has always lived at home. His mother, Gertrude, worked in the family court system, then the registrar's office at Lehman College, then in the Bronx district attorney's office as a trial separation assistant. She died of pancreatic cancer in 1988. Joel's father, Mike, is a retired accountant for the city of New York. His brother, Larry, ten years Joel's senior, went to college for three years and works as a freelance proofreader. Larry also lives at home — in the basement with his two cats, who aren't allowed upstairs because of Joel's allergies — though he has lived on his own in Manhattan and nearby in the Bronx. Larry is an expert-level Scrabble player too, but suffers no debilitating ailments like Joel. Neither brother has ever married, and Joel rarely if ever dates, a subject, like all others, that he will discuss gladly.

Joel was six years old when he began playing Scrabble with his family. He was fascinated by the idea that a combination of letters could make more than one word, and that he could find them. It was also a tolerable way of spending time with his mother, whom he describes as difficult and bitter. "Through most of the last ten years of her life I played hours and hours of Scrabble with her," Joel says. "Basically it was the only thing I enjoyed doing with her."

In high school, Joel played chess constantly, but never really liked the game; it was just a way of killing time. His peak rating was 2051, expert level but "squat on a scale where a master is 2200 and up, senior master is 2400 and up, and grand masters are 2600 and up. I had no chance of achieving a draw against any of those, that's how bad I was." In his twenties, when he worked downtown, Joel would stop at the Manhattan Chess Club on the tenth floor of the Carnegie Hall Studios most nights because he hated riding the crowded rush-hour subway home. Half the time he would read the paper, schmooze, or even play an occasional game of Scrabble, though only one of the chess masters, Asa Hoffmann, a hustler who had played hundreds of games against Bobby Fischer, was also a bona fide Scrabble player.

By then, Joel had played in a Scrabble club — in Phoenix, while visiting his parents, who had moved there briefly — and won most of his games against, he was told, expert players. When he tired of playing chess for money against Hoffmann, they switched to Scrabble. Asa crushed him, but Joel gradually improved. "When I beat him badly two sessions in a row I finally said, 'Okay, it's time to look up the New York club,'" Joel says.

Joel inhaled the two- and three-letter words, and received a 1570 rating after his first tournament. He qualified for the expert division in the 1989 Nationals in New York, finished 14–13, and his rating leaped to 1774. When his roiling gut forced him to quit working the next year, Joel turned to Scrabble. He really didn't need to work. There were no mortgage payments on his father's house, and a small inheritance from his mother allowed him, his father, and his brother to live comfortably. So Scrabble would be Joel's focus. Why not? "There basically wasn't anything else I was going to do in this life that well."

Joel leaves home a couple of times a week, usually for errands in the neighborhood or to direct the Manhattan Scrabble Club on Thursday nights. The rest of the time? "Sleeping, eating, playing Scrabble on-line, wasting time, procrastinating," Joel tells me.

He works at a computer (Ashley Judd is the screen saver) on a fold-down desk next to the kitchen. What used to be the dining room table is covered with unopened junk mail, stacks of paper, floppy disks, and tattered Scrabble dictionaries. There is an old portable radio, rolls of pennies, bags of plastic bags, and sheaths of takeout menus in the old, cluttered kitchen. (Except for breakfast, the Shermans have most of their meals delivered.) In the similarly cluttered living room, Joel shows me a charcoal drawing of him done by a woman at the Manhattan Chess Club and a sketch of his father made in the Philippines during World War II; they look alike — big ears, wispy hair, a large nose that makes an almost ninety-degree turn at the bridge.

Upstairs, Mike Sherman is sitting in his bedroom at a card table with his back facing the window, an aqua transistor radio and a bag of lollipops close at hand. He is playing Master Monty, the primitive electronic Scrabble game that dates to the early 1980s. On an old cardboard set so worn that he has had to pencil in the values of some of the premium squares, Mike plays a half dozen games a day by himself. He punches his word into Monty, which three minutes later spits out its counterplay and updates Mike's rack. Mike occasionally joins his sons at tournaments. It keeps him active. Mike is eighty-five years old.

Joel hands Mike his hearing aid. Mike cleans off the wax.

"I just want you to know that the house looked different when my wife was alive," Mike says in his gravelly voice. "I do what I can. I clean some. But I can't cope with that mess. With all that paper lying around."

Mike occasionally pressures his sons to get nine-to-five work, but seems resigned to their choice. "I worked for sixty years," he notes. "That didn't come from me."

Joel and I head back downstairs, and I ask him about his "job," full-time game player, which is how he asked to be described in press material at the 1997 Worlds. Surely Joel studies all the time, I had thought. But he has no collection of word books, or any sort of books, for that matter. "I don't read," he tells me back at his computer. "The only reading I do is on this damned screen. Because looking at printed matter puts me to sleep. It's been doing this for years and years. If I open a book and sit there and try to read it, my eyes shut on me."

Even if it's a word-list book?

"Faster."

The words were never enough. Joel slogged through the early stages of studying — the pages and pages of high-probability bingos in Mike Baron's book. Joel hated memorizing, but he was a natural anagrammer. He could just see the words. When he got bored reading word lists, a computer program called Lexability revived his interest. For a couple of years, he studied on the computer for an hour or two a day, four days a week.

"I would put it at five-tenths rack preparation, two-tenths board awareness, and three-tenths board preparation," he says of the game. "And what I mean by board preparation is making sure that the board is always amenable to my having a good play."

"It would seem fundamental, but not everybody can do it," I say. "What's the difference?"

"Possibly my concentration on those factors when other people are concentrating on word finding. To me the word finding is the easy part. My brain just does it."

"And the memory part?"

"That's the hardest part."

I laugh.

"I just don't feel like I retain well," Joel insists.

"You must, though. You've memorized eighty, ninety thousand words."

"I don't exaggerate my shortcomings. I'm painfully aware of them."

It's true, Joel's strength doesn't derive from a love of the words. (It's also true that he doesn't exaggerate his shortcomings.) He wasn't an innovator. He didn't create his own word lists. "I'm an opportunist," he says. "I piggybacked on the work other people did. I don't deny that for a moment." But he did have an affinity for patterns, and word patterns held more meaning for him than chess patterns. Joel can rattle off words of Greek origin which end in OS and pluralize with OI instead of I. He knows which words ending in US take an I plural and which take II, and which ones ending in UM pluralize with A. He knows whether words are botanical or anatomical, minerals or mathematical terms.

But the strategic conflicts of the game are what drive him. Joel spends hours, usually after midnight, analyzing board positions and evaluating play sequences, and then posting lengthy analyses on CGP about specific racks. Here's one example. Your opponent opens the game by playing the word FOU (an adjective meaning "drunk"). A question is posed: From a rack of EOOPVWZ, what do you do? Play VOW above FOU at 7F, forming OF and WO, or POOVE (an offensive term for a gay man) below it at 9I, forming UP? Here are the choices:

	A	B	C	D	E	F	G	H	I	J	K	L	M	N	O
6		TLS				TLS			TLS				TLS		
7			DLS			DLS	V	O	W	DLS			DLS		
8	TWS			DLS			F	✦	U			DLS			TWS
9			DLS			DLS		DLS				DLS		
10		TLS			TLS			TLS				TLS		

or

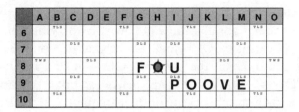

Via its simulation feature, which assesses the strength of plays, the computer program Maven determines that VOW is superior. Joel disagrees, in a manner that demonstrates the depths to which a few letters on a Scrabble board can be analyzed:

> POOVE and VOW score equally. POOVE draws two more tiles with plenty of valuable things in the pool. POOVE does not leave hooks on easily lucrative lines that accept tiles other than S. I is a very likely draw, so at the very least, the WZ leave from POOVE threatens WIZ 8M for 50 points. The V on column L means opponent is not very likely to take that spot across row 8 for a three-tile play of his own. Opponent might play thru the E of POOVE but if he does, ZOWIE K8 is still a minimum 34 points for a highly likely IE draw out of five chances with 9 I's and 11 E's unseen. Worst case scenario is opponent plays thru the V, and somehow fails to give back any big Z play, and that's really hard to do. While EPOZ is clearly a superior leave to WZ, on a board that requires hooks on every line that are not part of this leave, drawing three tiles instead of five simply is not supportable.

Not everyone agrees, and that's classic Joel. Other top experts routinely bash his analysis, in this case for foolishly opening the board with POOVE and for keeping the rancid W.

"Joel Sherman sees WIZ and ZOWIE and says, 'Cool, I have synergy,'" Bob Felt rebuts. "But where are we going to play these *non*-bingos? Play off WZ next turn, and guess what? After three turns our rack is a random draw — we have done *nothing* toward building a coherent rack. . . . One of my advantages as an expert is I understand how to build racks. The notion of throwing away that advantage seems bizarre to me."

Jim Geary, whose rating is on par with Joel's, e-mails me privately. "Joel's latest piece of shit is so misguided I want to ralph." It underscores, Geary says, one of Joel's basic theoretical shortcomings: He worries too much about things not worth worrying about. In the case of VOW versus POOVE, Joel worries that his opponent will take advantage of hooks on the back of FOU — FOUL, FOUR — or the front of VOW — AVOW — that he, Joel, doesn't possess. But he could get them easily himself because of their frequency in the bag.

Geary addresses another position deconstructed by Joel. A 1300-level player named Scott posted to CGP that he held AINNRRT, a bingo-prone rack except for the duplicated N and R. Scott asked what the experts would do. He realized that he was five-sixths of the way to RETINA, the third-most fruitful six-letter bingo stem, with an open board early in the game. So his inclination was to make a small play, such as RAN, which would have left him with INRT, or to exchange an N and an R, leaving the even better AINRT. There are lots of E's in the bag, which is good for Scott.

Joel pooh-poohs the idea. He says that Scott needs to be concerned about the possibility that his opponent could hook a Y onto the word WITCH already on the board. WITCHY would net at least 38 points, because the Y would land on a triple-letter score that would count in two directions. "This enormous hot spot indicates turnover should be of great concern to you," Joel writes. "If you don't have a reasonable way to block that spot, and you don't, you have to beat your opponent to the Y." Joel suggests playing TRAIN or RIANT, improving Scott's odds of drawing the Y by playing off more tiles.

"Wrong. Wrong. Wrong," Geary writes. "The most important factor, which 1300 Scott correctly guessed, is that he has TRAIN on his rack with a bunch of E's left. How many ways is Joel an idiot? Let us count." Jim counts to nine, starting with the fact that the Y hook is not that big a deal because there are only two Y's in a bag that now contains seventy-three tiles, and it's not that hot a spot anyway because the theoretical average play is 35 points, compared to WITCHY's minimum of 38. Trying to block the spot is wrong.

"Not only are we screwing ourselves to turn over good tiles for just two tiles in the bag that could even be used in this non–hot spot that's not going to make much of a difference in our lives if we do in fact miraculously hit it, Joel has us wasting turns to block opponent from doing same," Geary writes.

Joel's obsession with the potential Y hook has him eschewing a basic goal: building a bingo rack from great tiles, especially early in the game, when taking a lead can be decisive.

"Fishing for bingos from high-probability racks is often correct," Geary goes on. "Fishing for Y's from high-probability racks is wrong on two counts. One, the Y ain't that big a deal AND it's hard to get. Two, that's exactly the wrong thing to be doing with this potentially nice rack. And, most important, when you get five great synergistic letters together, you don't want to burn them. Especially when the missing piece is one of 11(!) unseen E's. Joel wants to shatter this combination in which even weak players see the potential energy.

"In summary," Jim writes, "Joel Sherman has very many bad ideas about Scrabble. If you write a chapter entitled Joel Sherman: Man or Myth?, please feel free to use this analysis in its entirety. Or maybe call it Jim Geary: Backbiting Also-Ran. Who knows which is right?"

G.I. Joel's peers can question his ability, world championship or not, and laugh at his physical tics, but it's hard not to admire his quirky devotion. Other than Joe Edley, who works for the Scrabble hierarchy, Joel is the only player who devotes his life to the game. More than Edley or Cappelletto or Butts — whom I believe Joel will come to resemble physically later in life — Joel is Mr. Scrabble.

Joel once played hundreds of games against Maven in which he allowed the computer to select his moves for him in an effort to determine whether Maven "cheats" in its tile assignments (by giving itself better letters, as some conspiracy theorists suspect). When Ron and Susi Tiekert moved to Atlanta, Joel took over the Manhattan club, and he e-mails thorough weekly summaries to members. His posttournament musings often include detailed hotel and restaurant reviews, like this one, about a porridge he ate in Singapore: "Whatever the heck it was, I liked it enormously, it was a very satisfying and nourishing breakfast, plainly and cheaply produced yet flavorful, and left my tummy quiet as a mouse, at least until lunchtime." How can you not love that?

Joel has won more than forty tournaments in his career. In the previous year, he lost about $2,000 playing Scrabble, meaning that after paying for entry fees, transportation, hotels, and food, he was two grand in the red. The year before that, when he won the Worlds, Joel netted $27,300. Despite the meager wages, when someone asks Joel what he does for a living, he answers, "professional Scrabble player." (Not that many people do ask. Joel rarely encounters anyone who isn't a Scrabble insider.)

"The point is to be good enough at it that I can say seriously to somebody that I make a living at it," Joel tells me. "And to get the game promoted enough that that can be a real possibility. It's very frustrating to me that we have not yet managed to develop an audience for the game. I don't mean participants. I mean literally people watching. People could watch Scrabble a lot more often than they would watch chess. Scrabble has more mainstream appeal. It is more easily understood than chess."

"Watch what?" I ask him. We've just played a game against a computer robot called ACBot over the Internet. "Watch you play TREHALA and then run to the dictionary?"

"I'd sooner have them watch me make a five-letter play that has four overlaps," Joel says. "The point is to see us use all of what we know and be inspired by that to use more of what *they* know. That is, the spectator should be inspired to use more of what the spectator knows."

"Which is?"

"The maximization of resources. That's why a five-letter word with the four overlaps is the interesting thing to see. Because that's not necessarily going to involve something not everyone knows. It's just going to involve using what you know and using all of what's in front of you."

That may be one of the game's intellectual beauties, but it doesn't bring Joel's dream any closer to reality. Hell, I'd like to travel around playing Scrabble for a living, too, and have people watch me do it; that might even motivate me to take what little innate talent some experts sometimes tell me I seem to have (could I qualify that any more?) and develop it faster. Frustrated Scrabble experts love to compare their game to chess, the national organization of which boasts eight times as many members as the NSA. As Joel posted to CGP:

I just don't see why Garry Kasparov can make millions playing chess, and perhaps a dozen or two other grand masters can earn respectable livings as professionals at their game of choice and the same can't happen in Scrabble. Those respectable livings are available because the game's mass appeal is exploited by manufacturers and publishers of accessories and ancillary products used by hundreds of thousands or even millions of enthusiastic if far less talented players. This has happened with golf, tennis, bowling, and chess. The result is that the burden of supporting these professionals is spread out over so many consumers that it is barely noticeable to the individual consumer.

But chess was a public phenomenon exactly once, when Fischer played Spassky. And the Scrabble played by Joel, even by me, is so radically different from what's played at home as to render it even less accessible to the casual player than top-level chess. It's a circus act — all those words! And it's controlled by a single company (responsible for dozens of other products) which does very well, thank you, selling a million or two sets a year without spending hundreds of thousands more promoting a pro Scrabble tour that no one would watch. Hasbro isn't likely to lend out its sacred trademark for sponsorship by other companies, as some players want. The company is more likely to license a World Championship Wrestling version of the game. The expert players just don't matter that much.

But Joel will play whether or not ESPN shows up in the Bronx to profile him or Hasbro begins making a G.I. Joel action figure. He has no other purpose in life. After winning the Worlds, Joel had his fifteen minutes of fame — a *New York Times* profile, an appearance on the *Today* show, a visit to his old elementary school, P.S. 89, to receive a citation from the state assembly as an "outstanding citizen." One expert reported that his doctor, after learning he was a competitive Scrabble player, asked him, "Have you gone up against that Sherman guy?"

Since the championship, Joel seems happier, chattier, friendlier. And cockier. He signs his e-mails "G.I. Joelgernaut." After Joel bragged about scoring 600 at the club and trashed his opponent, one CGP wag wrote, "So nice to see that being the World Scrabble Champion has heightened Joel's sensitivity to his opponents' shortcomings."

But who could begrudge the Joelgernaut a celebratory sack dance? *It's all he's got!* "I'm an accidental overachieving underachiever. An unlucky person with a failure complex," Joel tells me, "who somehow managed once in his life not to."

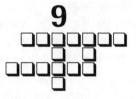

9

1291

T HERE ARE 3,199,724 unique combinations of seven tiles that
can be plucked from a virgin Scrabble bag of ninety-eight letters and two blanks. That's the good news. The bad news is
that you can draw only one of those combinations at a time. It
could be AEINST? with its sixty-seven possible bingos. But it also
could be IIUUUWW or any other rack of dross.

Mathematicians have determined that the possibility of choosing an acceptable seven-letter word from a fresh bag is 12.63 percent, or just over one in eight, and that's pretty good news, too. Except for one other thing: Those seven letters could be EEEGRUX or
CMMOPSY and you don't know that EXERGUE and COMSYMP
are acceptable words. Even worse, they could be AELLRSY and you
see RALLYES but chicken out and learn later that it is a word and
means exactly what you thought it meant (the plural of a kind of
auto race). Or, even worse than that, the tiles could be AAFIWY? and
you fail to see the one obvious bingo, FAIrWAY.

"You," of course, is me. And I can't help it. Despite the downside, I
am attracted to the combinations and what they represent: boundless possibility, the opportunity for success, the test of the mind and
of the forces of probability. I like playing the odds, reaching into the
darkness of the Scrabble bag and extracting my destiny. I like knowing that there's a chance of something great.

The problem is that the better you get, the more your frustration
grows. You see greatness, but you can't touch it. It's happened to me

before. I quit playing golf when I couldn't get my game down to the low eighties; it was just too frustrating. I was constantly reminded of my shortcomings. It's the same in Scrabble. The scorecard tells you when you fail. The Franklin tells you when you fail. A Greek chorus of second-guessers hovering over the board tells you when you fail.

"YONIS was a forty-eight-point play," one of the Washington Square Park regulars informs me in the middle of a game early in my playing career. "You missed a forty-eight-point play."

"I didn't know the word," I demur. "I don't know the fours yet."

"YONI, yeah," he says, repeating the word, which is a Hindu symbol for the vulva. "It's some Indian pussy."

In a way, the living room player is lucky. He has no idea how miserably he fails with almost every turn, how many possible words or optimal plays slip by unnoticed. The idea of Scrabble greatness doesn't exist for him.

But greatness is a vanishing point on the horizon, an object that recedes just a little farther when you think you're getting closer, a desert mirage. The best players can't stop racing toward it. They are driven by the possibility of solving something that in truth might be insoluble. They can learn more and more words, maybe even all of them, but there's always the risk that the crucial one will prove irretrievable at the necessary moment. They push and push and push anyway, because they have no choice. Perfection may be the goal, but it's really about the search, about the chance of wringing something magical from those 3,199,724 racks.

I want to join the race, and I guess I have. But when I play the game, I play scared. I don't see the possibility of greatness in 3,199,724. I see instead the threat of humiliation, the dread prospect of failure. And that — as much as my word knowledge, my performance at tournaments, and my rating — is what must change. I need to believe.

The cumulative evidence is incontrovertible. In eighteen tournaments in eighteen months, I have compiled a record of 104 wins and 115 losses, a winning percentage of .475.

I'm as predictably mediocre as a low-revenue baseball team. Call me the Minnesota Twins of Scrabble. My rating is stuck in the 1200s, inching up and falling back. In seven tournaments in the previous seven months, I have *lost* rating points (I poked my head above 1300 for one tournament), which in the "enthusiast" division, as the netherworld of Scrabble is euphemistically referred to by some, is okay for enthusiasts — the blue-hairs and the hobbyists, the nonstudiers, hoi polloi. But it's not okay for a supposed comer like me, who hangs out with the experts as if he were one himself, a sportswriter who confuses covering a team with playing on it. In one stretch, I dropped a remarkable seventeen out of nineteen tournament games (albeit against higher-rated players).

"I still can't believe you aren't stomping on those lower divisions," my now-expert friend Dominic Grillo tells me. "You seem to have the desire to learn and a decent word knowledge. You should be doing better."

But I'm not. I've even become something of an enigma among other players climbing the ladder.

"We were talking about you on the way over here," a young Boston-area player named Scott Pianowski, a chunky sportswriter, tells me during the annual Waltham tournament. I have a 4–5 record in the third of four divisions when we talk on the final morning of play. (I go on to lose all three games that day.)

"You were?" I say.

"Yeah, that you're a better player out of competition," Scott says. "I mean that as a compliment. Really. I've seen you study boards and come up with anagrams I didn't see. I wish I had your word knowledge."

Indeed, my word knowledge probably is better than my rating. In other words, despite my lackadaisical study habits, I know more words — more fours, more bingos — than someone with a similar rating. That's why, despite my personal dissatisfaction with my play, I consider myself underrated. As do others. At Waltham, Ron Tiekert picks me to be on his team in "rotisserie Scrabble," a $5-per-person pool in which entrants select two players from each division and tally their combined results. And yet, I also know that if I can't win games *during* tournaments — as opposed to kibitzing a board in a casual late-night game, when Scott is impressed with my play — I don't deserve a higher rating.

I candidly assess my game, and here is what I find:

I am plagued by recklessness, thinking it a substitute for word knowledge. My score sheets are filled with phonies. SOLDATA*, DECOATED*, RECOATED*, MAILORS*, LAYE*, LIVIDEST*, GAVELER*, AVARICED*, CENTERER* (actual word: RECENTER), ARIETIC*, EVEREST*, ARRRG* (AARGH, AARRGH, AARRGHH), MOXIEST*, RETONES* (ESTRONE). Sometimes I get away with this junk. Most of the time, however, I am unmasked. As Edley pointed out after that last Catskills tournament, I'm even getting a reputation as a player of phonies.

I also lose because I don't challenge words (such as CUELIKE*, TRAMPIER*, and ENTEROLS*). I am cowed by my opponents' ratings; at the Hartford "team tournament," where individual games count toward a team performance, I played "fourth board" on an expert division team with Matt, Marlon, and Matthew Laufer, the Washington Square parkie, and posted a 1–11 record. I demonstrate that I really don't know the fours, because I routinely miss them in endgame situations, when they can be valuable ways of "going out," or getting rid of all your tiles before your opponent does. I exceed my time limit regularly. I fail to execute tactical maneuvers that could yield victory. I chicken out on plausible bingos, such as . . .

"RATLIKE?" I ask Marlon between rounds at one event.

"Yes," he replies, meaning it is indeed an acceptable word.

"Fuck!" I say.

After the last game in Waltham, I retreat to my car, angry. I lost the finale in classic fashion. I couldn't find the high-probability bingo INULASE. I misplayed the endgame. And I went over on my clock by five minutes, costing me 50 points. I bang the dashboard, dislodging the face of my compact-disc player. "Well, that was a three-hundred-dollar loss," I say to myself, shocked back to reality. I pick it up off the floor and stick it back on. It still works.

"Somehow I find a way to be intimidated," I confess to Joe Edley.

"If you're intimidated you can't compete," he replies.

"I want to win," I whine. "I really want to win."

"It's not only thinking it," Edley says, "it's feeling it and not having any other distractions."

I have journeyed back to National Scrabble Association headquarters. It's time to get serious. Edley and I are sitting in his office. It is a cramped, paper-strewn space devoid of personal touches. On the bookshelf are *Seven Habits of Highly Effective People,* the British word sources *Official Scrabble Words* and *The Chambers Dictionary,* and other word books, including the two Edley has written. Tacked to the wall is the score sheet from the Waltham tournament where Edley lost his first eleven games and finished with a 2–11 record.

Edley isn't the dangerously thin, bearded ascetic he was in the 1980s. The beard, for one thing, is gone. With his circular, bumpy face, hairy ears, and inquisitive head tilt, he looks less like Darth Vader than Yoda. Edley is wearing unpleated, baby blue slacks, black aerobics-style Reeboks, a too-tight short-sleeved white oxford shirt with blue stripes, and a navy blazer, collar askew. A few weeks earlier, he had surgery to repair a detached retina, a scleral buckle. ("That's a good word. CALLERS, RECALLS, CELLARS," he says, noting its anagrams.) He had to lie face-down for several days. When I ask him about it, he responds with a shrug of acceptance. "If I lose one eye, I'll have another eye. If I lose both eyes, I'll be blind and that'll be another challenge in my life. That's how I look at life." That equanimity, genuine or not, helps explain his success at Scrabble.

I tell Joe that I've moved from over-the-board anxiety to what seems to be an actual fear of success. When I'm leading, I think the game is over and I've won; when I fall behind I think it's hopeless and I've lost. In either case, I imagine the moment when I will make a crucial blunder.

Edley lectures me anew about entering a happy, confident state of mind that will allow me to find the words when I need to. "If you at least believe that it's in your power you will do far more to find the creative best play than someone who thinks it's beyond them," Joe says.

Like a doctor searching for a diagnosis before he can suggest a remedy, Edley moves on to a different aspect of my Scrabble corpus. He wants to analyze my study habits. "What have you been doing?" he asks. "Because you've developed a certain level of skill now. You're pretty good at anagramming."

I let the compliment slide. I think I'm a lousy anagrammer, particularly after observing Matt and Marlon and Joel.

"I've basically been paper-studying," I say. "I'm up to number twenty on the high-probability stems," meaning Mike Baron's list of the Top 100 six-letter combinations that take a seventh letter.

"How do you study?" Edley asks. "What do you do?"

"I mostly read and reread and test myself by writing them down."

"Give me an example, like if you want to study a stem, what do you do?"

"I go through it in my head or on a piece of paper. I'll familiarize myself with the stem by reading all of the words it forms. I'll write down the stem and the letters that go with it and then fill in the blanks. The four-letter words I've been doing mostly by reading on the subway, reading them and reading them and reading them. I've written down all the ones I don't know twice."

Not a foolproof method. In one game, I challenge the word FIDO and lose because of it. It means a defective coin. After the game, I check my study list. "The real indignity," I write in my notebook, in capital letters, which I do when I'm upset, "is that FIDO isn't on my list of fours. I must have skipped it inadvertently. So of the hundreds of fours I copied down, the one I missed kills me."

Rather than looking at words and trying to memorize them — the lazy man's idea of studying, *my* idea of studying — Edley recommends that I combine studying with anagramming. He pulls a red, 8½-by-11, spiral-bound word book off the shelf, one that groups words by length and lists them according to their alphagrams. The alphagram of a word is listed in one column, with the correct answer or answers in another column to the right.

"There are only four or five pages of fours," Edley says. "There are more fives. I would xerox the page and blow it up a hundred and forty percent. Then I'd cut it up into pieces and have cards. I could make a deck of cards out of four-letter words and five-letter words. You have the alphagram and the word next to it. Just by spending a certain amount of time going over anagrams, that's how you learn them.

"What you're doing with the stems is not bad, but it's not time-effective at all," Edley says. "It's better that you have the words you want to learn and you look at them in alphagram form. You can't look at the words spelled correctly. It's a big waste of time. It's not going to help."

"It's not training my brain?"

"That's right." Studying by unscrambling alphagrams, by contrast, is "a can't-lose proposition," Edley says. "It's why I love to study. You

get a thrill from it. You see a jumble of letters and you suddenly figure out what the word is. Eureka! Oh, wow! That's a positive experience. You feel better. It's something biological.

"Basically you have to get to the point where you can visualize the
letters in your head, manipulate them in all of the common ways you
can think of, and don't allow yourself to get frustrated. And look at
the answer if you can't find it in a short time. And just go back over
them."

"A lot of the people who play this game seem to have this predis-
posed anagramming ability," I say, "or have the mental alacrity where
they are drawn to creating a study program." I mention a postdoc-
toral researcher at NYU named Mark DiBattista, who showed me a
computer program he wrote that generates all of the seven-letter
bingos containing single-point tiles only and all of the bingos containing six single-point tiles and one two-point tile. "I don't have
that bug."

"You don't have the interest in studying that way?" Joe asks.

"It's not the lack of interest. It's the feeling of being overwhelmed
and not knowing where to begin — and this is after a year of playing.
Should I be studying seven-letter words? Should I be studying the
fours? Should I weave in the fives? It's the feeling that it's too big to
even break down."

Joe gets Zen on me. "Studying Scrabble words is like walking
around the world, but as you start walking your feet start getting bigger. Every step you take is taking you farther. The more you study, the
more ability you develop and the easier it becomes to learn more.

"But you want to maximize your use of time. Don't go over words
you're never going to miss. Don't waste your time going through letters that aren't anagrams. Only look at the combinations that are
words that you want to know. Decide which words you want to
know."

"How do you decide?"

"Okay. There is a huge number of words. You just have to decide
to take small quantities. One hundred words at a time or two hundred words at a time and study them and move on."

Edley takes the word book and leaves the room. Down the hall, he
begins photocopying on giant yellow cardboard the first few pages of
seven-letter bingos, which are listed in order of their probable emer-

gence from a full bag. Unlike learning Baron's stems, there's no easy way to create mnemonic devices; you just have to learn to unscramble the words. Each page in the book is divided into eight columns, the alphagram on the left and the word or words contained therein to its right:

EHINRST	HINTERS
EIIMNRT	INTERIM
	MINTIER
	TERMINI
EEINRTV	INVITER
	VITRINE

"You can just start studying this list and go through it," Edley says. "This book is all about learning the words. If you were to start studying the sevens, the first few pages of these, you'd be doing all right. The other thing is you should really learn all the fives."

"Ugh."

"It's not that hard."

"The fives seem so overwhelming. The fours seem completely manageable and I'm still only halfway there."

"You're blocked by that feeling, and that's hindering you. You're telling yourself things that are defeating you. First of all, you have to tell yourself that it's not overwhelming. You're hypnotizing yourself to defeat yourself. You have to start telling yourself, 'I can do this.' If your reality check wants to seep in, you can say, 'It's a lot of work, there's a lot to learn, but I can do this.' You don't have to be a genius to do it. You just have to spend the time to practice."

When I suggest that not everyone is a gifted anagrammer, Joe agrees that specific skill functions are necessary.

"And I'm clearly not a natural," I say.

"You think so?"

"I'm not. But maybe that's just more of a defeatist attitude."

"Start studying and you might see things differently."

Edley sends me off with a sheaf of cardboard bearing the fours, the fives, and fifteen hundred sevens. As soon as I get home, I chop them to the size of tarot cards, four columns of words to a card, two each of alphagrams and solutions. I start studying with the sevens. I take the bottom card from the deck, flip it over, and cover the right-hand column of the first list on the top card. Then I try to unscramble the alphagram. The first card is easy, mostly review:

AEEINRT	ARENITE
	RETINAE
	TRAINEE
ADEINOR	ANEROID
AEINORS	ERASION
AEINOST	ATONIES
AEILNRT	LATRINE
	RATLINE
	RELIANT
	RETINAL
	TRENAIL

If I fail to solve an alphagram within a few seconds, I uncover the first letter of the answer, which helps. If I still don't see the word, I place a dot next to it so that I'll know which to review. I manage to get through about eighty words, or a full card, on a one-way commute to work if I can ignore my fellow subway riders and the overhead ads for computer training schools and skin doctors and mental health assistance and spousal abuse hotlines. I'll repeat the same card two or three times before moving on to the one beneath it. Studying in twenty- or thirty-minute chunks, Edley and others have advised, improves retention.

A four-letter word has just twenty-four possible letter combinations, which may seem like a lot. Understanding, however, that the combination of vowels and consonants will render most of them implausible should make the possible solutions relatively simple. And yet I stumble over common words. When I see AHLS, my first impulse is to say HALS*. The next day, when I go over the same material, I say (aloud) LAHS*, when LASH is simple and obvious. When I see AHMT, the first combination I say in my head is MHAT*. When I see AKLT, I pronounce the logical answer "talc" rather than "talk." The brain plays tricks, and I realize that learning the words is about training my mind to be patient as well as nimble.

After a few weeks, I tell Matt I've been studying for about an hour a day. "Then your rating will be a thing of the past," he says. "Of course, you *should* do eight hours a day. But then your life would be a shipwreck."

Marlon makes a New York appearance, crashing on my floor. We rise early on a Saturday morning and drive to the trusty Comfort Inn on Long Island. This month, the attraction is especially great: nine games instead of the usual seven. In the living room, or in the park — or in a games parlor once upon a time — sessions can extend well into the double digits. Ron Tiekert recalls a nonstop, nineteen-hour session in the 1970s at the end of which he owed his opponent $6. The decade before that, Lester Schonbrun once played for two straight days, with bathroom breaks, at the Flea House against a chemist named Aaron, who, when it was over, handed Lester $100 and thanked him for the good games. But in a tournament, where you can't just keep playing, or stop a game, or chatter, where the logistics of coordinating a large group of players slows things down, nine games in a day qualifies as a marathon. More games, however, is always preferable to fewer games.

The groupings put me in a good mood. My 1291 rating is the second-lowest in a group of twelve players in the second division of four, and the top rating is 1667. That sets me up to earn major points. I think about my latest talk with Edley, about breathing deeply, about concentrating and remaining calm. Whether any of my new words materialize is irrelevant. The mere fact that I've been studying consistently has convinced me that I have improved. I have never felt this confident.

One rack at a time, Edley says. The first one that I draw in the tournament is AEMNTX?. I'm playing Marie, the woman with the icy stare. She intimidates me. I exhale, hunch over, and shuffle. MAX, TAX, EXAM. My brain processes. I search for a bingo, but at the same time consider what would be the best possible "leave" if I can't find one. MAX, for instance, would leave me with ENT?, a four-tile combination that is almost sure to yield a bingo soon.

Suddenly, I have a eureka moment, the kind where your breath catches and your heart races and you have to control an urge to shout it out because *what you know is a secret.* Scrabble is poker with letters. It's neither polite nor smart to gloat during a game; it'll back-fire. But when I see it, I want to leap out of my chair. TAXiMEN! The X lands on the double-letter score, and the N on the star. I have seen the word played in a game before, so I'm sure that it's acceptable.

"Ninety-six," I announce. "The blank is an I."

Marie challenges. I know it's going to be a good day.

JIVER, JEW, COBS, FALL, CAW, DOG, ORZO. Short words, but my points mount. Marie can't score. I'm ahead 303–88. I play sE-QUELS and sip the nectar of revenge. Down she goes, 477–282.

I win the next game, 431–390. And the next, 392–322. And the one after that, 382–336. And another, 411–315. And one more, 374–348.

Six and oh.

I'm as methodical as a contract killer, seeing words the way Ted Williams could see the seams of a baseball spinning toward him at ninety miles per hour. I'm not particularly social between games, wearing as I am a mask of cold, professional indifference.

For a change, my opponents play the phonies (BRUNG* and FIELTIES* — puh-*leeze*) and I challenge them off. I play actual words, and they challenge erroneously. If I know the word, I find it. With a rack of ABIKNW? and an open G on the board, I play WINGBAcK, which draws a challenge. WINGBACK! A backfield position in football! I play FORESTED and ANTEATER and JANGLERS.

After Game 6, Marlon trots up.

"You win?"

When I nod, he shouts, "Yes!" and offers a fist to bump with mine.

I drop the seventh game (no blanks, poor tiles).

"I didn't think you could go undefeated," says the pesty Mark Berg, a short, nasal, sports fanatic who is a regular at the Manhattan club.

"Thanks for the support, Berg," I say. But I shrug him off. There will be no YER*s this time. I know I'm going to win the tournament.

In Game 8, I rack up 521 points — including 111 points for SKEINED — and rout my opponent. The only way I can drop out of first place is to get blown out in the final round. I don't even consider the possibility, and I do something rare, for me: win in the endgame. A 42-point play on the penultimate turn ensures a 377–358 win.

I finish 8–1 with a spread of +641. I capture the division by two games. I walk away richer by $80 and a game of Pictionary (for SKEINED, the high single play of the tournament). I scored an average of 411 points per game (by far a personal best) and yielded just 340. And I wasn't even that lucky: nine blanks and nineteen S's in nine games, in line with the odds. I was even focused enough to record my games rack by rack for later review.

Marlon offers to calculate my new rating on the spot. From a master list that tournament directors receive, I write down the ratings of all of my opponents. Standing on the motel steps, smoking a cigarette, Marlon does the math on my notepad. I don't understand what he's saying.

"Fourteen seventy. Five times two to five. Fourteen fifty and then fourteen hundred. Three. That's a hundred. That's three hundred. Fourteen thirty, fourteen fifty-six. I give 'em all five. One, one, four, four, five, is giving up twenty-five. Fourteen forty-two."

"Yo, you is hundred fifty below the field," Marlon says. That means my incoming rating of 1291 is 150 points below the average rating of my opponents that day. "That's six-point-three. And you lost one game. That's five-point-three. You multiply the factor — point-seven because you hundred fifty below your field — times nine rounds. Five-point-three times is your multiplier. Your multiplier is twenty — anything below eighteen hundred is twenty. That's a hundred six. Anything over five points per round is bonusable. Nine rounds times five is forty-five. Every point you go over forty-five is bonusable. You had a hundred six. That's sixty-one. Add it to the one-oh-six. You're going to do about a hundred seventy points."

My new rating, by Marlon's calculations, will be 1461. Goodbye, blue-hairs.

"That's living the dream, baby," Marlon says. "Fuck winning the tournament. Hundred seventy points! That's *goooood*. You should be *skipping* home."

"About time, wouldn't you say?"

"Worth the wait. Wow! Hundred seventy points. That shit is *mind*-boggling. You had your kick-ass tournament."

"Took me a year."

"So what? Doesn't matter."

I feel relief and, for the first time that day, anxiety: Now I have to live up to the new number. I drop off Marlon at the apartment of a

Scrabble player in Queens and lend him half of my winnings; he says the IRS is mailing him a check for $2,200 and he's going to break down and take a job working with his uncle at an insurance company. I'm dubious.

We soul-hug, and I drive off, believing that my rating accurately defines who I am.

"Okay. I'll take credit for that." Joe Edley laughs. It's Monday morning, and Joe has heard about what happened over the weekend. "So how's the method?" Edley asks, referring to alphagram study.

"Great. It's helped me see the words better," I say. And it has. During the tournament, I believed I could anagram with more skill than before. "I don't know if the studying made a specific difference, but my attitude was totally different."

"How'd that happen?"

"I don't know. I didn't do what I normally do, which is think about the outcome in advance. I stayed focused."

"That's certainly one of the things you need to do."

I give Joe my opening rack. "TAXIMEN!" he says. "That's nice. The X on the double letter. Beautiful." Then I set up the ABIKNW? rack with the open G on the board. "WINGBACK," he says after a few seconds. It had taken me a couple of minutes to find it, and another minute to ponder how sure I was that it was a legitimate word. "You make high-class plays like that, you'll win."

"Even when I was trailing I felt I was going to win."

"I wouldn't be surprised if you exceed your expectations."

"We'll see," I say skeptically.

"But the typical sixteen-hundred player isn't going to see TAXIMEN or WINGBACK," Edley says. "Anyway, I'm pleased. I hesitated to believe it was anything I said. But it was a pretty dramatic change. You're on your way."

My new rating arrives in the mail one week later, on one of the computer printouts with which I've become so familiar. I rip open the envelope and study the page for several minutes, scrutinizing each of my wins and the performance of other players. Then I look at my individual tournament scorecard, the one I filled out after each round, which is returned with the ratings cross-table. The long string of W's

interrupted by one L, my game-by-game scores and those of my opponents, my cumulative record and cumulative spread. All of the letters and numbers are handwritten neatly. Cold, unemotional, and
businesslike. Each of the W's appears absolutely identical. Saving the
best for last, I run my finger over the cross-table and find the number. Marlon was right: 1461.

10

The Words

JOSEPH LEONARD looks much younger than his sixty-five years. He has smooth, light skin and a full head of sandy gray hair parted on the left and brushed forward. Joe wears gray slacks, a short-sleeved white button-down shirt, and black slippers when he greets me at the door at the precise time we had arranged via snail mail. Joe doesn't have a telephone because he finds interruptions disturbing. He can't afford a computer.

The walls of his one-bedroom, government-subsidized apartment in Center City, Philadelphia, are white and bare. There is little furniture. The living room contains a small, rickety bookshelf that bows under the weight of dictionaries and other volumes, a stand holding folders and more dictionaries, a bench bearing a stereo and record player that Joe bought in 1967, and a desk with a manual typewriter and rows of pencils that Joe frequently rearranges during my four-hour visit. The apartment is spotless, solvents lined up like soldiers on a kitchen ledge. Joe keeps the shades drawn because he suffers from extreme astigmatism, though he pulls one back a few times to peer into the street below. He tells me he leaves the old, brick walkup only occasionally, to buy food, mail letters, examine books in a Barnes & Noble or a library, and pick up the medication he takes to treat anxiety and panic disorders.

Joe was raised in northeastern Pennsylvania coal country by an aunt and uncle; his father died of cancer when Joe was eight, and his mother died three years later after falling through a basement grate at a supermarket. He was a county champion speller in the tenth grade, and he recalls playing Scrabble as early as 1949. He can't play now, though, because the pressure of the game makes him panicky. At Lehigh University, Joe was hospitalized after a nervous breakdown. He graduated with a degree in chemical engineering and worked in Philadelphia for the Defense Supply Agency in the 1960s and early 1970s, first as a chemist and then in a medical group in which he wrote specifications for dental equipment and other supplies. As the Vietnam War wound down, Joe was reassigned to the chemicals lab but didn't like the job. The stress was too great. Joe hasn't worked since.

I have come to visit Joe because no one has been more devoted to words and to the dictionary used to play Scrabble than he has. I first heard about him through Matt Graham and Mike Baron, who dubbed Joe the "Word List Master General" and dedicated the first *Wordbook* to him. We've been corresponding for months. Joe responds to my letters with long, single-spaced missives composed on a manual typewriter. Nearly all of his letters include at least one page-long explanation of mistakes in various Scrabble dictionaries or other word lists that I ask him about.

"He has a personal relationship with words," Matt Hopkins, a Philadelphia player who has befriended Joe, tells me. "His word knowledge is staggering. He understands the etymology of words. He once explained to me the derivation of MYNHEER and MIJNHEER from the Dutch." But Joe's treatment of the words about which he knows so much is narrow, detached, and inflexible. He's attracted to the rules of lexicography and list making, not the beauty, wonder, or irony of language.

Joe has scrutinized every page of well over a dozen dictionaries, including a few unabridged ones, by hand. The first was a rhyming dictionary, into which he handwrote additions. He shows me his copy of a dictionary of pseudonyms, to which he has added hundreds of his own entries. He has scoured telephone books for names that are palindromes, atlases for place names that contain each of the letters AEIOU just once, and almanacs for errors in population tables.

When the original *Official Scrabble Players Dictionary* was published in 1978, Joe tells me, he immediately found numerous errors, and set about cataloguing them. But first he drew on the *OSPD* for the pioneering word lists he contributed to the incipient Scrabble newsletter.

Joe wrote down all 21,734 seven-letter bingos in the *OSPD*. He would type a word and then handwrite its alphagram below it, cut up each pair, and sort them alphabetically according to alphagram, placing the slips of paper in what turned out to be five hundred Baggies. Then he typed up the alphabetized alphagram list, the first of its kind. He did the same thing with the 26,455 eight-letter words. Subsets of these lists graced the newsletter.

"It was rather time-consuming, but I enjoyed it," Joe tells me, kneeling on the floor of his living room with his legs splayed behind him.

The original *OSPD* was created when the growing tournament scene highlighted the need for a reliable, easy-to-use word source. The official arbiter of the time, *Funk & Wagnalls Standard College Dictionary*, was confusing. Some words were found only on long lists of undefined derivatives starting with UN, RE, or MIS, or ending with ER or MAKER. Comparatives were allowed only if the first part of speech listed was an adjective; so SMARTER could be challenged off the board, while MAINEST* was allowed. Some words lacked parts of speech, and other words were just missing, including BUSLOAD, COVEN, and SURREAL. Foreign words like JA*, OUI*, NYET*, and BITTE* were allowed.

Selchow & Righter, which owned the game at the time, chose Merriam-Webster Inc. to oversee publication of a new dictionary. It was decided that the book would contain words that could be found in at least one of five collegiate dictionaries in print at the time — *Funk & Wagnalls* (1973 edition), *Merriam-Webster's Collegiate Dictionary, Eighth Edition* (1973), *The American Heritage Dictionary of the English Language* (1969), *Webster's New World Dictionary, Second College Edition* (1970), and *The Random House College Dictionary* (1968).

Player volunteers did much of the compiling, and they and Merriam-Webster made lots of mistakes. Joe Leonard found scores of them. There were omissions; several words, including GRANOLA and MELTDOWN, could be found in all five of the source dictionaries but somehow didn't make the *OSPD*. Misprints were copied from the source dictionaries, such as DUODENAS*, WAEFU*, and PAPULAN*, which turned out to be a sixty-year-old typo in *Funk & Wagnalls*. New misprints were created, like CRESIVE* instead of CRESCIVE. There were missed parts of speech, words overlooked because of complicated or confusing entries, erroneous plurals — name a mistake, the *OSPD* had it.

Many of the errors were corrected in addenda printed in the Scrabble newsletter. Joe kept his own master list. Scouring the source dictionaries page by page and matching them against the *OSPD*, Joe by 1982 had compiled a list of two thousand words that should have been in the *OSPD*. As new editions of the source dictionaries were published, Joe checked them for new words and other changes and passed his findings on to the Scrabble association. By 1989, Joe's master list was fifty-five hundred words long. A final typed version, starting with AARGH and ending with ZYMOSAN, came to forty-four pages, two columns of words per page, including part of speech, inflections, and source dictionary. Leonard sent it to Joe Edley, who was coordinating efforts for a second edition of the *OSPD*.

Leonard's list had to be refined because Merriam-Webster didn't want to include words in the *OSPD2* if the source dictionary was no longer in print. For instance, some words contained in the eighth edition of *Merriam-Webster's Collegiate* but not the ninth, such as DROPPAGE* and MAINLINER*, were disqualified. More oddly, words found in the original *Funk & Wagnalls* which inadvertently had been missed by the compilers of the original *OSPD* were excised from Joe's list, too.

With the redactions, Joe's list was used by Merriam-Webster in full. This reliance on the work of an unpaid, unseen, amateur lexicographer — albeit a meticulous one — was almost comical. At the end of his list, Joe included examples of foreign words in the *OSPD* which needed to go. But he stopped at the letter E, with ENFIN* (if anyone had asked, Joe would have supplied the full list), and when the *OSPD2* was published, only those words were deleted; foreign words found later in the alphabet lived on. Joe accidentally skipped over the word KVELL, which was in *Webster's New World,* and to this day it's not playable in Scrabble.

"In short," Joe writes in one of his letters to me, "one could say that *OSPD2* . . . was almost solely my effort." He estimates that he spent more than eight thousand hours — four years full-time — working on the lists on which the revised dictionary was based. He never asked Merriam-Webster, the National Scrabble Association, Selchow & Righter, Coleco, or Hasbro for any money. And he never got any at all.

Dictionaries are designed to appear authoritative. They're thick, sturdy, and precise, with pages of explanatory material and complex notational schemes that create an aura of august finality. People refer to "the dictionary" as if there were just one, divinely inspired, like the Bible, and passed down through the ages.

But dictionaries are as subjective as any other piece of writing. Which words are included in them and which words are removed or ignored are decisions made by lexicographers based on shifting criteria, varying standards, and divergent publishing goals. Dictionaries serve different agendas, contain different numbers of entries, and have different rules. *Webster's Third New International Dictionary* — the grand, 2,726-page tome published in 1961 which sparked an outcry for its perceived linguistic permissiveness — contains 450,000 entries. The tenth edition of *Merriam-Webster's Collegiate* has 160,000 entries.

What's considered a word by lexicographic standards? Depends on what you count. Linguists thirty years ago estimated the size of the English lexicon at more than four million words; today it could be double that. For starters, there are millions of chemical compounds and other scientific words. "There are in addition," Sidney I. Landau wrote in the 1984 book *Dictionaries: The Art and Craft of Lexicography,*

> nonce words (words coined for a particular occasion), dialectal words, slang, neologisms (new words), exotic words (words introduced from other languages but not yet naturalized), trade names, and words derived from place names, such as *The New Yorker* [magazine] or *Michigander*. . . . Does one include all obsolete words, and all forms (or spellings) of each of them? If one admits lexical units larger than words, where does one draw the line? . . . Are proper nouns to be considered words? Are compounds like *pull toy*?

Noah Webster's two-volume *An American Dictionary of the English Language,* published in 1828, was the first great American dictionary. It contained seventy thousand entries — twelve thousand more than in any earlier word source — including for the first time in a reference work commonly used nouns such as *glacier* and *malpractice,* verbs such as *electioneer* and *revolutionize,* and at least one neologism, *jeopardize.* Webster said that "the business of the lexicographer is to collect, arrange, and define, as far as possible, all the words that belong to a language, and leave the author to select from them at his pleasure and according to his own taste and judgment." Or, as Thomas Jefferson wrote, "Dictionaries are but depositories of words already legitimated by usage."

But lexicographers don't always agree, and everyone considers himself a lexicographer. That's why the *OSPD* and the *OWL* — the *Official Tournament and Club Word List,* the volume that simply lists the acceptable words, sans definitions — arouse more passion than any other aspect of Scrabble. As with any dictionary, the main argument is over what should and shouldn't be in these books. Marlon Hill thinks there are too many spellings of words such as WADMAL (five), WRESTLE (six), and GANEF (eight). "Pick one," Marlon says, ignoring the fact that alternate spellings are based on citations in common usage found by lexicographers. Others have fought over the years for the exclusion of words labeled foreign; some of these (DA*, DES*, VIN*, VON*) were removed from Scrabble when the *OWL* was adopted in 1998, some were not (AMI, DE, JEU).

Dan Pratt, a mathematician with the Department of Defense, quit the NSA's dictionary committee, and tournament Scrabble, partly because the last dictionary revision didn't go far enough. Pratt refused to talk to me about the *OSPD* because, he said, he was too frustrated to rehash his battles. But he wrote an article for the word journal *Verbatim* in 1999 in which he bemoaned inconsistencies in the *OSPD* derived from the fact that it's an agglomeration of words from a bunch of dictionaries, some of which are out of date. He suggested a sweeping word putsch.

"If future word-game dictionaries accepted only words appearing in two standard reference works, we would have a stabler dictionary environment that might please both the word lovers and the pros," Pratt wrote, "and perhaps we could even consider weeding out many of the words that no longer appear in any readily available reference, and maybe even the most suspect of those vouched for only by one."

Most experts aren't such strict constructionists. They are curious about the source and history of the words they play, and even critical of the legitimacy of some words. But they accept that the Scrabble "dictionary" isn't really a dictionary at all. It's a book designed to keep players from spending all of their time fighting over what's a word. "People keep confusing dictionaries with a narrowly defined word list to be used as a prop for a game," a Canadian expert named Albert Hahn posted to CGP.

The entries in the *OSPD* include only part of speech labels, inflections, and truncated definitions; no pronunciations or etymologies. And the definitions can't always be trusted. Scrabble players love to joke about the *OSPD* definition of TUP: "to copulate with a ewe." Hahn thought it was funny, too, and wondered whether this act was so prevalent that it needed its own word. That was until he looked up the word in an actual dictionary. It means to screw a sheep, all right, "but it refers to the ram," Hahn wrote.

If the *OSPD* were a full-fledged dictionary, or the *OWL* were a word list based on usage, it would be updated more frequently. Since publication of the *OWL*, there have been three new printings of the tenth edition of *Merriam-Webster's Collegiate*, adding dozens of new words. They include such now-familiar terms as BREWPUB, CINEPLEX, MESCLUN, MINIBAR, MORPHED, MOSH, SPAM, and ECHINACEA, not to mention a bunch of new currencies from Eastern Europe and elsewhere which would be fabulous short Scrabble words. But those words need asterisks on this page. They can't be used in the game yet.

The times when the Scrabble dictionary *has* been updated, it hasn't been cleansed. More than a thousand words were added in the two most recent revisions, but only a handful were deleted. Meanwhile, there are words in the *OSPD* that can't be found in any standard college dictionary currently in print. They've survived just because they're there.

Take the word AL. It's an East Indian tree, according to the *OSPD*, which defines AAL slightly differently, as an East Indian shrub. AL appeared in *The Random House College Dictionary* "at just the wrong time for *OSPD* purposes," Dan Pratt wrote in *Verbatim*, "since it now will live, apparently forever, even though the current edition of *Random House* and all of its competitors omit this extremely obscure rarity." But while AL and AAL survive, those words that Joe Leonard found in *Funk & Wagnalls* that had been skipped during the creation of the original *OSPD* never had a chance to live on in infamy.

The Scrabble dictionary did receive one purging, but it wasn't the one the players wanted.

In late 1993, a Virginia art gallery owner named Judith Grad was having lunch with two elderly Jewish friends. The conversation turned to the couple's passion for Scrabble. And when they pulled out their *OSPD* and showed Grad the word JEW — defined as "to bargain with — an offensive term" — she was horrified.

Grad looked up other words — KIKE, HEBE, YID, NIGGER, DAGO, SPIC. "I was livid," Grad told a local newspaper. "It's a game. Those words have no business in a dictionary used to support a game." She started writing letters, first to Merriam-Webster and Hasbro's game division, Milton Bradley. She didn't like the responses.

"It is certainly not the intent of the dictionary to perpetuate racial or ethnic slurs or to make such usages respectable," Merriam-Webster's editor in chief, Frederick C. Mish, wrote. "However, such slurs are part of the language and reputable dictionaries record them as such."

"As a dictionary, it is a reflection of words currently used in our language," Milton Bradley President Dave Wilson told her. "It is important to note that Milton Bradley Co. does not condone the use of these words, nor do we advocate the use of offensive terms. If it were up to us, none of these words — nor the sentiments behind them — would exist at all."

Grad wasn't satisfied. She contacted the Anti-Defamation League of B'nai B'rith, the National Association for the Advancement of Colored People, the Zionists Organization of America. Nothing. Finally, the National Council of Jewish Women began a letter-writing campaign, which attracted some attention in the Jewish media, and the Anti-Defamation League picked up the baton anew. The ADL wrote to Hasbro Chairman Alan Hassenfeld. It accused Hasbro of "literally playing games with hate" and urged that "hateful and demeaning epithets be retired."

Growing up, Hassenfeld had played Scrabble with his mother, Sylvia. "Words that were critical of people — those were absolutely out," Hassenfeld tells me. "You'd have your mouth washed out, and choking on soap bubbles you'd come back in. No. No dirty words." Without consulting Merriam-Webster or the National Scrabble Association, Hassenfeld acceded to the ADL's demand: The company announced that fifty to one hundred "offensive" words would be removed from the *OSPD*.

The Scrabble community went ballistic. A handful of players, notably some devout Christians, backed the decision. But a huge majority, led by a number of Jewish players, accused Hasbro of censorship. Words are words, and banning them from a dictionary would not make them go away, they argued. Plus, the players tried to explain, the words as played on a board during a game of Scrabble are without meaning. In the limited context of scoring points, the meaning of HONKIE, deemed offensive in the *OSPD*, is no more relevant than the meaning of any obscure but commonly played word. Jewish players unblinkingly play YID, and African Americans won't hesitate to play NIGGERS if it's the correct strategic move. (Outside the playing room, of course, the words have context. DARKIES showed up in a final game of the 1990 Nationals, but it was changed to DARKENS when the board was displayed on *Good Morning America* the next day.)

Hilda Siegel, a daughter of Russian Jewish immigrants and a member of the National Council of Jewish Women, organized an anti-expurgation petition drive that produced nearly eight hundred signatures from players in thirty-five states. "There are huge numbers of words which may be offensive to one or another individual or group," the petition read. "However, a book purporting to be a dictionary cannot pretend that those words do not exist." Players threatened to quit the NSA, boycott tournaments, and even sue if the words were excised. John Williams received hate mail and threats at the NSA offices.

Meanwhile, though, Williams had to help compile the list of words to be eliminated. Hasbro executives jumped on the political-correctness bandwagon, which didn't make the task any easier. "I have concerns about some of these words," Williams recalls a senior Hasbro executive telling him. "BLOWJOB? Am I to believe that this is good in Scrabble?" TUP appeared on a list of potential deletions prepared by the corporate owners until Williams pointed out that it was about the ram, "not two farm boys."

Williams heard from the head of a Romany group representing Gypsy interests who demanded that the verb GYP be delisted (it wasn't). One letter asked whether CRIPPLE (no) and WETBACK (yes) would be purged. Another writer declared that he found GUN and WAR to be the two most offensive words in the English language and (facetiously, one hopes) demanded that they be removed. "Don't surrender to the language police," said another.

The list, which was never made public (though Scrabble players deduced its contents), contained a total of 206 deletions, the root word, plurals, inflections, and alternate spellings of about seventy different terms. Most of the words were predictable — profanities, ethnic slurs, slang terms. Then there were a few absurdities: FART, LIBBER, FATSO, JESUIT, PAPIST, PISS, and TURD. BADASS and PISSER were kicked out despite lacking the dictionary label "offensive" or "vulgar."

"Being offended is so subjective, it's ludicrous," Williams said in one of the scores of interviews he conducted. "But we're trying to take an academic approach."

It was a battle between censorship and sensitivity. Hasbro told Williams not to utter any of the banned words in interviews. He felt as if he was being forced to defend an indefensible position. On the one hand, Scrabble was a proprietary game and Hasbro had the right to protect its corporate image and interests; it owned the Scrabble dictionary, which of course wasn't an actual dictionary but a tool used to play its game. On the other hand, Williams was a player himself who understood that removing words from the dictionary on other than lexicographic grounds was just wrong; it didn't make the words disappear.

So behind the scenes he tried to negotiate a compromise: two books, one for the general public, one for the competitive players. But some top players didn't trust that it would happen. So there was blood in the water at the Nationals in the summer of 1994. More than two hundred players streamed into a ballroom at the Universal Hilton Hotel in Los Angeles wearing T-shirts protesting the expurgation and waving placards demanding that it be reversed. Minutes before addressing the crowd, Williams called Dave Wilson at Hasbro. Then he made a triumphal announcement: "The words are ours," he said.

Hasbro agreed to publish the two dictionaries. The one sold in bookstores, the *OSPD3*, would carry the label "for recreational and school play" and exclude the so-called offensive terms. A separate list, including the deleted words and eschewing definitions entirely, would be printed for use in clubs and tournaments. The players cheered.

In 1988, Joe Edley received one of Joe Leonard's lists of words for possible inclusion in the planned *OSPD2*. The words were typed straight across the page with just a couple of spaces between each one, so Edley asked a member of the NSA's dictionary committee, a longtime player and club director in Portland, Oregon, Karen Merrill, to retype the list in columns.

A short piece about Merrill, written by Edley under the headline "Club Spotlight: A Leader in the Northwest," appeared in the Scrabble newsletter two years later. The fourth paragraph of seven read, "Karen was also instrumental in helping move forward the publishing date of the revised *OSPD*, which currently is some time in 1991. She joined the Dictionary Committee in 1988 and helped put the new word list into readable form for Merriam-Webster to edit."

Joe Leonard had yet to be acknowledged for his work. Edley had written him saying that he understood Leonard couldn't accept money for his efforts (which Leonard says wasn't true), but that the Scrabble Association would seek to compensate him some other way. (Edley says he was planning to offer Leonard a copy of the *Oxford English Dictionary* and to write a story about him in the newsletter.) Leonard asked for a lifetime membership in the association, reimbursement for the cost of the source dictionaries he had purchased, and at least two copies of the *OSPD2*. He never heard back from Edley because of what happened next.

Shortly after the article about her appeared in the Scrabble newsletter, Karen Merrill received an angry letter from Joe Leonard. He was upset that she had received credit for work on the new dictionary while he had not. By that time, Leonard's final, forty-four-page master list had been passed on to Merriam-Webster, which relied on it almost exclusively in preparing the *OSPD2*. Merrill forwarded the letter to the NSA, and Edley told Leonard he owed her an apology. Edley said Leonard would receive credit for his work "when the time is appropriate."

Merrill then began receiving obscene and threatening postcards written in what appears to be Leonard's precise handwriting or typed on a manual typewriter. Merrill says the postcards, some of which bear Joe's signature, arrived every few weeks for about a year. Then they stopped, and Merrill says she received a second apology from Leonard. (Joe never admits to me that he wrote the postcards, but he never explicitly denies it either.) On the advice of Hasbro attorneys and U.S. postal authorities, John Williams revoked Leonard's membership in the Scrabble Association. The *OSPD2* was published in 1991, but Leonard was neither credited nor compensated.

Despite the imbroglio, Joe kept researching words. When Hasbro ordered the expurgation of the allegedly dirty words a few years later, the NSA had a chance to revise the dictionary anew. Players compiled a list of about a thousand words from the tenth edition of *Merriam-Webster's Collegiate*. Joe, naturally, found about 160 additional words missed by those who did the searching, from ADZUKI (which was listed under the entry for "adzuki bean") to YUPS (a plural of the noun YUPPIE). He found but didn't include BOFFED and BOFFING on his list because of the expurgation debate, and they remain unplayable even though they are in *Merriam-Webster's*.

I ask Joe why he kept searching for new words even though he was persona non grata with the NSA. He says in a letter that the list "was doing me absolutely no good just being here in the apartment, totally done in pencil. So I thought once again, 'Why not share it, so that all others who use what would be *OWL* can also benefit from it.' And so I did. I just figured the players of the game deserved to have those additional words."

Joe forwarded his list to a Scrabble player with whom he corresponds, who passed it on to Joe Edley, who printed it in the newsletter. Edley was told the words came from Leonard, who was still banned from the NSA. Regardless, they were included in the *OWL*.

Leonard never received any thanks or compensation for his latest contribution.

Almost nine years after he was kicked out of the NSA, John Williams agrees to reinstate Joe's membership on the condition that he doesn't "vent all [his] frustrations" at the organization. Joe is perplexed by the statement, and mentions it in several letters to me.

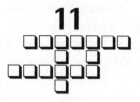

11

Matt

MATT GRAHAM lives on the Upper East Side in a brownstone walkup so thoroughly subdivided it has more doors than an amusement park fun house. His low-ceilinged studio on the third floor is eight feet across at its widest and about thirty feet long: a crypt for Shaquille O'Neal. The contents make it appear even smaller, a claustrophobic shrine to Matt's multiple interests.

His main passion is books. More than forty shelves groan under the weight of hundreds of them, maybe more than a thousand, stacked two-deep in some places and ceiling-high in others. There are, naturally, scores of books about words: more than a dozen standard dictionaries; dictionaries of etymology, slang, euphemisms, and rhymes; books about the history of language, semiotics, wordplay, linguistics, foreign tongues; *The Esperanto Wordenboek;* volumes by William Safire, Edwin Newman, Dmitri Borgmann, and just about anyone else who has written about language. There is a wall of books about games, how-to-win books on chess, backgammon, Othello, Go, Monopoly. A stack of books about smart drugs and the brain. A separate section of sports books, many of them about his first and second loves, basketball and Indiana University basketball.

Then there are the games, also stacked on the shelves, some unopened. There is Scrabble in many variations, of course, plus knockoffs like WRDZ and Word Wise. There's Ipswich and Keyword, Qwink: The Quick as a Wink Word Game, Big Boggle, Quip Qubes.

Piled in netting suspended from a wall are dozens of stuffed animals, including some of the ones Matt totes to tournaments. Other animals crowd Matt's bed, and when I sit down in one of the apartment's two chairs a giant character from Maurice Sendak's *Where the Wild Things Are* stares up from the floor beside me.

Matt's desk occupies the narrowest part of the apartment, a short hallway leading to the entryway (where the sports books are, along with a newspaper box featuring the defunct early 1990s sports daily *The National*). On it is an old desktop computer, dozens of bottles of vitamins and smart drugs, some of which Matt acquires via mail order, more stacks of books, cassette tapes, a display for a Spiderman game, and a Scrabble board ready to be used.

The two windows let in little light, the bathroom is dirty, the refrigerator in the microscopic galley kitchen contains more vitamins than food.

Matt spends most of his time in this tiny warren. He's never had a steady job. ("I had a paper route," he deadpans. "And I was good. I was a good paper boy.") He thinks jobs are part of society's problem; if someone doesn't want to work, he shouldn't have to. Jobs are about money, and money is just about stuff. If he had more money, what would he have? A bigger apartment, nicer possessions, an easier time with women. Fuck all that.

Money for rent and vitamins — Matt's two biggest expenses — comes mostly from his mother. An occasional standup performance or victorious one-on-one Scrabble session provides some walking-around money. Matt has chosen two virtually moneyless professions — if playing Scrabble can be considered a profession — and both keep him isolated for long stretches in his apartment, where he sleeps odd hours and studies words when he feels like it.

Matt is one of Scrabble's best raw anagrammers. He has awesome word knowledge, which he attributes to an innate ability to retain words augmented by his warehouse of supplements. And he loves the words for their intrinsic beauty, going poetic with appreciation for words that display symmetry, balance, or other aesthetics.

"I feel like Salieri to his Amadeus," Eric Chaikin says. "I feel like I can hang in there, but pure letters and anagramming, he's just automatic. His brain just works that way."

Matt's most impressive trait is an imagination only a few other experts can match. He just finds mind-bogglingly creative plays. Late in a tournament game in Ocean City, New Jersey, Matt held a rack of EHIIPRT. But his opponent blocked the sole place for him to play the only bingo on that rack, PITHIER. The logical move would have been to play off HIP, keep EIRT, and hope for a good draw. However, Matt noticed an N and a C on the same row with seven spaces between them. He played NEPHRITIC. Almost no one else would have even considered the possibility of playing, forget about finding, a nine-letter word *between* two letters.

In a game at the Nationals in Chicago, Matt topped his Ocean City find. He was losing by a bingo with just one tile in the bag. His rack was DEEIOSW. But there is no seven-letter bingo on that ugly rack, and no eight was to be had on the board, either. So with the clock running down, Matt did the unthinkable: He produced a nine-letter bingo through a disconnected T and R, which required hooking OX to make SOX. It's a feat of mental dexterity akin to juggling five balls and tossing in a flaming torch for the hell of it: STOREWIDE.

The sort of flexible thinking that produced his two personal favorites is what he is most proud of in his comedy, too. Matt could have been a star, he says, if only he had tailored his act for the lowbrow masses and landed a pushy agent to score a six-figure TV development deal. Instead, Matt stuck with his cerebral brand of comedy, full of offbeat images and knotty wordplay.

"I recently trained my dog to sit every time he hears a bell. And then I put a bell around his neck. Doesn't get around much anymore. Not much of a watchdog — but a super gargoyle. Haven't seen an evil spirit lately, and that's upped my holiday mood."

"Last Friday, my roommate sent me out to get some canned fish, because we're having some Catholic survivalists over for dinner. Weirdest thing happened. I'm coming up the steps, I stumble, all the groceries fall down the stairs. Except for a can of salmon, which falls up the stairs. Bizarre experience, but it gave me an idea. Couple nights later I was driving the wrong way down a one-way street. Cop pulled me over. I told him I was spawning. He said, 'Young man, I have reason to believe you're DUI. You know what that is?' I said, 'Do I!'"

"As a child I was in and out of institutions — visiting my parents. My mother's schizophrenic. Of course, I prefer to think of her as a 'people person.' And my father, he's manic-depressive. Has these terrible mood swings. Once he sent me a postcard. It said, 'Having a wonderful time. Wish I were dead.'"

When I first see Matt perform, in a crowded SoHo bar, he bombs. He whines about feeling sick, mocks audience members in a hostile tone, and shifts uncomfortably on his feet. Later, though, he gives me a tape of his three appearances on *Late Night with Conan O'Brien* (his ex-girlfriend is a staff writer). In the first appearance, Matt is nervous and stiff. In the second, he is composed, relaxed, and connects with the audience. He kills. In the third, when the audience jumps on a punch line, Matt sarcastically thanks them for laughing in the wrong place, and someone boos.

Matt on stage is Matt in Scrabble: smart, sophisticated, extremely creative, but volatile, hair-trigger angry, easily provoked, self-conscious, paranoid. "Just one chromosome up from the guy in *Silence of the Lambs*," one Scrabble veteran says.

Pushed by a new girlfriend to be more responsible for himself, and helped by his old one, Matt in mid-1998 decided to find a job. *Saturday Night Live* was looking for writers, Matt knew one of the cast members, and a few weeks before the Nationals, he was hired for the fall season.

"This motherfucker go from two feet in the ground to this job with six figures," Marlon Hill, my other penniless Scrabble genius friend, said. "I was, like, just lemme know when Toni Braxton be on that motherfucker."

Still, Matt was down because his girlfriend had broken up with him. Matt had been dwelling on the breakup, and drinking a lot. A couple of weeks before the Nationals, though, he stopped. He said his anagramming was strong and his board vision had returned. "I'm just bursting," he said a day before leaving for Chicago on the train with Marlon. "I was just so numbed out and drinking so much. I took one night off and I was finding all these dazzling plays. The mental focus, the focus that allows me to lead a more tranquil life, is in place. I'm psyched. I think I can play great Scrabble."

It was like that before the 1997 Worlds: Matt had been on a partying jag, stopped two weeks before the event, studied round the clock, and finished second. But the success didn't materialize in Chicago, where he drew poorly and couldn't mount the charge he did at the Worlds in Washington, and Matt sat sulking in the rear of the ballroom as the bland, unflappable Brian Cappelletto collected his $25,000 check.

Matt started at *Saturday Night Live* in September. In October, he was fired.

More than a month after his firing, Matt told me what happened. He said he was cranking out twenty jokes a day for his segment, "Weekend Update," but he couldn't get any of them on the show — only one the first week, and none the second, third, or fourth. The segment producer told him it takes time, but no one was helpful and nothing he wrote seemed to be good enough. *SNL* had always had a reputation as a petty, high-schoolish place, where being in with the right crowd mattered more than what you did.

"It's like you're like the pariah," Matt told me. "I'm not the best guy to deal with that. I've never had a job. I know people say, 'What did Matt say? What did Matt do?' so I haven't talked to anyone about it. It stunned me beyond belief. It matters to me what other people think."

For six weeks, he had holed up in his apartment, consumed with the firing. "Last night I didn't even sleep," he said. "I've slept one hour in the past forty-eight or seventy-two. I just think about it. Even when I'm in a good mood I think about it.

"But I have Scrabble to look forward to."

Hanging around with Matt makes me wonder whether Scrabble isn't a substitute — for work, for ambition, for confronting the realities of life. Any chess hustler or cardsharp or Nintendo junkie can testify to the seductive power of games. I feel it myself now, too; I'd need to be strapped to a mast like Odysseus to avoid the siren song of a Scrabble board.

On one level, the game I have chosen is just an intellectual pursuit, a compelling strategic challenge; Scrabble is one of the games played at the Mind Olympiad held in London every year. On another, though, it can't *not* be a substitute for something, an escape. Matt once said that Scrabble "has been such a blessing. It seems like anything that means that much to you, even if you're not religious, even if you're atheistic . . ." His voice trailed off. He tried to make the game make cosmic sense in his life, to justify it. He noted that Hasbro was celebrating the fiftieth anniversary of Scrabble that year on February 5. His birthday.

But can playing the game, for however many hours and to the exclusion of whatever else in one's life, be harmful, the way a drug addiction is harmful? Or is Scrabble somehow different? For Matt, for Marlon, for G.I. Joel — the most extreme players in the Scrabble subculture, for whom the game is the sun in their solar systems — there is a tangible goal: being the best at a competitive pursuit. Winning. Matt and Marlon and Joel don't play Scrabble because they can't stop and it makes them miserable. They play because they believe they are good at it and want to win — win money, prestige, respect, the label of being the best at something.

So I don't consider Scrabble an obsession in a clinical sense: a disturbing preoccupation with an unreasonable idea. For Matt — or Marlon or Joel or me — I think of it as an obsession in the colloquial sense, a compelling motivation. As mystical as we may think the language is, none of us has as yet credited this word game with, say, extrasensory capabilities. We just love to play it. G.I. Joel has accepted that Scrabble is his life, and it doesn't have to be remunerative. Joe Edley has accepted it, and has made it remunerative. Marlon has accepted it, too; he is unconflicted about living with his mother and studying Scrabble all day, and about quitting a perfect job — beta-testing computer versions of Hasbro games, including Scrabble.

And Matt? He's never so secure. Having only Scrabble to look forward to, I thought at the time, might not be the best solution to his depression over losing the *SNL* job. Scrabble would be a temporary fix. But Matt was enthusiastic about playing in the team tournament in Hartford a few weeks after his firing.

Scrabble did serve its purpose there, distracting Matt from contemplating his career. He named our team "Compony Pyknic" — acceptable words both — and joked around all weekend. Despite my lame 1–11 performance (this tournament took place several months before my victory on Long Island), Compony Pyknic still managed to take first place, and Matt said, "We've got to decide whether you're getting a full share or not." (I did keep my full $45 cut of the winnings.)

During the awards ceremony, there was more opportunity for laughter: a "Scrabble moment," as Matt calls what happens when a Scrabble player demonstrates exceptionally inconsiderate or self-centered behavior, usually in pursuit of a game. Edie Berman, the game's matriarch in the Boston area, was reading a heartfelt letter she wrote to her close friend and Scrabble partner, Muriel Sand, who had died recently. It was a touching moment embodying all that is good about the game — camaraderie and friendship, the love and loyalty and devotion that so many people find in a hundred tiles and a board. But the respectful hush in the room was broken by the castanet rattle of tiles in a bag. Jan Dixon was engrossed in a game with Marlon, talking loudly and shaking the bag vigorously, oblivious to the fact that a woman was reading a letter to her dead friend. "You've got to be the first Scrabble player to play through a eulogy," Matt told Jan with a smile. "Have you ever played at a funeral?"

Back in New York, though, Matt began feeling increasingly paranoid. He freaked out on stage during a comedy set, telling the audience that "if I don't come back, here are the names of the people who did it." Matt had been ingesting well over a hundred pills a day, maybe fifty or sixty different kinds. But the most worrisome addition to his arsenal was GHB, gamma hydroxybutyrate, a flavorless liquid that induces unconsciousness and recently had been banned in several states. Matt had been taking GHB — which he raved about in Hartford, showing me the bottle of lime-colored fluid — to help him sleep, increasing the dosage as his anxiety and depression over losing the *SNL* job deepened. Mixing GHB with alcohol is extremely dangerous, and Matt also had been drinking a lot.

Matt first began taking smart drugs and vitamins after he got good at Scrabble. When they met in 1992, Marlon remembers, Matt was taking just a few pills. At a tournament in early 1998, Matt decided not to join Marlon and me for lunch, saying, "I'll have an apple. I'm not hungry. I've taken so many damn pills," only to change his mind and come, and then decide to sit in my car listening to a CD by the rock group Cake which includes a cover of the Gloria Gaynor hit "I Will Survive."

Matt says he knows exactly what each pill and potion does to his body. He subscribes to nutritional newsletters, reads books about smart drugs, studies the side effects and contraindications. But now some combination of the drugs and his life circumstances had made him unsteady. At one point, he stayed in his apartment five straight days. A short time after, he called his closest friends, who took him to see a doctor.

The books, the games, the stuffed animals. The hyper behavior. The comedic frustrations. The Scrabble brilliance. "He wants to be the mad genius," one of his friends told me. "But he's going to be the dead genius."

Marlon came up from Baltimore to visit. "He has some rainman qualities," he said of Matt. "Somebody whose mind is so scattered that it takes him a long time to answer. That's somebody's mind that work on another goddamn level. It's a fine line between genius and insanity. That motherfucker is tiptoeing on. He's probably walking backward on it." Marlon thought Matt should leave New York. "Too many fucking people, too much fucking time in that little apartment. Who wouldn't go fucking crazy?"

What Matt had done to his body, countless others had before him and countless others would after. Like other expert performers, Matt had begun taking brain-enhancing drugs to improve his memory, sharpen his concentration, build up his stamina. Matt's ex-girlfriend Janine DiTullio, the *Conan O'Brien* writer, took him to a doctor who has treated other expert performers who develop drug problems, including pool players and bodybuilders. "You took it to get an edge playing Scrabble," Janine said the doctor told him. "You're way past needing an edge."

The doctor told Matt he had to flush out his body and brain, and the way to do that was to give up all the smart drugs; Matt told him about his life, told him he was taking up to 150 pills a day, and when Matt started rattling off the list of products, the doctor stopped him.

"You're taking stuff that was made in somebody's basement," he said. But he added reassuringly: "You have a strange lifestyle. That doesn't mean you're mentally ill."

All this for Scrabble. For a board game. For words. "Words are, of course," Rudyard Kipling wrote, "the most powerful drug used by mankind." They had come to dominate Matt's life. At a comedy gig once, during a joke about female genitalia, Matt wandered off into a confusing digression about Latinate plurals. "That's me," he said. "Caught in the web of words."

The audience didn't get the reference to the title of the biography of James Murray, the first editor of the *Oxford English Dictionary,* who devoted his life to words and died before he could see the work completed. Matt once told me that he imagined himself in old age like Murray, who is pictured in the book with a long, white beard like an Orthodox bishop's, surrounded by hundreds of thousands of slips of paper stacked floor to ceiling and containing the word citations that formed the great book.

Matt loved *The Professor and the Madman,* Simon Winchester's book about the relationship between Murray and Dr. William Minor, a clinically insane American surgeon convicted of murder who sent nearly ten thousand citations to Murray for the *OED.* And Matt is the first person to tell me about Joe Leonard. Matt revels in the image of the reclusive "Word List Master General" doing nothing but scouring dictionaries. He wanted to accompany me if I tracked Leonard down. (I chose to make the visit alone.)

For Matt, as perhaps for James Murray, William Minor, and Joe Leonard, words are the objective reality of life. They are codifiable and indisputable, and the game Matt plays using them is decided by a score on a piece of paper. No one can say he sucked, the way they could on stage or at *SNL,* without being disproved by the won-lost record, by the intuitive brilliance, by the deep insights. The dictionary is finite, but what you can do with it in the confines of the fifteen-by-fifteen Scrabble board is boundless. And Matt is better at it than just about anybody.

But a question lingers in my mind: Did the game create the personality or was the personality attracted to the game? Was Scrabble the symptom or the cause? And how could you be sure? "I'm sitting up here memorizing Scrabble words," Eric Chaikin told me from his Catskills retreat when we talked about Matt, "and I'm thinking, That's the result."

*   *   *

The Eastern Championships in Danbury. February 1999. Matt was glad to be getting away, and determined to get healthy. "I'm going to be washing out my brain of all the shit I take," he promised after I met up with him, Eric, and Marlon at the hotel just off Interstate 84 where the tournament was held. "I've already reduced it by a third, the vitamins. I'm getting away from the city, which helps. And I'm playing fucking Scrabble. And this was a fun tournament last year."

Eric and I shared a room, and Matt took a rollaway bed in the corner.

"I brought way less shit," Matt said.

"Just get off it," Eric said, referring to the drugs.

"Yeah," Marlon said.

We all agreed Matt should just quit. But we also understood that he was physically addicted, and pressuring him wouldn't help. The conversation moved away from Matt. Marlon was threatening to take a job, stocking trains for Amtrak, a solitary task he thought would suit him.

"I can't work for nobody," Marlon said. "I can't stand people. People are just too damn stupid."

Matt arranged his pills in the white plastic container he carries to meals. A third might have been a good start, but he still had brought about twenty bottles, including Blast-Off, the high-caffeine potion, and other smart drugs. He called Janine to check in. He paced the green carpet.

Marlon said he always expects to get fired from a job. "I'm the happiest poor motherfucker you'd ever meet in your life."

"I do exactly what I want," Eric said. "I do words and friends, which is exactly what I want to do. But I've got no friends." He was joking; Eric has a stable of friends, but he'd been camped out in the Catskills alone for a while.

"You don't need no friends," Marlon said.

"I simplified so much I'm ready to complicate again," Eric said.

"Amtrak's looking like a fucking dream to me now," Marlon said. "It's not close proximity to assholes. Offices — you get into office politics, the bullshit."

"I could get you a phat job on Wall Street if you didn't always have to say exactly what you were thinking," Eric said.

"I could take *over* Wall Street," Marlon said.

Matt was ravenous but quiet at dinner, and so exhausted from antianxiety medication that he lost three of four games the first night. He wrapped a red T-shirt around his eyes and buried himself under the covers with two stuffed animals. The next day was no better. "My meds have me wiped out right now," he said in the morning, before losing five of six games. At 2–8, unprecedented for him, Matt joked that you have to experience the lows to appreciate the highs. I wasn't sure he was referring only to Scrabble.

At meals, there was none of the jovial anagramming banter that distinguished Danbury a year earlier, and we left hurriedly after eating so that Matt could get to sleep. Incredibly, on Sunday and Monday, Matt won eight of the final ten games to finish an even 10–10 for the tournament. (I went 9–11, still untutored by Edley and mired in mediocrity.) Matt was subdued as I drove him home.

12

The Owners

WHEN I SEE the denuded Scrabble boxes rolling down an assembly line at a Hasbro plant in East Longmeadow, Massachusetts, I experience a giddy rush of excitement. I'm like Charlie inside the chocolate factory.

The 1.2-million-square-foot plant abuts the headquarters of Hasbro's games division. It's the company's last factory in the United States. Most of its toys and games are now made at company-owned factories in Europe or, increasingly, outsourced to Asia. In 1998, Hasbro shuttered a Vermont factory that had churned out a million maple Scrabble tiles a day for twenty years, an event that prompted a wave of sentimental news stories about the loss of another American icon to cheaper, overseas labor. The tiles and racks are now made in China.

But the Scrabble box, cover label, and instructions are printed at the East Longmeadow plant, as are paper products for other Hasbro games. On the factory floor, wooden pallets stacked thirty feet high hold sheets of Monopoly money and Get-Out-of-Jail-Free cards, Clue score sheets, boards for Life and Chutes and Ladders. Production on the ten assembly lines is scheduled according to demand. Monopoly is cranked out periodically on three shifts round the clock, about ten thousand games per shift. Right now, Pokemon and Star Wars products rule; when I visit, Hasbro has recently acquired the company that made Pokemon and embarked on a costly licensing deal for Star Wars items.

Scrabble is assembled on Line 7, beneath a giant banner for the game Battleship. The average run is twenty-six thousand units of the standard cardboard version in two weekly shifts. (Deluxe Scrabble, with the rotating plastic board, is assembled occasionally on Line 4.) I watch boxes as they are "spotted" on a Scrabble label — a new red-brick color scheme designed to liven up the packaging — on which glue has been automatically applied. A giant arm plunges the box into the label and folds over the sides at the rate of thirty-three boxes a minute.

As a box travels down the hundred-foot-long conveyor belt, a worker places into one end a sealed plastic bag of tiles. Next comes an upright cardboard divider that displays the rules of the game, then four racks from a pile of thousands, then a gray plastic tile bag, then the cardboard game board, into which an information slip from the NSA is fed, and finally the cover. The box is shrink-wrapped and packed with five others, and the half-dozen games ride an elevator to another conveyor belt, where they are relocated for shipping. My tour guide, a Hasbro executive named Gary Brennan, pulls a warm box off the line and hands it to me. I notice later that it depicts inaccurate tile values on the back: six points for a J instead of eight, two for a C instead of three, eight for a K instead of five. (I tell John Williams, who tells Hasbro, and the next time I inspect a box, the errors have been corrected.)

The factory produces well over a million of the standard, travel, deluxe, and Spanish sets combined per year. Sales exceeded two million in 1998 and would do the same in 1999. As I stand watching the Scrabble boxes roll by, I wonder, Where do all those sets go? And how do they get sold with little or no advertising?

Industrywide, companies turn over their product lines at a rate of close to 100 percent for toys and 25 percent for games. But certain brands are perennials. Hasbro found that sales of Candy Land, for instance, tend to parallel the birth rate three years earlier; when kids turn three, they inevitably receive Candy Land. Scrabble sells year in and year out because parents buy it for their children and newlyweds add it to a living room bookshelf. These games are cultural talismans, signposts in an American life. For Hasbro, they are annuities. American leisure time increasingly is dominated by television and computers, but Hasbro is selling more board games than ever, about 95 million units a year. So entrenched are its games that the company now promotes games playing rather than individual games, bunching Scrabble with other chestnuts — Monopoly, Life, Clue, Yahtzee — in a marketing gimmick called "Family Games Night."

"It would be hard to launch some of these perennial brands today," Mark Stark, a marketing vice president at Hasbro Games, says during my visit. Scrabble doesn't sizzle with action, so it's hard to advertise on television. "It's there because it has endured the test of time and become a part of the culture," he says.

At a meeting of "Team Scrabble" — which consists of Hasbro marketing, licensing, and promotions executives, representatives of an outside ad agency, as well as John Williams and a colleague from the National Scrabble Association — I'm asked to explain tournaments, basic rules, and the words. The Hasbro executives show me a recent analysis of Scrabble's brand strategy which doesn't even mention the competitive side of the game. And it strikes me that the people who own the rights to Scrabble don't know much about the subculture around it.

Does that matter? If the competitive realm could help Hasbro sell more sets, presumably the company would take advantage of it, and executives say they do care about the tournament scene. "I'd love to see Scrabble achieve the same level as chess, where you have grand masters that are internationally known and you have the tournaments and there is funding," Dave Wilson, now the president of Hasbro's games division, tells me later in his surprisingly toy-free office in East Longmeadow. "I think it would be terrific to do that."

But on a daily basis, Hasbro sees more to gain in the eye-rolling ideas enthusiastically discussed at the meeting: inflatable Scrabble furniture, an eighteen-karat-gold set, a special golf edition, a licensing arrangement with the gambling industry (Hasbro already has licensed Monopoly-themed slot machines), a deal with Pepsi to put Scrabble on soft-drink cups at movie theaters.

It's up to John Williams to bridge the gap between the corporate and competitive worlds — a gap that doesn't exist for any other proprietary game because no other proprietary game exists in such a competitive world. Williams tries to decommercialize Hasbro's ownership role; for instance, he notes, the NSA's big event isn't known as the "*Hasbro* National Scrabble Championship." It's important to give the players, he tells Team Scrabble, a feeling that they, not some faceless corporation, control the game. Hasbro's Stark agrees: "That degree of ownership they have is something you don't want to disturb."

From the perspective of some top players, though, Scrabble shouldn't be owned by anyone. If a corporate parent is an unfortunate necessity, they believe, then it should do more to support the players. Hasbro, the complaints go, unfairly cracks down on players who want to write how-to books. It harasses Internet sites that infringe on the game's copyright (though erratically so — Hasbro's struggling interactive division, which the company would sell in late 2000, all but ceded cyberspace to games players). It doesn't stage enough big-money tournaments or allow outside corporate sponsorship. It doesn't spend enough through the NSA to support the clubs and attract new players to the game. And, at a time when cheerleading, bass fishing, and the National Spelling Bee show up on ESPN, it hasn't managed to get the sport on television.

"We'd like it to be the PGA Tour," the veteran Scrabble expert Merrill Kaitz tells me, pointing out another game with a burgeoning pro tour, the strategy card game Magic the Gathering, also now owned by Hasbro. "That's an ideal world."

The resentment stems from the fact that the players, as Lester Schonbrun once told me, "created the whole world," and keep creating it, organizing tourneys (prize money in all events but the Nationals and Worlds comes out of player entry fees), making plastic Protiles and custom boards, writing software, creating Web sites. The players love the game, and praise Hasbro for events like the Nationals, but feel used because they generate free PR for the world's biggest toy company.

"I and a few other of the game's best competitive players believe it's only fair to expect some reasonable remuneration for putting in the time and effort to become one of the best at anything," G.I. Joel once wrote to Hasbro's Dave Wilson. "Golfers, bowlers, tennists, and, yes, chess players all have the dollar incentive to excel, and showcasing the best players has always been good for product sales in those sports. But Scrabble still lags behind. Why isn't this as ludicrous to you as it is to those of us who have chosen to excel at the great game whose copyright you own? And just so you know a little more about the fine art of anagramming, please note that LUDICROUS + I = RIDICULOUS."

Of course, people who drink the Kool-Aid have little perspective. Hasbro probably devotes more time and money to the competitive Scrabble scene than to those of all of its other games combined. The reality is that network executives aren't clamoring to televise Scrabble, and Fortune 500 companies have more productive uses for their sponsorship millions. "Where would I rather be? In fifty NASCAR events or on a banner at the Scrabble championships?" Williams asks. "There's this myth that some company is willing to pay a million dollars to sponsor tournaments and Hasbro is holding back."

Could Hasbro do more? Sure. But it doesn't. "They're not only in the Scrabble business," John Williams told a town meeting for players at the 1998 Nationals. "*You're* only in the Scrabble business." To illustrate how far apart the concerns of the two are, Williams said he had received a letter from a player maintaining that if Scrabble adopted SOWPODS, adding thousands of British words, the game "would go into the toilet." The same week, Williams said, he was asked by a Hasbro executive, "What do you think of a Hard Rock Cafe version of Scrabble, where if you play a rock star's name you get extra points?"

In fact, nothing is guaranteed. Williams has to present a budget to Hasbro every year, and he's never assured of approval, especially of late as Hasbro has struggled. "It's dangerous to assume that they're going to continuously pump a very big sum of money into this ad infinitum," he says. Further downturns in the toy industry, a lawsuit by a player, a new marketing executive who really doesn't get it — anything could lead the company suddenly to spend less on competitive Scrabble.

The players aren't completely naive about the bottom line, or the reality of their world. "Behind it all," Kaitz says, "[we're] wishing our game did have more potential than it really does, that intellectual games were more valued in our society than they are."

When Alfred B. Swift opened a toys and games wholesale business amid the horse-and-carriage clatter of lower Manhattan in 1867, the industry was in its infancy. Playing cards had been made in America since colonial times, but board games didn't emerge until the middle of the nineteenth century. Leading the field was W. & S. B. Ives of Salem, Massachusetts, which in 1843 introduced the Mansion of Happiness, in which landing on a space denoted as a virtue (Piety, Honesty, Temperance, Gratitude, Prudence, Truth, Chastity, Sincerity, Humility, Industry, Charity, Humanity, or Generosity) advanced one toward the Mansion of Happiness, while landing on a vice (Audacity, Cruelty, Immodesty, or Ingratitude) sent one back toward the start. In 1860, a struggling draftsman and lithographer named Milton Bradley created one of the first mass-produced games, the Checkered Game of Life, which had similar moral overtones.

One of the first games that Alfred Swift shipped was Parcheesi, which was almost identical to pachisi, the national game of India since at least the fourteenth century. Swift soon after acquired the copyright to the game, but when his business took a downturn he signed it and the business over to one of his creditors, a paper-box manufacturer named Elisha G. Selchow. Selchow planned to sell the company, but he was so impressed by its manager, John Righter, that he kept it going and made the young man a partner.

In 1874, E. G. Selchow & Company received a trademark, one of the first in the United States, on Parcheesi. Selchow became the sole sales representative for Milton Bradley, and sold dozens of other popular games and puzzles with names like Pigs in Clover, Richter's Building Blocks, and Fuld's Ouija Board. Along with Milton Bradley and Parker Brothers, the renamed Selchow & Righter led a tide of games sales that capitalized on a changing society in which leisure had become morally acceptable and new technology enabled mass production and transcontinental distribution.

Selchow and Righter were hardworking, religious family men. "They were definitely against liquor and gambling," a company history compiled in the 1970s says. "They definitely rejected any game or accessory that could in any way encourage gambling. No roulette wheels, no horse race games, no poker chips, no poker or pinochle type playing cards, no paper play money, no metal coin play money, etc." (The dice in Parcheesi were acceptable "for it appears they believed that [dice] would never encourage one to gamble.") Harriet Righter, a daughter of John Righter who succeeded him as president, passed on acquiring Monopoly from its inventor, Charles B. Darrow, because the game used play money.

Selchow dropped out of the wholesale business but started manufacturing Parcheesi in 1927. The firm wanted to keep things small. It wasn't an innovator. It didn't take risks on new products or develop any hit games. It didn't pressure buyers and retailers to stock its line, and didn't advertise directly to the public the way Milton Bradley did with Chutes and Ladders and Candy Land, and Parker Brothers did with Monopoly, Go to the Head of the Class, and Sorry! Selchow had Parcheesi, and that was fine.

That Scrabble wound up in the hands of a cautious, conservative, unglamorous company made perfect sense. The game, after all, was invented by cautious, conservative, and unglamorous Alfred Butts. Just as Alfred had one success in life, Selchow built a business on one product, Parcheesi. Just as Alfred had no idea about how to bring his invention to market, Selchow didn't approve of the hard sell. Alfred stumbled across an investor who helped him get his game made and marketed; Selchow stumbled across its games. No owner made Scrabble the legend it is now. The public did.

From the start, Selchow's involvement with Scrabble was pure chance. In 1949, a retired buyer for the Marshall Field department store in Chicago named Lester Twitchell stopped in on Marion Stringer, a longtime company employee who worked at Selchow's office in the Toy Manufacturers Association building in Manhattan. Twitchell and a friend, James Brunot, had just acquired a game they had renamed Scrabble and wanted to offer it to Selchow.

"What an odd name and what does it mean, if anything?" Stringer recalled thinking. "It was certainly not very attractive in appearance, with its nondescript playing board, crude racks, and heavy cardboard lettered square pieces." They played a bit. "I did not dislike the game," Stringer wrote in the company history. "I thought it had some merit. But at that time word games were out."

A year later, Twitchell and Brunot visited Harriet Righter at Selchow's Brooklyn headquarters. "I looked at it and said, 'It's a nice little game. It will sell well in bookstores,'" she recalled. But Twitchell and Brunot said they wanted Selchow just to make the boards. They ordered two thousand, disappeared for a year, ordered four thousand more, and then another ten thousand.

It was the summer of 1952, and Scrabble still was being sold by word of mouth. Some Selchow executives didn't even know it existed. When a customer called Marion Stringer to place an order for Scrabble, she remembered the game's name but told the caller Selchow didn't make it. A few minutes later, a man who worked in a neighboring office told Stringer he had played a fascinating game over the weekend called Scrabble. Within the hour, a Macy's buyer called in a panic because the chairman, Jack Straus, "had just come in to get a game of Scrabble and was annoyed to learn that his toy department had never heard of it." Stringer tracked down Brunot's Production & Marketing Company in Connecticut and learned that Selchow had been manufacturing Scrabble boards for two and a half years.

Miss Righter, as everyone called her, dispatched her factory manager to inspect the little Scrabble operation. Brunot and his wife, Helen, carried chairs onto the grass next to the old one-room schoolhouse at the country crossroads where the game was being manufactured. They confessed that they were burned out. They couldn't handle the flood of orders. Toy companies were pressuring them to sell. A few months later, a Selchow contingent led by Miss Righter went to Connecticut and reached a deal to take over the manufacturing and marketing of Scrabble.

Selchow & Righter didn't have to figure out how to sell the game. Buyers thronged the company's offices and calls jammed its switchboard. Scrabble "became a raging battle by day and a nightmare in our dreams," Stringer wrote. But Selchow decided not to contract any manufacturing outside of its Brooklyn factory. For three years, it allocated shipments to give customers a fair share. Finally, realizing the game was here to stay, Selchow built a new factory and offices in Bay Shore, on Long Island. Selchow assumed production of the travel and deluxe editions from Brunot, and introduced Scrabble for Juniors, the rules of which were devised by Marion Stringer. Through the sixties and seventies, sales remained steady and the company's profits were modest, just as Miss Righter had wanted.

In the 1960s, television became the games industry's chief medium. Quiz shows like *The $64,000 Question, Password,* and *Concentration* were turned into popular boxed versions. In turn, the business began producing so-called "skill-and-action" games like Kerplunk, Mouse Trap, and Connect Four because they were easier to advertise on TV than static board games with complex rules. But

Selchow didn't change. Scrabble and Parcheesi sold themselves, so that's what the company sold. Its catalogues were filled with boxed puzzles and slow-moving board games. Selchow periodically rolled out dull brand extensions, like Scrabble Crossword Cubes, but refused to push products on stores or the public. "They were not marketers," says Gene Murtha, a toy-industry veteran. "They were manufacturers with a sales network."

Into the 1980s, there was little pressure on small, privately held outfits like Selchow, Ideal, Lakeside, and Pressman — no stockholders to report to or share price to worry about. Salesmen got favors from buyers to get products onto the shelves. If you had a staple, like Scrabble, or a hot newcomer, like Uno or Aggravation, you could make it without being a marketing heavyweight in the mold of Hasbro or Mattel.

Thanks to its two perennials, Selchow's revenue — 80 percent of which came from Scrabble — trailed that of only Milton Bradley and Parker Brothers in the games business. Yet the company maintained such a low profile that many people in the industry didn't even know how to pronounce its name (SELL-shau rhymes with "now"). In the late 1970s, when Selchow needed a new president, rather than recruit from the toy industry its board tapped Richard Selchow, a grandson of Elisha Selchow. An engineer by training, Dick Selchow had never worked in the family business. He had spent ten years with a plastics molding company, then in R & D at a semiconductor plant. When he agreed to take over, Dick Selchow was the full-time business administrator of his Episcopal church in Greenwich, Connecticut. At Selchow & Righter's spartan, one-story headquarters, the new president of the number-three U.S. games company worked at a metal desk.

Dick Selchow was a competent caretaker. But he made one visionary and ultimately calamitous move: He acquired Trivial Pursuit from its two Canadian inventors. After a slow start, a couple of well-timed magazine stories triggered a craze unprecedented in toy-industry history. Selchow sold 1.5 million units of Trivial Pursuit in the second half of 1983, tripling company revenue. Then the rush started. It was like James Brunot trying to meet the demand for Scrabble from the Connecticut schoolhouse. By February 1984, Selchow faced back orders of a million units; by August, they had hit 11 million. Selchow sold more than 20 million units of Trivial Pursuit worth about $750 million at retail in 1984, tripling the size of the *entire* U.S. games industry.

Little Selchow was in over its head. Shipping agents grew testy. Overwhelmed salespeople didn't return calls. Customers were hung out to dry. Eager to meet demand, Selchow kept the factories churning out boards and cards and boxes. Then the market for the game crashed, and Selchow couldn't shed its inventory, which reached 20 million units. Like James Brunot before him, Dick Selchow and his company just weren't prepared.

Unable to manage the inventory fallout, with no family members interested in succeeding him, Dick Selchow decided to sell the company. Hasbro made a lowball offer. Coleco Industries, trying to rebuild via acquisition after the collapse of its big hit, Cabbage Patch Kids, paid about $60 million in cash, plus notes. In May 1986, Coleco pledged to keep Selchow's management and employees. In December, Coleco announced that it would shut down and sell both of Selchow's Long Island factories.

Most Selchow executives had cashed out but were irate nonetheless. They hadn't trusted the brash, smooth-talking Coleco suits who persuaded the timid, honorable Dick Selchow to sell them his cherished, 119-year-old family business. Coleco, they believed, coveted Selchow as much for the tax write-off as for the three solid brand names — Trivial Pursuit, Scrabble, and Parcheesi — that would give it instant credibility.

Dick Selchow stayed on as a consultant, only to watch his employees lose their jobs and his family business lose its identity. "He felt betrayed," says Gene Murtha, who was Coleco's marketing vice president at the time. "Absolutely betrayed." Less than three years later, Dick Selchow suffered a stroke and died. He was sixty-seven.

Selchow & Righter's tradition of stewardship over innovation was nowhere more evident than with its prized word game. The formation of Scrabble Crossword Game Players Inc. in 1973 as a subsidiary was pitched to the new ranks of competitive players as a way to market their emerging world. In reality, Players Inc. was intended to ensure that the company retain control over that world, because protecting the trademark on the name Scrabble was more important to Selchow's survival than promoting a tournament scene.

The *Official Scrabble Players Handbook* made the company's priorities clear. The first chapter was titled "What Is Scrabble Crossword Game Players Inc.?" The second was "What Is a Trademark?" "SCRABBLE is always capitalized and is *never* the name of the game," the manual stated. To protect trademarks from becoming generic terms, companies use them as descriptive adjectives rather than as nouns. The Scrabble handbook explained that Selchow's products actually were named Crossword Game, Crossword Game for Juniors, Sentence Cubes, and Crossword Cubes. "SCRABBLE is their point of origin," the manual said.

The company was wise to protect the name so assiduously: The name was all that it had. But almost from the beginning, the players believed Selchow didn't understand their needs. As Players Inc. became more involved in establishing tournament rules and other guidelines, the players chafed. The first head of Players Inc., a Selchow executive named Lee Tiffany, didn't play Scrabble and had little interest in learning about those who did. Asked by a player how he could run the organization if he didn't play, Tiffany replied, "I don't have to wear Kotex to sell it."

Tiffany's successor was Jim Houle, who had been a manufacturing executive before being assigned to run the players' organization. To Houle's credit, the number of Scrabble clubs grew in less than a decade from a handful to more than two hundred, and the newsletter became a forum for the evolution of Scrabble theory, which Houle encouraged. But Houle didn't involve the players. The experts wanted their voices heard in building the competitive scene, but aside from filling the newsletter, they weren't. Not one player worked for or was involved in decisions made by Players Inc.

On a corporate level, Scrabble chugged along. After Alfred Butts made himself known to the company, Selchow trotted him out on a publicity tour. It spent some of its Trivial Pursuit cash on print ads — cartoons depicting characters in awkward positions (Santa Claus stuck in a chimney, the Statue of Liberty encased in scaffolding, Gulliver tied down by the Lilliputians), saying, "I'd rather be playing Scrabble." The ads were placed in mainstream publications, a first for Scrabble. Another first: a television commercial, using the same theme.

Selchow also used its Trivial Pursuit money to expand the Scrabble line (most of the products flopped, like Scrabble People, plastic building blocks shaped like people into which letters were inserted) and to back a television show (hosted by Chuck Woolery, *Scrabble,* which bore little resemblance to the actual game, ran from 1984 to 1990). And Selchow put on its most lavish event to date, the 1985 Nationals in Boston, which attracted three hundred players.

There the conflict between the experts and the company came to a head. John Nason, Selchow's marketing vice president, knew Players Inc. was perceived as ineffectual. So in Boston, he asked John Williams — the brother-in-law of a former colleague at J. Walter Thompson, who had been helping with Scrabble public relations — to moderate a roundtable with a handful of experts. Dick Selchow wanted to hear their grievances. Jim Houle wasn't invited.

"As it is now, the game does not belong to the players," the expert Albert Weissman proclaimed in a letter read at the meeting. The gripes poured forth. The official newsletter was published inconsistently. Qualifying tournaments for the Nationals were a disorganized mess.

Then there were complaints that Selchow had become too zealous in protecting its trademark. In one instance, it had sought a court injunction to stop publication of a book by Joel Wapnick, who settled by agreeing to give the company 25 percent of any royalties. Jim Neuberger, the New York lawyer, who should have known better, said: "I don't see why anyone has to get a license from Selchow & Righter to publish a book that they want to publish about this game that we all love."

The Selchow executives were learning how much the players cared — that they sincerely believed the game was so much a part of American culture, or at least their lives, that it shouldn't belong to anybody. But the company stood its ground. "It is a valuable trademark and we want the publicity," Dick Selchow said. "It is good business for us to get royalties."

"You have to understand we are in the games-making business. We are not in the altruism business," John Nason added. "We conduct these tournaments and we invest money in these tournaments so that the world at large will know about Scrabble, will go out and buy Scrabble games. You have got to know this."

Dick Selchow listened to the players and promised to make changes. Afterward, he told John Williams to revamp the newsletter and begin overhauling the players organization. Then Dick Selchow sold the company.

Coleco was the antithesis of stodgy Selchow. For a year, it treated Scrabble like a hot item, commissioning a TV commercial aiming the brand at a younger adult market. (In it, a man and woman bantered while playing Scrabble; all the viewer saw was a deluxe board spun back and forth.) Sales spiked above 1.5 million sets in 1987. But it wasn't enough to save the company. By the middle of the next year, Coleco was in Chapter 11. By the time Hasbro acquired its assets the following year, Scrabble was wounded.

"They almost lost the brand," says Dave Wilson. "They weren't games people to begin with. They came from the toy business, where if something is good one day and a year from now or two years from now it's not so good, well, move on to the next. It goes, it dies. I'd commit suicide if on my watch Scrabble died."

At the annual International Toy Fair, Hasbro's showroom on West 23rd Street in Manhattan is a bombardment of bright colors and brighter lights. Four actors dressed as futuristic NASCAR racers greet visitors who emerge from a tunnel illuminated with neon signs flashing the names of some of Hasbro's four-hundred-plus products. The ninety thousand square feet of showrooms are a sprawling testament to the power of children's culture in America and an almost obscene paean to the breadth and depth of the world's number-one toy company. Nerf. Star Wars. World Championship Wrestling. Monopoly. Trivial Pursuit. G.I. Joe. Tinkertoy. Play-Doh. Room after room, familiar name after familiar name, slogan after slogan. It is a blend, notes John Williams, of the classic and the opportunistic, with the opportunistic usually receiving top billing.

We cruise past the NASCAR guys, past Barney the purple dinosaur, past enormous cardboard displays featuring the Pokemon logo, and hang a left into a room dedicated to board games. Attempting to retool the image of some older brands, Hasbro has dedicated reasonably prominent Toy Fair real estate to its "Kool Kids" campaign promoting baby boomer–era lines: Battleship, Mouse Trap, Perfection, Connect Four, Twister, Trouble, Operation. Farther down the same corridor, in a quiet rear corner, far from the glamorous displays staffed by smiling young actors hired to deliver cheery spiels, are the even older and stodgier chestnuts: Monopoly, Life, Sorry!, Clue, Yahtzee.

Here Scrabble gets its modest display. Various versions of the game are mounted on a wall. Next to them four placards describe the activities of the National Scrabble Association. They note the number of NSA clubs, tournaments, and members. They mention the burgeoning School Scrabble program and the 2000 Nationals to be held in Providence, Rhode Island, just a short drive from Hasbro's headquarters in Pawtucket.

For Williams, getting his informational material on the wall at Toy Fair for the few buyers and journalists who will pause to inspect the old standards on the way to the hot, new games is a small coup, of which he is proud. But to the passing eye, it's boring, and even among the stalwarts in their familiar packaging, the Scrabble display looks hopelessly square.

"Actually, it's the best we've ever been represented," Williams says. "Last year, the Scrabble display consisted of these three boxes," he says, pointing to the wall.

Still, Scrabble is lost amid the acres of World Championship Wrestling action figures and Pokemon gewgaws. Even when it sells two million sets in a year, Scrabble doesn't make or break Hasbro. Generating annual sales of about $25 million, Scrabble is a consistent, but ultimately insignificant, source of revenue for the $4-billion-a-year company.

Hasbro may not get it — it being the fact that never in the two-hundred-year history of the U.S. toy industry has there been such a highly developed community for a proprietary game; that there is intellectual heft to Scrabble; that it isn't a board game at all in the way that Clue or Monopoly is a board game, contrived, redundant, and temporal, but rather a brilliant, organic, seemingly inevitable creation in the same way as chess or backgammon or the Mona Lisa. But Hasbro knows enough to keep funding Scrabble, at levels that may or may not be sufficient to encourage growth in sales and in the ranks of tournament players.

Williams tries to balance the fanaticism of the top players he at once jokes about and admires with the reality of the toy industry. He can't offend the Hasbro executives who could boot competitive Scrabble off the corporate gravy train. He knows that Scrabble will sell with or without tournaments (though not as much without). But he also knows that inside Hasbro, where landing the Next Hot Toy is more important than tending the old-fogy ones, the game amounts to little more than a pimple on Barney's ass. Which is why amid the sonic boom of Toy Fair, Williams and I talk in a quiet, lightly trafficked, far corner that most visitors politely blow right past.

That's the paradox of Scrabble. It may be the trademarked property of a major multinational corporation, and it may never attract the money and attention that it "deserves." But it transcends the little display at Toy Fair, transcends the pedestrian boxed games with which it is lumped, transcends the benign neglect of the Selchow years and the stable but, from some players' perspective, disappointingly uncreative ownership of Hasbro. What the game does for the people who play it, for me, can't be measured in commercial terms.

"They may *own* the game," Williams tells me of the company on which his job depends, "but they'll never come close to your devotion to the game."

13

1461

Amerca's good-time game." That's how Hasbro describes Scrabble in the only television commercial the company has made for the game in the last decade. It's a hokey, thirty-second montage of nuclear families, mostly white and blond, laughing around a board. So it stands to reason that few things could be more American than playing such a treasured game on the Fourth of July.

But wholesome is not the image delivered this Independence Day by my next tournament venue: Reno. I'm greeted at the airport by the why-waste-a-minute image of slot machines next to the baggage claim. The Megabucks prize scrolling across a red neon ticker in the main terminal is up to . . . "$7,000,000!!!" THE BIGGEST LITTLE CITY IN THE WORLD, as the sign stretched across the tawdry main thoroughfare proclaims, consists of pawnshops and jewelry stores and quick-loan joints — and all of them at once at Palace Jewelry and Loan. I feel a weird blast of air conditioning as I walk past Harrah's and the Nugget: The gambling pit opens onto the sidewalk. Art Deco clubs like the Nevada and Harold's, which boasts "50s and 60s nostalgia," lie dark and shuttered. CHECKS CASHED UPSTAIRS, one sign reads. Reno is a place to borrow money and gamble it away, or marry your sweetheart at the Candlelight Wedding Chapel and honeymoon at the Thunderbird Motel.

What would Alfred Butts think? My hero, counting letters on the obituary page of the *Herald Tribune* so that sixty years later Americans could play Scrabble and blackjack in one afternoon.

But Reno is The Tournament. As befits a superlative-happy gambling mecca, this year Reno is The Longest Tournament. Ever. Thirty-nine games in the main event plus twelve in an optional "early bird." That's a total of fifty-one games over eight days, a *They Shoot Horses, Don't They?* exercise in Scrabble machismo or masochism, I'm not sure which.

Reno is the second-most-popular Scrabble tournament after the Nationals, and in odd-numbered years, like this one, it is considered the championship stand-in. About three hundred players, including two experts from Thailand who barely speak English, have descended on this tacky gambling mecca. Most of the best in the land are present: G.I. Joel, Brian Cappelletto, Joe Edley, Jim Geary, Lester Schonbrun. Everybody plays Reno.

The tournament has been run for years by a contractor named Johnny Nevarez, a buff Californian in his early forties who, with his passion and tanned good looks, would be the perfect host for a Scrabble infomercial. Nevarez got interested in Scrabble while in college. He and his friends would get stoned and play. "Games would last four hours," he says.

Nevarez stages the tournament at the Sands Regency, one of the cheesier hotels in the city's casino district. It's a giant ashtray (G.I. Joel wears a surgical mask throughout the event), and soft rock pours like a sedative through the loudspeakers twenty-four hours a day. Working-class vacationers clad in Reno T-shirts and pastel nylon sweat suits dump nickels, quarters, and Susan B. Anthony dollars into the slots, some patterned after Hasbro's own Monopoly game. There are no high rollers in this joint. The room I share with Marlon fetches $39 a night, for two.

When I arrive, Marlon is lying on his bed, his naked, fireplug body wrapped in the sheets, watching Clint Eastwood in *A Fistful of Dollars*. He is crashing after a three-bus, sixty-one-hour journey from Baltimore via Washington, Toledo, and Chicago. His dogeared *OSPD* lies on a table, along with three tattered notebooks and several packs of off-brand toaster pastries and Parliament cigarettes. The early bird starts in five hours. Marlon is broke, and he says he needs to win some money — playing Scrabble, not gambling. He wants to pay me for this hotel room, and he still owes me $100 from a year ago in Chicago. Plus, he needs to make sure he has enough cash for bus fare home.

I'm happy to front Marlon money — he pays back when he can — but I can't help wonder. Marlon is a bright, self-aware, highly social man who won't take a job because almost all jobs, he theorizes, benefit white people. He gave up on the idea of working for Amtrak. Instead, he plans to win a lawsuit he has filed against the food company Giant.

A few months earlier, Marlon walked into a supermarket to buy a pack of cigarettes. The clerk asked him for identification. Marlon, who is thirty-four, felt as if he were being harassed. He raised his voice and asked to see the manager. He raised his voice again. Then Marlon says a security guard — a white security guard — grabbed him, threw him to the floor, and pinned his arms behind him. Marlon was arrested. No charges were filed, but he sued the company, alleging battery, false arrest, and false imprisonment. "I'm gonna get a whole lot," Marlon says. "That's malicious prosecution and shit. Brother man gonna get paid."

In addition to studying words and waiting for the trial, Marlon has begun writing what he describes as a tract about Pan-Africanism. I'm never sure if Marlon's by-whatever-means-necessary routine is bombast or if he's organizing a revolutionary cell in his bedroom. Marlon is a pussycat by nature, polite, funny, loving, and friendly with just about everyone in the Scrabble world, race notwithstanding. But he's also genuinely angry. When I ask him what he's going to do, he'll often reply, "Gonna burn down America!"

Marlon was born in Baltimore. His mother, Hattie, worked for years in the main post office downtown until she went on disability with diabetes and neuropathy in the early 1990s. Marlon knows his father, but he has never been part of Marlon's or Hattie's life. Hattie has lived in the same row house in the black working-class neighborhood of East Baltimore for more than forty years.

At age two, Marlon could recite the One Hundredth Psalm from memory; his relatives propped open a Bible to make it look as if he were reading. At age five, he *could* read, and soon was poring over the *World Book* encyclopedias that an uncle sold door to door. He remembers reading about World War II and the Kennedy assassination. "I knew that was bullshit," he says. "Ain't no way [Oswald] popped him by himself." So emerged Marlon the skeptic. An aunt inspired in him a sense of racial injustice; reciting the Pledge of Allegiance, instead of "and justice for all," she would say "and justice for *y'all.*" An uncle told him that white people "didn't want black people working with them because they didn't want us to know how dumb they really were."

Marlon never followed, or led. He had few close friends outside of his family. He never joined a gang because "peer pressure is totally lost on me." He went to the library but hated school — the bells telling him when to come and go, the obligation to study what he considered useless subjects, like the German class he quit in sixth grade.

Marlon was bused to special schools because he tested well but fought with other kids, cut classes, and got bad grades. He turned down a scholarship to a private school and wound up at a technical high school learning electrical construction and maintenance. He played one game of high-school football, in ninth grade, rushing twelve times for 173 yards and three touchdowns, but he quit because he didn't start the next game. "I didn't feel I was getting respect."

Marlon went to Morgan State University, a predominantly black college in Baltimore, for two years, but quit because a white teacher stiffed him on a grade on an English paper. "You are a big fish in a little bowl. There are many bright minds in the big bowl," Marlon says the teacher wrote atop the paper. "Meaning I wasn't no more than a smart nigger at Morgan. It soured me totally. Here I am at a black university and I have to go through this shit.

"I'd a been a great football player, a great boxer, a great anything I would have done," he tells me. "If I'd a gone to school, I'd a been a great doctor, a great lawyer, anything."

"Whose fault is that?" I ask.

"I don't see it like a fault. That I'm not plugged into the matrix is not a fault. I'm glad I'm not plugged into the matrix."

The Hills played cards, family and friends gathering for long, competitive games of whist. One night, lightning struck a nearby church while they were playing. It was a sign from God: no more cards. So they switched to board games. Scrabble became a favorite. The Hills always looked up words in their dictionary, and over time learned dozens of two-, three-, and four-letter words, and bingos, too. Marlon's older cousin Cheryl eventually agreed to let ten-year-old Marlon play Scrabble with her. They became a family of living room experts, with strong memories and an intuitive sense of board strategy. "Twenty, twenty, twenty, bingo," Marlon recalls his Uncle Harrison instructing him. The meaning: score about twenty points three turns in a row while setting up your rack to bingo.

But throughout high school Marlon refused to enter a tournament. "What muhfukka 16 wanna be in the company of da flippin' socially retarded nerds that constitute the upper levels of the Scrabble stratosphere?" Marlon e-mailed me shortly after we met. It wasn't until he was twenty-seven, in 1992, that he did. On the Saturday of July 4 weekend, Uncle Harrison told Marlon they were going for a ride, but he wouldn't say where until they arrived at a hotel downtown. Marlon was pissed, but after starting off 4–0 he agreed to return for the second day of the tournament. He wound up 10–0, and afterward experts gathered to meet the new black kid who could play. One of them told him about the Nationals later that year in Atlanta and mentioned the prize money. "When I found out you could win ten thousand, I said I'm into this goofy fucking game," he says. His initial rating was 1765.

On the train to Atlanta, Marlon met Matt, who hustled him out of $17, and he met Richie Lund, who dubbed him the Muhammad Ali of Scrabble because he was running his mouth. Marlon went 12–15 in the expert division, boasted that he would win a Nationals within five tries, and was interviewed by Joe Edley for *Scrabble News*. "I knew I had skillz, but no pillz," he wrote me, meaning he had talent but no word knowledge.

Marlon quickly discovered that winning at Scrabble was a mild but important form of empowerment. He could beat the Europeans — the people responsible for the school system, the government, and four hundred years of racial injustice on the continent — at a game of the mind. Doctors, lawyers, engineers, Ph.D.s — whoever. Playing Scrabble, Marlon could stick it to the man. It was even sweeter when he beat someone whose condescension was plain.

"It definitely does not validate my existence," he wrote to me. "But it makes some shit easier to take."

The spiral-bound notebooks without which Marlon never travels are filled with his eclectic brand of Scrabble study and his sometimes inflammatory musings on race, religion, and life. On one page, Marlon has written every six- and seven-letter word he doesn't know by heart. On another, he offers himself a test of seven-letter words that have a tough anagram. He underlines the first letter of the anagram. For instance, in LIGULAS the anagram is LUGSAIL; PALSHIP, SHIPLAP; ALMONDS, DOLMANS. In another book, Marlon has over time manually recorded all of the nine-letter words he does not know. Even top experts play nine-letter words sparingly; after all, to do so you must either play through a two-letter (or longer) word already on the board or through disconnected tiles. "It's just words I want to know," he says. "If the possibility of them turns up during a game, I know to be looking for them."

During his sixty-one-hour bus ride, for inspiration Marlon reconstructed a game he played against Brian Cappelletto at the 1996 Nationals in Dallas. Marlon calls it "the nine-thousand-dollar game" — the difference, more or less, between the $10,000 prize for finishing in second place, which Marlon would do if he won the game, and the $900 for fifth place, which is where he would wind up if he lost. Marlon committed to memory every play in sequence. He beat Capp — only Marlon calls him Capp — and shocked the Scrabble world, finishing 19–8 and second to Adam Logan, the Harvard math graduate student who ran away from the field with a 24–3 mark. It was, and remains, the high point of Marlon's Scrabble career.

The victory led to a profile in the *Baltimore Sun*, which led to the job testing game software for a Baltimore company whose main client was Hasbro's interactive division. Marlon tested computer versions of Monopoly, Battleship, Mastermind, Risk, and Scrabble. On his own time, he played ten thousand games against the Scrabble CD-ROM, proving, he says, that it cheats (drawing better tiles for itself than for its opponent). Marlon loved the work, and he was good at it. But he quit a few months after I met him, citing a racial incident. He worked briefly as a security guard at Morgan State, but quit that, too. Now his job is Scrabble, Marlon says, and changing society.

At Reno, Marlon swears he won't let a string of recent bad luck influence his play. To help achieve that goal, he composed during the bus ride his "Rules of Engagement." For the early-bird event, Marlon has four rules.

1. WIN THE GAME.

2. STAY FOCUSED.

3. KNOW THE LEDGE. "That's knowledge," Marlon says, explaining to me, the hip-hop-challenged white boy, that the phrase comes from a song by the rapper Rakim.

4. ICE FOR BLOOD. "In a short tournament, calm the fuck down," Marlon says.

Marlon has different rules for the long tournament. He says that in a short tournament you just try to win the few games and not take any chances. In a long event, you need to rack up a big point spread, because that often is what decides the overall winner.

1. PLAY MY GAME. "If you're a boxer, you don't fight somebody else's fight, like Sugar Ray did fighting Duran," Marlon explains. "My game is an open game. In a long tournament, play my game." For instance, Marlon insists that in a long tournament, if handed FACTION on his opening rack, he would not make the conventional placement of the F on the double-letter score but would slot it two spaces to the right, sacrificing 8 points for the remote chance of playing LIQUEFACTION from the triple-word score.

Nearly every top player would judge this strategy as idiotic. "That's why people think you're crazy," I say.

"People have no fucking idea," Marlon replies. "People have no idea what is fucking going to happen to them. I'm calculating more than just about anybody who can play."

2. STAY FOCUSED.

3. WALK A TIGHTROPE (EARLY BUT NOT LATE). "String the board wide the fuck open," Marlon explains. "Flirt with danger. Slot T's in the triple-triple line. Slot E's in the triple-triple." Why take the risk? I ask. "I'm a stronger player," he says. "I know the dictionary now. I'm probably ninety percent on the dictionary now."

4. BREEZE IT, BUZZ IT, E-Z DUZZ IT. Marlon is quoting from a *West Side Story* song. "I got to remind myself that all the time," Marlon says.

Indeed, losing his cool is Marlon's biggest weakness. But it is also the personality Marlon chooses to cultivate: the brilliant but unpredictable ghetto boy, as apt to drop ELUTRIATE in a game as he is "motherfucker" in a conversation.

It's not just his skin color, it's how he chooses to wear it. There are plenty of African-American Scrabble experts, including one ranked higher than Marlon, Lisa Odom of Minneapolis, who's also the highest-ranked woman. But none of them makes a point of race, while Marlon struts his blackness, from the wooden Black Power fist and African-motif necklace he wears — "Green is for land. Red is for the blood of the people" — to what Matt Graham calls Marlon's "high Ebonics" speech. Marlon knows standard English; he chooses to speak the way he does. During games, Marlon turns his chair around and straddles it, sucking on a toothpick or two. He'll show up late and let his opponent start his clock. He'll chatter to himself, usually growing frustrated over bad racks. "God-*damn*," he'll cry, quieting a room of players.

Of course, no one takes Marlon's act entirely seriously. He's never threatening. He laughs at himself when ribbed. He has forged caring friendships with many players; he greets me with a soul handshake and chest bump, while the sweet Rose Kreiswirth, a middle-aged expert from Long Island, gets a hug and kiss on the cheek. Marlon's ready good humor, courtesy, and lovable charm don't stop his outbursts. If they did, Marlon wouldn't be Marlon. Even Marlon doesn't always view himself as entirely out of the mainstream. Asked to pick seven Scrabble tiles that best describe him, he replied, "M-A-R-L-O-N, plus a blank. MARLON is NORMAL. And the blank is unlimited potential."

If he's ever going to be feared and respected, like Cappelletto and Edley, Marlon needs to exploit that potential and play it cool. Otherwise, he'll forever be a sideshow — the loud, irreverent, outrageous Black Player, good but not great. Not that Marlon worries about how he's perceived. He knows he's smarter than most people.

"Never in my life have I felt inferior," he tells me. "Never, not ever. Ain't never looked at a white boy and thought that motherfucker is better than me. Under no circumstances. Stupidity when it confronts intellect does not retreat. Intellect when it meets stupidity ain't got no choice but to retreat. 'Cause the first thing you say is, 'Oops, you stupid.'"

I come into Reno with my 1461 rating ranked about 650th in North America, a long way from about 2,000th, which is where I began my quest for Scrabble proficiency. But in the three weeks since my tournament victory on Long Island, I've lost momentum. I'm exhausted from moving into a new apartment, I haven't studied much, and I'm my usual nervous self. While I finally have achieved a respectable rating, deep down I feel like a fraud.

In the smoke-filled hallway, within earshot of the jangling arcade noises of the omnipresent slots, I'm listed on the player sheet under my old rating, which bothers me. I want to be known as a 1461 player, a solid intermediate. While a mistaken rating could work in my favor by lulling opponents into complacency, I'm more concerned about how I'm perceived. Still, I win three of four in the early bird on day one, which ends at 11:00 P.M., or 2:00 A.M. Brooklyn time. My back is killing me, Marlon snores, I sleep badly, and the next day I lose seven of eight games.

At least it's not the main event. There are thirty-nine games to go. But playing in a long tournament when things aren't going well is like enduring the stages of grief. My inauspicious 4–8 record in the early bird speeds me past denial and hope and straight to resignation. Sure, I made a few nice plays — spotting KANGARoO down from a K, turning ETIC into ENERGETIC — but most of it feels random, out of my control. Talking to Joe Edley and being Joe Edley are not the same thing.

I had longed to escape the novice division to get away from the blue-hairs, but I've discovered that they are among the intermediates, too, just with inflated ratings. The trick to avoiding them is to get out to a fast start, because the players with the best records play one another, and the little old ladies never have the good records. In the main event, I do that, racing to a 6–4 start.

One mystical sequence in Game 3 is memorable. On my first turn, I play a seven-letter word, PArOTID. On my second turn I play an eight-letter word, DREARIER. On my third turn I add ING to my opponent's previous play, making a nine-letter word, REVOLTING. And on my fourth turn I make a ten-letter word, placing UN in front of my opponent's earlier bingo, REALIZED. Seven, eight, nine, ten. The sequence combines all of the joys of the game: creativity, symmetry, linguistic flexibility, mathematics, and luck. I win the game, 490–403.

The effects of study are immediately apparent: four-letter words like CUIF, WEIR, YECH, and VROW all instinctively fly from my fingers in early games, as does OUTBARKS (I've studied the OUT words . . .) and OVERFAR (. . . and the OVER words). And when my higher-rated opponents win with plays like OUTHOMER and SUBRENT, well, what can I do? But then I endure a 2–5 stretch after the 6–4 start. My slump isn't about not "knowing the ledge" but losing the cool, playing phonies (like ZINCE*, when ZINC would have done) and failing to think through winnable endgames, blinded by a haze of complexity and worry.

At 6–7, I write in my notebook, "Back to playing the blue-hairs." At 7–8, I scribble, "Breakout is turning into a breakup."

I'm not the only one struggling. In the middle of Game 19, over in the expert section, Chris Cree leaps from his table and storms out of the playing room, shouting "Goddamn it!" and slamming the door. The tile shuffling stops, and for a moment the room goes hush.

Chris Cree is best known in the Scrabble world not for his steady run of top-notch play, his folksy Texas twang, or his successful forklift business. Nor for his golf-course attire, country-club Republican politics, endless cigarette, unfailing generosity, adept guitar strumming, or well-timed *Goddamn!*s when the tiles don't fall his way. No, Cree is a legend because of what happened at the Scrabble Superstars Showdown at Bally's in Las Vegas in 1995.

It is 7:30 A.M. Cree has been drinking beer and playing blackjack all night. In the last forty minutes, he's come back from the dead, from $15,000 in the hole, to pull even. Then the cards really start falling, and Cree keeps betting, $5,000 per hand, three hands at a time. Then eight or *nine* hands at a time. He can't lose. From 8:00 to 9:00, Cree wins $177,500, pushing his winnings during the Scrabble tournament to nearly $200,000. Mike Baron has been monitoring his inebriated friend, prodding him to stop — not because he's drunk, not because he's just won two hundred grand, but because the Scrabble tournament is about to resume.

"They're starting your clock," Baron says. "It's time to go."

Cree hasn't even been winning in the Superstars. But after collecting his check at the cashier's window, he goes to play Scrabble. He wins two of three, races down to the blackjack table at lunch, wins another $62,000. He plays four more Scrabble games in the afternoon, goes to his room, eats a shrimp cocktail and a cheeseburger, washes it down with a Pepsi, and sleeps. By the week's end, Cree has won $250,000 — five times as much as David Gibson wins in the most lucrative Scrabble tournament ever.

But when a *Sports Illustrated* reporter who is writing about Scrabble asks what he would have rather won, the gambling money or the Scrabble tournament, Cree doesn't hesitate. "Tournament," he says. "Glory. Glory. Glory. I want that glory."

Cree has had his share, taking big events like Reno in 1990, when he started 18–1, and the Grand Canyon in 1984. He finished fourth in a Nationals in the eighties, and he always seems to wind up near the top of the top division. But Chris has been on a year-and-a-half-long run of bad luck, and he's happy to tell you about it. That's why I love him: Among the expert Scrabble players, Chris Cree may not be the biggest whiner, but he's the biggest whiner who should know better. Either that, or the man who won $250,000 playing blackjack has been truly screwed by Lady Luck.

Over dinner in Reno in a hotel where his room is comped — one far swanker than the Sands Regency across town, and racier, too, this week thanks to the convention of swingers it's hosting — Chris explains why he can't stand Scrabble's unfairness. Take the game he lost that day to a weaker player. Chris sacrificed a dozen points to make what appeared to be, based on the tiles unseen to him, a logical late-game play. But his opponent beat the odds, hooking the word he had just played with SCENERY, an improbable combination based on the information Chris had.

"It just goes down as an 'L,'" Chris says. "No one will ever know all the anguish and thought and pain that went into it."

"And that frustrates you," I say.

"Very much. It does."

"But that's built into the game, isn't it?" I reply.

Chris points his steak knife at me in a mock threatening manner. "Perhaps," he says. "It. Is."

At age forty-five, Chris golfs to a handicap that fluctuates between six and twelve. He closed down the offices of his forklift sales company a year ago and now runs the business from his big suburban Dallas home. His devoted girlfriend sits behind him during Scrabble games, listening to the postgame tile talk with the patience of a priest in a confessional. All in all, a pretty good life, he admits. And yet this goddamn game.

Chris is as good as anyone at assessing Scrabble's probabilities. He is one of the most meticulous tile-counters around, not only tracking which ones have been played but keeping a running count of how many have been played. By doing so, Chris is seeking to minimize the odds of something unexpected happening. "When the odds don't go the way they're supposed to, that just pisses me off," he says.

Chris admits his word knowledge is inferior to that of the top twenty players. What turns him on is calculating those in-game odds — based on vowel-consonant ratios, the opponent's previous play, the unseen tiles — and winning despite them. "I want to win the game when *you* draw both blanks and all the S's. The games where the odds are against me," he says. "That's what gives me glory. Who cares about getting both blanks, four S's, and scoring six hundred points? That's not even fun."

In one game in Reno, Chris had the rack ADKMNNU. He deduced by his opponent's play that the one remaining tile in the bag had to be the J. So he played off his D and went out with JUNKMAN to win. Afterward, his opponent said, "How'd I lose this game? I had everything!" "Yeah, I know you did," Chris replied.

That's why he can't take it when the odds betray him, because he's thinking and his opponent isn't. He's not drawing blanks; he's expecting not to draw blanks, so he's playing more defensively.

"I keep track of it. I watch it," he says the next day, chain-smoking Marlboro Lights in the Sands Regency coffee shop. "Every tournament in the last year and a half, I've had fewer blanks than the number of games played. Today, I had two blanks in one game. I had no blanks in the other five. I came within ten or twenty points in the other ones. That's really frustrating when you have a chance for that glory, to win a game where somebody's luckier than a two-dicked dog, and you just can't do it."

"Why does it matter so much?" I ask.

"I want a return on my investment. I want a return of glory on my investment of time."

The next day, I happen by Chris's table during a game and notice his rack: AEEEEOU. Across the room, someone in the expert division yells, about something else, "Shit!"

"That wasn't Chris Cree!" Chris announces, and everyone in the packed playing hall laughs. "But I'll show y'all how to do it in *juuuuuuust* a minute."

Day five, 10:00 P.M. The tournament room. A few friendly after-hours games are in progress.

One of the players, a fiftyish Manhattan club member named Sally Ricketts, feels light-headed. She sits in a chair, and someone brings her water, but she starts getting woozy. Larry Sherman, Joel's brother, props her up in his lap, but Sally's fading. Finally, we lie her on the red carpeting. I call a player who is a physician, and he comes down from his room.

Meanwhile, the games go on. Players glance over at Sally lying on the floor being tended to by paramedics, but no one stops playing. Arguments over racks and moves and bingos and strategy — all continue uninterrupted. Sally is carted out on a stretcher, and over her protestations is taken to a hospital.

"That's fucked up. I'm sorry," Marlon says. "The lady lying there on the floor and we keep playing. Me, too. She could have been dying right the fuck there and we would have still been playing Scrabble. That's fucked up. We just kind of stuck with that bug a little bit too bad."

G.I. Joel, who is Sally's friend, asks, "What should people do? Stop playing? Crowd around, not give her air, pretend to care? At least they're honest."

Ira Cohen, a Los Angeles expert, has a practical concern. If Sally doesn't make it back to tournament in time for the morning rounds, "The pairings will be all messed up," he says.

Fortunately for the pairings, Sally is okay. She returns to the hotel later that night and plays in the morning.

Playing fifty-one games in eight days — *in a casino* — is a time-bending experience. A moment arrives where your quotidian anchors come loose, and you're not sure what day it is, or how much longer this can go on. You add up the numbers and figure it's got to be over soon, and then you realize you're 13–11 in the main event, out of the running. And there are still three days and *fifteen* games to go.

I'm not sure what day of the week it is; not that it matters. Play starts at 9:00, and Marlon has to wake me. "It's after eight," he says. "Get up."

"I don't want to play," I respond.

"I hope a lot of other motherfuckers feel the same way," he says. "Bring it on."

Marlon has shamed me. I do want to play. I always want to play. It's just that I'm sore, aching, and exhausted. My back is stiffer than Al Gore. The black, puffy rings below my eyes look as if they've been applied by a makeup artist for Kiss. My legs and arms feel atrophied, as if my reentry capsule has just plopped into the Pacific Ocean after a week in space. All of this means I'm doomed.

Failure, in other words, is a self-fulfilling prophecy, and I'm very much in self-fulfilling mode. The low point comes in Game 25, when I challenge a common three-letter word (FIZ) and then play back-to-back phonies against a woman for whom English appears to be a second language. Late in another game, I fail to block the only spot for my opponent's otherwise-unplayable Z. In yet another, I miss a wide-open play of QUAY for 36 points on the penultimate turn, playing QUiET for 23 instead, which sets up my opponent's winning 44-point QUIZ.

After Game 30, I'm 14–16, and I scribble some capitalized obscenities in my notebook. Not only have I reverted to my old playing habits, but I've given up.

In the quarter-century of organized Scrabble, only a dozen or so players have scored more than 700 points in a sanctioned game in North America. Nick Ballard, the Scrabble theoretician who published the newsletter *Medleys*, scored 792 in a club game in Chicago in 1980, but he used four phony bingos and never bothered reporting the result. When a skinny, nineteen-year-old, University of Cincinnati student named Bill Blevins, who worked at a Big Boy restaurant, scored 724 points in a club game, it was big news. Blevins made page 1 of the *Scrabble Players News,* but the game was tainted: His opponent was an eighty-three-year-old club newcomer, Daisy Webb, who totaled 176 points and let Blevins get away with five phonies. The tournament mark of 719, set earlier that year, stood.

In the next thirteen years, despite an enormous talent surge, the proliferation of study materials, and the addition of more than five thousand words to a new, second edition of the *OSPD,* the 700 club would be joined only seven times. Scoring 700 was nearly as rare as a round of 59 in a professional golf tourney or an unassisted triple play in baseball. You had to know some words, but, more important, the tiles had to flow favorably and there had to be available spots to play them for a lot of points. You had to be damn lucky.

So when Mark Landsberg scored 770 points in a tournament in Pasadena, California, in July 1993, it wasn't just rare, it was shocking: *770!* And not against some overmatched blue-hair, but against the highest-rated player in the tournament, Alan Stern. Landsberg started with a bingo, SHAMEFUL.

On his third turn he made a triple-triple, WOBBLIEr, for 176 points, through the second B, which he had placed there on his previous turn.

After Stern passed, Landsberg played INTRADAY, a double-double worth 98, which Stern unsuccessfully challenged.

Then Landsberg drew the second blank and played *another* triple-triple, UNCInATE, for 131, which Stern also challenged.

After five turns, the score was 512–113. The word judge who ruled UNCINATE acceptable rushed over to the tournament director and reported the score with a trembling voice. The final was 770–338 — the highest single one-game score ever, and the highest total of winning and losing scores. But Landsberg had no idea he was making history. "No one ever talked about the highest game," he says. "There was no such thing."

There was after that. Landsberg has dined out on 770 ever since. The license plate on his black Mercedes 560SEC reads MR 770. He shows up at tournaments wearing a matching cap and T-shirt bearing the number. He hired an agent to try to negotiate appearances with the National Scrabble Association, attempted to publish a book about the 770 game, and talked about it on CNN.

Whenever Landsberg sees anything priced $7.70, he buys it, like the chocolate silk pie he came across at a bakery in Laguna Hills, California, where he lives in a retirement community called Leisure World. The kid behind the counter gave Landsberg a look when he said he buys anything that's $7.70. Landsberg dragged him to the parking lot and showed him his car. "That's why I have to buy anything that's $7.70!" he exclaimed. *"I'm Mr. 770!"*

In Reno, Landsberg holds court one midnight in the tournament room before a dozen or so players who hang on his stories. Landsberg is in his early sixties. He wears eyeglasses with magnifying lenses that give him a bugged-out, Mr. Magoo look. An oversized, button-down denim shirt hangs to his knees. A few days before, Landsberg won the early bird and called John Williams to announce his retirement from tournament play. (Williams thanked him for the call and for his cooperation over the years, but he was perplexed; it wasn't as if the NSA had to prepare a spot for Landsberg's bust in some hall of fame.)

Landsberg says he started playing Scrabble seriously in the early 1970s in Los Angeles. He was studying English as a foreign language at UCLA after two years in the Peace Corps in Iran and five more years traveling around Asia and the Pacific. Doing what exactly? "I can't tell you," he says. "You have this tape recorder on." He describes himself as a "retired philosopher," and offers only that he worked as an independent games inventor, creating more than two hundred games, a handful of which made it to store shelves. From their sales he draws royalties.

Landsberg played at a place in the Westwood section of L.A. called the Word Club. Shortly after moving to California in the early 1970s, Lester Schonbrun found himself there looking for a game. He was flummoxed. The players had their own rules — 75 bonus points for an eight-letter word, 100 for a nine, 150 for a ten. They also decreed that, based on an inquiry Landsberg says he made of Funk & Wagnalls, RE could be affixed to any verb, and UN and ANTI to any noun. "So you could be ANTICAMEL," Landsberg says.

Landsberg wrote down his ideas about the game, enough for a twenty-five-page pamphlet. When he sent the material for approval to Selchow & Righter, which he knew was zealous about protecting its trademark, the manufacturer's newly formed subsidiary Scrabble Players Inc. said it was working on its own book, but was interested in working with Landsberg.

"We'll make you Mr. Scrabble," Landsberg says he was told. After a year of periodic, uncompensated consultation, Landsberg's lawyer told Scrabble Players it needed to pay Landsberg. "They said, 'We're sorry, we dropped the project,'" Landsberg says. But a year later, the association published *The Official Scrabble Players Handbook.*

Landsberg claimed the company ripped him off. "Everything was paraphrased," he says. "Everything was in the same order, including key words and the annotated games. The strategy part of this book was all mine. It was a derivative work. They couldn't have done their book without mine." He sued Scrabble Players for $10 million. He says the company offered to settle for $5,000.

For the next twelve years, Landsberg didn't touch a tile. The case of *Landsberg v. Scrabble Crossword Game Players, Inc.* went to trial in federal court in Los Angeles in 1975, and Landsberg won. The judge found that Scrabble Players had copied from Landsberg's work and awarded him several hundred thousand dollars in damages. But the Ninth U.S. Circuit Court of Appeals reversed the lower-court ruling, finding that what Scrabble Players had taken "was at most uncopyrightable ideas," like the notational system for games.

The court did order a new trial to determine whether Selchow had breached an implied contract with Landsberg. Three more years passed, and Landsberg again won at trial, though Selchow's lawyers tried to make him look like a word wacko. "Is it true that you believe REBANANA is a word?" he recalls one lawyer asking him. "No, no," he replied. "ANTIBANANA is a word."

Landsberg was awarded $800,000, payable over two years. The decision withstood appeal.

Selchow could afford it — by the time the company paid, Trivial Pursuit had filled its coffers — but it was a big embarrassment. "There wasn't twenty-five grand in the whole thing," Landsberg says of the original book. In the summer of 1987, Landsberg was in Las Vegas when he stumbled onto the Nationals. His settlement money was in the bank, and Coleco had just bought Selchow, so his anti-

Scrabble (hyphenated) feelings were softening. And, he learned, he was a Scrabble celebrity. One player asked for his autograph. Another had followed the case closely. "Do you know who you are?" she asked.

Landsberg played in the tournament (he finished 11–10) and decided to get back into the game. But the game had changed, with the word lists and regular tournaments and player ratings. What hadn't changed was Landsberg's love of words. In the 1970s, he had copied all of the seven-letter bingos out of *Funk & Wagnalls* and had a friend enter them into a computer; he still has the enormous green-paper printouts. His wife used a paper cutter to make thousands of flash cards. Landsberg just liked learning bingos, so he did. "I like impossible tasks," he says. "I wanted to learn every word."

And he played in an old-fashioned style: wide-open and bingo-friendly. Unlike all the new expert Scrabble sharks worried about their ratings, Landsberg just wanted to play. At Leisure World, he spots the retirees 100 points a game for fun. He invited Marlon Hill to his house for a week; the two played more than a hundred games. Landsberg revels in unspooling eight-letter anagrams from a computer study program in front of a crowd, as he does tonight in Reno.

"I'll tell you a secret," his wife says in Reno, the clock past one. "He's doing the nines now."

"To me it's like Disneyland," Landsberg says. "LOXODROME and APISHNESS and FENUGREEK and FEETFIRST. I played one the other day. IRRIDENTA.

"The game doesn't develop any intelligence. Except the study of the words keeps your mind in shape. That's why I'm going to do the nines. It'll take me maybe two years and I'll know all the nines cold. And then maybe I'll do the tens."

Another late night in the tournament room. The rainmen, and me, are playing Anagrams. That's the game in which players shout out words from a pool of tiles (two sets, no blanks) turned over one by one. Players take possession of the words they find and try to capture other players' words by adding letters from the pool and creating new ones. Whoever has the most words when the tiles run out wins.

It's the same game I played one night at the Chicago Nationals, and was complimented for finding WATERLILY*. Here in Reno, the competition is even tougher. I don't have a prayer.

TRUNDLE changes to UNDERLIT, then to INTERLUDE, and to DEREGULATING.

DIALECTS becomes LACERTIDS.

G.I. Joel gets RAWHIDE. He turns it into HEADWAITER.

"He was waiting for it," Marlon says. Marlon steals LACERTIDS by changing it into DISTRACTABLE, using an A, a B, and a T from the pool.

Joel steals RIDGILS by making DIRIGIBLES.

"What is a DIRIGIBLE anyway?" asks Trey Wright, a concert pianist in his late twenties who finished second to Cappelletto in Chicago.

How could he not know what a dirigible is?

"It's a blimp," I say.

"Like a blimp in the sky?" Trey asks.

"A zeppelin," Joel says.

Someone forms UPGAZED.

"This is stealable," Joel says.

"With one letter," Marlon says. "GAZUMPED."

Joel has ten words in front of him: WEDGIES, JURATORY, ECLIPSES, FIXATION, HEADWAITER, VAQUERO, ATARAXY, MAFFICK, DEREGULATING, and DIRIGIBLES. After creating MASCOTS, he has eleven. Then someone steals ECLIPSES by calling out SPECIALIZES, and Joel is back to ten. Marlon takes MASCOTS with IOTACISMS. WEDGIES becomes EDGEWISE. Eight.

"I'm a get it," Marlon says. "I'm a get your SPECIALIZES."

While Marlon is talking trash, Joel blurts out, "CONVEYOR!"

"Damn," Marlon says.

"You're too busy talking while I'm anagramming," Joel says.

Sometimes I can't believe these guys are in the same room together, let alone socializing. Yet they share a skill so central to their disparate lives.

Joel adds FOOTIER and GEOGRAPHY. "GEOPHAGY with an R," Marlon notes. Joel turns SCIUROID into RIDICULOUS. Then he gets MEZQUIT, bringing him to thirteen. Marlon has five. He says he's fixated on stealing CHAPERONES, which someone else has formed.

"OVERPREACHINESS," he says. It's challenged. "Aw, that's a good word," he says, after the *Merriam-Webster's Tenth* stored in someone's laptop says it isn't.

Joel shouts "VIXENISH!" a split second before I do.

"Man, I saw that," I whine. "I finally saw one." But Joel won't give it to me. Rules are rules.

He picks up FLUNKEY. Joel has nineteen words in front of him. I have zero.

Scrabble is like the pole vault. You're proud to have cleared one height, to have set a personal best, but then those damned officials raise the bar an inch higher. And when you dislodge it, and free-fall limply onto the mat below, you can't remember what it was like to have soared.

I don't believe, all evidence to the contrary, that I've improved at all. My doubts are reinforced on day seven, when I put together a 2–4 stretch, dropping to 16–20 for the event. When I'm blown out in Game 35 by Eileen Gruhn, a charming, witty, longtime intermediate player from Seattle, whom I'd beaten earlier in the tournament, the dejection must be obvious. Eileen gets maternal, or, more accurately, grand-maternal. "You have the skill and drive," she says, trying to cheer me up. "You're an excellent player. You'll be in the expert ranks soon."

A sucker for a compliment, I believe her for a minute — all evidence, again, to the contrary. With a few sentences, sweet Eileen has made the week worthwhile. Maybe she's right. Maybe I do have what it takes. What's not clear is whether that's a good thing or not.

During a walk along the pleasant, tree-lined Truckee River that cuts through downtown Reno, away from the casinos, an active but perpetually novice (and content to stay that way) player notes that I already have the hallmarks of an expert. I think I'm better than my rating. I declaim how the top players deserve a larger share of the prize money (a long-running debate in Scrabble). I rehash game positions. And I do it all a bit too energetically.

"You're slowly becoming not normal," she says.

I finish with an 18–21 record. Cappelletto wins the expert division with a 30–9 mark, reaffirming his dominance. He receives a standing ovation, high-fives, and hugs when he collects the $2,000 first prize. Marlon goes 19–20, out of the money — and out of money.

Afterward, he complains to a crowd about the terrible tiles he drew throughout the tournament. He needed a top-three finish, he says, to earn bus fare back to Baltimore. "The tiles," his fellow expert Joel Wapnick notes, "don't care about the bus." I lend Marlon another $100 to get home.

14

Lester

LESTER SCHONBRUN is a lanky man in his mid-sixties with a wispy, gray beard, a bald pate always covered by a floppy baseball cap, and a knowing smile. He has a deep yet gentle, inquisitive voice bearing the faintest traces of his New York upbringing. He wears circular wire-rimmed glasses with thick lenses, open flannel shirts over earth-tone T-shirts, and baggy pants, and he shuffles pigeon-toed in Teva sandals with socks. Lester looks like what he is: an old radical.

I hitch a ride from Reno to San Francisco with Lester, who has just finished third in the tournament, and his partner, Joan, an intermediate level player herself. Lester and I have been communicating by e-mail; he's been telling me, in installments, intimate facts about his life. An avowed if not card-carrying Communist, Lester has done everything from operate card-sorter machines for IBM mainframes to drive for a hippie cab company in Berkeley to manage the office of the party newspaper, *The People's World*. These days, he and Joan work as legal secretaries for a progressive Oakland law firm.

Lester is great company: well read, opinionated, honest, and generous. He has set aside afternoons away from work to take me around San Francisco, introduce me to a game-world legend friend of his, and attend a meeting of the purportedly wacky local Scrabble club. He also is my link to Scrabble's distant past and an old New York where you could wander into an establishment any time of day or night and get a game. The escapist allure of such a place — well, it's something I dream about.

Lester represents, for me, a saner side of the game. He's the most considerate and self-aware of my Scrabble comrades. He doesn't ramble on selfishly about racks. He compliments his opponents when they deserve it and is hostile only when they're jerks. (When one especially self-absorbed expert finally discovered Lester's political persuasion, he said, "I hear you're a Communist." Lester considered replying, "If you weren't always engrossed in recounting blowouts and marveling at your opponents' luck, you would have heard me chanting 'All Power to the Soviets' long ago.") Commie or not, Lester can admit that he likes playing for money. ("It screws things up in some ways," he says. "But I wouldn't go to a tournament if there weren't prize money. I hate to admit it, but a ten-thousand-dollar prize does seem to validate it in some way.") And, perhaps the biggest indication that Lester is socially housebroken, he can enjoy a good meal without calculating everyone's share to the penny.

Most significantly, Lester is candid about how this game has shaped his life. It's pretty simple. Lester has always felt as if he never fit in — in his family, in schools, in social situations, in the workplace. Scrabble offered structure in both the way the game is played and the universe in which it is played. Scrabble helped Lester escape from the world and make sense of it at the same time.

"The parts of life that are hard for me are when I don't know what I'm supposed to do," Lester tells me as we eat Subway sandwiches in the office of one of the law firm's partners. "In Scrabble, you're being tested. There's a very specific test at every step. The rules are crystal clear compared to other parts of life. It takes place in an area of my mind that I feel very comfortable with, that I feel very confident in.

"Plus, there aren't some of the complicating factors. Am I doing this for myself or am I doing it to make someone else rich? Does it have any positive or negative social connotations? In that sense, it's *true*."

Nearly forty years later, Lester can still conjure the scene: the decrepit walkup on 42nd Street next door to the New Amsterdam Theatre; the drab, second-floor room overlooking the sex shops and the porno theaters of Times Square; the faintly urinous odor in the stairwell; the old men hunched over their chessboards; his heart racing as he vaults the steps two at a time. The Chess & Checker Club of New York, a.k.a. the Flea House, was open twenty-four hours a day. There was a main room for chess, with checkers in the rear. An adjacent room housed bridge, and another more chess and Scrabble. It was the most vivid symbol of a time when games parlors offered a viable, if not altogether respectable, diversion for men of a certain age and temperament.

Lester began frequenting the place in the early 1960s. The proprietor, John Fursa, charged 20 cents an hour during the day to rent equipment to play. At midnight, the rates went to 30 cents, and then 60 cents at 2:00 in the morning. The Flea House was where the unheralded and, by conventional societal standards, unsuccessful, but often brilliant and charismatic, gathered to do what they did best and loved most: play games, usually for money. It was a smoky, stimulating refuge from the confusing world outside.

For Lester, the Flea House was a kind of home he had never had. He was born to working-class Hungarian immigrant parents in Astoria, Queens, just after the Depression. Lester's father, a carpenter who loved baseball's New York Giants and drank a bit too much, died when Lester was eleven. His mother ran a neighborhood candy store that failed, then worked as a seamstress in small, dingy factories to support her six children. For a time, seven family members crammed into a one-bedroom, one-bathroom apartment on the same ugly block as a Borden's milk plant.

At Bryant High School, "everyone was on track for the welding shop," but Lester was bright and his best friends were the richer Jews from Sunnyside who lived on tree-lined streets and taught him the guitar, chess, and leftist politics. When the mother of one of his friends said, "North Korea? North Korea didn't start the Korean War," Les realized they were Communists. Having watched his own mother sew toy parachutes in sweatshop conditions, he liked the working-class mantras of his middle-class friends. "I'd see people in my neighborhood working their balls off so the people I went to school with could have a good life," Lester says. "I thought, Why shouldn't *they* have a good life?"

Lester got into Queens College, but he wasn't motivated, and quit. A series of unrewarding jobs only hardened his political beliefs;

working for a zipper company, Lester saw forty immigrants toiling for almost no pay behind a closed door. Lester took a test and won an entry-level job at IBM. But he couldn't stand wearing a suit and tie, and didn't fit in socially, so he quit after a few months. The training qualified him for other data-processing jobs, and then he learned some programming, and he would take one job after another to support himself, never for more than six months at a time. "Just being confined to a job was too hard for me," Lester says. "Too many authority problems."

After a failed early marriage, Lester in his late twenties was living near Columbia University in a $40-a-month single-room-occupancy hotel when he met a group of chess-obsessed graduate students. They would play chess in the back of a bar called the Gold Rail from 10:00 at night until closing time at 4:00 in the morning. Then they'd head over to a player's apartment, drink tea, and play speed chess — five minutes per player — until midmorning. One night, when the apartment wasn't available, they went to the Flea House.

Lester was a competent chess player, good enough to beat all comers when he was a teenager, and to hold his own with his new friends. But against the Flea House hustlers, he was a patzer. Les could solve specific problems with the skill of a master, but he couldn't stomach the book learning required to excel in competition. "If I'm playing a whole game, I'm lost," he says. So when one of the Gold Rail guys showed up at the bar with a Scrabble set and a *Funk & Wagnalls* dictionary, Lester was game. "They play Scrabble at the Flea House," the friend announced, "and they use a clock!"

"I remember playing ORGANIZE down from the triple in one of the early games and feeling a pulse," Lester says. "An even sweeter memory was playing THROMBIN. I used to read *Scientific American* regularly, although I seldom got through any of the articles. But I picked up words, and that's where THROMBIN came from, just popping into my head. I remember with pleasure the worried and disgruntled look on my friend Henry's face as he challenged, and his disgust when it was good."

Lester would watch the Flea House Scrabble players and thrill at their ability to create so many seven- and eight-letter words. "I remember Henry saying, 'Just look for prefixes and suffixes.' Click. Bingo production soared."

With serial jobs and serial relationships, Lester found himself drifting more and more frequently to the Flea House, which changed for him from a gray, unhealthy lair populated by wacky old Eastern Europeans to an addiction "as strong as any drug." Soon, the men who seemed so aged and odd the first time he visited took on personalities. There was Freddie the Fish and Frank the Nazi Criminal and Israeli Jack and Sidney the Simian and a little man everyone called Mr. Rubenstein. Mr. Rubenstein would say, "Hello, how are you?" to no one at all, and he would tell the same joke over and over: "I went to a movie." "What did you see?" "It was dark in there, I couldn't see anything." The old Eastern Europeans "probably struck me as benign versions of my father, or my father at his most benign," Lester says. "Something about their whimsical, absurd humor struck a chord."

The Flea House was a meeting place for European Jews who had fled their homelands during and after World War II. They would trade intelligence about the Cold War and news of relatives back home, and argue about everything from politics and science to literature and sports. "If you wanted social intercourse, if you wanted information, it was the place to go," one of the regulars, a Hungarian Jew who fled after the Soviet invasion in 1956, tells me in Washington Square Park one day. "That was back when games players were intellectuals," adds Matthew Laufer, the poet and Scrabble player.

But mostly the Flea House was a place to play. One chess titan is said to have lost his delicatessen in a game. Huge, bald Nick the Wrestler, who had a role in Stanley Kubrick's early classic *The Killing*, said "check" whenever he made a move and "mate" whenever he had a check. Kubrick himself sometimes played at the Flea House, as did the conductor Leonard Bernstein, who would turn up after concerts. ("He wasn't much of a chess player," one of the old-timers tells me.) Bobby Fischer played there. The Flea House regulars were an eclectic mix of successful professionals, lost souls, brilliant misfits, certifiable crazies, inveterate gamblers, and convicted felons. "World-class people who knew how to play games and knew how to make it fun as well as interesting," Lester says. "It was an art."

Lester would order a bowl of Campbell's green pea soup, which John Fursa inexplicably served with a cube of sugar, and a salami sandwich (70 cents) and play chess, getting hustled for a quarter or half dollar a game. Players would spot him a knight, a rook, or play with less time on their clocks than Lester, but still he would lose. "That was the code, of course. If someone gives you odds, they're *supposed* to win," he tells me. "With the odds came the recognition that they had great contempt for you."

Scrabble was, in a way, Lester's revenge, particularly as his Communist leanings were derided at the Flea House. He proved to be the best of the Gold Rail gang at Scrabble, and eventually wanted to test his strength against the Flea House regulars, but didn't have the nerve. Their boards "looked like they were in a foreign language," and, besides, they played this game for money, too. Lester didn't want to be a "fish" — a sucker, an easy mark. But, for a while, he was.

Lester recalls the first time he was hustled at Scrabble. "This guy, Harry Feldheim, was watching a game between me and one of my Gold Rail pals. I held ALNOSTV. After I made my play, Feldheim asked me why I didn't play SOLVENT. I told him you can't spell it with an A. He looked it up and told me I was right. Next time I saw him he asked me if I wanted to play. He suggested stakes that were high for then, maybe a nickel a point. He tore me to pieces. That whole SOLVANT*/SOLVENT deal had been a ploy. He was a top player with no spelling problems." Another time, a player gave him both blanks and all four S's — on the condition that Lester put one on his rack each turn. "After three moves, I've got three S's on my goddamn rack and I can't make a play."

In the beginning, the hustlers spotted Lester as many as 175 points per game. But Lester was determined. He would do a puzzle in the *New York Post,* finding as many five-letter words as possible in a longer word, and he would use *Funk & Wagnalls,* the source at the Flea House, as a guide. Mostly, though, he improved through a combination of osmosis and schmoozing. He would play and watch others play. One marathon session against Al Tesoro, a physics Ph.D. candidate, lasted three days and three nights. Before long, even the hustlers wouldn't play Lester straight up. He was one of the best players at the Flea House, and by extension in the city, and perhaps anywhere.

Of course, the games themselves didn't really matter. The place was what mattered. The Flea House was where Lester could stretch across three chairs and sleep if he were temporarily homeless or just tired. It was where a scrawny, Camel-smoking regular known only as Tiger used to greet him by saying, "Lester! Lester! *Mein tuches ist dein shvester!*" — my ass is your sister. The greeting earned Lester the nickname Tuches. The Flea House was where an insecure Jewish kid from a poor immigrant family in Queens who was uncomfortable in workaday life and had unpopular political convictions could find a sense of accomplishment that eluded him in the outside world.

"One thing the Flea House had that the real world lacked was objectivity," Lester says. "If you were good, little else mattered. At first, this bothered me. [Some of the best] chess players were real sleazebags. They would hustle the innocent and sneer at them at the same time. I couldn't stand the fact that people I liked deferred to them, accorded them so much status. But gradually, I found myself sticking up for the hustlers when talking to my friends. It's like the scene in *The Godfather* when Al Pacino says to Diane Keaton, 'Now who's being naive?' Seeing the straight world, as I did and do, as being dominated by world-class superhustlers who are also hypocrites, I would say at least these hustlers didn't have any pretensions about it.

"When I started to have status, it meant a lot to me. I knew it wasn't because I kissed anyone's ass. But I remember the time that Al Tesoro made me aware of it. He said Scrabble had been a real gift to us. None of the big shots" — the world-class chess players who frequented the place — "would have ever said hello to us if it hadn't been bruited about that we were the best, or among the best."

Little else mattered outside of the neon-lit game room one flight up on 42nd Street. Jobs didn't matter. Friends didn't matter. Romance mattered even less. "Once I had two serious girlfriends at the same time, but all I could think about was getting to the Flea House. And they were dream boats, both of them," Lester says. "I just got bored with couples sitting around, gabbing. I itched to hop on the subway and get off and be right there." Still, Lester did manage to remarry. In 1966, he wed a potter named Ann, in a civil ceremony at City Hall. He went to the Flea House afterward.

Lester played in the first New York Scrabble tournament. It was staged in the late 1960s by the proprietor of a new games parlor on 72nd Street between Broadway and Amsterdam Avenue called the Chess House. A double round robin in which the ten entrants played

each other twice, whenever they could over two weeks, the tournament awarded a top prize of $35. (It wasn't, however, the first tourna-
ment anywhere; there was one in Sparks, Nevada, of all places, in
1961, and it's possible that others were held even earlier.)

Lester's Scrabble supremacy was being challenged by Mike
Senkiewicz, a recent Iona College English grad who spent four or five
hours a day at the Flea House hustling both chess and Scrabble.
(He later would become a U.S. backgammon champion.) Senkiewicz
had what Lester and other top players considered a limited working
vocabulary. But he did what no one else was doing. He combed
through *Funk & Wagnalls* and compiled lists. He trained himself to
count the tiles in his head as they were played, another unheard-of
practice. And he learned to play the endgame with precision. Senkiewicz had become a chess master not because he was a genius but
because he studied and calculated and concentrated. He applied the
same techniques to Scrabble.

Lester, on the other hand, was known as a clever strategist rather
than a prodigious memorizer. (Though when his friend Al Tesoro
spotted a *Funk & Wagnalls* on the bedroom floor of the apartment he
shared with Ann near Grant's Tomb, it got back to the Flea House
crowd. "Tuches sleeps with the dictionary," Tesoro reported.) But
both he and Mike played the conventional style of the times, which
would be discredited by the strategists and mathematicians who took
over the game in the 1980s: lay down a lot of tiles early in the game to
increase the chances of drawing the blanks and S's. "Rack balancing"
and "rack management" — keeping a healthy balance between vowels and consonants, and retaining bingo-prone letter combinations,
like EST, ING, or AENR — were just evolving. One or two bingos a
game was a lot.

"No one could touch us," Lester says. He and Mike staged hours-
long sessions at the Flea House. In the Chess House tournament,
Lester and Mike waited until the end to play each other — at the Flea
House, naturally, rather than the Chess House — by which time each
had 15–1 records. Lester drew all the good tiles, and won both games
and the $35.

But for Lester, something was changing. Times Square was deteri-
orating. Thugs seemed omnipresent at the Flea House. And many of
the regulars who gave the place its unusual charm — and him decent

Scrabble competition — were dying off or moving to other pursuits, like betting on horses. For good competition, it was just Lester and Mike. Lester began to feel uncomfortable spending so much time with Senkiewicz; they didn't have much in common outside of Scrabble, and he missed the camaraderie of the Flea House crowd and the Gold Rail gang. The combination of a job he hated — something to do with water meters, in Queens — and the long sessions with Senkiewicz began to feel unhealthy. Ann, frustrated trying to scrape by as a potter in New York, wanted to return to California, where she had gone to college. So in 1970, they moved to Berkeley, and Lester left the Scrabble scene behind just as it was about to take off.

Lester escorts me to the members-only Mechanics' Institute Library, founded in 1854, which occupies a stately building in downtown San Francisco. Lester visits to read, check out books, and play an occasional game of chess in the library's renowned Chess Room, which stages tournaments that attract international masters and even grand masters. He has arranged for me to meet a player who never enters a tournament but is regarded as one of the best, his friend Steve Brandwein.

Steve is a game-room legend. A short, shambling New Yorker, he appears meek and retiring but is cuttingly smart and dryly funny. Like so many games players, Steve is unconventionally brilliant. He dropped out of college but reads voraciously. He can more than hold his own in conversations on everything from military history to African cultures to Buddhism to the films of Werner Herzog. As Communism fell around Eastern Europe, Steve would bait Lester by calling him "Ceausescu," after the deposed and executed Romanian dictator. This day, he is razzing Lester about his opposition to U.S. involvement in the Balkan war that's raging; Lester has been joining peace marches lately. He also will kid him about his chess skills. "Don't feel bad, Lester," he said after watching him botch a game. "It takes just as much intelligence to make the worst possible move every time as the best."

Steve is considered one of the greatest chess players who ever refused, and still refuses, to play in tournaments; he knew and played against Bobby Fischer. He also is considered an expert at backgammon and bridge. He never studied Scrabble, but can play that at an expert level, too. But Steve lives hand to mouth, hustling some chess, working as a bookie, giving chess lessons, and doing odd jobs. He spends a lot of time reading. We talk about politics, and when Bosnia and the ethnic conflict involving Albania comes up, I mention that I visited the country a few years earlier. Steve asks if I've read anything by Ismail Kadare, the Albanian novelist, and when I can't remember the title of the one book I do own, he rattles off a list of them for me.

Lester introduces me to Steve, I realize, because he is the epitome of the games-playing mind and character: brilliant, unconventional, and unapologetic. He is Lester if Lester were more accomplished at chess and less well adjusted socially. Lester respects and admires Steve, not only for his fertile mind but for his decision — if it can be called that — to live on the fringes of society. And that's the fate of a lot of games players. Within their world, games afford respect and sustenance and a place to pass the time: outcasts welcome. But much of that world, like the Flea House, is gone, or, like the corporate-run Scrabble clubs and tournaments, bowdlerized. Lester wants to make sure I have an accurate understanding of the old games world, what it stood for, and why its outsider residents deserve respect. They were the ones, not Selchow & Righter or Hasbro, who created the rules and the tournament world that prospers now. "Hasbro didn't even invent it," he says. "They bought it. They got rich off of producing it. It is an example of one of the absurdities the capitalist system creates."

In some ways, Lester admits, he misses the old world. His life is comfortable now; he has been happy with the dynamic, eclectic, and cynical Joan for about twenty years (he and Ann split in the late seventies). Lester had dropped out of Scrabble after moving to San Francisco; it just wasn't interesting without stiff competition and the thrill of a money game. Also, Lester was trying to move on. Not until Ron Tiekert, who had succeeded him as the best player in New York, wrote a letter encouraging him to start playing again did Lester come to terms with the game. "I accepted the game world as an important thing in my life," he says.

Lester found new competitors, including Joe Edley and the future national champion Bob Felt. Joan took up the game, which made traveling to tournaments more enjoyable. Lester became one of the best again. His rating has been consistently near or above 2000 since I met him, and he is still considered a master strategist. Scrabble is a fixture in his life; he plays against the CD-ROM, attends an occasional one-day local tournament, and hits the biggies, Reno, the Nationals, the Worlds. Lester has qualified for the U.S. team that will play in Melbourne, Australia, in a few months.

These days, Lester calls himself an "armchair Communist." He joined the party in 1980 and attended a few meetings, but it's a belief system more than a cause now. At a Scrabble tournament, he once named his rotisserie team the "Stalinists." In Reno, he rooted for China against the United States in the Women's World Cup soccer final. "It's how I read the paper. It's how I see the news. I think working people should build the world. The working classes are getting screwed.

"I feel like I've discovered the secret of life," he says. "Things seem prescient to me and so clear and I realize after I've said two things there's a dead silence on the other side. But I like the fact that people know it and accept me. In a way, it's my contribution. To let people know that not all Communists are alike, not the stereotype."

Is it enough? Does he feel guilty that his principal pastime is playing Scrabble?

"Sometimes the obsession bothers me. I should be doing something else, like smashing imperialism." Lester laughs. "Or writing. Or anything."

I'm standing on the corner of Bush and Leavenworth in San Francisco waiting for the SuperShuttle van to the airport. I hear a voice from the sidewalk behind me.

"Scrabble, eh?"

Someone has spotted my NATIONAL SCRABBLE CHAMPIONSHIP CHICAGO 1998 canvas bag, which is adorned with the three-point tile C (for Chicago) in red. My deluxe board sticks out of the bag's top.

A homeless man, who appears to be in his late forties, stands next to a metal grocery cart with a single cardboard box inside. He is wearing a dirty purple sweatshirt and filthy chinos. His long, thinning brown-and-gray hair is tamped and scraggly, and a beard hangs halfway down his chest. His oversized brown plastic glasses are

fogged over with dirt. He is sucking the last life from a filterless cigarette butt.

"Yup," I say, returning my gaze down Bush for the van, which is
late, and unsure whether to pursue a conversation or not. What the
hell. "Do you play?"

"I used to play. I played in the Nationals in 1980."

I try not to act surprised, but then I really don't have to try, because I'm not. I don't doubt for a second that he's telling the truth.
But he must sense some disbelief — he knows that I see what I see —
because in the next breath he says that he beat Joe Edley in a qualifying tournament en route to the finals that year, which were held in
Santa Monica. It was the tournament that Edley wound up winning
after spending a year memorizing the *OSPD* on the overnight shift as
a security guard. The one he felt fated to win.

I suppress a smile — this is, after all, absurd. I've just spent almost
three weeks doing nothing but Scrabble. I've played seventy games,
met a games legend and several Scrabble giants. I've even attended
America's Most Dysfunctional Scrabble Club, which meets in a Carl's
Jr. fast-food restaurant in downtown San Francisco and features a
cast of characters out of *One Flew Over the Cuckoo's Nest*. I'm feeling the onset of burnout, questioning the utility — or is it futility? —
of trying to master this game. Now, as I'm about to be freed from
the Scrabble sensory-deprivation tank in which I've been locked, a
homeless guy stops me on the street to say he played against Edley.

"I was also an alternate to the Nationals in 1983 but had mental
problems and didn't go," he says.

He tells me his name is Don. Don says he hasn't played Scrabble
since 1986, but he recalls facing other West Coast Scrabble greats,
and names a few of them, including Lester, who he says whomped
him by 300 points in one game. As he talks, Don's eyes dart behind
his thick glasses and he nervously shifts strands of hair away from his
face. He explains that he was adept enough at the words, "but I never
fully understood the strategy. That's why I wasn't better."

I ask Don what happened to him. He says he graduated from
M.I.T. and came west to work as an aerospace engineer. But he was
laid off amid Defense Department cutbacks in the early 1970s, and
hasn't worked since. In the 1980s, he underwent electroshock treat-

ments that resulted in limiting his short-term memory. "Scrabble," Don tells me, "was good therapy."

I think of Matt Graham and some other players I've met in New York. Of the expert who studied at M.I.T. and worked at Harvard and speaks fifteen languages but now wheels a shopping cart crammed with books and toys around Manhattan. Of the club regular and Harvard graduate who was a top player in the 1970s, has had several nervous breakdowns, and now plays in a bizarre, low-scoring, defensive style and hums spirituals during games. I even think of Edley in his residence hotel days, not far from where Don and I are standing, working as a night watchman so he could memorize the *OSPD*. And I wonder again, which came first, the personalities or the game? Why are some people who like solving these board-game riddles also prone to weirdness, or worse?

Scrabble is becoming something I adore and fear at the same time. So while I want to know more about Don, I also don't. A blue and yellow van pulls up to the curb and a white-shirted young guy leaps out and grabs my bags. "That's my bus to the airport," I say to Don. Over my shoulder, I shout good luck. But I don't turn back to say goodbye, or to shake his hand. Later, I check the record. Don finished twenty-first of the thirty-two players in the 1980 Nationals, with an 8–9 record.

15

The Club

"MAAAATCH-UUUUUPS!"

In floppy gray slacks hoisted by red suspenders, G.I. Joel is standing on a chair in the middle of the narrow room where Scrabble Club No. 56 meets. Climbing the chair is about as much exercise as Joel gets in a week — his personal StairMaster — and he tackles the ascent before each of the four games on Thursday nights. From his perch, Joel shouts out who is playing whom and other important information. One week he announced that someone had left behind a bag containing Metamucil and a box of rectal suppositories.

Twenty to thirty people usually show up at the Honors Bridge Club on the sixth floor of a midtown office building across the street from the club's old home, the Allerton Hotel. Joel has been directing the club since Ron and Susi Tiekert moved to Atlanta the previous year, a few months after he won his world championship. The job has given Joel a sense of purpose. He likes being in charge, collecting the $11 entry fee, and determining the round-by-round pairings, which are based on ratings and then results. He likes doling out the prize money, adjudicating word challenges, and cleaning up the boards and racks when the night is done. He likes writing the weekly summaries he dubs "Honoraria" and distributes via e-mail, in which he recaps results, offers lessons, and dishes dirt. He likes trying to make first-timers comfortable — recruiting new players is Scrabble's toughest task, for the obvious reasons (the people) and some not-so-obvious ones (the intimidating atmosphere of competitive play). And Joel *loves* making announcements. Play doesn't finish until after 11:00, and Joel often doesn't get home to the Bronx until 1:00 A.M.

The transformation of Scrabble from Flea House hustle to ritualized hobby took place in the early 1970s, when new games parlors opened in New York and a younger crowd of players was drawn to the game. It's not clear why. Maybe it had to do with the coming of age of the first wave of baby boomers, college educated, disaffected, uninterested in the social crises of the day. Maybe it was because competitive Scrabble was an outsider's game, appealing in a way that chess no longer was amid the locust swarms that followed the Fischer-Spassky match in 1972.

For whatever reason, a regular Scrabble night sprang up at the Bar Point House of Backgammon in the East Village. There were games at the Olive Tree, a Greenwich Village coffeehouse. And you could play daily at the Chess House on West 72nd and Chess City at 100th and Broadway, which later moved to 75th and Broadway and was renamed the Game Room.

Where the Flea House had been the games-playing equivalent of a Wild West saloon — all bluster and braggadocio — the game rooms were goofier and more egalitarian, and the game itself approached more studiously. The new Scrabble experts weren't cranky old-timers who lacked jobs and happiness and decorum. To be sure, some of the old ne'er-do-wells helped fill the Chess House and Chess City, and hustling was still the code. But there were others for whom the games were a healthy supplement to life.

Jim Neuberger, a lawyer in the state attorney general's office, headed up to the Game Room most nights after work. A dishy former actress named Ann Sanfedele, who had had three husbands by the time she'd reached her early thirties, found herself unexpectedly drawn to the quirky games parlors. "For the most part, people who came to the clubs did not expect to develop friendships," Ann tells me. But they did. For the best players, the clubs conferred respect. "When I walked into the Game Room, I felt like John Travolta walking into a dance club," Neuberger says. Which is funny, because the Game Room in the late 1990s was the trendy China Club, a hangout for pro athletes and models; if only they knew.

Ron Tiekert also went to the games parlors every night. He lived in a single-room occupancy hotel on West 73rd called the Commander and worked as an editor for an educational publisher (a job he still holds). He requisitioned a copy of *Funk & Wagnalls* and combed through it, making lists of short words. Ron quickly became the best player in New York. He was regarded as gentlemanly, never hustling easy marks, making no more than $40 playing as many as fifty games a week.

The de facto Scrabble director at Chess City and later the Game Room was Mike Martin, a short, squat Greek American with a slushy, Donald Duck voice who gave everyone a nickname. Ron Tiekert was the Head Brillo. (Ron says the name referred to his centurion's helmet of curly hair; everyone else says it referred to the fact that he was a brilliant player.) Ann Sanfedele was Fancy Deli. Jim Neuberger was the Head Lobster.

If you got stuck with the Q, you had to pay Martin 50 cents; if you made a bad challenge, you had to put a quarter in the "goo-goo," Martin's term for the kitty he amassed for monthly prizes in categories he announced at random. He would hand out candy to unsuspecting players who had made a bingo using a particular letter. "It was part of the craziness," Neuberger says. "It was fun. It was great fun."

So when Joel climbs on his chair, or distributes 50-cent prizes for getting away with a particularly stinky phony or a British-only word or e-mails his regular commentaries on our play — lauding low-probability finds and triple-triples and discussing anagrams and interesting words — he's continuing a tradition. And I think Joel likes that, too.

The more my game has improved, the more regularly I've shown up at Club 56. It hasn't hurt that my prior Thursday-night commitment — group therapy — ended recently. Scrabble is my new group therapy. I have grown to like the collection of characters who frequent the club; they're not the yuppies I work with at *The Wall Street Journal* or any of my other more conventional friends.

The club members run from the clinically crazy to the socially inept, but the bulk are friendly, smart, and functional New Yorkers. There's Pam Grazette, a dental hygienist who always wears a floppy

The Club ❑ 217

white hat, and Jean Lithgow, a teacher and ex-wife of the actor, and Steve Pfeiffer, the New York Scrabble veteran, a fire-safety consultant who speaks with a slow, guttural Brooklyn voice that sounds like an idling car.

Paul Avrin is a bushy-haired, retired high school math teacher with aviator glasses who looks like a character from an Edward Koren cartoon in *The New Yorker*. He's trying to play in more than four hundred tournament games this year. Sal Piro is president of the *Rocky Horror Picture Show* fan club. He bickers endlessly with the schlumpy, barrel-gutted Mark Berg, who sells ads for those coupon books that clutter mailboxes. Mark's wife, Verna Richards Berg, is a nurse from Jamaica with a singsongy Caribbean lilt. They met playing Scrabble.

There's a bookie named Josh Silber and a piano teacher named Laney Berel. Judy Kass has written biographies; Jack Eichenbaum is a geographer who also guides tours of Queens neighborhoods; Mark DiBattista, the NYU post-doc, studies geophysical fluid dynamics; and Woody Chen is a mailroom clerk in a bank who screams his high scores excitedly. There's George Warnock, a buff guy with tattoos who serves as a guinea pig for drug company tests. There's Diane Firstman, whom I'd played in the park so long ago, a budget director for a city government agency who turns out to be smart, caring, and witty, not at all the gloating clock-whacker I'd first imagined.

Then there's Steve Williams, the Harvard grad with psychiatric problems. Steve started playing Scrabble in 1973 when he was hospitalized during his junior year at Harvard. He nearly flunked out because of his Scrabble preoccupation but did complete his undergraduate degree in American history. Steve later was diagnosed with manic depression and obsessive-compulsive disorder, and has been on a diet of antipsychotics and antidepressants. For years, he wrote columns for a now-defunct African-American newspaper, *The City Sun*, but his last full-time job, in a Medicaid office, ended in 1981. He lives with his father in the house in Queens where he was raised.

Steve was a daily player at the game rooms, staying all night and sleeping all day. He won the New York City championship in 1977, and was rated as high as 2030. But over time he began playing a claustrophobic brand of Scrabble. Steve shuts down the board with words that cannot be pluralized or extended in any way; to do so, though, he makes plays worth only a handful of points and often winds up outscored. His rating has fallen steadily into the 1400s.

Steve is a tall, bearded man with a downcast head and hunched-over, shuffling gait; his sense of humor is dulled or nonexistent. He remembers scores of games from ten and twenty years ago, remembers his records and point spreads at long-gone tournaments. He insists on counting the hundred tiles after every game. Steve takes an antianxiety pill thirty minutes before playing. Once, when he forgot to do so, he scored a total of 97 points in a game against G.I. Joel; Steve went over on his clock by nineteen minutes. "Some days when I'm practicing at home, my brain goes to pieces and I have to calm myself down after playing," he tells me. The game, though, is Steve's center. "Without Scrabble, I'd be doing serious time in the hospital," he says.

If I wanted to be We Are the World about it, I'd say the Club 56 denizens are a cross-section of society. Black, white, Asian. Single, married, divorced. Straight and gay and unclear. Sane, less sane, not sane. Most are over forty. The gender split is about even. Some study and play Scrabble twenty or thirty hours a week. Some never study at all. Some have graduate degrees, some have high school diplomas. A couple are still in high school.

I circulate a questionnaire among the regulars to find out who they are and why they play. "I feel guilty about all the time I devote to Scrabble," a single mom, a children's textbook writer named Christine Economos, reveals after recounting her best plays, UNEVENEST and EIDERDOWN.

"It has been one of the most wonderful things to have happened to me," writes a sixty-two-year-old retired cop named Nancy Okolsky. "My parents brought me up to believe that games are for children. It feels so good to have grownups play with me. I feel like a teenager because I am still rebelling against my parents." John Scalzo, a forty-six-year-old city bus dispatcher, calls the game "a mission." A writer named Jim Piazza says it offers "the illusion of accomplishment" and the "camaraderie of nerds." Sharp and sweet sixty-nine-year-old Lois Kahan tells me she first played in 1948, when her father bought what must have been one of the original Production & Marketing Company sets.

Some of the players say Scrabble has given them a social life (the club in Queens meets on Saturday nights). "Without being corny, it is like having another set of family," says Jeremy Frank, a thirty-one-year-old court reporter. Some cherish the competition, others the words. "I love having unusual words at my disposal," Susi Tiekert writes from Atlanta, saying she misses the club "like C-R-A-Z-Y! . . . I like the different racks opening each game. I take pride in the fact that there is SOMETHING I can do better than the general public. And last but not least I have Scrabble to thank for a terrific husband."

Joel's brother, Larry, jokes, "I play strictly to meet chicks. The game itself sucks ass." And G.I. Joel responds, too, even though I know enough about Joel to diagram his large intestine. On the questionnaire, I ask what role Scrabble plays in people's lives, and Joel replies: "It made me a media sensation . . . for a few seconds. It consumes my life. It is my life. What's a life?"

Gambling is encouraged at the club. So when Joel shouts "Match-ups!" on this particular night, and follows with "Mark Berg versus Stefan Fatsis!" he adds, "The windows are open!"

Joel, a former OTB regular, means the betting windows, and everyone loves to bet against Berg. His rating fluctuates between 1650 and 1800. Berg is a games dilettante, good at many (he whomps me at table tennis one night), master of none — but he is renowned for his shaky word knowledge. He spells conventional words wrong. He is an inveterate player of phonies. He challenges words that he shouldn't. Joel calls his weekly 50-cent awards for the "best" phonies that go unchallenged "Berg Prizes." When you bet against Berg and win, you collect "Berg Bucks."

Berg, a tireless trash talker with a New York accent, decides that he is a 50-point favorite against me and welcomes all action. The betting — on me — is heavy. Diane wagers $3. Jack lays $2. George drops $5. Sal adds $3 to the pool. Ann Sanfedele lays down $1, in quarters. I bet a buck on myself. Berg can win $15 if he beats me by more than 50 points, or lose $15 if he doesn't "cover the spot."

"Wow," Berg says. "A lot of action on Stefan."

"Yeah," George says. "He's smart."

"He may be smart," Berg says. "But is he a good player?"

"He's a good player," George says. "I've seen him in the park."

At this point, I'm not yet a fixture at the club — still considered just a reporter and not a real player. My rating is low. I haven't earned the respect of the experts, or even the expert wanna-bes.

I go first. QUODS. Fifty points.

"Stefan's winning a hundred to nothing!" Sal announces gleefully.

On my fourth turn I find DERVISH for 93 points, giving me a lead of 173–128, not including the spread.

"You sure you don't want a draw?" Berg jokes. "Against a player of my caliber, take the half point." (In tournament games, ties are worth a half point to each player.)

"I'm up three dollars in Berg Bucks!" Sal gloats as the game nears its finish.

"Mazel tov," Berg says. Then he starts whining about his tiles. "This sucks. Early upset. Big upset in this round."

Without the spread, I win 412–361. Sal calls me the man of the hour. Players applaud.

"Where's my two bucks?" Jack demands.

"Show me the money!" Ann says.

"You the man!" Sal shouts. "You the man all night!"

I win three out of four games, and $15 as the evening's best intermediate player. Plus one Berg Buck.

I've started dreaming about Scrabble.

I'm playing in the Nationals. There is one long table of players, like a prison mess hall. It turns out that two high-school friends, Frank and Dave, and a couple of college acquaintances also are in the tournament. They've entered because I've entered, and I'm excited. But none of them has played Scrabble before, so I rattle off some basics. "Try to identify prefixes and suffixes," I say hurriedly. "Keep a balance between vowels and consonants. Don't play an S for less than thirty points unless you have more than one. Don't play a blank unless you can bingo or score an equivalent amount."

Then I realize that I'm late for my first game. I run to the table to find that my opponent — one of the middle-aged fat ladies who populate the intermediate divisions — has started my clock. I draw tiles, but they are the tiny wooden ones used in travel Scrabble. I can't get a good grip and keep dropping them. (In my recurring baseball anxiety dream, I can't open my glove to catch the ball.) Then I realize that I've drawn twelve tiles, eight on my rack and four on the table in front of me. But when I look on my rack again, there's a fish. It's a perch, wet and scaly, but clearly identifiable because PERCH is spelled out on its side. I can't find the tiles, though I think they're still on the rack. I call over the tournament director to decide what to do. End of dream.

I dream that I lose eighteen straight tournament games.

I dream that I'm playing another middle-aged fat lady. She lays down QUIZ at position H8, and simultaneously forms two other words, one using the Q and the other the Z: QUATING* and ZEATINER*. She announces her score: 300 points. She hits her clock. I should challenge because I am sure that ZEATINER is a phony. Then my mother appears and starts coffeehousing. I tell her to go away, but now I'm totally flustered. I forget to challenge.

I do have one happy Scrabble dream. After playing in the park one afternoon, I dream that I'm totally accepted there as a great player. Aldo Cardia, the subdued, chain-smoking restaurant owner, is smiling and laughing and joking with me as I explain the hierarchy of the park to a newcomer. This park is more sylvan than grimy Washington Square. I explain that when I first arrived, none of the top players would let me play. Aldo tells an inside story about my early days in the park. We share another laugh.

The down-at-the-heels chess players, with their speed games and low-stakes hustles and barker mentality, had controlled the southwest corner of Washington Square Park for decades. Other games were unwelcome. A Parks Department sign even said so: THIS AREA RESERVED FOR CHESS AND CHECKERS.

In the early eighties, the park was a tough place. There was a killing near the corner one summer night. The bathroom was considered off-limits because it was used as a gay pickup scene. Stabbings, fights, and thrown bottles weren't unusual. Drug deals proliferated. An addict nicknamed Flash would rip off unsuspecting players. Chess clocks were a popular target. One player whose clock was stolen saw it being used by another player a few days later; he had to buy it back.

"All you had to do was breathe deep to smoke crack," a parkie named Arnie Weisburg tells me. "So many people just laying around wasted all over the place."

When Arnie brought his little travel Scrabble set to the southwest corner in 1985, he couldn't get a game. No one played Scrabble. His first regular partner was Jerome, a homeless man who said he had worked as a microbiologist in a hospital lab specializing in scatology before he was convicted of murder in Pennsylvania and released on a technicality. But Jerome vanished after an old Flea House regular who had joined Arnie's Scrabble game cleaned him out one day.

Then others wanted to play, and Arnie, a retired chemicals sales-man, started coming down daily. The park was getting cleaner. The cop in charge of the Washington Square Park detail, a lieutenant named McKenna, was clearing out the crackheads and junkies; one time the police used water hoses to roust the druggies from park benches. But the sign still limited games to chess and checkers, even though the city parks commissioner had ruled otherwise; he sent a letter to a group of backgammon players who had complained when the chess players tried to have them evicted, noting that the sign should have read BOARD GAMES ONLY. NO GAMBLING. And when McKenna was away, an overzealous substitute ordered a cop to ticket Arnie for playing an "unauthorized game" at a table reserved for chess and checkers.

Arnie pleaded not guilty. A parkie made him a T-shirt that spelled out FREE WEISBURG in Scrabble tiles. "In the interest of justice," Arnie told the judge presiding over his hearing, "I ask for a dismissal." He produced the letter from the parks commissioner to the backgammon players about the erroneous sign. The judge laughed.

"What was the game you were playing?"

"Scrabble."

"Case dismissed."

The game gradually drew a bigger following. Players from the Manhattan club began showing up, like Matthew Laufer, the poet, and Jimmy Young, an ex–Flea House regular, and Alan Williams, the contractor who switched over from chess. There was a cab driver who would park nearby and play because he hated driving a cab. There was a Latino guy who wore a plumbing company shirt. After a few years the Scrabble players moved away from the chess players and colonized the park's northwest corner, beneath the towering elm known as the "Hanging Tree," where from 1790 to 1819 convicts from Newgate Prison were hanged and then buried in an adjacent potter's field.

The more I visit the park, the more I recognize how Lester Schonbrun must have felt climbing the dank Flea House stairs, his heart racing in anticipation. When I bike to Washington Square, my pace gradually quickens as I pedal up Sixth Avenue and turn right on West 4th Street, then left against the traffic on Washington Square West. When I take the D train instead, exiting at the front of the train and making a left on Waverly Place, I jog the last block. If no one is there, I'm virtually inconsolable. If I have to wait to play, I'm antsy. If I can sit right down, I'm blissful, though I never show it. I come to the park to get lost in the game, as addicted as the druggies who stagger around wailing about the need to legalize marijuana.

The park is Scrabble in its purest form, stripped of pretense and affect, like all games played on the street. The tiles are usually dirty. The bags often reek of too many hands reaching in too many times. The regulars use analog chess clocks, not the $100-plus digital variety found in formal play. They don't have special score sheets listing all of the tiles so they can keep track during play; notepads or scrap paper will do. Some write down the twenty-six letters and track the tiles played with slash marks. Most don't bother.

Disdain runs high, and no one, as I've learned, is loath to criticize a boneheaded play by another regular. The park isn't for the thin-skinned or insecure. One day, before the parkies know me well, I'm playing Christine Economos, who is a sort of park den mother; she lives around the corner and often lends the parkies a board and tiles if they're short. Matthew Laufer is kibitzing my game, and tells me I've just missed a bingo. Richie Lund, a Vietnam vet, is seated next to me at the green picnic table.

"Shut the fuck up!" Richie bellows at Laufer. He rises to face him. "Get the fuck out of here!"

It's like a David Mamet play. Testosterone rules. The parkies can be divided into two classes. The first is the money players like Richie and Alan and Matthew and Aldo and other experts who wander by. The stakes are usually small — two or three bucks a game, plus two or three cents per point — but they can escalate to ten or twenty a game.

The second class is everyone else. The best of the rest, and my favorite, is Joe Simpson, a tall, bearded, septuagenarian World War II veteran who always wears fatigues and a green beret that covers a bald, light chocolate pate. Joe, who spent three decades in air force administration, started playing Scrabble two days after his sixty-fifth birthday. That was six years ago. Joe is gruff, forever snapping at some poor parkie — usually Arnie or John, a skinny, retiring Woody Allen–ish figure. John always brings equipment but rarely plays, like an elementary school kid who knows he can't compete but hangs around the jocks anyway. But it's an act; Joe is a softie who enjoys playing the tough.

When I stroll into the park on a late-spring afternoon, Joe greets me like an old friend. "Where you been?" he asks.

"It's spring now," I say. "I'm back."

"You mean you're not a winter player?"

Meantime, his opponent is complaining. "I'm in trouble here," he says.

"Concentrate," Joe barks. "You're running your mouth a mile a minute."

I play three games against one of the low-skilled regulars, Herb, and win all three easily. Drawing all six blanks helps, but I also find words like SERIATED, BURGLED, and POTshARD. I'm back the next day, and Richie invites me to play doubles with him against Alan and Aldo. It's a sign of acceptance into the park culture, akin to my drubbing Berg at the club and earning pats on the back. This will be my third season in the park, but my first as a real player, one who studies and has ambition. The stakes are low — $1 a man and 2 cents per point. Richie does most of the work, and I ask and learn.

He's patient; when a move is indicated, he waits for me to make a suggestion before explaining the options and completing the play. He finds GARAGING to a G. He sees the only bingo in DIINORS (SORDINI). He explains why he prefers a leave of DERSS over a leave of ESSV. When I suggest VIM through an I, simultaneously forming MAX, Richie says, "Nothing wrong with that at all. Nothing." Richie and I lose six of eight games, and $13 apiece.

"Sometimes you see a lot," Aldo says, profoundly. "Sometimes you see squat."

"It's very embarrassing," Richie says.

The next day, we play more doubles, and Richie and I recoup $9 each; I'm thrilled when I find a couple of plays — FATWA, AIRLINER through an L — that Richie overlooks.

Richie is wearing his uniform: a black cutoff T-shirt, black jeans, and black sneakers. Three gold chains, one bearing an eagle, dangle from his neck. Richie is clean-shaven, with short hair that recedes from a forehead that hangs over his eyes. He's missing a few teeth. By day, he's a chemist for Con Edison, the power company.

Between games, Richie shows off some of his new tattoos. Bruce Lee, which he'd had done before the Nationals last year after his quintuple bypass surgery, was just the first. "That's the one that got me hooked," he says. On his right forearm is a painting by the Japanese artist Hajime Suriyama called *Cat and Telephone* — a cat with a telephone on its stomach lying on a bottle of Jack Daniel's. On one side of his left forearm is *Gladiatrix*, another Suriyama painting, of a futuristic female warrior. On the flip side is an adaptation of the exploding-head poster from the movie *Brazil*; in place of Jonathan Pryce's head is Richie's, with Scrabble tiles flying out of his crown. On his upper left arm is a painting by Donald Roller Wilson, *Cookie*, which depicts a baby orangutan; Richie says he is attracted to "the whimsical quality of it." He turns around and lifts his shirt. Stretching across his back, unfinished, is the *pièce de résistance:* Rousseau's *The Dream*, "which," Richie notes, "is in permanent residence at the Museum of Modern Art on the second floor. It's my favorite painting."

Richie has spent about $7,000 and more than sixty hours being tattooed, and he's not done. "I want to get some high art," he says. "Maybe a Magritte on my leg. I'm doing a Mount Rushmore with my four favorite composers. It's going to be Handel, Mozart, Beethoven, and Bach." Richie slaps his knee and laughs. It's a deep, sinister, *Goodfellas* guffaw that insists you join in or risk bodily harm. He invites me to come watch him get tattooed. Suddenly he says, "It smells strongly of urine over here, doesn't it?"

I meet Richie on a Friday night at the East Village tattoo parlor of Anil Gupta. Since that day in the park, Richie has had the composers etched into his lower right arm: Mozart in lavender, Bach in orange, Beethoven in green, and Handel in blue. Richie removes his shoes and his right sock and sits in a dental chair. He swallows a couple of Tylenols with codeine and lifts his right pants leg, revealing the work in progress: the funeral mask of King Tutankhamen.

Anil dons surgical gloves, trains a lamp on Richie's leg, and rubs King Tut with lotion. He flicks on the tattoo gun, which emits a high-pitched buzz. It punctures the skin at a rate of about fifty pricks per second using anywhere from three to fifteen needles. Anil is using seven needles to paint the red ink along the edge of Tut's gold mask. Richie bites on a plastic bottle cap to dull the pain.

Richie Lund is the Fonzie of Scrabble: He's so cool that you wonder why he's hanging with the nerds, but his mere presence legitimizes everyone around him. It's not just the black clothing or the gold chains. Not the welcoming charm or lack of condescension. Not the brilliant plays or sudden eruptions. (In Waltham, once, another player gave him the finger and Richie screamed, "Give *me* the finger? I'll break that finger off and shove it right down your fucking throat!") Not the dark, penetrating eyes or the unblinking gaze over the board. None of that. What makes Richie Lund special is knowing that the pain of a tattoo is literally just a pinprick compared to what he has gone through to get this far.

As Anil switches to yellow ink for Tut's mask, Richie tells me his life story. He was born in 1948 in Brooklyn, which accounts for his accent. The family moved upstate and then, when Richie was sixteen, to Parker, Arizona, where his father worked for the Bureau of Indian Affairs. A year later, at seventeen, Richie graduated from high school and joined the marine corps. And a year after that, in 1966, he was sent to Vietnam. "I wanted to go out there and get some adventure in my life," Richie says. "I was sent right into the shit, man." He flew directly to Da Nang. "Two days later I was up the DMZ dodging mortar shells. Nothing in between."

Richie was a radio operator with the Fourth Marine Regiment of the Third Marine Division, assigned to night watch patrols, carrying a PRC-25 portable radio weighing twenty pounds, plus batteries, on his back. Richie did a thirteen-month tour. Dong Ha. Cuaviet. Cam Lo. Con Thien. Right on the DMZ, the focus of heavy action. Camp Carroll. Phu Bai. Camp Evans. Richie saw it all. A buddy blown up by a land mine. Bodies dangling from trees. A camp full of dead Green Berets.

Richie came home a broken man. "Bellicose, warlike, always getting into fights, starting to do drugs, downers, drinking," he says. "My mom didn't recognize me. I had this vacuous look in my eyes. I was gaunt. I looked like death warmed over."

Then he volunteered to go back for thirteen months more. This time he was assigned to the Fifth Marine Expeditionary Brigade of the Third Marine Division. On the second day of his second tour, in the spring of 1967, Richie wound up at Khe Sanh, in the middle of the Tet Offensive. "It just got worse my second time over," he says. "I knew if I got through Khe Sanh, I could get through anything. That was as bad as it got over there."

Richie bites on the cap and grimaces.

Like many veterans, Richie couldn't readjust. "I was as much of a mess on the inside as I was outside. I wasn't about to accept help from anybody. My attitude was fuck everybody. I wasn't even angry — just out of it. I didn't want to fucking think about anything. I was one of the lost boys."

Richie shunned his family and old friends. He wandered. Arizona. Colorado. California. Oregon. Washington. He visited other vets. He rode a Harley-Davidson Sportster until he wrecked it in California. He took a job repossessing cars in Phoenix. Still drinking, still getting wasted, still spiraling downward. He was accused of punching a cop (Richie denied it) and spent a couple of weeks in jail in Tucson. It was a hidden blessing. The father of a fellow marine was an influential lawyer in Tucson who helped place Richie in a yearlong detox and rehab program.

Richie moved back to Brooklyn, sober, to live with his grandmother. He decided to go to college under the G.I. Bill. He finished second in his class at a community college and then earned a bachelor's degree in chemistry from Brooklyn College. Under a Vietnam veterans outreach program, Con Ed hired him in 1979 as a chemist. For years, Richie has conducted environmental analyses to check for asbestos, PCBs, and the like. He's just been transferred to an administrative job in the department.

It's hard for him to talk about Vietnam and its aftermath. He leavens the conversation by asking rhetorically, "Can you believe that?"

and guffawing. He shifts the subject to tattoos and the quality of Anil's work, showing me around the studio and pointing out impressive designs.

Richie adjusted to working; he liked it. At Brooklyn College, he saw a flyer for a Scrabble club in the borough. He had played with an aunt and uncle in Brighton Beach since returning to New York, and when he was growing up his parents had played chess, Scrabble, and other word games. He went to the club and met Steve Pfeiffer, another Vietnam vet. Pfeiffer shared word lists and they talked Scrabble, but rarely Vietnam. Richie decided he wanted to master the game. Why not? Scrabble was the ultimate distraction from everything that had come before. How could you think about the horrors of war when you had to memorize one hundred thousand words? Scrabble helped Richie forget. He devoted a year just to learning the words. (No lesser an authority than Brian Cappelletto once credited Richie with having the greatest Scrabble word knowledge of all time.)

"I just wanted to be a top player. I wanted to be top at something. I pretty much knew I wasn't going to be top in my profession. Given what I had previously been through, it was an accomplishment just to get a job."

Richie played in a few tournaments in New York, earning an 1800 rating, but outside of a handful of local players, no one knew who he was when he traveled to Boston for the 1985 Nationals. Ron Tiekert won, Joe Edley finished second, and Richie came in third. On the pivotal move in the final game, against one of the top players at the time, a Canadian lawyer named Stephen Fisher, Richie cemented his place in Scrabble lore by plunking down TWINBORN. Fisher challenged. It came back good.

"Me! A virtual unknown!" Richie says. "And he didn't know the word!"

Other experts began calling him Mr. Twinborn. Richie had found a new, less harrowing world to replace the inhumane one he had encountered in his youth. It wasn't an exaggeration to say that Scrabble saved Richie Lund.

He started playing regularly in tournaments. He won a bunch of East Coast events. He finished in the top five in three Nationals. He finished fifteenth in the Worlds in New York in 1993. But he always remained enigmatic. He'd drop out of the scene, disappear from the park for months at a time, and then suddenly reappear, ready to play. When he did, other players wondered, "Is Richie okay?" He was Scrabble's cipher, which, of course, only burnished his legend.

For a while, he burned out; studying was no longer fun. But, like a few other retired stars, Richie reemerged when the lucrative Superstars Showdown in Vegas in 1995 was announced. He returned to the park and entered a weekend tournament on Long Island attended by all of the top players in the east. He hadn't played in a tournament in a year. "I annihilated the field!" he says, belting one of his happily threatening laughs. "Won ten in a row in the middle of the tournament. Only lost three."

He entered the Superstars with the second-highest rating in North America, 2080, behind only the defending Nationals champion, David Gibson, who also came out of retirement to play. Richie didn't do well, finishing thirty-fourth. But he invited his family. Richie wouldn't board an airplane, so he hadn't seen his parents for eight years, his sisters for thirteen and twenty-four. Scrabble had made him whole again in ways that Richie can't describe and doesn't necessarily even want to think about.

Anil puts the finishing touches on King Tut's funeral mask. He squirts green soap on Richie's leg to clean off the stray ink. He's done.

"Oh, man," Richie says. "I'm so glad."

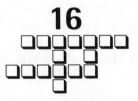

16

The World

S TROLLING GROGGILY through the airport in Auckland, New Zealand, eighteen hours after leaving New York, I see two men sitting across from each other, bowed over what appear to be word lists. I walk up, and say, "I can spot Scrabble players anywhere."

These aren't just any Scrabble players. Finding Joel Wapnick and David Boys quizzing each other at a snack bar a few days before the World Scrabble Championship is like stumbling across Andre Agassi and Pete Sampras hitting balls at the public courts in Central Park before the U.S. Open. Wapnick, a fifty-three-year-old, mild-mannered music professor at McGill University, has sad eyes, a hang-dog face, and a shuffling carriage. He was the North American champion in 1983, and runner-up at the Worlds in London ten years after that. Boys is a coffee-gulping, cigarette-smoking, thirty-five-year-old workplace underachiever with the energy of a Jack Russell terrier. He won the Worlds in 1995.

We're all traveling to Melbourne, Australia, for the 1999 Worlds. I'll be observing, not playing, as ninety-eight players from twenty-nine countries square off across the board. The U.S. team of fourteen will be the largest. Boys and Wapnick represent Canada, which has six players.

I buy a cup of chamomile tea and a blueberry muffin and join them. At this moment, they are drilling each other on eight-letter words that are acceptable in the British word source *Official Scrabble Words*, or *OSW*, but not the North American one, the *OWL*. Learning a lot of British-only bingos is a key to success at the Worlds. Boys has a list of seven-letter words to which an added letter forms a British-only bingo. He is quizzing Wapnick on the G's. So when Boys says, "PATSIES," Wapnick responds "GASPIEST#."

"OVERALL," Boys says.

"OVERGALL#," Wapnick replies.

"NOVELLA." Wapnick is stumped. He has slept thirty minutes in the last thirty-two hours.

"LONGEVAL#," Boys says.

Wapnick began playing Scrabble in 1975. It was a game well suited to his mind; mathematics and music are related in the brain. When he decided to learn the dictionary, Wapnick settled on rote memorization. As we wait for our connecting flight to Melbourne, Wapnick tells me how he did it. First, he broke down seven- and eight-letter bingos according to their component vowels; his first list starts with words containing three A's; SALADANG (a wild ox) is the first word on it. Wapnick memorized the words in order of appearance, in blocks of twenty. Every twenty-first word is a "guide word" and every 201st word is a "super guide word."

"Take the list that starts with GALATEA," he says. "GALATEA, ANNEALED, AGITATE, SALARIED, ASSAILER, SEASONAL, IGNATIA, ADNATION, LAGUNAS, DELEGATE." He utters the ten guide words in three seconds. "Those are words numbered one, twenty-one, forty-one, sixty-one, eighty-one, and so forth. So let's say I have something like A-A-E-I-D-L-R-T. If I don't see LARIATED immediately, what I'll do is say to myself, 'GALATEA, ANNEALED, AGITATE, SALARIED. It's got to be after SALARIED.'" That's because words containing the same vowels are listed according to the alphabetical order of their consonants. So DLRT (the consonants in LARIATED) would come after DLRS (the consonants in SALARIED) on the AAEI list. "Then I'll go through the twenty words: SALARIED, LARIATED, ASSAILED. LARIATED is there. I can go through the twenty words real fast."

I ask him to do so, and he does.

"SALARIED, LARIATED, ASSAILED, DILATATE, ATTAINED,

DATARIES, DIASTASE, SATIATED, GERANIAL, ALGINATE, GAS-ALIER, TAILGATE, ANEARING, ANGARIES, ARGINASE, AERAT-ING, ALLANITE, ARILLATE, NASALISE, ARTERIAL."

Seven seconds.

Wapnick carries with him a wad of five stapled sheets of paper that, in microscopic type on one side of a page only, contain sixteen thousand *OWL* bingos. It represents an excerpt from his bible, a 425-page tome titled "My Word Book." The system has served him well. In addition to his championship, he was runner-up at another Nationals and a Worlds — but lost the final three games in both to finish second. This year, after a bad tournament, he started studying from scratch. "I went back to my very first list, and I recited it over and over about fifty times in my head, so it was totally automatic. It occurred to me that if I did this with all of my old lists that I could get them back."

Strolling around his suburban Montreal neighborhood every evening lost in a haze of words, he did. In the past, Wapnick had been able to practice two or three pages of two hundred words apiece in one study session. Now, he was doing twenty-two hundred words in an hour. "It was so automatic. It was fabulous." He managed to memorize about four thousand British-only words. But then the new academic year started, his study time slipped, and now he isn't confident. "This particular tournament, I don't think it's going to pay off," he says.

Boys, by contrast, is optimistic. He quit his job as a shipper at a medical equipment company in order to prepare for the Worlds; he's returning to school to study computer programming. Marathoner-thin, with a close-cropped haircut, sunken cheeks, and nicotine-stained teeth, Boys looks like an extra from a World War II movie. He crosses his legs and bounces the dangling foot incessantly. For Boys, Scrabble is like Ritalin: It calms him down and gets him to focus, if only temporarily.

Unlike a Wapnick or an Edley — players who exude a scholarly sobriety about the game — Boys is a "whatever" kind of Scrabbler. He plays the tiles instinctively, doesn't overintellectualize board positions after a game is done. His early study involved reading the *OSPD* — no word lists, no flash cards, no system. He doesn't subscribe to Wapnick's technique. "I hate memorizing," he says. "I'd rather find the word in a half a second on my rack than go through a list and spend a minute."

When he won the Worlds, Boys studied thirty hours a week, and he's well prepared again. Boys won't say it, but he wants to become the first person to twice win this tournament, which has grown in prestige as top American and Canadian players become more serious about studying the British words and as the rest of the world closes the talent gap.

"It's the whole world," Boys says. "Not just North America." He flips to a list that contains seven-letter words plus a Y. "PORTALS," he says.

Wapnick recites the alphagram, ALOPRSTY. Stumped again.

"PASTORLY#," Boys says. "BURNERS."

"It's not SUNBERRY#, is it?" Wapnick asks.

It is.

Since the Worlds are played using a combination of the North American and British word sources, players who regularly use only one of them have to learn words in the other. And that's mostly the North Americans. The United States, Canada, and Israel are the only countries in the world that use the *OWL* as their word source. England is the only country that uses only the *OSW*. The rest of the world plays the game using both sources, which is known as SOWPODS (an anagram of the letters contained in *OSW* and *OSPD*, the North American source until the *OWL* was published).

The elite players in England, however, don't even bother playing *OSW*-only Scrabble anymore. They play SOWPODS exclusively. That's something the best North Americans can't afford to do; there are just too many good *OWL* players, too many *OWL* tournaments, too few opportunities to play the world game, and too much geographical distance between the best SOWPODS players at home to limit study to the combined book. This shift has left the North Americans at a disadvantage.

The British book is fatter than the North American one, so the U.S. and Canadian players have to learn more "new" words than their British counterparts. For instance, there are twenty-five British twos that a North American player has to learn for SOWPODS but only twelve American twos that don't fly in Britain. The twos, though, are easy to learn. Harder are the 257 British-only three-letter words; 1,252 British-only fours; and close to 18,000 British-only sevens and eights. All told, there are 40,240 two- through nine-letter words unique to the British word source, nearly twice as many as there are American words for players across the Atlantic to assimilate.

But in Scrabble, the world is converging. The biggest and most lucrative tournaments outside of the North American Nationals and the Worlds are held in places like Singapore and Bangkok, where corporations and governments are advancing prize money and support. And the world is deciding that a universal word source is the way to go; Australia has crossed over to SOWPODS play from the old *OSPD*, and England gradually is switching over from *OSW*.

Only North America has been reluctant. For more than a year, a debate has raged over whether to adopt the international rules. Hyperbole and name-calling have been rampant on both sides of the fence. The pro-SOWPODS players, the antis say, are a handful of elitist snob experts who play in the world championships and are trying to ram forty thousand ridiculous words down the throats of the masses. The anti-SOWPODS players, the pros say, are a bunch of lazy Luddites who don't understand that North America will be left behind if it doesn't convert. Tens of thousands of impassioned, often venomous words have been spilled on the e-mail forum CGP. At Reno, players donned NO SOWPODS buttons. To which Jim Geary replied, "Why not just wear a sign saying, 'I'm an idiot and I don't understand all of the issues'?"

There are a few. The biggest is that most players don't want to learn more words. SOWPODS contains 35 percent more two- to eight-letter words than the *OWL*. "This is a monumental change," says New York expert Paul Avrin, who hasn't studied in years. "It cannot be compared to the relatively small amount of words added in the previous dictionary revisions." Another point is that the British words would change strategy. SOWPODS is more creative and offense-minded, because more words equals more possibilities and more opportunities to score; individual scores above 500 points are routine. The extra two-letter words alone allow for more parallel plays, that is, placing one or more tiles on top of others, which improves the chances of playing bingos. And the British twos include

ZO and QI, the latter especially important for dealing with the clunkiest tile, which often ruins the flow of games. In SOWPODS, it becomes more difficult to shut down the board, a common, stultifying tactic in *OWL* play. The pro forces see this as a positive change; the antis say defense should remain part of the game.

But the loudest wailing has been reserved for the words themselves. The British list is based on *The Chambers Dictionary,* which all agree is a lousy source for a word game. *Chambers* is crammed with Shakespearian and Spenserian archaisms, not to mention thousands of Scottish words, like THEGITHER#, which means "together." There are Latin words not labeled with a part of speech, and there is at least one word, PRENZIE#, from Shakespeare's *Measure for Measure,* that, the definition admits, might have been a misprint. "If there were only a few of these, it would be fine," U.S. team member Ron Tiekert tells me. "But there are tons." And some of the British-only twos are ridiculous: PH, the measure of the acidity or alkalinity of a solution, is in there because the P is lowercase, and therefore meets the definition of a word (and the plural is PHS), while CH is defined as obsolete English dialect for "I" when fused with a verb, as in "cham" for "I am" and "chave" for "I have."

On CGP, every time an anti-SOWPODS-er trots out a list of supposedly weird British words, a pro-SOWPODS-er defines them to prove they aren't so weird. If an "anti" suggests that the recent additions to the North American book are reasonable, like ANTIDRUG$ and REBOOT$, but the British words are insane, a "pro" points out that we also added words like TUGHRIK (a monetary unit of Mongolia) and KUVASZ$ (a large dog with a white coat).

Some see the fight over specific words as beside the point. "English is a weird language," Bob Felt says. "Words come and go." Bob Lipton, one of the most vocal SOWPODS backers, notes what should be obvious. "If you take *any* subset of words that includes words listed in one dictionary but not another, you will see a list of words that is generally unfamiliar to most people." Scrabble, say Lipton, Felt, and others, is just more fun when more words are available.

Others see the SOWPODS movement as another step on a slippery slope. Having a word source sans definitions was bad enough. "Quaint as it seems," Larry Sherman posted, "many of us signed up for this cruise because we enjoy language. Five or six years ago, I could actually define most of the words I placed on a board. But as SOWPODS advocates blithely remind us, today's letter combinations are just 'game pieces.' The same gentlemen who daydream about lucrative corporate sponsorships" — Larry is referring to his brother, G.I. Joel — "are not concerned that much of a SOWPODS board would look like Greek to their prospective audience."

The logical solution is to clean up both word sources; the *OWL* is still sullied by words that no longer appear in any U.S. dictionaries. A cleanup, however, would require corporate oversight, and no one believes that Merriam-Webster or Chambers or the companies that own Scrabble care enough about the game's minutiae to get involved.

At the time of the Worlds, the debate appears to be approaching a resolution. The NSA has promised to schedule a referendum on whether to adopt SOWPODS — but not on whether to clean up the dictionaries. Meantime, it has asked the Scrabble clubs to vote on whether to test-drive SOWPODS for a month. At one Thursday-night gathering, G.I. Joel stands up on his chair to stump for SOWPODS. He says he hates *Chambers* — "as a reference volume, it's an abomination" — but he likes what it does for the game. One reason to try it is "to be recognized as the most courageous club in America." I am one of thirteen club members to vote yea; I love the idea of more wide-open games, and I'm still learning words, so what's a few thousand more? But SOWPODS loses by three votes. Joel keeps handing out 50-cent prizes anyway for the best SOWPODS words that don't get challenged off the board, and off to Australia we go.

To prepare for watching the Worlds — and for playing SOWPODS on the side — on the plane from Los Angeles to Auckland I memorize the twenty-five British-only two-letter words, which is a snap. Learning all 256 British threes, however, seems ridiculous. So I write down a few with entertainment value — DOH, EEK, FAB, GUB, HOO, ISH, PST, UEY, UFO.

The words aren't the only thing separating North America and the rest of the Scrabbling world. The World Scrabble Championship is a showcase for one of the oddest relationships in the toy industry, perhaps in any industry. While Hasbro controls the North American rights to Scrabble, in the rest of the world they belong to Hasbro's rival, Mattel Inc. It's as if Ford and General Motors were forced to manufacture a car together, or Coke and Pepsi had to share a soft drink. Scrabble is like a child caught in a custody fight between warring parents. In this case, visitation rights for the Worlds, by an unofficial agreement between the two companies, are on an every-other-year basis. "It's quite possible that a high-level Hasbro executive and a Mattel executive never had a conversation about this," John Williams says. "It's like North and South Korea."

Hasbro and Mattel have battled for decades. Hasbro and G.I. Joe were long synonymous with the boys market, Mattel and Barbie with girls. In the 1960s, both companies tried and failed to build board-game businesses from within. So they bought their way in. Hasbro had the upper hand. In 1984, it acquired Milton Bradley — which made Life, Yahtzee, Candy Land, Chutes and Ladders, and dozens of other familiar games. Five years later, Hasbro landed Scrabble by outbidding Mattel for the assets of bankrupt Coleco. In 1991, Hasbro beat Mattel again, acquiring Parker Brothers and classics like Monopoly, Sorry!, Risk, and Trivial Pursuit. By 1994, Hasbro had gobbled up more than half of the $1.1 billion U.S. games market.

But Mattel tried to catch up. It bought International Games, maker of the popular card game Uno, and then it pulled off a stunning coup: It outbid Hasbro for J. W. Spear and Sons, a mom-and-pop British firm that controlled the international rights to Scrabble. Spear had long been close to Scrabble's old mom-and-pop North American owners, Selchow & Righter. Spear launched the game in Britain in 1954, policed the Scrabble trademark (though it was plagued by ripoffs worldwide), and hired linguists to translate the game into twenty-two languages, from Arabic and Afrikaans to Hebrew and Russian. "Only the Japanese and Chinese couldn't do it," Francis Spear, the grandson of the company founder, tells me.

After Hasbro acquired Scrabble in 1989, it took a 27 percent stake in Spear. So when Francis Spear decided to sell in 1993, it seemed a fait accompli that Hasbro would be the buyer. But some Spear board members considered Hasbro's initial offer of $47 million far too low. Hasbro raised it to $71 million. Still not enough. The board sought a "white knight," and Mattel stepped in, eventually offering $90 mil-

lion. Hasbro dropped out. "We believe the Mattel offer is very generous and above a level which we could justify in business terms," the
president of Hasbro International said.

Hasbro had passed on an opportunity to lock up worldwide rights
to one of the most popular board games in history. Plus, Mattel had
beaten Hasbro in a showdown over a games company, which would
have been embarrassing enough had that company not made a game
Hasbro owned back home. Even worse, the appeal of Scrabble overseas had been growing annually, and there was a huge market waiting
to be tapped.

The NSA was hounded for free Scrabble sets by clubs in places
like Nigeria, where Scrabble was a government-sanctioned sport. Pi-
rated versions sold by the thousands from Italy (where it was called
Scarabeo) to India (where there were dozens of knockoffs). Un-
sanctioned tournaments in Thailand were attracting more than one
thousand adults and schoolchildren. Newspapers in the Philippines
and Malaysia reported tournament results. "Hasbro didn't understand that the game transcended cultures," an industry observer says.
"They didn't do their homework."

So now the Scrabble world was divided. But while Hasbro was
deepening its commitment to the competitive side of the game, hosting ever bigger Nationals, Mattel cut funding to the British players
organization and in 1998 decided not to sponsor the British national
championships, instead spending money on a school program and a
publicity stunt in which the army played the marines on a giant
board in Wembley Stadium. Mattel executives "see that there is a part
of the PR that should be related to the players, but they don't see that
the PR is always positive," says Philip Nelkon, a top British player
who handles Scrabble marketing and media for Mattel.

Overseen by Mattel U.K., six thousand miles from the company's
California headquarters, Scrabble barely registered on executives' ra-
dar screens. Even more problematic, Mattel simply wasn't a games
company, despite its efforts to become one. "It's about Barbie," a
Scrabble insider says. Scrabble's boosters at Mattel U.K. "are trying to
convince Barbie and Hot Wheels people what this stuff is about."

As 1999 approached, doubts surfaced about whether Mattel even
would stage the Worlds. Barbie sales had tumbled, profits weakened,
and a major management shakeup was announced in early 1999. Un-

derstandably, a Scrabble tournament was a low priority. John Williams suggested contingency plans to Hasbro in case Mattel backed out. A few months before the event, though, Mattel approved a budget. The scale would be smaller than Hasbro's blowout event two years earlier, with total prize money of $35,000, including a $15,000 first prize, compared to the $50,000 ($25,000 for first) that Hasbro paid. The Carlton Crest Hotel in Melbourne, where the tournament is being held, is a Motel 6 compared to the elegant Mayflower Hotel in Washington. Hasbro gave each member of the U.S. and Canadian teams $3,000 to help cover expenses; the British players got about one-quarter as much from Mattel U.K.

I'm rooming with G.I. Joel in Melbourne. Since arriving a couple of days earlier, Joel has been suffering from his usual range of maladies, plus back pain that has led him to sleep against an ironing board propped against his headboard. Except for playing in two warmup tournaments and taking a trip to the zoo with a Filipino player on whom he has a crush, Joel has scarcely left the hotel. He's played lots of Scrabble in the lobby, which has been commandeered by tournament players.

The four-day, twenty-four-game event begins in the morning, and tonight Mattel hosts the traditional player reception. As the defending champion, Joel will be center stage, and he intends to make a grand entrance.

Joel looks presentable, if a little lost, inside a navy blue suit complemented nicely by a maroon tie adorned with Scrabble tiles. We're ready to go, but then he gets animated, and I get worried. He pulls out a pair of Scrabble boxer shorts (which match the tie) and pulls them over his pants. I notice a stack of T-shirts on his bed. Joel unfurls one of them — from the 1996 Nationals in Dallas — and wraps it around his right leg.

"Joel, you can't," I say.

"Sure I can. Why not?" He's giggling.

Then he asks me to help him tie a T-shirt from the 1998 Nationals in Chicago around his left leg. Reluctantly, I oblige.

"That seems to work," Joel says.

I think: For whom?

Finally, Joel unfolds a third white T-shirt, this one from the 1997

Worlds in Washington, the event that he won, the event that validated his existence as a human being. I can't imagine what Joel has planned for this garment, given that he already is wearing a shirt, tie, and jacket, and his thighs are swathed in Scrabble T-shirts that dangle below his knees like chaps. But Joel is undeterred. He squeezes the T-shirt *over* his suit jacket, gazes at himself in the mirror, and laughs.

Joel prompts a few chuckles and a lot of head shaking when he enters the reception. The narrow, nondescript conference room hardly befits a world championship in any sport. The hors d'oeuvres are skimpy and the décor doesn't exactly shout class. Five flags featuring the Mattel corporate logo — a spiky red circle bearing the company's name in capital letters — hang limply from the walls. Two smaller banners read WORLD SCRABBLE CHAMPIONSHIP 1999.

I remind myself, though, that it's not about how much money the sponsoring company spends. It's about the international love affair with the English language and this game. The Nigerian squad sports *fila,* or traditional caps. The Kenyan team arrives dressed in long, colorful outfits known as *kitange,* which they also peddle in the hallway, pulling matching shirts and hats from a duffel bag. The nine English team members wear yellow golf shirts adorned with a rose, the national flower; a springbok leaps on the kelly green shirts worn by the three South Africans.

The Filipinos — emerging talents in the Scrabble world — meet the Pakistanis. The Thai mingle with the Singaporeans. I meet Adebayo Johnson Fasuba, a thirty-eight-year-old structural engineer from the Seychelles, and his teammate, Dhanapala Silva, a sixty-year-old schoolteacher. Keichiro "K.C." Hirai, a young Japanese translator playing in his first Worlds, is dressed in a bright jacket known as a "happi coat"; he tells me about the six hours of words-on-tape that he has recorded, about how he is developing a version of Scrabble in hiragana, about his study of compound words — "SNOWLAND, SNOWSUIT, like that," he says. "My next dream is to increase the popularity of Scrabble in Japan," K.C. says.

In this room there are Trinidadians and Maltese, Saudis and Scots, a Frenchman and an Indian, and more Sri Lankans, three, than I've ever met. There is an editor from Poland and a metallurgist from Malaysia and a plumber from New Zealand and a husband-and-wife team from Oman. There's a Pakistani doctor and a Bahrainian chef and a Kenyan veterinary surgeon. There is a management consultant from Nigeria who sold his battered Honda for $1,000 to drum up cash to travel to the 1997 Worlds, and his countryman, an army colonel who was chief of logistics for peacekeeping forces in Liberia and Sierra Leone.

That these people have come together to celebrate the English language even though many of them speak it as a second or third language, and sometimes just barely, makes the scene both touching and bizarre. Most of the nations represented here have at least colonial ties to Great Britain, and others traded with England. But some have no logical link to English or Scrabble. Thailand, which boasts some of the game's rising stars, avoided European colonization. Today English is taught in Thai schools but rarely used outside the classroom. Regardless, the common language here isn't English but words, and there's a difference. "You don't have to know how to speak," Laurentiu Sandu of Romania tells me.

No players at the event better reflect Scrabble's cross-cultural tug than Sandu, who goes by Dan, and his teammate, Catalin Caba. Dan and Cata traveled thirty-five hours to get here, from Bucharest via London and Singapore. They each earn about $200 a month — better than the average Romanian income of about $80 — and hit up family members, friends, and employers to raise more than $2,000 to pay for the trip. Dan, a thirty-year-old commercial inspector in city hall in Bucharest, scrounged $500 from a cereal company where an aunt works. Cata, a twenty-six-year-old computer engineer for the national electric company, paid the airfare out of his own pocket and hopes to be reimbursed by the utility.

In the waning days of his repressive dictatorship, Nicolae Ceausescu, the "Giant of the Carpathians," banned Scrabble as a subversive evil. "In the past was the Communist era," Dan explains. "Now it's open to go to other places, and with Scrabble there's an opportunity."

Dan has a round head, close-cropped brown hair, a gaunt face with prominent cheekbones, and a mouth of gapped, brown teeth; still, there's a faint glimmer of Paul Newman, circa *Cool Hand Luke*, in Dan's bright eyes and wry smile. Beefier, with long black hair and slumping posture, Cata could pass for the bass player in a 1970s high school garage band. When I meet them, they, too, are wearing national costumes, Dan a black vest called a *bunda,* adorned with red and green geometrical patterns, and Cata an *ie,* a white, open-necked shirt with black and blue decorative stitching around the collar, shoulders, and sleeves. A Canon automatic camera hangs from Cata's neck.

Dan is the Scrabble veteran of the duo. He began learning English at age ten, but "Russian was of more importance." Opportunities to practice English were, and remain, rare. "I know many words, but to speak . . . ," he says, struggling to convey a thought. Regardless, seven years ago he introduced competitive Scrabble in English to the country, and now is the national champion in both languages. (Romanian Scrabble sounds like a challenge: thirty letters, six hundred thousand words, thirty verb inflections.) Dan also plays duplicate Scrabble — which he pronounces DUPP-li-kate — in which both players use the same rack of letters. He plays it in French.

At the 1997 Worlds, Dan gave John Williams a pennant that says FEDERATIA ROMANA DE SCRABBLE and a bottle of Transylvanian wine whose label features a drawing of Dracula. Dan finished seventy-eighth out of eighty players, ahead of contestants from Guyana and the Seychelles, with a record of 5–16. "Not so good. It's not okay," he says.

Not okay? I think. *You can barely speak English.*

Dan wants to win ten games this time. "Double," he says, only he pronounces it DOO-ble.

Cata began playing Scrabble in English just three years ago and didn't start studying lists until this year. "We know many words but we don't know to put letters in front or back," he adds. "Hooks," says Dan. *Whooks.* "Hooks are big problem."

Peter Morris of the United States captured the first World Scrabble Championship in 1991. Mark Nyman of England won in 1993. David Boys of Canada did it in 1995. And my roommate, G.I. Joel, won in 1997.

In Melbourne, Scrabble's resident bookie, Jim Geary, has made Nyman the favorite at 6 to 1. Two Americans (Brian Cappelletto and Joe Edley), two Canadians (Boys and Wapnick), and a New Zealander (the little-known Nigel Richards) are 7 to 1. Who knows? A

Thai, Filipino, Sri Lankan, or Nigerian might emerge as a contender. It's bound to happen someday: Two people speaking broken English battling for supremacy of a game using English words. Everyone studies the same lists, learns the same strategy, plays against the same computer programs.

But the focus is on the Americans. When the U.S. team poses for a group photo at the reception, a flock of players from *other* countries gathers to snap pictures. Cappelletto, Edley, Sherman — these men are Scrabble gods. "I just had to have a look at him!" a middle-aged Aussie woman says to me at a warmup tournament (in which I play, going 3–3). "Joel Sherman! The world champion! I tried not to let him see me looking."

When I ask about his performance at the three previous Worlds in which he has participated, Kunihiko Kuroda of Japan offers his proudest achievement. "Four years ago," he says, "I beat two Americans."

Of course, the Americans are less interested in fostering Scrabble World Harmony than they are in being themselves. Bob Felt is at his disheveled worst, shirttails untucked, pants unbelted, face unshaven, hair uncombed, wandering about the hotel lobby re-creating for anyone who will listen, and even those who won't, some random Scrabble position. G.I. Joel bounds around like a kid on a sugar high. Joe Edley talks about his energy level from behind a baby blue surgical mask he has donned to ward off cigarette smoke. ("There goes the Darth Vader of Scrabble," Jim Geary says. "Oh! Now he *looks* like the Darth Vader of Scrabble.") At a restaurant, Brian Cappelletto reads aloud the description of an item on the menu while a waitress shifts uncomfortably. "Brian," his girlfriend finally admonishes. "Don't perform it. Just order it."

The Americans' quirky behavior — and the presumption that they are the best — is a bit much for the English team. After all, Nyman is considered the best SOWPODS player in the world. The British dominated in 1993, taking three of the top five spots and four of the top fifteen in 1997 (of course, the Americans took first through fourth places). And yet when the nine members of the English team assemble for a group photo, no one from other countries takes snapshots of them. It raises a question that rankles the Brits: Are the Americans really better? Or just weirder?

"Most of the Americans are a bit larger than life. It's a function of national characteristics," asserts Philip Nelkon, Mattel's Scrabble man, himself a four-time British national champion. "I think the U.K. players are just as intense as the U.S. players, but they just don't show it. I'd say we have more regular guys than you do." He says that "Sherman-Edley types" — eccentrics unafraid, even eager, to flaunt their eccentricities — would be unusual in the U.K. Or, as the English player David Webb, a forensic accountant, sums up the Americans: "I can't imagine *being* any of them."

"All the Yanks seem to live at the center of their own universe with only a dim recognition of, and no interest in, life outside it," Webb tells me. "Conversational gambits are treated as genuine inquiries into their universe, but there is no recognition of any need for reciprocity. There is a camaraderie about the Brits abroad which simply doesn't exist with the Yanks. We enjoy our company and care about the team and how everyone is doing. I have never seen a Yank showing any interest in a fellow countryman's performance, or indeed that of anybody else.

"Having said all that, the Yanks are rather good at Scrabble and are the only nation we actively set out to beat every two years."

From the earliest days of the Flea House, the Americans played for money and blood. But the English were genteel. For years, they played a collaborative game the object of which was not to win but to score as many points as possible. Players would exchange frequently or burn two or three tiles until they could bingo. There were unwritten rules: Vowels were to be left adjacent to premium squares, allowing for high-scoring, two-direction plays for the X, J, and Z (ZO was always acceptable in British Scrabble). The triple-word-score square was not to be used except for triple-triples, or "nine-timers" in British parlance. Players would try to slot an E in the second position on the triple line to facilitate nine-timers. The benchmark for scoring was ten points per tile, and the combined score in games was about 1000.

As long as both parties cooperated — and they didn't always — Scrabble became less a competitive sport than a team project. Nelkon once scored an 804 in the British nationals. The British tournament record is 849. Phil Appleby, in a friendly game, racked up 1049 points, which was listed in *The Guinness Book of World Records* as the highest-scoring game ever. Appleby played OXIDIZERS for 374 points, on a triple-triple line that stayed open for several turns, and LACQUERS for 221. "I missed another nine-timer later on," he recalls. "I should have scored twelve hundred."

Now, Appleby says, the old British approach is "so contrived it's almost embarrassing." By the mid-1980s, aware of the popularity of the Scrabble scene across the Atlantic and growing bored with their "please, after you" game, the British experts gradually switched to the American system of play. In 1989, Appleby and Nyman traveled to Reno for the North American championships. The Brits were floored by how well the tournament ran and how many players — 221 — entered. "It was the most mind-opening experience," Appleby says. "It was on a scale we'd never seen before."

It was so . . . American. Bigger, rougher, brasher. More players, more money, more competitive. And it instantly underscored the cultural difference between the Brits and the Yanks. In the United States, Scrabble was all that mattered. In England, it wouldn't be right to appear so unabashedly obsessed. Whereas G.I. Joel will tell anyone with ears that winning the 1997 Worlds validated his existence, the notion that Scrabble is more than just a game strikes the British players as overblown and self-aggrandizing, which is how they view many of the Americans. "Scrabble doesn't validate anything," David Webb snips.

I ask John Williams about the differences between the two teams. After nearly twenty years observing the experts, Williams is the Jane Goodall of Scrabble. The North Americans, he believes, have something that none of the Brits do. Williams sees it in the calculating focus of Joe Edley, the nervous intensity of David Boys, the fast and aggressive play of Adam Logan, the self-loathing drive of Joel Sherman, the I'll-hit-you-so-hard-I'll-kill-your-whole-family gaze of Matt Graham (who isn't in Melbourne because he didn't qualify, and wouldn't have come anyway because he doesn't fly). He sees it in the unstinting, unforgiving desire to win. It's not just not caring what other people think. It's not just a lack of self-awareness and self-respect. And it's not a show. It's a desperate, at-all-costs, life-isn't-worth-living-without-it, insecure, overachieving *need* to win.

"That's who we are as a culture," Williams says. "We were spawned by underdogs." He adds, "It kills the Brits that we're so good."

Mark Nyman comes closest to combining the British and American ways of Scrabble. He looks like the well-adjusted yuppie he professes to be, wearing black, rectangular Dolce & Gabbana eyeglasses and a black Donna Karan sweater. But over the board he gnaws his fingernails and tugs his thinning hair as if pulling taffy. Nyman is the only British player the North Americans actually *fear*. With reason. Much like Cappelletto, his American child prodigy counterpart, Nyman has a prodigious, possibly eidetic memory, uncanny anagramming abilities, and better strategic vision than his peers. Hell, he once finished second in the North American championships, where he had to avoid using the British words that filled his brain. It was like shooting pool with a pencil.

Fearful of being portrayed as an American-style Scrabble weirdo, Nyman takes pains to minimize his commitment. Despite his demurrals, though, Nyman has crafted a life around anagrams. It began when he appeared as a teen on a popular television game show called *Countdown*. Two contestants are shown nine letters and have thirty seconds to find the longest word. (The show was piloted in the States a decade ago but was rejected as "too cerebral," Nyman says. "Or so I'm told.") Mark won eight shows. Later, he was offered a full-time job as a contestant researcher. Today, he coproduces the show.

Like some top American players, Nyman quit Scrabble for a time. He had nothing left to prove and he was tired of the pressure. And yet he still loved the travel and the words and the competition. So he did more prep work for the 1997 Worlds than for any other tournament. He fell short, and now he wanted to show the cocksure Americans, who felt they were better than ever because they had begun devoting themselves to SOWPODS, that he could still play the game.

"I want to be the best," he says. "I want to be the world champion again."

17

The Worlds

THE FIRST GAME of any Scrabble tournament — in Melbourne at the Worlds or in some motel by the Long Island Expressway — is always the tensest. There is the promise of the new, the boundless hope for perfect tiles, the misguided belief that possibility can temporarily outmuscle probability in a game governed by those twin, warring concepts. As the defending champion, G.I. Joel is seated at Table 1 for the first game. He dips a tissue into a water glass and cleans off his personal Mattel-made playing board (the premium squares are the same color as on the Hasbro boards, but the remaining ones are kelly green rather than tan). Using two seconds, Joel's opponent makes the first play of the tournament: QAT.

As I stroll around the playing room to capture the initial moments, a familiar competitive tension courses through my body. I'm on high alert: eyes widening, breaths deepening, neurons straining to see what they see. Bob Felt plays WHORING. Jim Geary drops down YAWING. Phil Appelby plays DZO#. Brian Cappelletto opens with QUINA#, placing the last three letters atop the FOH played by his opponent. Steve Polatnick of the United States plays three bingos in a row — GOALIES, ALIZARIN, and NOSTRILS — but his opponent, Pui Cheng Wui of Malaysia, makes LEAFERY#.

Joel Wapnick sets up DEA?ING on his rack. Wapnick has been a virtual hermit since we arrived, venturing out of his room and his word book only for twice-a-day, three-mile walks around Albert

Lake across the street and an evening meal with other players. He glances up to find me standing a few feet away and shoos me off.

My Romanians, as I paternalistically think of them, become my Everymen. Especially Cata. His command of English as a spoken language is virtually zero; but he makes and studies lists (his favorite: the four hundred words acceptable in both Romanian and English), so a "Scrabble word" will spring unprompted from his brain. Cata has drawn Lester Schonbrun in the first round. This pairing is a big thrill for the U.S. team's only Communist. (He can't wait to tell his friend Steve Brandwein.) After three turns, Lester is ahead 147–40, when Cata tries to turn LINTERS into FLINTERS*. "It sounds good to me," Cata says as the word is looked up. "It's no good," Lester says gently. "Zero," Cata says dejectedly, picking up his tiles.

I wander around the room, and then return to Cata. He is losing 457–237, but he's made a bingo, StRIPES, and he holds the second blank! He hunches far over the table — his back arched like a prehistoric man in a *National Geographic* drawing, his face inches from the board, a pile of dandruff marking the black tablecloth like a fresh snowfall. He pulls RUY to go along with his ELT? and shakes his head. *Come on, Cata,* I think, *don't shake your head. You can find a bingo!* I want to channel my thoughts into his brain. *UTtERLY! cUTLERY! cRUELTY!*

Cata doesn't find any of them. Lester wins, 532–287.

"He's amazing. Just imagine if I was playing in Romanian," Lester says to me. He has Cata autograph his program.

Unlike Cata, Dan is oblivious to his linguistic shortcomings. After losing by nearly 200 points to an Englishman, a wounded smile reveals Dan's boulevard of broken teeth. "Fine. It's okay. It's okay," he says, falsely. "He had better letters."

Not without reason did Jim Geary make Brian Cappelletto a favorite to win the Worlds. For the previous two years Brian has been far and away the best Scrabble player in North America. Of all the players I talk to in Melbourne, only David Boys seems unintimidated by Brian's accomplishments. "*Brian,*" he says in a breathy, mock-reverential voice. "The fear of him. The myth of Brian. The fact that people sit down, and think, 'Wow, he's so much better than everybody else.' He still hasn't proven himself at SOWPODS."

Indeed, that's his one shortcoming. Brian finished tenth at the 1997 Worlds, and unlike Joe Edley or G.I. Joel he hasn't polished his SOWPODS skills by playing in lucrative tournaments in Singapore or Bangkok. So when Brian loses to a British player in Game 1, an Australian player in Game 2, and a player from the United Arab Emirates in Game 3, I wonder whether Boys is right. Maybe Brian isn't prepared. Regardless, in Game 4, ninety-seventh-place Brian Cappelletto is sitting in the very last chair, at the very last table, Table 49, of the tournament room. He is paired with the player in ninety-eighth place, the only one in the room with zero wins and a worse spread than he: Brian is playing one of my Romanians. He wins 502–269, but it's little consolation. Brian is embarrassed.

After six rounds, just one player is without a loss: Nigel Richards of New Zealand, an unflappable, thirty-two-year-old water company technician who is regarded as knowing more words than any other player. Nigel had been playing for just four years, but already he is a legend: Nigel played CHLORODyNE# through three disconnected letters, SAPROZOIC through ZO#, and the obscure American word GOOSEFISH$. Nigel has read the entire 1,953-page *Chambers Dictionary* and says he is able to recall words simply by conjuring mental snapshots of its pages.

At the end of the first day, Nigel is in first place with a 7–1 record, ahead of three other players who have the same number of wins but smaller spreads, G.I. Joel among them. Ten players have six wins. Cappelletto makes a comeback, clobbering his last five opponents of the day. Wapnick also has five wins, as does Edley, who is disgusted nonetheless and all but blows me off in the hotel lobby.

Before the second day's play starts, I peruse e-mails from around the world posted on a bulletin board in the hallway. There are messages for Edley, from his best man and fellow Scrabble expert Jerry Lerman, and for Logan, Boys, and Wapnick, the Canadians. There is one entirely in Polish for that country's lone representative. (*"Wczorajsze wyniki przekazal em Twojej Zonie,"* it begins, demonstrating why the Z and J are not power tiles in Polish Scrabble.) There are e-mails for the Pakistani team and for the Filipinos. Chris Cree, the lovable, complaining Texan, who has been following the tournament on-line, has sent one for Cappelletto: "Sure, give everyone a head start. You are the best that there is. It will work out."

G.I. Joel had insisted he wasn't prepared for Melbourne. In the weeks before the trip, he had a cold, an "air bubble" in his back, and back pain. I e-mailed him to ask how he felt. "Still crappy. I have a feeling I'm not going to enjoy the trip, and playing in the tourney is going to be a waste of time, because I haven't been able to study. I've just been watching a lot of baseball games and resting even more than usual. I've got a week left to improve, but I'm not feeling very positive at the moment. Aarrghh!" A week later, the air bubble was still there and his back still hurt. "I literally wrenched it trying to cough up some mucus," he told me on the phone. "Ever since then I've been jamming down antihistamines to make sure I don't aggravate the back coughing up mucus." But the antihistamines had left him feeling foggy and his stomach queasy. And the aspirin to dull the back pain had made his stomach more acidic.

He seems fine now. In Game 11, against Nigel, Joel plays GHARRIES to go up 423–347, then draws ACIOST? and instantly plays AgNOSTIC through an open N for a 501–375 lead. He breaks out a hotel spoon and a small pie tin containing a tart, leans back in his chair, and starts eating. Eyes twitching over the board, mandible pumping on the tart, Joel wraps up the game to go to 10–1 and first place.

Cata, meanwhile, has staked out Table 49 as his permanent home. His record of futility grows — 0–4 with a spread of −641; 0–6, −1165; 2–9, −1476 — and with it my empathy. Every time I wander by his table, Cata is a picture of pain, his back hunched over like a question mark, chin resting in folded hands, mouth agape, staring at the Scrabble set as if it were a Ouija board, only no answers are forthcoming.

But every time I pass by, Cata also seems to have a blank on his rack. He misses ARMORIeS, then PREENInG. A game later he'll be blessed with ELORST?, but won't find any of the three dozen or so possible seven-letter words. Then it'll be EELNR?? — a perfect balance of vowels, consonants, and blanks — yielding a plethora of bingos but no hope to Cata.

This time it's AENORT?, with more than a dozen possible bingos, at least three of which Cata probably knows (the common anagram group SENATOR, ATONERS, TREASON). As he shuffles the letters, it's clear Cata doesn't know the obvious hook — using his O to turn WEIRD into WEIRDO. In the meantime, his opponent creates an even *easier* spot, playing the word MOO, to which Cata could add an N, S, or T (or a D, L, or R, not to mention an I, K, or P to form British-only words). He's got three minutes left on his clock with at least half the tiles still in the bag. Cata plays off an O and draws a C.

He shuffles and shuffles and shuffles. Suddenly, he lays down CERATiN, hooking the N to MOO. I'm elated. Cata is anxious when his opponent challenges — under the "open challenge" rule at the Worlds, players do not lose a turn for challenging an acceptable word, only for playing a phony — and then relieved when it is good. Cata probably plays the "Scrabble word," CERATIN, about which he is unsure, rather than the common word, CERTAIN, because they have equal meaning to him, which is no meaning at all.

Afterward, I tell Cata and Dan about WEIRDO. "Someone who is strange, a strange person," I say.

"No, I didn't know," says Cata.

"Weirdo?" says Dan, as if spitting out a piece of rotten fruit.

For all the competitive intensity, for all the sniping and personal enmities stockpiled over years, the shared bond of Scrabble wins out. Players mock Bob Felt but indulge his need to yak about racks. G.I. Joel can be pesty, demanding, and embarrassing, like a little brother, but he is also sensitive and smart and proud of his talent. I sit around the table at a Chinese restaurant in a Melbourne suburb with Lester and Joan, my favorite socialists; with Ron and Susi Tiekert; with G.I. Joel's brother, Larry, and their cranky father, Mike; with Lisa Odom, the top-rated American woman player and top-rated African-American, too, and her partner, Steve Pellinen, an expert player himself; and with Jim Geary, the pudgy, sarcastic, brilliant poker player, and I think: What am I doing here with these people? And why am I so comfortable?

I have traveled halfway around the globe to watch a Scrabble tournament. I wouldn't be here if I wasn't writing about the game, of course, but I feel as if I'm where I belong. I enjoy the Scrabble chatter that dominates dinner, and the background conversation, too, getting to know some of my Scrabble comrades better as regular people. They are no longer just "characters" in a literary sense but friends, and the game itself has established an emotional permanence in me that goes beyond winning and losing. I'm not sure it's rational — believing as many do that a board game possesses a sort of cosmic power, something commensurate with our capacity for wonder — but I feel it nonetheless.

I feel it as I wait for the elevator on the fifth floor of the hotel, where G.I. Joel and I are bunking. I lean over the wall and glance down the atrium to the lobby below where a half-dozen friendly games are taking place. I hear the rustle of the tiles and the white-noise game chatter. From up here, the boards look like matchbooks and the players are nearly indistinguishable. I love the scene so much I want to float down and hover over the boards and osmose the words and the tactics and the ambience. It is so hazy and yet so palpable that I almost want to cry.

I feel it again late on the night before the final full day of play. G.I. Joel had a bad afternoon, falling to 11–5. Three players are at twelve wins, including Wapnick and Nyman. Eight players are bunched at eleven wins — Boys, Sherman, Cappelletto, Logan, two Brits, an Australian, and a Thai. Nigel Richards has ten wins. The consensus favors the Americans heading into day three, or at least the consensus of Yanks thinks it does.

But at 11:00, the competition is secondary. A crowd of us has just returned from another meal and Scrabblers of varying nationalities fill the lobby, a few playing, most sitting in circles drinking and talking. Paul Epstein, a taxi driver–rock musician from Ann Arbor, Michigan, finishes a piano set of Rolling Stones and Beatles tunes — he plays "Back in the U.S.S.R" and I wonder if Lester notices — and then G.I. Joel takes over.

Joel often says that what he *really* would like to have been in life, had he not been cursed with his body and looks and nasal passages, is a singer; after he won the Worlds, Joel had hoped to go on David Letterman, talk about Scrabble, and perform, but the appearance never materialized. Without fanfare, he sits down at the black baby grand and attacks the keys. He's a banger, with a heavy foot to boot, and he's serious, curled over the keyboard as if it were a Scrabble set.

He belts out a deep vibrato that makes all of his colleagues stop and listen.

I soak in Joel, tiny Joel, hammering away at the keys, exorcising his demons, now at the piano as before over a bunch of letters, exposing himself without fear or shame, with joy.

G.I. Joel is singing Billy Joel.

You may be right, he croons, *I may be crazy.*

The next morning, remarkable things happen. At Table 3, Nigel Richards plays THIONINE$, a violet dye, Adam Logan plays FLIGHT, and the relevant section of the board looks like this:

	A	B	C	D	E	F	G	H	I	J	K	L	M	N	O
1	TWS			DLS				TWS				DLS			TWS
2		DWS				TLS				TLS				DWS	
3			F				DLS		DLS				DWS		
4	DLS		L	DWS				F				DWS			DLS
5			I		V	E	T	E	r	A	N	S			W
6		TLS	G			TLS		R		G	O	O		TLS	A
7			H				DLS	R	DLS		B	L	I	N	D
8	TWS		T	H	I	O	N	☆	N	E		DLS			D
9			DLS				DLS	T	DLS				DLS		
10		TLS				TLS		E		TLS				TLS	

Three turns later, Nigel lays down USE, forming UG#, SH, and ETHIONINE$, which is an amino acid.

	A	B	C	D	E	F	G	H	I	J	K	L	M	N	O
1	TWS			DLS				TWS				DLS			TWS
2		DWS				TLS				TLS		O		DWS	
3			F				DLS		DLS			U	DWS		
4	DLS		L	DWS				F				T			DLS
5			I		V	E	T	E	r	A	N	S			W
6		U	G			TLS		R		G	O	O		TLS	A
7		S	H				DLS	R	DLS		B	L	I	N	D
8	TWS	E	T	H	I	O	N	☆	N	E		DLS			D
9			DLS				DLS	T	DLS				DLS		
10		TLS				TLS		E		TLS				TLS	

On the next turn, Adam makes *another* extension by playing BAM to the triple-word score, forming BUG, ASH, and METHIONINE, another amino acid.

Adam's final play used three letters and scored 78 points. "I don't quite know how I knew the words; maybe memory from organic chemistry or from some popular book on the subject (*Gödel, Escher, Bach*?)," Adam tells me in an e-mail after the tournament. "And I think I'd heard those hooks mentioned before in a Scrabble context. I saw the possibilities as soon as he played THIONINE, and, believe me, when he played USE, I was very glad to see that I'd just picked the M!"

In the same round, Joel Wapnick turns the word GLOM into the nonbingo, triple-triple EGLOMISE$ for 99 points. And when Brian Cappelletto beats Mark Nyman — despite Mark's play of CAThOODS#, which *Chambers* defines as the state of being a cat or having the nature of a cat — he moves into first place on the leader board. Brian has gone from ninety-seventh place to first place, from Table 49 to Table 1. After nineteen rounds, Jim Geary's two favorites — Brian and Mark — are running first and second.

I stop by Brian's old stamping ground, Table 49, and, sure enough, Cata has another blank on his rack: CINOSU? This time, however, he finds a word! AUCtIONS! Who's the Giant of the Carpathians now?

Dan, it turns out, also is making some impressive plays. "The best game of mine," he excitedly tells me, and then recounts his top plays.

"ACTINIDE," he says. *AK-tin-i-dee.*

"STRIVERS," he says next, getting the pronunciation correct.

"And hoe-ax."

Hoe-ax? Hoe-ax? I wonder whether HOEAX is good in the British book. I check his score sheet.

"Oh," I say, grinning, "*hoax.*"

"I have eight," Dan says. Eight wins is truly remarkable, I tell him, as many as a Canadian and an Australian.

"But it is no good," he says. "Ten is good. I want ten. That would be double." *Dooble.* "Double the last time."

After Game 20, the first six spots are held by players from six different countries — England, Canada, the United States, Australia, Nigeria, and New Zealand. When the Brit (Nyman) beats the Australian (John Holgate) in Game 21, he does so by playing MPRET# at the very end, a word he has never before used in a game (it's a former name for the ruler of Albania). Nyman's endgame is so impressive that the spectators around Table 1 actually applaud. After twenty-two rounds, Nyman and Wapnick are 17–5. Only Cappelletto and Boys, both 15–7, have a chance to catch them. G.I. Joel is out of it at 13–9.

Nyman loses to Ron Tiekert. Wapnick loses to Boys. If Brian wins, he will have risen from the ashes of Table 49 and given himself a chance to silence his SOWPODS critics and advance to the finals. He's playing a Brit, Andrew Fisher, and has a lead of about 20 points in the endgame and the tiles to win. Then Fisher plays EPEE, hooking an E to the word RONT#, forming RONTE#, for 35 points. Brian thinks it's a desperation play, and challenges. It's ruled good. Brian is stunned. He loses by 5 points.

"I just didn't know a British five," Brian says when I ask him what happened. "RONT and RONTE. I just didn't know the pair. I just didn't know the hook. I didn't know the hook." Brian is flush, on the verge of tears. "Five points," he says. He grabs his girlfriend's hand and slinks down the hallway, head bowed.

"The magic number," David Boys says, "is ninety-two."

That's by how much Boys has to beat Nyman in the last game to make the finals. Wapnick, who is in first place by virtue of a larger spread than Nyman, would have to lose by more than 200 points not to make it.

Six hours earlier, Boys had written off his chances. He lost his first two games of the day and was mired in twentieth place. Plus, he had a persistent migraine headache. Boys played through the pain, winning five in a row. Now he's in the hallway, dancing on the balls of his feet, a nervous whirl that brings him inspiration. He recalls a scene from a 1970s slapstick comedy. "You ever see *Gumball Rally?*" he asks me. "The Italian guy rips off his rearview mirror, and says, 'What is behind does not matter!' Whenever I get in this situation, I think of that." Into the playing room he bounds.

Meanwhile, at Table 49, in the last two seats in the house, Dan and Cata are paired in the final round.

"The two Romanians," Dan says.

"No problem," says Cata.

Nyman takes an early lead. Boys comes back. Nyman goes ahead again. On his score sheet, Mark doesn't bother with the actual tally; he records the game as if he had started with a 91-point lead, because all he needs to do is not lose by more than that amount. He bites the fingers of his left hand, which he holds with his right. Boys cradles his migrainous head and wipes his face. He lays down two tiles, then picks them up, then checks his tracking. He has a blank, but awkward tiles to go with it, and not enough points. When the bag empties, Mark knows Dave can't bingo. While he will lose the game, and the two will finish with identical 17–7 records, Mark will have a larger spread and meet Wapnick in the finals.

Mark glances over at his girlfriend, who is standing behind the rope, and he nods repeatedly. He sees me standing to his left, and winks.

The game ends. Mark taps his pen three times on the table and stands up. The game occupies the last page in his score pad, a spiral notebook with soccer balls on the cover. His clock reads 00:01.

"So it's 1993 all over again," Boys says, referring to the Nyman-Wapnick final that year.

Wapnick comes over after vanquishing Ron Tiekert.

"Good luck to both of you tomorrow," Boys says, gracious in defeat.

Wapnick turns to me, insecure already. "Mark's incredible, and I have a terrible record against him," he says, calculating right there that he is 3–9 against Mark, including 1–2 this week and 2–3 in the 1993 finals, where he lost three games in succession. "And I still am not prepared."

I dash over to Table 49. "So who's the Romanian champion?" I ask.

Cata shrugs and tilts his head toward a beaming, teeth-flashing Dan.

"He needs the victory," Dan says, "and I need the beer."

I'm not sure what this means, but it sounds like it would work in a Michelob commercial.

Dan finishes in ninety-first place with nine wins, fifteen losses, and a spread of −2008 points. Not quite *dooble*, but amazing nonetheless. Cata is dead last, with three wins, twenty-one losses, and a gargantuan spread of −2991.

"Today, bad luck, but I don't accuse," says Dan.

"No problem," says Cata.

I love these guys.

That the two finalists are a Canadian and a Brit seems just. Canadians finished first, third, and fourth in the standings; Brits were second, fifth, and sixth. Ron Tiekert wound up as the top American, in seventh place. Brian Cappelletto, after a stunning 14–2 run, lost four of his last five games to finish in eleventh place. G.I. Joel also ended with fifteen wins, and in fifteenth place. Joe Edley finished 13–11, and Jim Geary was 12–12. "All that effort. Nobody knows," Geary says. "I put my whole life into this tournament. It's so sad."

For the finalists the next morning, there is no playing-room buzz, no shuffling of tiles from other tables, no distractions like challenges or spectators hovering nearby. As in Washington in 1997, the best-of-five-games match is held in a small room equipped with video cameras to show the games on closed circuit to the other players. Computers will simulcast them over the World Wide Web. By virtue of my reporter/insider status, I'm one of a handful of people (a word judge, annotators recording every play, the technicians, a Webmaster, and corporate execs) who can be in the room during the match. In the main playing hall, now cut in half of its tournament size, three screens — one for the board, one for Nyman's rack, one for Wapnick's — face twenty rows of chairs. G.I. Joel is happy to be tapped as one of the two color commentators (along with an Australian player). He wears his Scrabble tie for the occasion, but not the boxers.

Wapnick arrives first and unpacks his clock, his Canadian flag, and his lucky fire-engine red plastic rack that came from a 1950s Scrabble set purchased by his mother. A techie tapes the rack to the table so it stays in camera range. Wapnick looks shaky. He had a quiet dinner at the hotel, studied British four-letter words, and was in bed at 10:30. Nerves woke him at 4:00 A.M., and he managed to sleep for only another hour. I ran into him at breakfast, where he was seated alone, eating pancakes. "I am looking forward to this being over, regardless of what happens," Joel told me. "I want to relax."

Joel is "a little more apprehensive" than in 1993, when he lost to Nyman in the finals, and over the pancakes relived that nightmare for me. Joel won Games 1 and 2. Mark won Game 3. Then Joel took a 179-point lead in Game 4. Mark played the X for 52 points, drew both blanks, bingoed twice, and won by 9. In Game 5, Mark played BEDAWIN# to a triple-word square, opening a volatile area of the board. Mark came back again, and Joel lost.

"The scary thing is I thought about that game every day for the next three years," he said. "That's why I'm apprehensive."

Mark arrives a few minutes after Joel. He pulls out his own rack, a dark wooden one he received as a gift after winning the 1993 Worlds.

While the technicians complete their checks, Mark and Joel head out into the main hallway and chat with the other players. When they're escorted into their playing room, everyone applauds.

"I've got seven," Joel announces, meaning tiles.

Thirty-three seconds later, he lays down CHAPLET. "Eighty-six," Joel says.

It will be that kind of game. Joel runs out to a big lead, and there's little Mark can do. Joel plays FILTHIER, a double-double worth 109 points. Mark responds with SEADROME for 74, but opens a triple line. Joel pulls both blanks to go with AELRW and takes his time. First he lays down WALKERs, but picks it up before hitting his clock. "He's just jerking Mark off," Geary says in the spectators' room, where nearly a hundred people are gathered and I periodically visit. Finally, Joel plays WARbLEs for a 334–134 advantage.

Thanks to the camera, everyone sees Joel's tiles descend into view as he places them on his red rack. One by one they come: I E E S R V C. "Oooohhhh!" SERVICE or SCRIEVE, which Joel selects. Now he's up 412–160. Mark's cooked, but when he finds INSOMNIA through an M, the room erupts in admiring applause; no one had spotted it, and Geary deadpans, "He's pretty good."

Final score: 624–307. "That was fun," Mark jokes. "If luck evens itself out, I should be all right."

The pressure seems unbearable. Not only are Mark and Joel playing for the world championship and $15,000, they are doing it before a phalanx of cameras, with the best Scrabble players in the world besides them gathered nearby heckling every move. Mark and Joel have no sense of the comments and catcalls of their colleagues. It's dead quiet in the little room where they are playing. I'm not sure whether the silence makes it easier or harder for them to concentrate.

Mark draws better tiles in Game 2 and wins, 444–330. The players join the crowd afterward. It's amazing: the two competitors for the world championship not only mingling with the vanquished but having to endure, and respond to, their second-guessing while the event is still in progress.

Both players sigh a lot in Game 3; neither is getting great racks. Mark looks as if he's daydreaming. A moth invades the playing room, bumps into one of the cameras. Joel draws seven consonants. Mark twists his thumb around in his mouth, systematically gnawing all sides. The hum of the air conditioner is the only sound. Joel hooks an S onto ZAMIA, and Mark challenges. The natives, meanwhile, get restless.

"He's challenging a word he's known for twenty years!" shouts Ron Tiekert. "It's a frivolous challenge." Ron is implying that Mark is deliberately challenging words he knows are good in order to buy some time to think. It's one of the perils of the free challenge rule.

Joel leads 130–112. Mark, holding six vowels, gets rid of three with

URAO#, leaving AEI. "I think that's a bad play," Tiekert says. It might be, except that Mark draws LOPR and plays EPILATOR# on his next turn to cut Joel's lead to 202–197. They trade bingos (GINGLES# for Joel, KINETICS for Mark), and then the game turns in Joel's favor. He draws a blank, then an E, then the Q, then an N, then a U. The crowd begins oohing and shouting. Joel plays QUIeT atop the INETI in KINETICS for 69 points — a high-scoring overlap made possible by SOWPODS, as Joel made the word QI# — and a 386–280 lead. Mark pulls a bingo-prone rack; if there were an N on the board he could play ANTIWEED, but there isn't.

"I like WEB," Tiekert says. "It's the kind of play he made when he made his big comeback in ninety-three." Ron shouts out the daring play, which would create bingo possibilities. "WEB is the play," he says. "It opens the board."

"WEB *hardly* opens the board," G.I. Joel says into the microphone. He's been doing scant play-by-play, just periodic suggestions and goofy inside jokes that only the North Americans can understand. He sometimes condescendingly rebuts the suggestions of others, as he has just done with Tiekert.

"WEB is one hundred fucking percent the best play," the normally good-natured Tiekert snaps. "I'm tired of his egotistical commentary."

"Well, he *is* the world champion," Geary says.

For another couple of hours anyway, I think. G.I. Joel gets no respect.

Mark loses the game. He passes up the free lunch with the Scrabbling masses and heads off with his girlfriend. Droplets of perspiration bead on his upper lip. Joel retreats to his room with a 2–1 lead. An hour later, he emerges, shutting the door behind him — and forgetting his score pad and room key inside.

Joel and Mark say hi to each other, sit down, and play resumes. Mark, going first, pulls junk out of the bag — EEINNOU — and sighs. Clearly, he's rankled by his bad luck. Of the six possible blanks in the first three games, Mark got just one. Make it one for seven: Joel lays down ISOgRIV$, attaching the S to Mark's opening play of EN-NUI. Mark is frustrated, biting his nails madly.

Mark catches a big break when Joel lays down FUROUR on his second turn. Mark instantly stops the clock and shakes his head. "It's no good," he says. Joel is holding the bridge of his nose with his right hand. The judge confirms. "Phew," Joel sighs, shocked and embarrassed at playing a phony in what could be the deciding game of the world championship. To lose again to Mark after being ahead, well, that might be too much to bear. Mark draws CCDEEIM and exhales, his lips flapping at his continued misfortune. He makes a small play, MICE for 21, and Joel burns some unpromising tiles for a 94–60 lead.

Finally, Mark gets a blank, and plays lAICIZED for 90 points. Two plays later, though, Joel bingos back with STIFLERS. A few turns later, Mark bingos again with EMBOGUE#, but Joel on the very next play replies with TABORETS. It's 340–333 in Mark's favor, and there are just ten tiles left in the bag. The J, Q, and X have yet to be played.

But when Joel lifts DEGOTXY from the silky green sack, there's a surge of excitement among the chattering experts.

"This looks over!" Tiekert says. "This looks over! This looks over!"

"He's got DEOXY!" someone shouts.

"DETOX! DETOX!" Edley says.

"It's over!" Tiekert repeats. "The match is over!"

Mark plays JO for 42 points and a 49-point lead. But Joel sets up DEOXY$ on his rack, and I race back into the playing room. When I arrive, Joel is reshuffling. His hands are trembling. He drops DEOXY on the board, forming TO, AX, and BY. "Okay," Joel announces, exhaling. "Fifty."

"Three eighty-two, three eighty-three?" Mark says.

"Yeah."

"You went ahead?" Mark checks.

"Yeah."

"Shit."

Mark runs his left hand through his hair. He holds his pen in his right hand, which is shaking. His right leg is jumping uncontrollably. Mark touches the Q. He reviews Joel's tiles: GRT. There are two places for Joel to get rid of them by playing GIRT. Like a premonition of one's own death, Mark sees it and can't stop it. He's going to lose by 1 point. He plays QI# for 28 points. Final score: 403–402.

Joel looks at me and pumps his fists.

"Congratulations," Mark says.

"Thanks," Joel says. "This isn't a dream, right?"

David Boys is the first player to reach the room, and the two Canadians embrace. I think about running into them at the Auckland airport ten days earlier, quizzing each other between flights, Boys supremely confident, Joel filled with self-doubt.

Mark is red-faced and shell-shocked. The tournament organizers ask him to stick around for satellite interviews back to England. "I'll just go off and have a fag and I'll be back," he says.

When Joel reaches the main playing room for the awards ceremony, he's mobbed. "This is great!" he says, pumping his fists again and walking on tiptoes, like a kid on Christmas morning. Everyone applauds when he finishes an interview for a video news release, in which he eloquently answers the "Why?" question: "Scrabble is a passion. It's something that all of us who play it are enthralled by. It's got so much beauty in it, and creativity and excitement, that it's irresistible once you get into it."

I remind Joel of our airport encounter, how he complained he wasn't prepared, yet went on to win twenty-one of twenty-eight games and take the title. "I *wasn't* prepared," he says. "There were so many words I didn't know. I still feel shaky. Especially those four-letter verbs. They drive me crazy. But maybe next time I'll prepare better."

G.I. Joel removes his identification badge, which reads 1997 World Champion, crosses out his last name and the year, and writes in "Wapnick" and "1999." Nyman sets down a pint of Victoria draft beer he has procured from the hotel bar, and collects his check for $6,000 to a standing ovation. Philip Nelkon then asks G.I. Joel up to the stage, and it's like the old Miss America crowning the new one.

"The last time I get to touch this," G.I. Joel says, passing the trophy to the other Joel, who gets a thirty-second standing ovation, during which he sheepishly bows and holds the trophy aloft. After Nelkon asks G.I. Joel to leave the stage — he seems reluctant to go — the new world champion delivers a short speech. He thanks Mattel and Hasbro. He thanks David Boys. He thanks G.I. Joel. He thanks Mark Nyman. "I really don't know how anybody could have done better today with the tiles that he had," Joel says.

After the furor (wink, wink) subsides, I sit down with Joel Wapnick in a side room. G.I. Joel pokes his head in. "Mind if I listen in?"

he asks. Well, I do, but don't say anything. What is it, I ask Joel W. (knowing that Joel S. will answer, too), that makes you devote the years to this pursuit? Unlike my roommate, Wapnick has a wife and two children, a successful academic career, a well-rounded life. Why be an obsessive, too?

"I guess you could ask that of any athlete or anybody who is expert in any field of competition," the new world champion says. "It's very important. It just is."

"It's our personal form of self-expression," the old one says.

"I think that's a good way of putting it," says the new one.

"We are artists and this is our way of expressing our art," says the old one.

"There's also something kind of nice," Wapnick says, "in being world champion of something."

18

1416

A
FTER WINNING his last game to salvage a .500 record, Jim Geary sat at the playing table in Melbourne and remembered: How he had created flash cards for every British-only bingo — seventy-five hundred seven-letter words, nine thousand eights, ten words to a card, with anagrams on the back and the British words written in red ink "because of the Redcoats." How he had studied them while lying on the couch cradling his newborn daughter, Colleen. How he had stuffed the cards into two shoeboxes that he toted everywhere but Australia (five pounds, too heavy). How he had got a reprieve on his master's thesis in information systems engineering from a professor who told him the tournament was more important. How he had wanted to win so badly. All that effort, he thought, and for what? *Forty-sixth place.*

"We're sitting there after the game," Geary recalls in an e-mail report that he posts to CGP, "and I'm just drifting off in some kind of resignedness like a zebra that's just been dragged down by a lion and doesn't fight, doesn't yell, doesn't kick, just gets a glazy look in its eye and walks toward the light at the end of the tunnel. I feel all self-control just floating out of my body, not caring what anyone in the world thinks of me at that moment."

Tears build, and the moment begins to overwhelm him when . . . when Bob Felt sits down and launches into one of his soliloquies. "Jarred back to the zeroth astral plane," Geary writes, "I quickly gather my things and head down to the bar."

Geary's tournament diary — which runs to forty-five single-spaced pages on my printer — reveals how deeply my favorite pastime is connected to real emotions, and not just those resulting from winning or losing, but will and determination and passion and compassion and schadenfreude and humor, the whole human buffet, in fact, of hungers, disappointments, frailties, and insecurities. That may have to do with one's dedication, or it may have to do with the nature of the game itself — the positional battle, the complex geometry, the mathematical calculation, the compulsion to play again. The prominent chess journalist Frank Brady once wrote that the strategy of the game and the shifting arrangement of the pieces made chess a form of artistic expression. "It's a sad expression, though — somewhat like religious art," he wrote. "It's not very gay. If anything, it's a struggle." The inherent beauty of the game — the rhythmic dance that transpires on the board — is eclipsed by the very somberness of the pursuit.

Geary embodies that conflict. He loves the aesthetics of words — in Melbourne he dreams of finding the British word QINGHAOSU# — and plays beautifully. A few years ago, holding a rack of BEEIORW, he determined that playing off the B and an E would yield a 1 in 68 chance of drawing an A and a T that would give him a rack of AEIORTW and allow him to play, through the disconnected letters Z and O already on the board, the word WATERZOOI. It happened. He will happily detail his great plays and label them as such but then always leave room to berate himself. (His Web site, jimgeary.com, bears the slogan "Something to bore everyone.") In one game at the Worlds, he challenges a five-letter Z word, saying, "It's not in ours." Then, "a lightbulb goes off, and I say, 'Wait, it *is* in ours.' And [my opponent] adds that it's not even good in theirs." Later, after taking a long time to play LASAGNE, which has two North American anagrams (GALENAS, ANLAGES) and two British ones (ALNAGES, LAGENAS), he writes, "Another Brit must wonder how he lost to an idiot who took five minutes to find the only playable common bingo."

On the first turn of the second game in Melbourne, Jim lays down KATY*.

I start to think, "Hey, that's not a word," when I luckily remember the Cab Calloway song "She Caught the Katy" from the *Blues Brothers* soundtrack. As soon as I punch the clock, I feel sick. Probably confusing it with the British fours JUDY and MARY. It comes off, and he plays SECRETED for a double-double and I'm down 160–0. Then things really start to go bad. I lose 515–368, and am now in 96th place out of 98 after two games. Worse, my confidence is shot, as I see losing a turn on a phony four as part of some big morality play where all my weaknesses are magnified at the wrong time.

At the midpoint, Jim is 7–5, but loses three in a row, the last to a Kenyan who, late in the game, "picks his fourth S to keep his second blank from getting lonely." Now 7–8, "I'm emotionally exhausted and hoping to catch an opponent from Neptune or something, and find I'm paired with another strong American, the equally frustrated Lisa Odom. I pick well, she doesn't. So at the end of Day 2, I'm 8–8, and will not be World Champion this century."

That night, at the hotel bar, I buy Geary a few Jack & Sevens, which ease the pain. He is desperate to finish above .500, which he failed to do in 1997. On the final day, Jim splits the first six games, and needs to take the final two to wind up with more wins than losses. In the penultimate game, against an Australian woman, Jim opens with an easy bingo, PEATIER.

Things turn south immediately thereafter as I can't buy an easy rack while she gets two blank bingos, GOATIeR# and StEALED#. Worse, I completely lose my mental control. Rather than focusing on my short-term objective, I am plagued with sadness and self-pity and frustration and anger as I think about all the effort that I had put into the game over the last few years just to come up a no-op at this tourney. I've never had a mental breakdown of this order of magnitude in the middle of a tournament game before. Usually, I can correct fuzzy thinking with autosuggestion right away, but this is like a dam breaking. I lose 406–427. I say nice game, and stagger away crushed.

Jim wins his final game to pull even, Felt intrudes on his contemplative moment, and it's over. A week later, Jim writes:

I can't sleep nights. I can't stay awake days. I want to play another twenty-four games right now. I want to show the world that I know how to play this game. Two years is an awfully long time to wait to redeem yourself. I can usually hit my horizon playing medium-stakes poker tournaments in about a month. The WSC's [World Scrabble Championship's] horizon could easily be ten years. I have to make a decision. It's tough to compete with an entire world playing one version of English Scrabble [SOWPODS] while I play a different one [*OWL*].

But not playing any Scrabble at all isn't much of a choice.

After Reno and San Francisco, before the Worlds, I've had enough. The fifty-one games, the round-the-clock Scrabble scene in the tawdry casino, the homeless former Scrabble player on the corner. I'm too committed to the game and losing perspective. On the one hand, I have agreed to write this book, which requires me to be a full-time Scrabble player (I've taken a leave of absence from my job). On the other hand, if I allow the game to dominate my life, as I have, how am I any different from Matt or Marlon or G.I. Joel (other than the fact that I'm still a weak player)? They're like Bobby Fischer, who told an interviewer in 1972 that he understood that chess wasn't "work" and that he was "out of touch with real life." Fischer said, "I've thought of giving it up off and on, but I always considered: What else could I do?"

That's the trouble with games, I think: seductive as hell, but ultimately a big fat nothing. What's the point? What's the higher purpose? I can't see any, especially while losing twenty-nine out of fifty-one. Scrabble feels sad and meaningless, its role in other players' lives imbalanced and pathetic. I don't want to end up like them, obsessed with a game. So I take a break. I go to the library. I read about the history of games and dictionaries. I search for references to Scrabble in popular culture. I do anything but study or play. I tell myself I don't need the game. Like Lester Schonbrun after he moved away from New York and his game-room lifestyle, I refuse to admit that the game is important to me.

In September, a couple of months after Reno, Matt Graham invites me over to play a session. I haven't seen him since the spring. Feeling trapped in his apartment, Matt left New York impulsively and took a train to Indianapolis to visit his parents. In Indiana, he was able to forget about *SNL*, his career, and his emotional troubles. When he returned, his old girlfriend Janine helped get him work as a fill-in writer for Conan O'Brien. We play three games at his apartment. Matt pulls all six blanks, and squashes me.

A few weeks later, Marlon is the trigger to play. He calls to announce that he's on his way to New York and needs to crash at my apartment. On a brisk, sunny day on the border between summer and fall, we head to Washington Square Park. Matt arrives in a snazzy new pair of black Nikes with light blue trim and a T-shirt showing Curious George passed out next to a bottle of ether. He's in a good mood, and when another expert, Avi Moss, shows up, we play doubles, Marlon and me versus Matt and Avi, five bucks per man per game. We split six games and tie one. I love the scene, the lessons, and the escape. I've missed it.

But I'm still not itching to study or play as much as I did before Reno — until I meet Matt in the park on an October afternoon at dusk. The games players are gone except for a few dallying parkies packing up their boards. This time, Matt's wired. The Conan job has ended and there's a possibility of a staff position. But Matt is angry at the world again, recalling slights and complaining about encounters that most people would quickly forget. I haven't seen him this agitated since before he got sick, and I feed off of his emotions. I'm already a little antsy, in need of a Scrabble fix. I can't wait to play a few games against Matt's high-strung ass.

A few of us head to a diner on West 4th Street to play. But Matt is unhappy with the place. There's too much light, the ceiling is too low, there are five of us, an uneven number for games. He wants to go to a bar. So Matt and I leave. When we hit the sidewalk, he removes from his jacket a tube that once held chewable vitamins and empties out a palmful of pills, which he dumps in his mouth like cocktail nuts. He then extracts a two-liter bottle of water and drinks.

We go to the Peculier Pub on Bleecker Street, a college bar with sawdust on the floor, wooden booths covered with graffiti, and playoff baseball on the televisions. Matt is a regular. We commandeer a booth and set up shop. I win the first game, and Matt is agitated. After I play XYST for 51 points on a triple-word line that he inexplicably opened, he tosses his final rack — AAEIIT? — disgustedly onto the board. In more than twenty games we've played against each other, it is the first time I have ever beaten him.

"You ready to play for money?" Matt asks.

"Sure."

"Stakes?"

"How many points are you giving me? I'll take fifty. One and one," I say jokingly, knowing he won't play for just a dollar per game and a penny a spread point.

"Two and two," he says. "And I'll give you twenty points."

"Twenty points. Wow. That's generous. Thirty-five."

Matt wants to win, I can tell. He is ticked off after the loss and quickly downs his second beer. He has a crazy, shoot-up-a-McDonald's look in his eye, the next, familiar step in his mood cycle. After Matt builds a huge lead, bingoing with TREPHINE and MISeVENT, he stops paying attention, not tracking or even keeping score. I bingo with SALTINE and, a few turns later, after creating a hook spot with YIN which Matt, inexplicably again, doesn't block, I play DOsAGES (making AYIN) for 84 to cut the score to 375–348. Matt forgets that the Q is unplayed, and doesn't block a potential high-scoring spot. I play QAID for 34 to go out. With his tiles and the spread, I win by 20.

Now he glides from ticked to pissed. He wants to raise the stakes to five and five, which I point out is ridiculous, as he can easily win by 200 or more points, while I can't. We compromise at $3.50 and three and a half cents per point. I open with BENDY. He counters with AOUDAD, thinking I'll challenge, but instead I hook an S onto it and play JIGS for 42. He plays ETAGERE for 64. We're close when I play JIMPS* to a triple. I announce the score as 59, but after picking new tiles I realize I've made an adding mistake and recount. It should be 61, I say. Matt flips out.

"Wait a minute," he says, pausing the clock. "JIMP doesn't take an S. You announced the wrong score, and I was recounting and you flash-drew!" meaning I drew fresh tiles quickly before he could inspect the play. Once a player has removed a new tile from the bag, a challenge is no longer permitted. "I didn't even look at the word," he complains.

Now he's *really* pissed. Matt wants me to retract the play — which, I point out nicely, is ridiculous, since he failed to utter the customary "hold." (JIMP, meaning natty, is an adjective, so it can't be pluralized. I didn't remember that, and made the play honestly. Anyway, Matt sometimes flash-draws when he plays a phony, especially against weaker players, at least against me.) I offer to take it back because I don't have the confrontational instinct or the financial incentive he does. Typically, though, Matt changes his mind and accepts responsibility, but in a fuck-you sort of way. He clearly wants revenge — and he knows he has psyched me out. After I play BLANKET to a T for 36, Matt whines that I'm lucky. I'm ahead 257–203, and Matt is in danger of losing his most precious commodity: money. So he does what any self-respecting expert taking advantage of a lower-rated player would do: He plays a phony bingo, STROVEnT* for 92. I hold the play but am too intimidated by Matt's mass-murderer mien to challenge. Two turns later he plays ACRIDEST for 89. (It's good.) Matt wins 501–353.

Matt thumps me in a fourth game, but by now I don't care. He has drunk five bottles of Anchor Steam beer, which doesn't seem to impair his ability to anagram and doesn't diminish my satisfaction over having beaten him twice after two years of steady drubbings. I happily hand over the $10 he's won. I got what I came for: games. And I got something I didn't anticipate, too. I walk out into an autumn rain knowing that I need this game, and there's nothing I can do to make that feeling disappear.

The compulsion to play, the game's unavoidable lure, the testosterone rush of beating (and provoking) Matt — it all rekindles my competitive fire. Melbourne supplies inspiration of a different sort. I am glad to be there without having to face the pressure of tournament play. Just observing lets me enjoy the camaraderie and good sportsmanship, the artistic beauty of the performances, the high-stakes tension, and the Berlitz-class hallway banter. The game seems to make emotional sense. For the first time, I feel secure in my decision to live in Scrabble's world.

After five months off, it's time to rejoin the tournament scene. I pick up Matt and his three duffel bags — one for clothes, one for Scrabble paraphernalia, and one for his dozens of bottles of vitamins and smart drugs, plus a teddy bear and a Koosh ball — and we're off on a three-hour road trip to Bird-in-Hand, Pennsylvania, in the heart of Amish country.

Several hours from any big city, Bird-in-Hand seems an odd place for a Scrabble tournament. But then most Scrabble players aren't like me. They come to see friends, to sightsee, and to shop, and Bird-in-Hand, with its arts and crafts stores and black-clad locals driving horses and buggies, always attracts a big field. To me, the tournament venues are all the same: Danbury, Chicago, Long Island, Hartford, Bird-in-Hand — one giant hotel conference room that exists solely so I can have a place to play this game. I'm on the road for rating points, money, and glory. I especially need the points: After Reno, my rating tumbled to 1416 from 1461.

Joe Edley has sent me a fresh batch of forty-two hundred seven-letter words, which I cut into neat stacks and study daily. From the Web, I download LeXpert, a word study program that allows users to create word lists of any permutation imaginable and quiz themselves using video flash cards. I print out all of the fours, and the top seventy-five hundred high-probability sevens — duplicating the cards, but the sheets feel easier to manage. John Williams reminds me of something he told me when I started playing: "It's easy to get pretty good pretty quickly by learning a few tricks and playing a lot. Then you hit a wall — unless you start devoting yourself to this dubious proposition."

The wall analogy is a good one. The term usually refers to the point between mile eighteen and twenty-five of a marathon, where a runner's muscles shut down because of a lack of glycogen. In other pursuits, it's come to mean the dividing line between proficiency and mastery, that indefinable point at which the accumulation of skill or knowledge stops being easy and requires deliberate, consistent effort. I probably hit my Scrabble wall at Reno. I had left the blue-hairs behind. But to reach the next level of competence, I had to start working diligently to break through the wall.

The week before Bird-in-Hand, I dispatched three experts at the club and lost to a fourth on the penultimate play. I called Joe Edley for a pep talk. I vowed to concentrate, play smartly, be sensible, and breathe deeply. Ten wins, I said aloud in the car before picking up Matt. Ten out of twelve. Ambitious, but doable. Nine would be okay. Eight wins is two out of three — a reasonable expectation. We leave New York in plenty of time, I figure, for a leisurely dinner and some downtime before play.

Five hours later, I'm standing in a shot-and-a-beer bar straight out of *The Deer Hunter* — pool tables, mounted antlers, John Deere caps — searching for Route 340. It's 8:15 and we're at least ten miles from the hotel. A guy wearing hunting fatigues points us in the right direction, and we pull into the hotel at exactly 8:30, when Game 1 is to start. Dinner consists of a Clif Bar, a banana, a clementine, and a handful of raisins wolfed down in the car.

Now I face three games on too little sustenance and the residual anxiety of tardiness. I don't have time to compose myself, to take some deep breaths, to prepare mentally, the way Edley insists. I rush into the playing room, which I notice immediately has an unnervingly low ceiling, too-narrow tables, and glary, fluorescent lighting. I set up my board, and within two minutes I'm shaking the tile bag.

I'm overcome by uncertainty and ill-preparedness, an all-too-familiar sensation undiminished by my tournament hiatus. The first seven tiles out of the bag and onto my rack are BDOPRRR. When I drop down BRR for 10 points, some of the panic wanes, like a junkie who relaxes when the heroin begins coursing through his veins. I hang onto the third R to turn BRR into BRRR (even colder!). My opponent plays BOUND vertically from my B. I now hold ADEOPTR. Before even locating the possible seven-letter words (ADOPTER, READOPT), my brain instructs my hands to surround her N with my royal blue plastic tiles: PRONATED. The R and the D both strike double-word-score squares.

"Ninety-four," I say, smacking my clock.

My mood shifts. I'm one with the board now. I win the game, 464–294. I eat more food, but it doesn't help my ability to pick tiles; I don't see a blank or an S in Game 2, and write off the loss to the tile gods. An early blunder in Game 3 (missing the easy bingo EN-RAGES) leaves me questioning my ability anew, but I recover (playing SERGEANT on the following turn). Then my Scrabble persona changes, I think maybe forever.

On my next turn, I dump off a W and a Z, making WIZ and saving ADHS?. Out of the bag come an I and a second S. A duplicate letter, even an S, is mathematically considered a hindrance, and when I see it I assume I'll have to wait a turn to bingo. But before the idea settles — before even touching the tiles, before even considering the seven-letter bingo possibilities (and, it turns out, there are two, SANDHIS and SHAIRDS, neither of which I know) — for reasons I cannot begin to fathom, I think: I hope he puts down an I.

From my brain to my opponent's ears, he drops down the vowel-dump INIA in a wide-open quadrant of the board. What occurs next is an incomprehensible snap of recognition, an inexplicable firing of synapses, the pathways of my brain aligning for a moment in happy synchronicity to allow the retrieval of information whose source I will never be able to pinpoint. I put down the D. Then the A. Then an S. Then the H. My fingers dance over the existing I. Then the blank. Then my I. Then the other S.

"Seventy-four," I announce. "The blank is a K."

The satisfaction is not so much recognizing the word, or even knowing its meaning — a dashiki is an African tunic — but in feeling like a player who spots the uncommon word, makes the creative move, whose brain snaps to attention at the precise moment, unlocks the file drawer containing the solution to the puzzle at hand. I still don't understand anagramming and memory. I still don't feel prepared to ask the deepest questions of the masters. For now, I'm satisfied with knowing that DASHIkIS happens. I roll to a 387–277 win. Now I'm starting to believe.

Marlon has a new hairdo. He's letting it grow out. He's considering dreadlocks.

"You're all nappy," I say as we exchange a quick soul handshake and a hug in the expert playing room.

"Nappy," Marlon bellows, "is happy."

In recent months, Marlon had occupied himself with his harassment lawsuit against the Giant supermarket chain and, naturally, with word study. Still living at home with his mother, he has ruled out conventional jobs. He is determined to expose America for its racism and classism. He's been reading John Henrik Clarke's *Africans at the Crossroads: Notes on an African World Revolution* and begun writing.

"I'm gonna have two books written before you finish this one," Marlon tells me. "One of them, you know what it's going to be because you know me: America with three Ks." The other book, Marlon says, will be about the same subject — our unjust nation,

AmeriKKKa — but written in a street voice. "I might have to do one in a pen name because they ain't gonna believe it came from the same person," he says.

If Marlon seems more dedicated to his cause, he has reason. A few weeks earlier, he tells me, he was harassed by a cop while sitting on a train en route to a Scrabble tournament outside Baltimore. Marlon was thinking about the previous night's games when a transit officer "comes up to me and says something. I probably didn't respond to him quick enough. He probably thought I was a drug dealer and could be high."

"White guy?" I ask.

"Oh, yeah. It progressed probably because of the way I answered him. I'm ticked off. I probably said, 'What?' or 'What you say?' It immediately gave him something to jump on. It gave him even more reason to be a jerk."

Marlon says the cop took his identification and said they were getting off the train to check Marlon's record. It probably didn't help matters when Marlon said, "If I had a record would I be going to a Scrabble tournament?" County police joined the transit cop when the train pulled into the next station, and they made Marlon wait while they conducted the background check. When it came up clean, "they apologize profusely," Marlon says. "And then they talk about good luck in the tournament." Marlon lost five out of six games.

The story is vintage Marlon: Victimized by his skin color, he provokes authority rather than walking away. I admire Marlon's convictions, but I also wonder whether they don't hurt him. In the Giant case, he could have simply showed the clerk his ID and bought his cigarettes rather than protesting. And he could have accepted the company's $50,000 settlement offer. He didn't. Marlon had sued for $250,000, and thought he could win a bundle at a trial in front of a predominantly African-American jury. It was about principle, and about his self-image. Matt noted that Marlon's rejecting more cash than he had made in a year ran true to character. "The man who turns down bingos," Matt said, referring to Marlon's unorthodox belief in passing up bingos in some situations. Marlon once threw a blank back in the bag when he held both of them.

"I had what I thought was a good jury," Marlon told me after the trial. "I had six women — five of us and one of y'all." But the trial in the Circuit Court of Baltimore City didn't go well. Seven people testified. The defense witnesses said Marlon began swearing immediately after the salesclerk asked to see his ID. Marlon said he didn't. The defense witnesses said Marlon cursed again when he was asked to leave the store. Marlon said he didn't. They said Marlon pushed a security guard with both hands before he was wrestled to the ground and handcuffed. Marlon said he pushed only the guard's hand away after the guard touched him.

"There were so many people who came in and testified that it happened. We had absolutely no witnesses but Marlon," Marlon's lawyer told me. But Marlon blamed the lawyer for missing inconsistencies in the testimony. "One guy had me pushing the guard what would have been ten feet," Marlon said. "Another had me pushing him one foot. Another lady had me pushing him and *me* going back ten feet."

Marlon, I think, would make an excellent lawyer.

The jury awarded Marlon $10,000. "I thought it was a miracle I won the case," said his lawyer, who received 40 percent of the award. With his $6,000, Marlon bought a computer. He says it's all he wanted. But the system, as usual, let him down. The lawyers let him down. The jury let him down. The criminal justice bureaucracy let him down.

"This was a wake up call for me," Marlon wrote in one of his notebooks after the trial. "To remind me of how things are. This was a slap in the face: Wake up and handle your business."

After the first three rounds at Bird-in-Hand, players gather in the expert room at midnight for a champagne-and-chocolate-cake reception. A few people set up boards to extend the Scrabble evening into morning. Others gather round the chart listing the expert division standings. (Matt won his first three games.) Others renew acquaintances, make plans to check out the Amish (or at least their tchotchkes), and relate their astounding plays, awful racks, and impossible blunders.

"Yo, Marlon, I made a play for you tonight," I say.

"What's that?"

"DASHIKIS."

He immediately gives me a soul handshake and one of his deep, appreciative laughs. "That's good!" he says. "That's *damn* good! How you know that word?"

I'm starting to notice that the intensity of Marlon's cause is inversely proportional to his performance in Scrabble. The angrier he gets, the worse he plays. While I was in Australia, Marlon drove to a series of Florida tournaments with the Baltimore expert Gordon Shapiro, a round, retired trucker with W. C. Fields's face and Archie Bunker's sensibilities. In three tournaments, against relatively weak competition, Marlon went 7–5, 8–4, and a horrifying 6–10. His rating plummeted to 1732 — lower than his inaugural rating. Worse, the NSA received complaints about Marlon's behavior — cursing during games, storming out of the playing room, shouting in the hallway — and was considering taking action against him. "It's gotten to be too much," a Scrabble official tells me.

The mathematics of Scrabble — of life, really — dictate that, over time, in randomly occurring phenomena, like choosing seven tiles from a bag of one hundred, luck tends to even out. Edley has taught me to respect probability, never to complain about my tiles, to believe that I can control even the tiles I pick. But Marlon doesn't believe in probability. He believes only that his luck sucks, and that he is still better than just about every player out there. "There are less than ten people, RIGHT NOW, I would not play" for $1,000, Marlon posted on CGP. In Bird-in-Hand, he puts the number at seven, including Edley, Matt, Ron Tiekert, Brian Cappelletto, and Samson Okasagah, a Nigerian expert now living in Washington, D.C.

"Adam Logan?" I say, mentioning the red-bearded mathematician and 1996 Nationals champion.

"Yes." Marlon would play him.

"Lester?"

"Yes. He's old."

"Wapnick? Sherman?"

"Deh-fu-nit-ly."

On Saturday afternoon, after the seventh game of the tournament, Matt rushes to find me in the intermediate playing room, which is on the opposite side of the hotel swimming pool from the experts' room.

"Marlon's erupting," he says.

I've just played OFFBEaTS to a triple-word score for 104 points late in a game. Displaying classic Scrabble behavior, I'm more interested in showing off my brilliant play than in hearing about Marlon.

I get Matt to admire the play, then I cross the pool for an update. Marlon has been drawing bad tiles and losing, and letting everyone know about it. His usual chorus of "God-*damn*" and "This is ree-*dick*-uh-luss!" has been punctuated by profanities. He's storming out of the playing room during games. He berated the New York expert Lynn Cushman for playing AZIDO in a spot permitting a high-scoring counterplay when, in Marlon's estimation, she should have played the Z more conservatively.

"Well, Marlon, when you draw these tiles you can play them the way you want," Lynn told him, before he raced out of the playing room one more time. "He's behaving like an eight-year-old asshole," Matt Hopkins, a skullcap-wearing Philadelphia player who's helping to run the tournament, tells me in the hallway. "If it was my tournament, he'd be out the door."

When I spot Marlon before Game 8, he is frowning deeply and staring sullenly into the void. He looks like a teenager in after-school detention.

"Stupid shit keep happening to me," he tells me later. "I'm losing in ways not even fucking imaginable." He admits to acting up, especially against Lynn, but he's in no mood to apologize. She made a dumb play, he says, and then benefited a turn later.

"I went ballistic," Marlon says. "Make a totally fucked-up play and get rewarded for it. I told everybody to kiss my ass."

I'm staring at EEGLNS?.

Instantly, I think FEELINGS. Then the song "Feelings" comes into my head and I can't get it out before it's stuck on one of those endless loops, distracting me during a close game. "Nothing more than FEELINGS," it screams, and I can't even play the word, or any other bingo, on the tightly packed board. I open things up with GLENS to a triple-word score, saving E? ("... trying to forget my...."), and draw BFFOT, and the song is *still* there ("... FEELINGS of love ...."). I make my (brilliant) play OFFBEaTS ("... wo, wo, wo, ..."), draw a challenge, pull the X and the second blank, slap down PaX for 55 ("... again in my heart ..."), and wind up winning 454–289.

I do the math: From the time "Feelings" began its torturous soundtrack, I outscored my opponent 237 to 63. I never realized how much I loved that song.

There are twenty-six players in the second division (of three) at Bird-in-Hand, and I'm in the middle of the pack. I know a handful of the players from previous tournaments, but none scares me. In fact, I walked into the Eagle Room (who names hotel conference rooms?) a little full of myself. The two weeks in Australia hobnobbing with the stars, a string of victories at the club and in the park, even my first two wins over Matt in the bar — I think I'm prime time. I've long forgotten my Scrabble malaise. No one rated under 1700 intimidates me (much), whereas just a few months ago I was awed by the number next to a player's name.

Plus, the simple act of engaging in regular word study has boosted my confidence; I'd been through all of the fours twice in a week, solving the anagrams for each, highlighting in yellow the words I miss, and then reviewing those. Once I got over the panic owing to hunger and lateness, I surveyed the room — dingy compared with the Worlds, with its wide, cloth-covered tables adorned with the little flags — and thought, "You're *not* going to lose *here*. You're a favorite. Now go prove it."

On Saturday morning, I down a banana and a Clif Bar and run three miles though the manure-scented Amish country air. I win the day's first two games to improve to 4–1. I drop a squeaker. I rebound with the FEELINGS game and take the final game of the day, as well, getting away with a famous phony, UNTIMED*. At 6–2, I'm tied for the best record, walking on manure-scented air.

Over dinner with Matt down the road at the Intercourse Village Restaurant — pork chops and applesauce for me, crab cakes for Matt, the check for me — we talk about Marlon's outbursts, and how they hurt his game and his reputation. Matt suddenly is the rational member of my little band of Scrabblers. He swallows a plastic container's worth of pills.

"It's just a self-perpetuating cycle that makes him not get better at what he wants to be good at," Matt says. "There's a good amount of talent there. That's not what the problem is."

The problem is self-control, about blaming luck, about not taking responsibility for his game. "I've talked to him about it. But it doesn't seem to help. He's let himself down as a player, and he doesn't put the best face on himself. It's too bad. He's got so many good qualities no one knows about." Matt describes Marlon with terms I've never heard him use before to describe a friend — intelligence, warmth, depth of humor — and I recall that Marlon was one of the few people Matt turned to when he was sick.

I point out that the problem may not be Marlon's letters but Marlon's weltanschauung.

"Surely he doesn't think The Man is fixing the tiles," Matt says.

He doesn't have to think it's racial, I say.

"Right. It's just that he's getting fucked over."

The next morning, I lose Game 9 with a bad blunder, playing a phony (REAIRING*) when patience would have revealed an actual word (GRAINIER). I'm 6–3 and starting to think negatively. I've blown tournaments with late droughts before, and every time, I'm convinced, it's been because of my attitude. I repeat my mantra: I can win, I can win, I can win.

Despite pulling only one of the four S's, I draw well enough to win Game 10 against Ann Mirabito, a direct-marketing executive who aspires to experthood. Ann is curious, analytical, socialized, and sportsmanlike — a rare Scrabble grand slam. So I'm not disappointed when we're paired again in Game 11, especially since I have the psychological upper hand.

I make a bad play on the second turn of the game — eschewing GOLDEST, about which I'm unsure — but quickly counter with a phony, VALENTS*, which Ann lets go by, thinking, like me, that it has to be a plausible variation of COVALENT. (LEVANTS, a verb meaning to avoid a debt, is the real word in that mix of letters.) On the next turn, I unhesitatingly plunk down LUNCHER for 81 points. Ann challenges.

"The play is acceptable," Charlene, the word judge, announces.

I wasn't sure of the word, but figured it made too much sense not to be good — to lunch is a verb; ergo, one who lunches is a luncher. It's not a risky move of the kind I like to think I only used to make, but a smart, logical, grounded decision. I draw EIIJKNT and stare at my rack, and the board, for nearly two minutes. I'm ahead by 204–93, cruising to an easy victory. I could play it safe with JEU for 30 points (leaving the ugly IIKNT) or take a chance with a creative play: INKJET, for 34.

I weigh the options. I wonder whether INKJET has made it into our word source; many computer-related terms (LAN*, INTERNET#) haven't. Then I weigh the risks. If it's good, and Ann challenges, I'll pile up spread points. If it's not, I'll still hold a commanding lead. So I play it. Ann challenges. Charlene returns to the table and thumbs through the *OWL*.

"I know INKJET isn't a word in WordPerfect's spell-checker," Ann says. Given the score, and her general perky demeanor, I'm not offended by the coffeehousing.

"The play is acceptable," Charlene says, her voice rising with surprise or respect or both.

"Ugh!" Ann sighs, slumping over. I'm up 238–93. I play HAJI for 40. Ann exchanges. I lay down HERTZ for 34. I've been able to make four consecutive plays and built a 312–93 lead. Later, Ann opens up a bingo lane, allowing me to add insult to injury. Down comes VIRTUeS for 66.

Final score: 487–266.

I take a deep breath. I realize that I am guaranteed to finish first or second in the tournament.

No one has kissed Marlon's ass, but he isn't thrown out of the tournament either. By Saturday night, Marlon had calmed down, despite his 3–5 record, and even apologized for his outbursts. "My behavior was deplorable," he says as we sit in the expert room, where a half-dozen games of Scrabble, Anagrams, and Boggle are in progress. When I suggest that he might be at risk of getting suspended or sanctioned by the National Scrabble Association, Marlon scoffs. "They can't kick my ass out of tournaments. My behavior was bad, but puh-*leeze*."

I think Marlon has been playing too much, and doing too little of anything else. He's like a gambler who can't refuse another hand even though he's borrowing money to get in the game.

The man in full emerges: Marlon as victim, Marlon as unlucky,

Marlon as oppressed — by the cops, by employers, by The Man, by the tile gods themselves. "You wouldn't understand," Marlon often says, leaving off the first half of the phrase ("It's a black thing"), whether he's talking about drawing a W and a U in tandem or fewer than half of the blanks or a string of consonants befitting a Bosnian city. But I do understand: Marlon needs to stand out more than he needs to win.

"That's it," Marlon tells me. "The Nationals is gonna be my last tournament."

I write down his words in my notebook, but I don't believe them for an instant.

I'm standing in the hotel parking lot. A group of Amish boys, no older than ten, walk by in straw hats, black pants, and white shirts, and I imagine how I would explain to them what I'm experiencing right now: how I'm about to play a big Scrabble game, how I'm eating a Snickers bar for energy, how I'm standing here alone, breathing deeply the malodorous air, because I need to focus on the game, to minimize distractions, to get away from the white-noise chitchat that fills the playing rooms between rounds.

Could I make them understand why this tournament is important to me? Why the act of playing a single round of a mass-produced board game against a middle-aged woman will affect my mood and self-esteem for days to come? Could I explain the player I walked past in the hotel parking lot this morning, mumbling to himself, who didn't look up, who looked mentally lost? Could I explain how I can relate to that sort of behavior, how this game has made the socially bizarre commonplace?

I visit the expert room for an update on Matt (he has lost two of three today, dropping out of contention) and to update my friends on where I stand. Marlon has chilled out enough to congratulate me on being in first place — I'm tied with one other player at 8–3, but my spread of +753 is more than 300 points greater than anyone else's in the division, which is how I know I'll finish either first or second. "Now go *do* it!" Marlon barks at me, slapping my hand.

My opponent is the other 8–3 player, Wendy Littman, a fellow Brooklynite who is in a wheelchair with multiple sclerosis. Wendy handed me one of my losses. She's a fine player, as her record and her 1506 rating would indicate. But nothing can faze me now. I feel confident, tough, centered. Like Joe Edley at the 1980 Nationals, I have this weird feeling that I'm going to win. The game is secondary; I already know the outcome.

So I play self-assuredly. Wendy opens with HARES, leaving an obvious front hook with an S. I casually lay down BASINAL, take my 71 points, and hope she challenges. She doesn't, and rebounds with the double-double SNEAKED for 48. I play NIXE and OOZY and go ahead 171–126 and feel as if I can't lose.

I doubt Wendy feels any pressure. She's played hundreds of games, won a few tournaments, and probably doesn't care much whether her rating goes up or down or even whether she wins the $250 first prize or the $125 for second. She's just playing tiles, I know. She doesn't take much time on her moves, doesn't get anguished. And why should she? It's just a game.

So when she plays VOLVO* for 33, I don't bother challenging because, I think, she doesn't seem like the type to play phonies. (VULVA, VOLVA, VOLVOX, VOLVATE, VOLVULI, but no VOLVO*.) Wendy chips away at my lead, and after I exchange late in the game with three I's and two R's on my rack, she moves ahead. Neither blank is on the board, and I start to worry. I retake the lead, and pull a blank. I get away with a phony three. The bag is empty. Wendy plays JILT to tie the game at 341–341.

I hold DTUU? and see DUSTUP, but no open P or S to make it work. I determine that she holds II?, and breathe easier. I've got less than thirty seconds on my clock and no time for analysis. I play DUsT for 13 points, leaving myself a U. Panic! There's no place to play the U! But then I see two N's a space apart (NUN) and another orphan N (NU) and relax. I realize I can't lose, and I don't. Final score: 354–347.

Wendy shakes my hand, and other players gather to offer congratulations. I'm trembling from stress and satisfaction. My final record is 9–3, +760. I played smartly. I didn't take foolish risks. I crushed the field on spread. I never thought I would lose — except for that fleeting moment late in the final game. Craving the affirmation of my peers, I head over to the expert room. Dominic Grillo, the young, muttonchopped, marathon-running engineer from New

Jersey, praises my word knowledge, saying, "This guy's playing words I don't even know." My club friends — Sally Ricketts and Lynn Cushman and G.I. Joel's brother, Larry — are pleased. Marlon bear-hugs me. Matt shakes my hand. The two of them may be coming unhinged, affecting both their lives and their Scrabble, but I'm finally discovering my game.

At the awards ceremony, the division director introduces me by saying, "He gave everybody problems throughout the tournament," and I smile at this high praise. I accept my check and a sixteen-inch-high trophy with Nike, the winged goddess of victory, holding a torch aloft on a purple stand. The inscription reads SCRABBLE TOURNAMENT 1999 FIRST PLACE INTERMEDIATE BIRD-IN-HAND, PA. I crouch next to Wendy for a photo.

This is so cool. I haven't won a trophy in twenty years.

I call Joe Edley in hopes of collecting more kudos. But first I give him credit. I had talked to Edley the day before Bird-in-Hand just as I had when I won my first tournament six months ago. He laughs and asks me how I did it. I credit his tips on concentration, focus, patience, and stamina.

"Sounds to me like you're ready for Division 2." For a second, I stop breathing. Classic Edley, I think, the Most Hated Man in Scrabble at his condescending finest. This *was* Division 2, Joe, I want to say, and I won it, and by now haven't I established myself as a legitimate intermediate player — not that that means very much to you elitist experts? Sensing my jaw lying on the floor, though, Joe recovers. "To win it," he says.

I realize that he means the Nationals next summer in Providence. And he's serious. There will be six divisions at the event. The ratings brackets are set at 1900 and up for Division 1, 1700 to 1899 for Division 2, and 1500 to 1699 for Division 3. Players will be able to play up one full division. By then, I'll surely be well above 1500, if not 1600, so I'll be able to move into Division 2, where not a few experts will camp out.

In Bird-in-Hand, Matt joked that I was the George Plimpton of Scrabble. Well, now I'm thinking that I'm not wearing the number 0, the way Plimpton did when he played quarterback for the Detroit Lions. No one's giving *me* a free ride, letting me take a few snaps with the big boys. I'm clawing my way up — humiliating myself in after-hours games against higher-rated players, struggling to find anagrams that Matt tosses my way, failing to keep pace with the logological banter when the boys gather. I see myself less as George Plimpton than as an athlete who has to work harder to compensate for limited natural talent.

Now I have my goal: Win Providence.

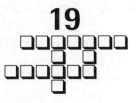

19

1501

O N THE THURSDAY after my triumph at Bird-in-Hand, I arrive at the club for the regular weekly session and hand G.I. Joel the $11 fee.

"How are things?" I ask.

"The same," Joel says, checking off my name on the club master list and writing it and my old rating on an orange slip on which I will record the evening's results.

"Good," I reply. "I guess."

"Not if you're me."

I smile and take a couple of steps into the room.

"Oh, Stefan?" Joel says.

"Yeah?"

"Way to go."

At tournaments, I always feel as if I'm playing for Joel, as if he's a coach who lives for his team, or a kid in a hospital bed for whom I've promised to hit a home run. Tournament results are posted on CGP, so club members know that I was a winner, and inside the playing room I'm greeted with everything but ticker tape. "Kickin' some tush!" Jeremy Frank says, and slaps me on the back. "Way to go, kid!" Sal Piro gushes. Even the petulant Mark Berg offers congratulations.

In the second game of the evening, against a weak opponent, I open with a deliberate phony, MEAOW*. On the next turn, she takes the bait, pluralizing the fake word, and I challenge that off of the board and gain a turn. It's a devious tactic that requires you to have more knowledge than your opponent. It's also praiseworthy. At the next table, one of the old-timers watches the sequence. "You've become one of us," she says.

During a game, there is precious little time to perform the complex calculus involved in making a play: assessing the seven letters on your rack, analyzing the state of the board, determining the possible moves, and deciding which among them maximizes your chances of winning and minimizes opportunities for your opponent. Instinct rules, but in this case instinct is acquired, the product of hundreds of hours of play and study. Even as transparent a ploy as playing a deliberate phony to lure your opponent into tacking an S onto it is a product of that learning.

Scrabble theory grew up in the early 1990s. The computer program Maven was accepted as a force in deconstructing the game. The newsletters *Medleys* and *Rack Your Brain* laid new mathematical and strategic roads. They were deep geek. *Rack Your Brain* devoted an entire issue, ten pages, to analyzing a 5-point endgame play. There was even a Scrabble humor 'zine, *Moxbib,* named after a word coined by Joel Wapnick to denote a ridiculously absurd phony. (*Moxbib* included features such as a list of the two-letter combinations *not* found in the *OSPD* and a TV guide with shows like *Scrabble, She Wrote* and *700 Club,* on which two players "relive their 700-point games of a decade ago.")

Maven was the key to theoretical study. It asked which was more powerful: the brain, with its intuitive muscle but chaotic operation, or the computer program, with its orderly function but no intuition. Of course it wasn't a new question. Games have been considered an ideal model for studying artificial intelligence since the late 1940s, when the first paper on programming a computer to play chess was written by a researcher at Bell Telephone Laboratories in New Jersey. Early chess move analyzers — with names like Turochamp and Machiavelli — simulated the play of a computer one move ahead, or one ply, by attaching scores to each possible position and making a move based on the best possible score. Later, a program called SOMA attached material values to each piece — the queen 9 points, rooks 5, knights and bishops 3, pawns 1. SOMA measured mobility based on which squares were being attacked, and created values for exchange sequences. Initially, computers didn't do the actual work; the scientists performed the calculations, known as simulations, by hand.

In 1983, during a summer internship at IBM's research center in Yorktown Heights, New York, later the home of the famous Deep Blue chess program, a Harvard undergraduate named Brian Sheppard came across an article about a Scrabble computer program in a journal on artificial intelligence. The article said the program averaged 19 points per turn. Sheppard considered himself a terrible Scrabble player, but he felt he could do better than that; he had heard that experts averaged well over 20 points. That summer, he wrote a simple program and typed in about twenty-five thousand words from the *OSPD* — every word of five or fewer letters plus the J, Q, X, and Z words. The program averaged about 23 points per move. Brian went back to school.

Three years later, bored with his job, Sheppard picked up the Scrabble program again. This time, he manually entered every *OSPD* word into the program. With little built-in strategy, the revised program averaged 30 points per turn. Sheppard named the program Maven after a computer he once had worked on, only later learning that the word itself meant "expert."

To make Maven play smarter, Sheppard needed an "evaluator" so the computer could make informed decisions, rather than just playing words for the highest possible score, which had resulted in the program sticking itself with terrible leaves. Sheppard had the computer play thousands of games against itself and he recorded the results, giving the letters point values, as the chess programs did. For instance, Sheppard kept track of how many extra points the program scored when it kept an S, and that became the value of the S: +8 points. An E was worth +4 points, a blank +25, the Q −13. Two I's on a rack was −10, while UU was −12. Sheppard rated one combination, QU, which turned out to be neutral. He assigned a negative value to opening a triple-word-score line, to prevent the computer from doing that willy-nilly. And he assigned values based on the balance between vowels and consonants left on the rack.

"I figured that on each turn three things change," Sheppard tells me when I call him. "You score points, you change the tiles on your rack, and you change position." So, in making a play, Maven determined that the value of a move equaled the score of the play plus the value of the rack leave plus the board position. The board was neutral in almost all circumstances because it was a resource shared by both players. Maven computed a value for each possible play in a turn and picked the best one.

Then Sheppard got in touch with two Scrabble experts in Boston, who coincidentally had been testing another computer program. Sheppard invited them to play Maven. "It absolutely kicked their butts," he says. Maven wasn't perfect — it screwed up endgames, it had dictionary glitches, it didn't assess positions optimally, and it was often needlessly offensive. But Sheppard reasoned it was ready to take on the pros. Another Boston expert was testing his program in a tournament and invited Maven to enter, too. Against the likes of Joe Edley and Bob Felt, Maven finished with an 8–2 record, good for second place.

Though he had never played seriously — he knew so little about Scrabble that in writing his code he called racks "trays" — Sheppard had developed a program that could beat the very best. And in the process he disproved much of the conventional wisdom about the game. By letting the computer play itself, Sheppard determined that it wasn't worth sacrificing points to avoid placing a vowel next to a double-letter-score square to prevent a big comeback play. The notion of tile turnover — moving as many tiles as possible to shoot for the blanks and S's — also proved mathematically insupportable; turning over more tiles encouraged the computer to keep more *bad* tiles, hurting its longer-run chances. General theory held that opening the board was bad because it gave the opponent first crack at new bingo lines; Maven's play determined there was no penalty for openness, except on the triple-word-score lines.

Sheppard perfected the program's dictionary so Maven wouldn't play phonies or challenge good words. He improved its ability to play endgames so it could block plays and not get stuck with tiles. Then he met Ron Tiekert, who told him about a test he had done involving a single rack of tiles.

At the time, the mid-1980s, only a few top players were combining strategy and mathematics. Tiekert, for instance, had tried to figure out whether A or I was the "better" letter. Starting with an A he drew six additional tiles and made a play. He returned all seven tiles to the bag, removed an I, and drew six tiles to go with it. Tiekert repeated the test over and over to see which yielded a higher score or fruitful leave most often. He did the same thing with a few two-tile combinations, and then applied the same logic to full racks. He wanted to figure out the best play to open a game.

Opening-rack analysis was pure, uncomplicated by board position or score. One of Tiekert's racks intrigued him: AAADERW. There were three obvious plays — AWARD, AWARE, and WARED, scoring from 18 to 26 points. But Ron had a hunch that AWA (Scottish for away) was the right move. It went completely against conventional wisdom. AWA scored just 12 points, and it moved two fewer tiles than the other choices, so by the popular thinking of the time it had to be a loser. But Ron realized that its leave of ADER was likely to produce a bingo on the next turn or two. Also, AWA didn't allow one's opponent access to double-word-score squares, and it couldn't be made plural with an S as AWARD could.

Ron had heard about backgammon experts who would spend hours replaying the same position to determine the "right" move. Ron figured such a test would work in Scrabble. At a table in his room in the Commander, the SRO where he lived, Ron pulled AAADERW from the bag. First he placed AWA on the board. Then he drew a rack of tiles for a mythical opponent and made the best play, recording the score. Then he replenished his own rack with three letters and made the best play, recording that score. Next, he placed AWARD on the board. He took the same rack he already had pulled for his opponent and made the best play. Then he drew two more tiles to go along with the three he had drawn to refill his rack after AWA and made the best play. He did the same thing with AWARE. At the end of the three turns, he added up the scores, giving bonus points based on the quality of the leaves.

Ron repeated the exercise one hundred times and totaled the results. Just as he suspected, AWA resulted in the highest average score after three turns. That didn't mean that AWA was guaranteed to produce a victory. It simply indicated which move was better from a probabilistic perspective. Ron submitted the rack for discussion in an expert newsletter and waited to see the response. No one else picked AWA, and most didn't even mention it as a possibility.

If a computer could be harnessed to perform such a test, Ron surmised, it would help players better understand their decisions. So when Ron met Sheppard, he told him about his manual test and suggested that Maven tackle such problems. Sheppard wrote a program that ran a thousand trials of each rack position, and it verified Ron's finding that AWA was the superior play. Sheppard added the "simulation" function, or "sim," to Maven.

By the early nineties, more and more top experts were relying on Maven. It helped them to see when and where they made mistakes. "Everybody has leakage," Charlie Carroll, a Minnesota computer programmer and a top player at the time, tells me. "Where are you losing points? Are you missing bingos? Are you missing overlaps? Is it in the endgame? This was the perfect tool." Joe Edley — who was contemptuous after losing to Maven in the program's tournament debut — eventually required that every game analyzed in the National Scrabble Association newsletter be checked against the program. (Hasbro eventually hired Sheppard and bought Maven to create a Scrabble CD-ROM, which is considered stronger than any human player; it beat Matt and G.I. Joel six games to three in a match arranged by *The New York Times Magazine* in 1998 for a story on Scrabble's fiftieth anniversary.)

Brian Sheppard and *Medleys* editor Nick Ballard began pushing mathematical theories. Their main contention was that Maven's tile values could be considered not only by a computer but a player over the board. Maven ranked the tiles from best to worst, like so: blank, S, E, X, Z, R, A, H, N, C, D, M, T, I, J, K, L, P, O, Y, F, B, G, W, U, V, Q. Scrabble is a zero-sum game, Ballard and Sheppard theorized, with the value of the hundred tiles totaling zero. Players could perform running calculations of the value of plays and of the bag during a game. The long-term goal was to give *everything* a numerical value so that evaluating candidate moves would become mechanical, requiring players just to add up a bunch of numbers.

Some experts scoffed, others marveled. But once Maven began simulating plays for them using the tile values, lightbulbs clicked on. Not only was there computer analysis to back up moves, but Maven could help answer questions. What letters were better to keep or trade? At which point in the game was creating board volatility best? What was the cost of particular plays and counterplays? "It was a puzzle," Carroll says. "It was different than chess, which has been analyzed to death for hundreds of years. You got to figure out stuff that no one had ever figured out before."

There are few theoretical breakthroughs anymore. The Scrabble debate has migrated on-line to CGP, which, like any chat room, is polluted by sniping, bad jokes, self-aggrandizing commentary, and inconsequential banter; I automatically delete three-quarters of the posts. But when board positions are posted, the quality improves. Computers are consulted to conduct simulations consisting of thousands of trials, known as iterations. Some players love sims, a few dismiss them as irrelevant; Marlon says either you win a game or you don't — every game is different — and a sim doesn't influence that. Too many players, especially the programmers, he says, consider Maven's judgments to be gospel. "Sim is doo-doo," Marlon says.

But sims reveal not whether a play wins or loses a *specific* game but whether the play yields a higher probability of winning over all other moves. "Humans can't do sixty-five hundred iterations in a twenty-five-minute game, so functionally you have to go with your intuition," Bob Felt says. "At end, intuition is distilled experience, and simulation provides reams of experience. The point of doing simulations is not to find out what play you should have played, but to change your thinking so you are more likely to make the play you should make in the future."

So while I gape at the tileheads, I also try to think more like them. In a tournament game, I draw an opening rack of CEEGPP?. I play PEP. Afterward, I wonder whether PEP was best and ask G.I. Joel for help. After 6,910 three-ply iterations, Maven says PEG wins 56.1 percent of games, followed by PEC, CEP, and then PEP. I picked the fourth-best move, which wins just 47.5 percent of the time. (Joel tells me that the G doesn't naturally blend well with either the C or the P. The best consonant combo among these three letters is CP, he says, and the C is a keeper because it's a good bingo tile.)

Poring over the e-mails and theory articles and old Scrabble games played by the masters seems to be changing how I think. Chess players learn by committing great games to memory and dissecting the positions of Fischer, Morphy, Capablanca, and Botvinnik. Substitute the names Edley, Cappelletto, Sherman, and Gibson, and Scrabble is no different. Over the board, there is no way I can calculate whether the "equity" of a particular leave is -4.5 points or -3.5 points, or that the T has a value of -0.8 points while the N is -0.2. But I can understand why it matters, and use the information to think more logically, rationally, and mathematically — more deeply.

It's part of the organic process of getting better at something. The payoff from studying words is obvious; I recognize more words and play them. The intuitive changes occurring in my brain are subtler: having a better spatial sense of the board, spotting bingos instantly, reaching into a full bag and knowing I have drawn exactly seven tiles, instinctively knowing that one word is better than another at a given point in a game. To paraphrase Supreme Court Justice Potter Stewart's comment on pornography, I can't yet define a good Scrabble play, but I'm starting to know one when I see one.

I don't sleep well at Scrabble tournaments. The soft hotel mattresses with their down-free pillows and synthetic blankets are uncomfortable. And there's always a roommate, a snoring Marlon or a jittery Matt. I roomed solo at my first few events, but began feeling foolish, the journalist solidifying his outsider identity, refusing to be one of the crowd, and wasting his money; the extra hundred bucks per tournament seems needlessly extravagant, especially with Matt or Marlon borrowing bus fare or cadging meal money.

The twenty-game Eastern Scrabble Championships over Presidents' Day weekend doesn't promise to be a restful event. A blizzard has dumped eight inches on Danbury and paralyzed highways around the east. Players are straggling in late, if at all. Six players get into car accidents en route; one guy totals his vehicle, hitting his head on the windshield, and then simply abandons the car and takes a train to town. (That's nothing. A tornado once destroyed part of an Ohio hotel that was staging a tournament; play continued in the unaffected section.) A total of 113 players finally make it.

I've talked myself into believing that this event will define my progress. It's a strong field. But my rating went to 1501 after Bird-in-Hand and now is up to 1524. I've been studying hard and have been exercising regularly to build up my energy level; upon arrival at the Inn at Ethan Allen, I head to the tiny gym and ride the stationary bike (thirty-five minutes), then run on the treadmill (fifteen minutes) before the evening's opening rounds. I stock up at the local

Super Stop & Shop: a half dozen bananas, three oranges, two bottles of water, five Clif Bars, three Think! bars, one Fresh Samantha Super Juice with Echinacea. I'm prepared, for Scrabble or a few days in a fallout shelter.

But play starts more than an hour late because of the snow, and Friday night's three games don't end until well after midnight. I go 2–1 but am exhausted. The clock in our hotel room is an hour fast, which neither Matt nor I realizes until the following morning. So when I climb into bed, I think it's 2:00 A.M. Panic sets in: I'm over-tired, I'm not going to get enough sleep, I'm not going to be alert in the morning, I'm doomed to play poorly. When I awaken from a state of borderline consciousness after a fitful night, I think it's 9:00, but it's only 8:00.

Nonetheless, by the end of Saturday, I have a 7–3 record and am in third place out of the thirty-four players in Division 2. I eschew after-hours Scrabble in the game room, but make the mistake of checking the name of my first Sunday-morning opponent. It's Amit Chakrabarti, who is leading the field with a 9–1 record in his very first tournament. A native of India, Amit is an experienced SOWPODS and Internet player; at the suggestion of Bob Felt and G.I. Joel, who have played against him on-line, Amit was placed in Division 2 by Ron Tiekert, who runs Danbury. Amit is a prototypi-cal expert: a computer science Ph.D. candidate at Princeton whose résumé (I look it up later on his Web site) includes a paper he cowrote titled "A Lower Bound on the Complexity of Approximate Nearest Neighbor Searching on the Hamming Cube."

"Good luck," Joel says sarcastically when I tell him whom I'm play-ing. I toss in bed thinking about how I'll have to play differently against this guy who belongs with the real experts.

Despite my good start, suddenly I don't feel the same cocksureness as I did when I left Bird-in-Hand. The field is stronger, the ratings higher, the players more experienced, and the competition stiffer in the last half of the tourney. I try to be Edley-like. I tell myself in the mirror that I'm going to win, but I'm not convinced. It seems to take hours to fall asleep, and then I'm awake again, too early. It's either too hot in the room or too cold. Matt's presence unnerves me. Why didn't I bring my sleeping pills?

I lose to Amit, who indeed proves to be a skilled player with strong word knowledge (and gets good tiles to boot). Then I split the day's remaining six games and head into Monday in eighth place with a 10–7 record, all but mathematically eliminated from contention thanks to a play that will haunt me that night and for several more to come. In a high-scoring shootout in Game 16, my opponent, Ann Sanfedele, the New Yorker who has played since the seventies, opens a fat spot late in the game, playing QUIRE vertically, starting in the second row, forming UN, IT, and RE.

If I have an S, I can simultaneously form a word ending in S and SQUIRE on the triple-word row. And I do. My rack is ANKRUVS, and I have fifteen minutes on my clock because Ann and I have been slapping down bingos and counterplays as if rushing to catch a train. But I can hardly control my glee. Like a kid given a plate of chocolates, I gobble up the spot, quickly playing RANKS, the first thing I see, for 42 points and a fat 394–316 lead. That's that, game over, I win, looking forward to Game 17. I hit my clock.

The chocolate creeps up my throat. Uh-oh. I've created a user-friendly bingo line under the R in RANKS. And both blanks are, in Scrabble lingo, unseen. I draw AEEGTUV. Yuck. Ann plays PICrATE (a chemical salt) for 76, placing the E under my R, and she draws the second blank, which I know because there are no tiles left in the bag. I use the next thirteen minutes trying to conjure a win, which I fail to do. If I had played KNARS or KNURS (bumps on a tree) or, better yet, VANS, I realize, I wouldn't have given Ann much chance to bingo anywhere other than the existing spot on Row 15 (through the E), because the K takes only an A after it and no two-letter words start with V. So dejected am I that, after dinner (with Ann and others), I even play a couple of late-night games, violating my pledge to abstain.

I toss and toss and toss in bed some more. My Scrabble sleepless-ness, I realize, isn't about idiosyncratic roommates or hypoallergenic pillows. The game traps me in a purgatory of anxiety. I fret about KNARS and KNURS. Bump on a tree? Bump on my head. I mentally replay the endgame scenarios.

Then I think happily about finding MILLiArE (a unit of area) in a late-night game, but regret missing the more defensive and creative MILLcAkE (the residue from pressed linseed), which is how a 1900-rated teenage Scrabble savant named Joey Mallick signs his e-mails (MILLCAKE being the shortest word using all of the letters in Joey's last name). MILLiArE reminds me of DECIARE, a bingo I've just learned. Thoughts of one game lead to the next, and I smilingly recall the six-tile overlap I made by placing, on consecutive turns, BE-LATED next to RETINAE to form RE, EL, TA, IT, NE, and AD simul-taneously.

But pride yields to inadequacy as my consciousness streams. I re-call playing GURNIES* in Game 17, but getting away with it, but then lying about it, telling someone that REUSING didn't fit on the board. I ponder what would have happened had I correctly opened my game against Amit with FOB, leaving AENR, instead of a phony, BARONE*, to which Amit hooked the T in his bingo FRIGATE to form BARONET. I think about racks I had and racks I didn't. Tiles spill abstractly from my head and float in the ether as in the tattoo on Richie Lund's arm. I remember a recurring childhood night-mare: giant wooden triangles and squares and parallelograms press-ing against my head so that I can't think. Were those wooden blocks a foreshadowing of the Scrabble tiles that haunt me now?

I attempt a return to Earth, calculating what would have to hap-pen for 10–7 me to catch the 12–5 leaders: Can three people not win two games? And four more not win three? Okay, if Ed and Amit lose their first two, and Roy and Jamie split, and Ann loses twice, and I don't lose at all . . . Why did I blow those two close ones on Saturday? Why did I botch my opening play against Amit? Why didn't I play KNURS or VANS?

I spot the red digits on the bedside clock. It's 7:10 A.M. I pull the covers over my head. I worry about oversleeping. Matt didn't place a wake-up call. The maid knocks at 7:12. *7:12!* I yell for her to go away. The racks won't leave my head. At 8:20 I abandon all hope of rest. I want to touch the tiles and hit the clock. Adrenaline will out.

Rise. Wash. Stretch. Dress. Eat.

Play.

"Freedom, time, utility, chance — such concepts coagulate around the game player," Alexander Cockburn wrote in his 1974 book *Idle Passion: Chess and the Dance of Death.* "Why do some players become addicted to the game of their inclination? Why does the long-distance runner torment himself with endless miles consumed each day; the racing-car driver confront death on such unfavorable odds; the gambler return to lose more; the chess player exhaust so many hours at his game? . . . Humanism has watered the pastures of leisure and of games with much uplifting speculation. But in the world of games lie areas of darkness, of taboos, of cruel instincts and vile desires."

Almost all of the greatest chess players were afflicted with various neuroses, breakdowns, and mental illnesses. Cockburn saw chess as a psychological condition, and applied Freudian theory to the game itself and the personalities consumed by it. More broadly, he asked, "How do people cope with idleness, boredom, pointlessness? What happens when they do have to work and plot their lives around this activity?"

While the Matts, Marlons, and G.I. Joels display many of the antisocial traits of expert games players, in Scrabble most top experts balance their devotion with outer lives. Some are downright normal, people I haven't written about here for that very reason, like Jim Kramer, a bearded, soft-spoken professional proofreader from Minnesota, ranked third in North America, and Jere Mead, a Latin teacher at a suburban Boston high school, who is ranked fourth, and

Bob Ellickson, a Yale Law School professor and 1900-level player whom I meet in Danbury.

The best female players fall into the relatively normal category, too. There just aren't many of them. More women than men play competitively, yet the top experts are overwhelmingly male. Only one woman has won the Nationals — Rita Norr in 1987 — and her eighth-place finish in 1998 was the only other time a woman finished in the top ten. Only one woman, Lisa Odom, represented the United States in Melbourne, and none did at the 1997 Worlds. There have never been more than six women in the top fifty, lately there have been just three, and there are no new women phenoms on the scene. At Danbury, I calculate, Division 1 is 30 percent female, Division 2 is 35 percent female, Division 3 is 60 percent female, and Division 4 is 90 percent female.

It's no different in other games. Men outnumber women in competitive chess by about twenty to one. High-stakes poker is almost all testosterone. The television show *Who Wants to Be a Millionaire* initially was slammed for the paucity of women able to get past telephone qualifying and onto the show. In relation to chess, Cockburn said, women "are happily without the psychological formations or drives that promote an expertise in the game in the first place. One could even add that women have never been allowed the cultural space to foster that lethargic yet zealous commitment to a useless pursuit that has fostered the bizarre careers of the great champions." In Scrabble, the answer might be simple. "Probably because they have lives outside of this shit," one male expert says.

Scrabble's top women don't disagree. At Danbury, I ask three top women players — Rita Norr, Jan Dixon, and Lynn Cushman — to talk about gender and Scrabble. On the last night of the four-day event, we head up to the hotel room Jan and Lynn are sharing. It's not like talking to the top men. The three women have been friends for twenty years. When we sit down, they don't expound on racks, debate positions, or trade anagrams. They talk over one another, sharing stories and gossip, and laugh endlessly. Transcribing the tape of the session isn't easy.

Rita began playing Scrabble when she was a young mother living in the Park Slope section of Brooklyn. Her furnace broke down one night and a friend came over with a Scrabble set. They formed a neighborhood Scrabble group, saw an ad for a tournament, and Rita went. Rita had read only a few basic lists in the Scrabble newsletter, but she turned out to be a natural. "I was always good at math and logic kinds of things and most of the people seemed to be computer or logic types," Rita says.

When she won the Nationals in Las Vegas, Rita had three kids at home and a husband in the movie business who traveled two weeks at a time. She was finishing a bachelor's degree in computer science at Brooklyn College. "Scrabble sort of saved me," says Rita, who has a soft, round face and speaks in the flat Midwestern tones of her Michigan childhood. She entered the Nationals rated 1911, just out of the top fifty. With three games left to play, Rita didn't even realize she had a chance to win; Joe Edley had to tell her. She accepted the $5,000 first prize on behalf of all the women in the game.

Jan grew up playing Scrabble and other games in a competitive Delaware household with four brothers. "Ping-Pong, pool, cards, Scrabble, Mastermind, Stratego, canasta, pinochle, chess," Jan says in her loud, 78-rpm, mid-Atlantic voice. Her family used a *Funk & Wagnalls* dictionary. "I realized how good I was when I was about twelve years old and we were in Kentucky and I was playing an aunt who was an English teacher and I was mopping the floor with her. I thought I must be pretty good at this if I can beat an English teacher."

Jan's first tournament was in 1981 in the Poconos. The top three finishers were women. "I had no idea women couldn't compete at this," Jan says. Within two years, she had a 2000 rating. "That was the only time I ever did what I would call real study."

"She was focused," says Rita, who barely studies now.

"I was very focused," says Jan.

Jan was in her midtwenties with two children and midway through a divorce when she became a top player. Another top woman of the day had a similar experience. "We both got to our peaks when we were going through the bad marriage, trying to make our decision, trying to get our own self-esteem," says Jan, who works as a tax accountant. "And that's where we put our focus when we were getting out of the bad marriage."

Lynn, a New Yorker, played a little Scrabble with her mother after college, but none of her friends was interested. A flutist who earned a master's degree from the Juilliard School of Music, Lynn was teaching at the 92nd Street YMHA when she met a pianist interested in Scrabble. Lynn soon discovered the clubs and tournaments. But then law school and seven years at a big Manhattan firm precluded regular play. When the firm folded, she got serious and studied formally until cracking the top fifty.

Over the board, each is serious and scholarly. Rita is the most calmly analytical. Lynn is aggressive and forceful; she hates losing. Jan, whose specialty is a killer endgame, is the most "male," eager to analyze specific board positions, willing to brag about her abilities, most prone to Scrabble moments, like the time she played noisily during the eulogy for a Scrabbler at the Hartford tourney. I ask them why no woman has done what Edley did: dedicate his life to the game, memorize the OSPD cover to cover.

"Joe had to worry about Joe," Jan says. "Rita and I had children. We had a life." She goes on, "I just think we're much more well rounded. It's just one thing that we happen to both be good at and enjoy. But it's just one aspect of our lives. Players like Joel Sherman don't have a whole lot more. That is what they do."

Lynn says it's not only the fact that men seem more willing to focus on Scrabble exclusively. They may be more hardwired for games, just as they are hardwired to memorize batting averages and reenact Civil War battles and play video games.

"It's what they prioritize," Jan says.

"That might be it," says Rita.

"The willingness to do it?" I ask. "The drive to do it?"

"No, no," Lynn says. "If you look in music, you find great pianists who are women, great violinists who are women. It's not drive. Why are women successful in music at a rate greater than they are successful in Scrabble?"

"But there is a part of it that's drive," Jan says. "I'm not much of a studier. When I play, I'm very into it. I look up lots of stuff. But when I'm home, Scrabble does not exist. A lot of people have said if I really studied and made the effort some of these players make, I'd be one of the very top players."

"So why don't you?" I ask.

"I've got two children. I've got a grandchild. I've got a house. I've got a job. I baby-sit two nights a week. I baby-sit every weekend that I'm home. Scrabble is not a priority unless I'm at a tournament."

When I say that the great anagrammers seem to be men, and the most obsessive ones at that, Jan points out that some women are great anagrammers, too. But I note that I never see them sitting around playing Anagrams at one in the morning during a tournament.

"Men need to prove themselves," Jan says.

Lynn reluctantly suggests that woman may not be programmed for competition, particularly against men. There's the testosterone issue; women don't storm out of playing rooms, punch walls, or curse aloud over bad luck or poor play (though I did see a woman once dump over a board during a tournament game — against her boyfriend). There also may be behavioral differences that make women afraid of succeeding in an aggressive manner, afraid of offending someone. Just that day, I mention, I squeaked out a win against Wendy Littman, the woman I beat in the final round at Bird-in-Hand, and she said to me afterward, "I'm glad you won because you looked like you were so upset."

"You don't want to cause that kind of upset. I've felt that," Lynn says. "It amazed me to realize it was going on with me because I wasn't brought up like that. I was brought up to think, Achieve, you're smart, you're talented, you can do whatever you want to do. To an extreme. But somehow I had that other thing going on, too. I keep coming back to the idea that the brains do work differently."

Jan and Rita don't share the maternal notion of not wanting to cause hurt in others, but all three agree that they don't have the obsessive dedication to memorizing words that many men do. They're just not interested. They don't pore over old games in *Medleys*, spend hours interpreting Maven simulations, or calculate the equity of rack leaves. What they know, they know, and they stay competitive by way of skill and strategy, not sheer word knowledge.

At the Los Angeles club one night — Rita is divorced and living in southern California — she was playing Trey Wright, the classical pianist who finished second at the 1998 Nationals. "He had this rack, OUSFRAB," Rita says. I note that she doesn't automatically put the letters in alphabetical order, the way most top male players would. "And he said, 'Well, if I had a J, I had FRABJOUS and if I had a T, I had SURFBOAT.' A weird rack like that with the F and the B and the U — women don't look at a rack like that, and say immediately, 'We have these two bingos,' know immediately that there are only two bingos and these are the only two letters I need to play.'"

Most women, the women say, look to see if they can find a word. They don't drill all of the answers into their heads. Jan recalls a game against Joel Wapnick years ago.

"He plays REOVIRUS," Jan says. "Now, I know REOVIRUS is a word. But he says, 'Oh, yeah, it's from my E-I-O-U list. And he starts blah blah blah SOUVENIR blah blah blah REOVIRUS blah blah blah.'"

"A system," I say.

"Men are more methodical," Rita says.

"I feel I don't know half the dictionary," Jan says.

"So how do you succeed?" I ask.

Jan mentions that she's good at cleaning up bad racks, seeing options on the board, and making intricate small plays — not in finding obscure words. They concur that, in the absence of regular study, they remember enough words from twenty years of playing to remain competitive at a high level. Also, I think they're modest about their word knowledge.

"Well," Rita notes, "we're not [rated] 2000 either."

The next morning, Rita wins one out of three games, but it is enough to finish the Eastern Championships with a 15–5 record, and first place.

I bang the playing table with my right hand and turn away in revulsion, barely suppressing a full-fledged Marlon. Through clenched teeth, I push out a "Dammit!" I want to hurl the board against the wall; if I had a golf club, I'd snap it over my knee.

I have just lost the first game of the final day to Trevor Sealy, a friendly player from Toronto who has a 1600 rating. The score is 391–385. I lose on time; exceeding my clock by less than one minute, I'm penalized 10 points.

After we complete the paperwork, I mutter "good game" and bolt from the playing room, nearly whacking an incoming player with the door I push too hard. I blurt out "sorry" but don't break stride. I make for outside, and am thankful I can see through the glass doors without risk of maiming an innocent. Larry Sherman is standing there, hands in the pockets of his high-waisted jeans, getting some fresh air.

"Fuck!" I scream. Twice. Three times. I'm pacing, turning in circles, thrusting my head heavenward, shouting more imprecations into the dead winter air. Larry studies me curiously, as if I'm a trapped wildebeest and he's Marlon Perkins in an episode of *Wild Kingdom*. I half expect him to start taking notes.

Larry is deadpan and imperturbable. I've never seen him lose his cool over a game, more often than not defusing frustration with a self-deprecating joke. At the club a few months earlier, plagued by a bout of slow play, I had scribbled "PLAY FASTER" at the top of my notebook. Larry happened by at that moment, grabbed my pen, and added "STUPID!" But he's always been a trusty adviser, including on the subject of time. He knows it's my Achilles' heel. When I find Larry awaiting me outside, it's as if I've just walked into the principal's office.

He patiently listens to my self-hating tirade, smart enough to know that advice won't help now. Instead, he artfully spins my negative into a positive: "You know, the better you've gotten, the more seriously you seem to take it. That's good."

Sure, I think, but getting better hasn't stopped me from screwing up. And because I've improved, the magnitude of the screwups seems greater — particularly when they're the same mistakes I made as an amateur. I seem to be approaching both Scrabble expertise and Scrabble neurosis in lockstep.

I head back inside. I'm mathematically eliminated, as they say in baseball, but with a couple of wins I still can finish as high as third place. I open my next game with an aggressive, 46-point phony, VEXILY*, which stays on the board, flustering my opponent, whom I have to shut up more than once when he coffeehouses. I win, 438–399. Now I'm 11–8. My final opponent is Noel Livermore, who has been rated as high as 1899 and whom I beat earlier in the tourney. We've got a nice one going, one with a little beauty (I play ILIA, he plays CILIA, I play CILIAE*, which stays on the board). He's ahead by 80 points when I draw the first blank and play EROTIcA. I follow up by pulling the second blank. After a couple of small plays, I'm down 252–199. My rack is AMNSTU?, which makes plenty of words on its own (fourteen, actually). But the board isn't bingo-friendly. Noel has been shutting the tap, but he's left one unlikely opening: through the first I in CILIAE*, which would require at least one hook, an R or S onto NEVE. I shuffle and shuffle and then, in what in replay feels like a continuous slow-motion sequence, like the Six Million Dollar Man in full stride, my brain seeing and my hands grabbing and the letters moving, I lay down hUMANIST.

	A	B	C	D	E	F	G	H	I	J	K	L	M	N	O
1								N							
2						Z	O	E	A	E					
3							V					E	H		
4						C	E	E				R	E		
5		h	U	M	A	N	I	S	T			O	X		
6							L			C		T			
7			J				I			R		I			
8			E	G			A	★	R	Y		c			
9			O	U	R	I	E					A	T		
10			N		A							I			
11					I						D	T			
12					L					W	A	R	T		
13					S	N	A	I	L	E	D		Y		
14							R			B	O	G			
15				A	U	T	O	E	D						

Noel looks stunned. He thought he had shut down the board entirely. He compliments my 78-point play. I have moved ahead 277–252, but Noel counters with HM for 32 (above the MA in hUMANIST). I follow with FOWL for 20 to retake the lead. The Q is unseen. I know it's going to come down to the Q. I draw the last two tiles: no Q.

All I need to do to win is prevent Noel from playing the Q. But there are two available places for it, and Noel also has the last U. I block the first spot (above IRE) and then Noel, inexplicably, misses the second one. I have plenty of time. All I have to do is play a single tile in front of AT. Which I do. And then I place an S at the end of it: 4 points.

I don't know why I put down the S. I thought I had figured it out. I thought I had considered everything. I thought there was no way he could play the Q. But he can. He places SUQ atop my S. Just like that, I have given him the game. Noel wins 357–332, but the final score is irrelevant. I have blown it in the most horrifying fashion: failing to execute an elementary Q-stick. I have demonstrated that I'm not worthy of being an expert. That I'll never reach my goals. That I can't play with Matt or Marlon or Joel. That I don't have it.

I politely rehash the endgame with Noel, who's appalled at his own failure to see QAT. Slumped over the table, I rearrange the tiles in the routine what-if scenario that follows tight games, but I move them like a kid shifting peas around on his dinner plate. I can't explain to Noel what happened, muttering that maybe I mistracked the S's, thinking I had the last one. But my score sheet indicates otherwise. I knew he had SUQ. I panicked and screwed up.

I have just enough frustration left in me to scrawl a two-inch-tall "FUCK" across the bottom of my score sheet. And then I abandon my board with the evidence of my incompetence still on it and morosely exit the playing room. I'm not mad; I'm devastated. Joe Edley asks what happened. I brush him off; I can't talk. Inconsolable, I beat back tears.

Three blown endgames in the last five games, to Ann, Trevor, and Noel. Instead of 14–6, which would have been good for second place, I finish 11–9, in ninth place. The same 11–9 as in Danbury two years earlier, in the second tournament of my career, when I lost my last six games. Sure, I've gone from fourth to third to second division in three appearances in Danbury. To what end? Still choking. Only now the magnitude of my chokes has grown.

Larry Sherman is right: The better I get, the more upset I get. The game now defines me. The higher my rating climbs, the greater the pressure. The more I succeed, the heavier my failures feel.

After I regain my composure and reappear in the playing room, one of the New York experts notes that it's possible my rating will climb over 1600. (Danbury is rated in two ten-game blocks, so my first-half 7–3 will propel me close to the next hundred mark while the second-half 4–6 shouldn't hurt too much.) "You'll be an expert," he says. I immediately scoff at the notion. While 1600 technically is considered expert status, everyone knows that 1700 is a fairer benchmark. Plus, I'm not worthy of the designation. And more than anything, I want to be worthy.

As I drive away from the hotel, I shudder at the realization.

I am become Joel: I need this game to validate *my* existence.

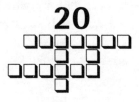

20

1574

A TLANTIC CITY. The casinos, the beach, the boardwalk, the mob, the Miss America Pageant, the Scrabble talent show. It's an annual rite. But it will be hard to top last year's winning performance: the ninety-six two-letter words sung to the tune of "The Star-Spangled Banner." At midnight after Friday's opening rounds at the Holiday Inn — just off the boardwalk, low rollers only — the Scrabble players gather in the main tournament room for the big show. Wine and cookies are served. Anyone can enter, a problem that is apparent immediately.

The first contestant is an introverted player whom I once saw standing outside a playing room holding a sign reading HOOTERS; he was looking for someone to join him at the restaurant for dinner. Here, he does "impressions" of almost every character on *The Simpsons*. Another player tries Johnny Carson's old Carnak the Magnificent routine. "Havana," he says. "What does Pat Sajak do when he laughs at Vanna White." The audience hoots. Next comes a parody, "Who Wants to Be a Scrabbillionaire," with inside jokes about G.I. Joel and Mark Berg, which gets a few chuckles.

I'm not sure whether the sight of the Scrabble players attempting humor deserves praise or pity, whether it unabashedly displays the camaraderie of the subculture or reveals its dark, pathetic center. Or maybe my reaction reflects a double standard; if I'm happy to play Scrabble with these people, shouldn't I accept them on this level, too? Shouldn't I hop up on stage and sing show tunes with Scrabble lyrics

("The blanks'll come out / Tomorrow! / Bet your bottom dollar / That tomorrow / There'll be blanks!")?

Well, no. The eccentricity of Scrabble players is, naturally, a question of degree. At the club one Sunday, a handful of players remain after a full afternoon of play. Someone notes that a certain player always brings along a Scrabble board even though there are plenty of boards at the club.

"Maybe he's playing somewhere else afterward," another player says.

"Maybe he's just weird," I say.

"We're *all* weird," G.I. Joel replies.

"He's weird enough to be called weird by the weird," Matt says.

As in any subculture, the extent of people's devotion and involvement varies. Most Scrabblers have a Scrabble life and a daily life, and the twain meet at clubs and tournaments or on-line. For others, Scrabble is the social center of the universe. Three middle-aged Scrabblers even share a house in New Jersey.

My friendships with Matt, Marlon, Eric Chaikin, and a few others certainly transcend the game. We talk about more than words and racks and anagrams. I pay for Matt's and Marlon's hotel rooms or meals when they ask not because I'm trying to buy their journalistic cooperation, but because they're broke and I trust them to repay me (someday). When Matt is at his emotional lowest, he phones, I hope, because he considers me a friend. I'm proud to call friends many of the people I play against at Club 56 on Thursdays, even if we don't go to the movies together or share intimacies about our inner lives. There are days when I'm sure they've forgotten that I'm a reporter. There are days when I know I have.

So even though I've gone native, I draw the line at talent shows. But just when I'm feeling too hip for this, it gets legs. Sheldon Silverstein, a retired accounts payable clerk from Brooklyn, does fabulous impersonations of Alfred Hitchcock and Humphrey Bogart. ("Of all the Scrabble joints in all the towns in all the world, she walks into mine," he says.) Jim Piazza, a New York writer who, on his day job, vets movie scripts for a Hollywood studio, recites a funny advice column, Dear Dr. Jim. Finally, with the clock approaching 1:00 A.M., Sal Piro, the *Rocky Horror Picture Show* fan club president, asks me to check his makeup, which I do, before he races into the room shouting, "The bitch is back!" Dressed in drag, with an orange wig, Sal introduces the Piro-ettes, three New York players who back him up on fifties songs set to Scrabble lyrics. My favorites: "Hey la, hey la, the Q is back" and "Going to first table, and I'm gonna play Edley."

Sal is truly disappointed when the audience awards the $50 first prize to Dr. Jim over the Piro-ettes.

After Danbury, my rating climbs to 1574, leaving me one good tournament short of the magic 1600 mark.

I'm glad, in a twisted way, that I'm not yet there. To have jumped from 1416 to "expert" in just two months after struggling so mightily for so long would feel cheap. An expert is supposed to be someone, according to *Merriam-Webster's Collegiate,* with a special skill or knowledge derived from training or experience. I don't have it. I want to earn whatever reward comes from being defined by a number. If that means slamming a few more doors and screaming a few more profanities, so be it. It means too much to me for it not to be genuine. No flukes allowed.

In Scrabble, there really aren't any, anyway. Some players bitch relentlessly about their misfortune. And, to be sure, chance is real; at a Sunday session at the club before Danbury, I drew a total of three blanks in nine games — about a 100 to 1 shot — and lost every game. Three blanks out of eighteen! The injustice! At the same time, Scrabble players like the fact that the game is orderly — one hundred tiles, strict rules, familiar patterns and procedures. "Scrabble is a sort of determinist world," Bob Ellickson, the Yale law professor, tells me over breakfast at a tournament. "It appeals to the people in it. Everything adds up to clean sums."

Ratings are nice and clean, too. Players can protest all they want that they are over- or underrated (usually the latter), but water seeks its own level. Players have miracle performances that catapult their ratings heavenward, but it usually doesn't last. Diane from the New York club went 11–1 to win my division in Atlantic City and her rating zoomed above 1700. She was back in the 1500s in short order.

At the annual Port Jefferson tournament on Long Island a few weeks after Danbury, an opponent says as we sit down to play, "I thought you were rated higher."

"In my mind I am," I reply.

I'm seeded second in the second division of the fifteen-game event. I have come for the usual reasons — the competition, the quest for experthood, the fact that I have no choice but to play. I'm starting to feel like a Scrabble mercenary: unswerving, driven, single-minded. I love the atmosphere, but fun is beside the point. At this event, there will be no distractions. I'm staying at Joe Edley's house nearby rather than in the hotel.

There is little hanging on the walls at Joe and Laura's two-story condo, no shelves displaying books or tchotchkes, and no end tables in the living room, just two aging sofas and a coffee table adorned only with class pictures of their preschool-age daughter, Amber. Her toys fill an adjacent room where Joe keeps a desktop computer, at which he plays and studies Scrabble while sitting in a metal folding chair.

For Edley, who lived under a tree for five months, I think material things are immaterial. He probably could live happily without the big television in the living room or any of the few other possessions he has. It's enough for Joe simply to wake up early, meditate, stretch, and perform tai chi in the living room. And, of course, study words.

Joe understands that I want to succeed, and Laura understands Joe. So they are accommodating. They let me decide what meals we'll eat together over the weekend. They insist I sleep in their bedroom. At dinner with them on Friday, before the first rounds, Edley approves of my decision to pass up dessert. He sends me off with a reminder to breathe deeply, concentrate, and be patient.

Thanks in part to Edley, something is clicking: I'm spotting bingos faster and more frequently, and absorbing the ones I read and anagram while riding the subway, pedaling at the gym, or couch-potatoing in my living room. The stack of seven- and eight-letter bingo lists that I tote everywhere is growing fatter. And I know I'm learning, because when I review the words highlighted in fluorescent green or orange they are surprisingly familiar. I find myself thinking, I didn't know that word? as if I were looking at a high school photograph and can't believe I ever wore my hair like that.

The idea that my brain is in training sounds obvious, but it's not something I consider as I pore over my lists. The day before Long Island, I sat in a Department of Motor Vehicles office (waiting for a new driver's license) and examined a three-and-a-half-page printout of the 1,322 acceptable five-letter words containing the letter Y. It turns out that I don't know 311 of them, from ENSKY to MUHLY to YIRTH. But where learning the words used to feel like a hopeless task, I now see how much I already have learned, and that it's not impossible, even if it's not easy. I accept now that learning words could be a lifelong process. After two decades, Edley still carries tiny flash cards wrapped in rubber bands, some handwritten in the seventies and eighties. While I'm at his house, Laura finds one on the floor and hands it to Joe. "This one is bingos ending in ER," he says. "I did this one years ago."

Achieving expertise doesn't require a secret password or some supernal force. I call Neil Charness, a Florida State University professor who studies the performance of experts. Charness tells me that researchers studying chess masters in the 1940s made what was then a monumental discovery: Chess expertise didn't result from greater intellectual capacity, as prevailing wisdom had it, but from the players' ability to retrieve patterns from memory. In other words, the more you know, the more you know what to look for. Knowledge is acquired in what memory experts call "chunks" and then applied to specific situations. (Chunks are familiar patterns or units of information.)† That knowledge becomes part of the routine cognitive processing that occurs during various activities, from playing chess to Scrabble to badminton to the violin.

Charness says I'm building the ability to make expert decisions. I've moved beyond "maintenance practice," or simply playing a lot of Scrabble, which is what hobbyists do (and what I did on my living room floor early on), to "deliberate practice," what Charness calls the "technical, draining, attention-demanding" work that can only be conducted in short sessions, a maximum of three to four hours a day in the case of writers and musicians. In a pioneering study in 1973, Herbert Simon and William Chase of Carnegie-Mellon University concluded that attaining an international level of expertise in chess requires about ten years of preparation, and they suggested it was no different in other domains. (Einstein had been studying physics for ten years before he published his first paper on special relativity.)

---

† A 1956 study showed that the outer limit of people's ability to reproduce information is units of seven, plus or minus two. Seven, of course, is the number of Scrabble tiles on a rack.

Other studies put the amount of requisite practice for expertise in many fields at ten thousand hours.

"Clearly, there are people who get there in less time," Charness says. "We're only beginning to start thinking about what might differentiate the speed with which people get to those points. There are probably individual differences among masters. But if I had to guess, my hypothesis wouldn't be innate differences but specific types of training they've engaged in." As for simply becoming an expert, he tells me, "the real predictor seems to be serious study alone."

So I study. I anagram and review and anagram some more. After club sessions and tournaments, I scour every rack of every game and check for missed words, which I record in a new slate blue spiralbound notebook. And it all pays off. In two club games, for instance, I play HETAIRAS (ancient Greek concubines), INPHASE (having matching electrical phases), VENALITY (openness to bribery), and CONGAING (dancing the conga).

My study doesn't yield just words from the prepared lists but trickier combinations that are difficult to find in a mishmash of unlikely letters. Against my friend Dominic Grillo, I play FIrEBUG (an educated guess that turns out to be acceptable) and follow it up with EQUINOX to an open X — tough because it's unnatural to view the X as the last letter in a word. The words get weirder. I play LOGINESS and ZINCOID and SHEKELS; JALOP, MUFTI, MAQUI, XENIA, and MEZES; APOGEAN and LIAISES. One night at the club, through the word DO already on the board, I play TOURNEDOs as a nine-letter triple-triple for 140 points, drawing a challenge. When G.I. Joel rules it good, he issues an approving smile.

After another club game, my opponent, Jean Lithgow, says, "You played that beautifully."

I fill my words notebook with plays I've missed, not to punish but to learn. Page by page, it slowly becomes a tapestry of linguistic randomness. ACAROID (105 lost points), COAGULA, OXIDASE, the chance to turn BLACK into BLACKOUT. I write down SODOMITE, which would have worked when MOODIEST didn't. EXODOI? A plural of EXODOS (a concluding dramatic scene). Most of the words or racks I botched may never materialize again. But so what? It's all part of the deliberate practice about which Neil Charness schooled me. WOOPS means to vomit. A RIVIERE is a necklace of precious stones. MONGO is a low-quality wool. There are three bingos in EGIMNPR: IMPREGN, PERMING, and GRIPMEN. The rack EFIPRST contains only one seven, PRESIFT — not PREFITS*, as I'd tried. I write down every unfamiliar word starting with Q, and every word starting with AIR, SEA, and ROSE.

Still, even under Edley's care, I stumble on Long Island. I'm 5–2, then lose three of four. After dinner with Edley, Laura, and Amber on Saturday night, Joe offers to replay a couple of my games in order to analyze my performance. I choose two losses that I believe were winnable. Sitting at the kitchen table, Joe dumps out the tiles from the British set I picked up at the Worlds, separating them by letter.

We spend ten minutes discussing my opening play and run a computer analysis that vindicates my move. My next two plays withstand Joe's analysis, and then my problem becomes clear. As soon as I tell him my next rack, AAILNTY, he says, "You missed the bingo."

"ANALITY, right?" I say. "I set it up on my rack and thought about it. I thought, I'd know it because it's BANALITY without the B. So I wasn't sure. I chickened out. I played INLAY."

"Yeah, INLAY was a big mistake," Joe says in the matter-of-fact tone that makes other players loathe him.

Two turns later, I did it again. With the rack of AEFILST, I set up FETIALS but couldn't remember whether it's a word. It is (priests of ancient Rome). I did bingo a turn later and took the lead a turn after that. My opponent drew the better-balanced late racks while I got six consonants and an I, and he squeaked out a win.

Joe points out that the sooner I bingo the sooner I have a chance to bingo again. Same deal next game. My first three plays were strong, Joe says. Then, with the rack of ABEIOT?, needing to start a seven-letter bingo with the A, E, or I (ruling out OBvIATE and nIOBATE, which I saw), I set up the rack in the following order: I?EBOAT. I thought, LIFEBOAT, FIREBOAT. I didn't think, IcEBOAT.

"Yeah, you've got to learn those bingos," Joe says.

The more you know and the better you get, the more frustrated you are by what you don't know — and what might have happened had you known. The more you know the more there is to forget. I see INFAUNAE but miss RUCK. I turn WITCH into SWITCH into

SWITCHEROO (winning high praise for creativity) but challenge LEA.

When I get home from Long Island, after an 8–7 finish that will send my rating down to 1532, I look up and write down in my notebook all of the bingos beginning and ending with BOAT. Not including plurals, there are thirty-six.

Words, words, words. Next to the 450,000 entries in *Webster's Third New International Dictionary* — not including certain plurals, verb tenses, neologisms, and technical terms — the Scrabble word list seems minuscule at 120,000. But when one considers that the working vocabulary of an average English speaker is commonly estimated at 15,000 to 20,000 words, the Scrabble task seems absurdly daunting.

How Scrabble players learn words is a bit like how people arrange a collection of books. Some players are random — paperbacks mixed with hardcovers, fiction with nonfiction, travel with sports. They'll anagram some sevens, read the dictionary, flashcard the fives, whatever rings their buzzer at a given moment. Others are Dewey-decimal anal — like Joel Wapnick with his vowel-order lists — and set out to learn words in rigid sequence, often for a fixed amount of time during a specific part of the day. Some players, like G.I. Joel, hate studying. Their method is the equivalent of leaving the books stacked in piles on the floor until forced to put them away.

How do players remember? Again, techniques vary. Lately, I've been trying to digest a couple dozen eight-letter words a day by using "anamonics," a term combining anagrams and mnemonics. In the early 1990s, a few superexperts took the most highly probable seven-letter stems. Using all of the letters that combined with a stem to form bingos, they created phrases. The idea was to be able to identify quickly whether a rack of tiles plus one more letter contained a bingo, rather than wasting precious minutes shuffling and searching for words.

So if you hold the stem SAINTED, remembering the phrase "GETS IMPROVED TOUCH" reveals all of the letters that combine with the stem to form at least one eight-letter word. For instance, SAINTED plus a C makes DISTANCE, plus a D is DANDIEST, plus an E is ANDESITE, and so on. For the stem LATRINE, *Medleys* editor Nick Ballard came up with the classic "MOVING FUNNY SPICES." For ATONERS, he created "FRUMPS BEING NICE." For CINEAST, he found "FANS OF THE DIRTY MOVIE BIZ." DIETERS produced "BLIMPS EATING CRAWFISH." Ballard devised anamonics for the top two hundred seven-letter stems, and other players did another three hundred seven-letter stems, plus two hundred six-letter stems (RETINA: "THE RED PUPIL PREFERS MUCH WINKING").

The only problem with anamonics is that you have to remember the stem, then the accompanying phrase, and then the words themselves. Some players, however, find that creating anamonic phrases helps with retention. My expert friend Martin Smith draws pictures to accompany his anamonics. For SALUTER, he devised the anamonic STIFF VET BOMBING and drew a picture of a stick figure with an erection saluting a flag while bombs fall around him. For the stem AEIORST, which doesn't form a word, he wrote ASTEROId. His anamonic is JJ UNHURT, DMV, and his picture shows a guy named JJ standing next to the DMV, which has been hit by an asteroid. Political correctness doesn't matter: For the anagram of the word GINGER, Martin, who is black, discovered the anamonic MY SLAVE. Whatever helps you remember.

Other players create songs or write stories to remember words. Steve Polatnick, a Miami lawyer and top-fifty player, tapes pictures from magazines next to words in his *OSPD*. He draws a skull and crossbones next to words that don't take an S but logically should. TELAMON (a male figure used as a supporting column), for instance, is pluralized with ES, he notes, while WANDLE is an adjective (meaning supple). Words related to Judaica get a Star of David. Piscine words are denoted by a fish drawing. Polatnick tape-records new words and plays them while driving. For fish-related words, he records the same sentence, with minor variations. "What'll it be? Filet of CORBINA or filet of CUSK?" He says, "I always use the last fish I learned and the new one."

Polatnick's dictionary is nothing compared to the one belonging to retired legend David Gibson. Gibson is a soft-spoken math professor from Spartanburg, South Carolina, who won the Nationals in 1994 and the Superstars in 1995 and earned the adoration of his fellow experts for his unmatched gentlemanliness and for sharing part of his $65,000 in winnings with them. ("He's a saint," Jim Geary says.) Gibson annotated all 668 pages of his copy of the second edition of the *OSPD*. Virtually every word bears some notation. Anagrams, anamonics, front hooks, back hooks, extensions, declensions, related words. All are crowded onto the page in neat, tiny, block capitals, each with its own explanatory code: a plus sign for the anamonic, front and back hooks in parentheses, component words separated by an equals sign. (For example, "LARGANDO = GARLAND + O = GRANOLA + D.") Gibson could recite the *OSPD* definitions almost verbatim and he did further research in "real" dictionaries on meanings and etymologies. He worked the book so hard that he had to have it rebound. Gibson put a new dark blue cover on it titled "David's Lexicon." He studied an average of four hours a day. Every day. For twelve years.

The most intricate mnemonic system, though, may be that created by the British player David Webb to remember all of the 412 (in SOWPODS) eight-letter words containing five vowels. (It's an important list because there are so many vowels in the bag, forty-two.) Webb described the method to me as we strolled to dinner through a park in Melbourne one night. Later, he sent me an e-mail elaborating.

Webb arranges a mix of five vowels in alphabetical order, say AAIOU. Then he sums the alphanumeric value of the first three letters, where A = 1, E = 5, I = 9, O = 15, and U = 21. So in the example AAIOU, A + A + I = 1 + 1 + 9 = 11. Then he converts the total into the corresponding letter in the alphabet. In this case, 11 = K. For the last two vowels, he uses an alphabetical list of the pairs in order, where AA = 1 = A, AE = 2 = B, AI = 3 = C, all the way up to OU = 14 = N and UU = 15 = O. Then he considers the letters generated by the two groups of letters as a pair. In this example, the first three letters (AAI) yield a K, and the final pair of letters (OU) yields an N. He associates that letter pair with an image. In this case, KN = KNEE. Then he uses the image to trigger a story: "A knee in the balls (BLS) of a cadet (CDT) gives him spots (SPT) so he goes to the Ritz (RTZ) hotel, where he sees a crocodile (CRC). He gives the crocodile buns (BNS) and hits him with rakes (RKS). Then the [English] football team Spurs (SPR) arrive followed by a sailor (SLR) carrying roses (RSS) and wearing a clog (CLG)."

Each of the consonant triples creates a word when combined with the vowel set AAIOU. The words prompted by his story are: ABOULIAS (AAIOU + BLS), AUTACOID, AUTOPSIA#, AZO-TURIA, CARIACOU#, OUABAINS, OUAKARIS#, PAROUSIA#, RAOULIAS#, SAOUARIS#, and GUAIACOL.

"Not all stories are of this length," he tells me.

Some comprise a single-consonant-triple such as that generated by AIIIO, which converts to (19, 11) = SK, which I associate with skiing. Skiing triggers the image of slaloming down a slope using cacti (CCT) as flags. CCT gives us the splendid word OITICICA.

This system may seem absurdly complicated and esoteric given its end product, but the five-vowel eights are a crucial list in Scrabble. The words are difficult to see and if you miss the bingo you are likely to score little and have a problem rack the following turn . . . It was my goal for many years to develop a memory system that delivered this list on a plate. I viewed this goal as a Holy Grail, not believing I would ever achieve it, but the technique came to me one evening out of the blue and it works. Although it took awhile to create and learn the stories, it now takes me only three hours every three months to keep the stories fresh.

I head over to Matt Graham's apartment, where the game itself is a Holy Grail.

We're playing "three and three" — $3 a game plus 3 cents per point in spread. Matt gives me 50 points to start, which I need, as I lose the first game by 2 points in reality but win with the spread, 480–432. In the second game, I draw the blanks on the final two turns, play UN-LOCK for 50 points and then go out with DOVeTAiL for 70 to win 500–410, not even needing the spread. That's when Matt tosses his tiles on the board and his clipboard on the table, and barks, "You ready to play without a spot?"

How far I've come. Just a few months ago, Matt first asked whether I was ready to play for money. Now, for Game 3, we leave the stakes the same but cut the spread in half, to 25 points. I get both blanks and win again, 432–374, again not needing the spot, to increase my edge to $11. To Matt, this money is meaningful, but the losing hurts him more. Not that I don't want to win money. It's just that I view playing Matt as an investment, and I budget $20 or so per session. Incentivizing gamblers is an excellent way to get them to play, and, with this gambler, for me to learn.

"I'm really not as bad a sport as it seems when I throw the clipboard," Matt says. "I'm just trying to have my way. But it really is amazing," he says, meaning the fact that I'm six for six on blanks in this session. It really isn't, but his ploy works: Matt persuades me to increase the stakes to six and six. As probability would have it, he promptly gets both blanks and crushes me in the fourth game.

The loss puts me $6 in the red. Matt squeaks out a win in our fifth game, dropping me in a $15 hole. I reclaim my 50-point spread, but he pulls both blanks again and hammers me, 492–362. Now I'm down $30. We play one more, still at six and six, and I win, 384–367, without the spread, leaving me down $23. Still, it's a morale-boosting session: I won three out of seven games straight up, and a fourth with a spot.

Before I leave, Matt shows me his latest health potion: activated charcoal, a "universal antidote and detoxifier that extends life" and has medicinal uses dating to the second century B.C., according to one of the vitamin journals Matt reads. The stuff is called Entera-Klenz Drink Mix. It turns your lips, teeth, and tongue black. Matt says he's using it to clean out his body. He hasn't had a drink of alcohol in four days.

"For the tournament?" I ask. We're heading to one soon.

"For the tournament," he says, "and because I've been going off the deep end."

I don't need to ask anymore what he means.

I'm on a playing binge. After the setback on Long Island, I head to the tournament that has been my bête noire: Waltham. I've stunk it up both times I've played there, 5–7 one year, 4–8 the next. Maybe it was the proximity of greatness in the form of the premier division, maybe it was my inexperience, maybe my stubborn refusal to commit the time to learn the words.

Now I'm playing in the expert division. Waltham is liberal about playing up; in this instance, anyone rated 1400–1700 has the option of joining the expert field. Still, when I check in and receive a name-tag that also bears my rating and the word EXPERT, I experience a tiny rush of pride.

Things start well. My first game is against one of the Scrabble misfit savants. He's a small, nervous, muttering man wearing large, rectangular glasses and a tight plaid short-sleeved shirt. I'll spot him later at the urinal saying, "I am stupidity!" (John Williams once remarked, "When you look up 'Scrabble player' in the dictionary, he's what you expect to see.") On my second turn, I find a word I'd just learned: the anagram of BARONET, which is REBOANT. (Marlon had said to me, "*Never* play BARONET. Always play REBOANT," because the odder word might draw a challenge.)

I feel locked in, my confidence unshaken when my opponent bingos with the blanks, playing UnBUCKLE and, appropriately enough, UrINALS. I find MOULDIER to tie the game. But my brain cramps in the endgame, spotting what would have turned out to be my only board-blocking, winning play, QURSH (a monetary unit of Saudi Arabia), but chickening out because of uncertainty. I lose a barn burner, 471–456.

Then I win three in a row, and find myself at Table 2 on Saturday morning. It's April 1, my thirty-seventh birthday. (When I was nine, in 1972, I calculated how old I would turn in 2000 but couldn't fathom that day arriving; it might not have seemed so terrifying had I known I'd be playing a board game full-time.) Chris Cree, the country club Texan, who's playing at Table 1, apparently thinks my presence at a top table is some sort of April Fools' Day joke. He does a double take, and a smile cracks his face. His voice goes deep country. "Whoa!" he says. "What're *you* doin' here?" I don't stay long. Jan Dixon whips me. I drop down to lesser competition and win the next game to improve to 4–2, but then lose three in a row, one especially painful because my opponent artfully manages to find a nine-letter bingo through a disconnected G and D — EStRANGED — a spot I chose not to block. (When I mention the play to him at a tournament two months later, he says, "You're *still* thinking about that?") After the final defeat, which plunges me to 4–5, I realize the numerical designation of expertise, alas, has been postponed again.

Not so fast. One win can foster the perceptional difference between happiness and disappointment. I'm riding an emotional Stair-

Master, up, down, up, down. So when I take two in a row and improve to 6–5, I'm up. In my mental ranking of records in twelve-game events, assuming even or slightly better opposition, 4–8 rates as a disaster, 5–7 is lousy, 6–6 is barely tolerable, and 7–5 is just acceptable. But seeded thirty-ninth of forty-two people, 7–5 in the expert division at Waltham would be a better birthday present than the blue baseball glove I got when I turned nine. And the thought crosses my mind that 7–5 could make me an "expert," too.

One game. My opponent is a longtime Boston-area player rated about 1800, a calm and friendly gray-haired gentleman I've never before met. Our game turns when I lay down EXpIRER for 99 points. It's a guess; many noun forms of verbs aren't words. So when he challenges, I'm not optimistic.

But it comes back acceptable, and turns out to be the only bingo in that rack of tiles, a cognitive achievement that makes me either lucky, good, or both. I pump my fist under the table and cruise to a 423–319 win.

At the club on a Thursday night a couple of weeks later, G.I. Joel is up on his chair, announcing the pairings for the third round of the evening: "Lynn Cushman versus Stefan Fatsis, who just beat Bob Felt!"

Some exclamations of surprise, a smattering of applause.

Perhaps searching for a dose of humility, I head to Washington Square Park. The weather has warmed and the usual suspects have emerged from their winter hibernation: Alan the contractor; Joe the World War II vet; John the Woody Allen lookalike; Aldo the diner owner; Jimmy the Flea House original, in a wool cap.

I feel insecure around these men in a way I don't anymore in the club or at tournaments. Their approbation is determined first by skill and second by familiarity. I'm a known face, but still a no-talent. The tournaments feel almost sissified compared to the gritty park — all those rules and scorecards and announcements and ratings, white noise obscuring what really matters: the game. No tracking tiles, no spinning the board after every turn. Just make words.

Bob Felt is there, we play, and order is restored as I lose. I win a couple of games against lesser lights. And as I sit down for one more, with Joe, the experts are hovering over the board. I open with HONDLER*, which I think should be good because HONDLE means to haggle, and HAGGLER is a word. They all know it's phony, but Joe doesn't and the play stays on the board.

When I play MAESTRI, slotting an M in the first column, the boo birds rise up out of their seats.

"Why'd you put it in the triple line?" Alan asks incredulously.

"Yeah, he should have played MISRATE," Jimmy says, as if I don't exist.

"MAESTRI was the right play," Felt says. "He just played it in the wrong place."

I believe this is known as character building.

Later, I play FIXER for 34 points. I look up and Alan is shaking his head.

"REFIX?" I say. I've just recognized the word, and the spot. It would have been worth 51 points along a triple.

He nods.

Whenever I reach a new numeric milestone in the game — 1200, 1300, 1400, 1500 — the significance of the achievement immediately diminishes as I begin looking another 100 points ahead. But the next one is 1600, and the designation of expertise. When I get there — not if, because I know I'm going to get there — I vow to be satisfied. I will have reached my goal. So when the cross-table from Waltham arrives in my mailbox and informs me that I am now rated 1598, I'm surprisingly content. It's only a matter of time now.

The Holiday Inn in Atlantic City beckons again, the big eighteen-game spring tournament (the one featuring the talent show is just twelve games long). With my new rating, I'm seeded near the top of the second division, which includes players with ratings as low as 1200; I'll need to win a lot of games in order to gain any points at all.

And I do. Seven of the first nine. Six of the last nine. I play newly learned, high-probability words like SOURDINE, TEGULAR, and INSETTER. My 13–5 record is good for second place and a hundred bucks. I'm perfectly satisfied.

Until I call Edley. He's initially complimentary. But then I tell him that the tournament director didn't seed the players using up-to-date ratings, so rather than fifth in the division, I ranked first. Thirteen wins, he says, might be worth a couple of rating points. "Probably not much more," he says.

At the club recently, I hung in there in a game against G.I. Joel. But I missed a bingo (KNEELER) and wound up losing.

"One mistake per game," I said to Joel.

"Mistakes kill," he said.

And then, in my notebook, I wrote, "I want to play until I don't make mistakes anymore."

This, of course, is folly. Mistakes are inevitable in a game in which humans are required to make decisions. But now, analyzing my Atlantic City games, it becomes clear: I have learned how to beat players rated below me but haven't yet eliminated the sort of conscious foolhardiness that kills. Four of the five defeats, I decide, were self-inflicted — phony bingos in two games; a missed "back hook" in another (turning LUTE into LUTEA, a word I'd just studied as I begin the fives); a Marlon-like decision to pass up a blank bingo for a 30-point play; getting unnerved by two bickering novice ladies sitting at the next table.

But the sting of my candid assessment wears off quickly, as it always does. There's the tingly anticipation of the next trip to the club, park, or tournament, another batch of words spilling out of my printer to be learned. A week after Atlantic City, I receive an e-mail from the ratings czar Joe Edley:

> It's official! You're now an EXPERT!
> Not much over the limit, but there it is.
> 1601.

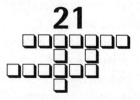

1601

JIM GEARY believes that games aren't worth playing unless they can be played to their theoretical maximum. In Scrabble, he says, playing the "total game" occurs only when you effectively control the game's three elements — your tiles, the unseen tiles, and the board. You synthesize information from the unseen tile pool. You see all of the strategic possibilities in the board geometry for both players. And your word knowledge allows you to exploit a rack to its fullest. It's being in the zone, a place Geary was when he extended EXISTENT along the bottom row to EXISTENTIALIsTs or made his legendary WATERZOOI play.

Take away any one of three elements, though, and, Geary argues, the game collapses. Without mastery of the vocabulary — the most widespread deficit among players — "trying to keep track of 'what's going on' is kind of a joke," he says. The point of making certain plays in Scrabble is to maximize scoring potential and to prevent your opponent from making certain plays. But if you don't know the words, you can't know which words you're missing and can't definitively know that you're stopping your opponent.

So who plays the total game? Not many players. When talk on CGP turns to the merits of winning the lower divisions at the National Scrabble Championship, Geary writes, "To be honest, the NSC is only Division 1. Every other division is just stamp collecting." The stamp collectors take up arms. Arrogant superexpert! they cry. The lower-rated players try hard! They're not "window decorations for the exalted few," one says. "There [is] a LOT of great Scrabble going on, by people who DO see it as a hobby, AND as serious study," another screams.

Blah, blah, blah. Geary's right. I've played more than a thousand games of Scrabble since embarking on this journey. I'm technically an expert now. But I've never felt like a pro — as if I had played the total game, or at least a game in which I could say I had considered all of the possibilities scaled down to my vocabulary. I know how good the greatest are. The rest of us are just hobbyists, because we're not playing the game to its mathematical fullest, the only place where it possesses analytical value.

But the only way to reach that place is to keep playing. I'm proud of what I have achieved. Eight months ago, my chances of qualifying for Division 2 at the Nationals seemed remote; I'd need a 1500 rating to play up, and I stunk. But then I won Bird-in-Hand, surged at Waltham, finished second in Atlantic City, and suddenly I was an expert. I run some numbers: Since my comeback, I have a 56–33 record in tournaments, a .629 winning percentage. After a one-day Long Island event, my rating improves to 1613. My contentment with achieving technical expertise lasted about a minute. I'm already looking ahead to the next century mark, which carries with it a tantalizing prize.

I do believe I can win Division 2 in Providence. But if I can reach 1700 I will qualify to play in Division 1 alongside the past and future champions, my mentors and backers, the people with the ability to play the total game. So that's my new goal. I have four weeks to gain 87 rating points. I'm going to have to collect a lot of stamps to do it.

First stop, Albuquerque, New Mexico. Every other year, Mike Baron hosts the Southwest Invitational L-Note Special — L-Note because the entry fee is $50 — at his well-appointed adobe home in the sagebrush scrub outside the city. Baron invites a cross-section of players, but the concentration is on the stars. Brian Cappelletto is going for his sixth title in a row here, and arrives with a 2095 rating, by far the best in the land. Jim Geary, rated 1987, is there, as is 1996-rated Trey Wright. Baron himself is rated over 1900, and Chris Cree, who flies in from Dallas, is at 1871. The opportunity for me to play such a lineup of Scrabble all-stars is incredible. And if I can beat one or two of them, 1700 is mine in one quick trip out west.

Baron and his wife, Pamina Deutsch, are terrific hosts. Mike lets me read his voluminous Scrabble archives. Over enchiladas at a famous cheap Mexican restaurant, Mike energetically rehashes his feud with Joe Edley. We pick up bagels and spreads for the next morning. At the photocopy store, we gather the personalized scorecards and score sheets Mike has made, and the giant scoreboard that will be taped to a living-room wall. There are snacks aplenty and shaded, backyard seating in the warm, dry New Mexico air with a breathtaking view of the Sandia Mountains. And there's collegiality unlike at any tournament; when you handpick the players, it's much easier to put together a reasonably well-adjusted group. Players fly in from Portland, Oregon; Boston; New York; Dallas; Chicago; Los Angeles; and Phoenix. A group of us stays at a bed and breakfast a mile away, and we enjoy alfresco breakfasts together. Scrabble for grownups.

With all the niceties, though, it's hard to work up a testosterone high. I have to be social and flip off the competitive switch when the game is done. I can't very well punch a bathroom wall or hurl obscenities into the air.

Ten or eleven wins in the seventeen games — my goal — would require at least two major upsets and beating all seven players rated near or below me. In Game 1, against an 1880-rated player, I bingo to empty the bag (CLARINEt, sticking the blank T between a U and an A, making UtA, a genus of large lizards). But then I draw the Q and lose. Two unchallenged phonies by my opponent are the difference in Game 2. I lose the third game by 18 points. Chris Cree takes me to school in Game 4. Then I finally win one. And then it's Murderers' Row: Cappelletto, Geary, Wright, and Baron.

Brian teaches me a lesson: Don't play scared. He opens with an easy bingo and proceeds to control a tight board, while I play off a few tiles at a time for too few points. I'm afraid to open up the board because I'm afraid he'll bingo. But since Brian has a 30-point lead, I can't win *unless* I open up the board. So it's death by a thousand cuts. I draw poorly, he builds a bingo rack, and then boom: ENHAnCER for 89, and a tight game becomes a 425–234 blowout. "I hate playing intermediates," he says, not meanly. "I feel like I *have* to play that way," he continues, referring to the closed board. The total game it isn't. I want to apologize for not being better.

Against substantially higher-rated opponents, there are two ways to compensate for the yawning gap in word knowledge. The most foolproof is to be very, very lucky: Draw natural bingos and be graced with obvious spots for the Q, X, and Z that you also pull, while the superexpert extracts unplayable dross from the bag. The second-best way to compensate for your shortcomings is to be a little bit lucky, but open up the board enough so that you'll have the opportunity to put down a bingo when fortune strikes. Against Brian, I stared at VIGOURS on my rack with no place to play it.

The worst way is for your superior opponent to have all of the luck. After Trey Wright beats me like a dusty carpet, I face Geary. We sit in the backyard, where I tap my leg nervously, steal wide-eyed glances at the clock, and shuffle frantically. I draw clunky tiles on virtually every turn, but I do well by them, playing awkward words like UNSEWN (30 points), DYKE (28), and MOULDS (31). Then I pick up both blanks at the same time and wring 122 points from them (PATZeR followed by GIRLIEs). While I'm playing Scrabble like a drowning man gasping for air, Geary is laying down a succession of mindless, high-scoring plays. QAT for 32, TOENAIL for 73, MIX for 38, RECLOSE* for 69 (which I neglect to challenge), HUH for 36, REF for 35. I'm trying to move a mountain; he's lying in a hammock sipping iced tea. Geary consumes less than ten minutes of clock time the entire game. Ho hum.

At this point I'm 1–7. I blow a 50-point lead and a sure win against Baron with the daily double of endgame sins: overlooking a winning "out play" *and* exceeding my time by a few seconds, incurring the 10-point penalty that in this instance turns a tie game into a loss. Polite guest that I am, I also lose to Mike's wife. My worst day of tournament Scrabble ends with a 1–9 record.

So much for 1700. I wrap up a depressing weekend with a 5–12 mark (the second day is losers versus losers, so I cadge a few wins). Brian takes first place again. In the fastest awards ceremony on record, he grabs his $385 in winnings and, like most of the players, rushes to the airport. Over the weekend, they'd seen nothing beyond Mike and Pamina's house, a hotel, and the road in between.

Baron e-mails me afterward: "Your quest for improving your skills (and getting that higher rating) is a noble one. Your rise in this past year has been almost meteoric! But *do* continue to enjoy each and every game, regardless of your or your opponent's ratings, and regardless of the game's outcome."

I wonder whether I'm becoming like Marlon, possessed of a gambler's addiction, so blinded by the need to inflate the number associated with my name that I risk having the opposite happen, losing rating points, let alone emotional stability. Post-Albuquerque, my immediate thought isn't the lofty "How can I become a better player?" or "How can I achieve oneness with the board?" It's "How can I still make it to 1700 before the cutoff for the Nationals?"

Now there are three weeks to the deadline — and two more possible tournaments. The first is a fifteen-gamer at a Howard Johnson's off Interstate 95 in Milford, Connecticut, the following weekend. The second is a one-day event the week after that at Columbia University, where G.I. Joel will direct a tournament for the first time. But after Albuquerque, I'm exhausted and demoralized, and as I drive into the New Mexico mountains for a few days of R and R, I tell myself to give up. Play at Joel's tournament, of course, but forget Milford. It's not worth the sacrifice: just one day at home, three hours of traffic, a weekend at a HoJo's. I see the writing in the sky: Surrender, Dorothy.

Then I find myself on a sidewalk pay phone in Taos dialing the woman who is organizing Milford.

Sure, she can squeeze me in. Yes, I'll play in the top division.

I cut short my trip and return home to study. HoJo's, here I come.

I'm burning to make up for my New Mexico humiliation, to replace all of the losses with wins, to reach my new goal. I'm also mentally numb and physically battered from playing so much Scrabble. For the first time, it feels like a job. Or like a bad relationship.

Intellectually, I understand that 1700 is arbitrary. But my construct is so clever! Embarrassed by my at-all-costs fanaticism, I start telling friends that I want to get to 1700 for journalistic reasons. Baron said it would be a much better story if I could conclude my Scrabble journey playing against the best. Jim Geary wrote me, "Readers won't give a shit if you go 70 percent in Division 2. They wanna read how you got your ass kicked in Division 1." I post the note above my desk for inspiration.

And then I drive to Milford. The escape from New York involves four and a half hours of relentless traffic on charmless, truck-heavy I-95. I go alone — no can-you-believe-the-injustice tales from Matt, no black-is-beautiful sermons from Marlon. No roommate at HoJo's at all. I'm there to work, not to have fun, which must be obvious. As I set up my board for the first game, I'm yammering to Larry Sherman about Albuquerque and my rating and this boneheaded play and that gross misfortune.

"You were such a sweet, young guy when you started," Larry deadpans. "Now it's like being with Felt. Sometimes it's like being with Marlon when you leave the room. I hope you're proud of yourself."

I laugh nervously. Larry's joking, but he's not joking. I'm becoming a Scrabble bore, but so what? I have a dream. I've already calculated that, with my rating down to 1564 after Albuquerque, eleven wins at HoJo's will get me to 1700; ten will get me close enough to plant the flag the next weekend in New York.

I didn't calculate what would happen if I win seven games and lose eight. Against 1900-rated Joey Mallick, I fail to block an obvious desperation setup, which Joey (who has played the words LEPROTIC and SUZERAIN) pounces on for 77 points and a 478–440 victory. This match earns me a prize for the high losing score of the tournament, a new sack for my tiles. Whoopee. Another inexcusable loss is to Gordon Shapiro, the retired truck driver from Baltimore who hauls Marlon around to tournaments. His legs weakened by hardened arteries, Gordon rides a motorized cart, muttering "Redrum!" like that kid in *The Shining*, and he drapes a white, monogrammed towel around his neck. I take an early lead on Gordon when I lay down a triple-triple, TADPOLEs, for 140 points.

"I gave you the fucking spot," Gordon says. "I must be fucking brain-dead. Tad-fucking-poles. Can you fucking believe that? Goddamn luckiest bastard I have ever seen."

I laugh, and think it's game, set, match, then neglect to block a hot spot, and post another high-scoring loss, 453–423.

The weekend isn't without its moments. A few recently learned fives (PAREO, a Polynesian garment, to lock up a game; HAMZA, an

Arabic diacritical mark, to steal another). A thoroughly well played victory over Bob Ellickson. The bumbling Mark Berg challenging the word ALLY. "Alley? Alley?" he says. "Allie Sherman? We have a challenge over here!"

I breakfast alone, at a nearby gourmet coffee shop. I lunch alone at the same place. Driving to and from meals, I crank at high volume some inspirational music (Steve Earle's "Transcendental Blues"). I dine alone at a burger place by Long Island Sound, studying lists and reviewing the day's games. I drive home alone, the weekend's work done, the dream deferred. Only thanks to my depressed rating will I recover most of the points lost in Albuquerque.

I'm a Scrabbling Sisyphus, sentenced to scratch and claw my way up the tournament ranks only to be knocked down again. But there must be a reason, a redeeming value to my toil. Camus argued that while the rock-rolling might have sucked, it was liberating. Sisyphus had been king of Corinth, but he served at Zeus's will. By defying Zeus — Sisyphus complained when Zeus made off with the maiden Aegina — Sisyphus unbound himself from his earthly servitude. Every time he walked down the mountain to roll the rock back up, he was free — free to think and free to be himself, opportunities denied in his temporal life.

My freedom is even more complete. *I* have chosen to push the rock up Mount Scrabble. Only my own shortcomings send it tumbling back down.

In rational moments, I recognize that I am improved. Anagramming, so mystifying at the start of this odyssey, is second nature now. Other tasks are even more routine. When I pull tiles from the bag, I record them in alphabetical order on my score sheet as automatically as if they were arranged by a computer. Out come the tiles — RLAOEMQ, say — and down they go onto paper — AELMOQR. (The longest word in there? I see it quickly: MORALE.)

I sense that the very physiology of my brain has changed. To find out why and how, I call Larry Squire, a professor of psychiatry, neurosciences, and psychology at the University of California School of Medicine in San Diego. In addition to being one of the country's leading experts on memory and the brain, Squire was a competitive Scrabble player in the 1970s. He explains that there are two important kinds of memory: declarative and nondeclarative. Both play a role in Scrabble. Declarative memory is memory for facts or events — in Scrabble, memory for the words. Nondeclarative memory is the unconscious recall of skills — for example, processing the spatial configuration of the Scrabble board. Declarative memory is the key to understanding how players absorb and recall the words and why top experts do it better than others.

Words have been common tools in memory studies for more than a century. In the 1880s, the German psychologist Hermann Ebbinghaus created lists of nonsense syllables in which he placed a vowel sound between two consonants, like NEK, LAZ, JEK, and ZUP. (Phonies all in North American Scrabble, though NEK is good in the British book.) Ebbinghaus memorized the lists and then tested his recall. He concluded that there is a distinction between short- and long-term memory, and that repetition helps the information stick around longer. Later studies showed that short-term memory can last only a few seconds, while long-term memory can last a lifetime.

In Scrabble, the goal is to transfer words from short-term to long-term memory through a process of encoding that occurs in various regions of the brain. This phenomenon happens through repetition or by applying cues such as word meanings, sequential lists, or anamonics. Lately, at Joe Edley's suggestion, I've been setting up the tiles on my rack in alphabetical order, because that's how I study racks on paper — the familiar letter sequence can help trigger recognition of a bingo.

As I study and play, Squire says, my brain is undergoing a long-term and complex architectural overhaul. Some of its ten trillion to one hundred trillion synaptic connections are getting stronger, improving my ability to recall words and make plays.

"The deeper the words are processed, the better they are remembered, the more cues are available for retrieving them later," Squire tells me. "Declarative memory sails along easily for people who are experts because they have such a deep encoding experience. A Scrabble player will look at the letters and he will be anagramming already — which letters they combine with, whether they have any uncommon letters. All of that is done without a thought."

This explanation accounts for why it's easier for me now than it was a year ago to see quickly all of the possible words in a rack of common tiles, to recall effortlessly words I've just studied, or to scan a board and see the potential hooks and hot spots. The part of my cerebral cortex that performs that last task, for instance, may have grown by a millimeter or so, Squire says. I probably have created thousands of new cells and hundreds of thousands of new neurons devoted to the activity of finding words and making decisions about how to play them. "You're making new connections, new associations," Squire says.

But I can't keep up with Matt or G.I. Joel or Edley. I haven't studied and played for years the way they have, so my brain hasn't changed to the point at which expertise is fully developed. It's not that they have "better" memories; it's that I don't hold in long-term memory as many chunks of relevant knowledge needed to solve particular Scrabble problems as they do. Their brains have become highly specialized for the perception and information processing specific to Scrabble.

A study by the Carnegie-Mellon professors William Chase and Herbert Simon showed that expert chess players could re-create perfectly a board setup from an actual game, while novice players could not. But when the same pieces were placed randomly on the board, the experts had no better recall of their placement than the novice players. Positions need to have meaning related to the expertise. So when Bob Felt dredges up some position from a decade-old tournament or Matt Graham says to me, "For some reason I remember plays from years and years ago," it's not just raw memory. It's their expertise talking.

But Squire notes that there's a genetic component to expertise, too, even if scientists and researchers haven't yet figured out how to define or measure it. "Mozart was Mozart. No amount of basketball practice is going to turn you or me into Michael Jordan," he says. "The brain we are born with is adept at being good at being a musician or a lawyer or a scientist or an accountant or a Scrabble player."

The New York City subway system is like a favorite library carrel. I get my best studying done there. When I board a train in my Brooklyn neighborhood, I have twenty to forty-five minutes, depending on destination, of total alone time, a perfect concentration increment. I like the fetal rocking motion. I like the periodic announcements. I like the strangers looking over my shoulder and wondering why I'm highlighting funny-looking letter combinations on a page of jumbled uppercase letters. Being engaged in a practice apart from the usual subway behaviors — newspaper reading, catnapping, CD listening, baby tending, battery peddling, panhandling — somehow makes me proud of my (a)vocation, proud of being different, and, therefore, able to focus better. No one said it has to make sense.

G.I. Joel's tournament is held on a hot summer Saturday in an unair-conditioned basement cafeteria at Columbia University Teachers College in upper Manhattan. That's a longish subway ride, just what I need to prepare. I already have calculated that six wins in the seven games will definitely stretch my rating from 1606, where I wound up after Milford, to 1700, and five will get me pretty close. On the Number 2 train, I review some fives. On my notepad I write "NO MISTAKES. Focus. Look deeply. Save time for endgame. Concentrate on minimizing errors.

"TRUST YOURSELF."

And then I repeat the mantra as I walk from the 116th Street subway station to the Columbia building four blocks away. *Trust yourself. You can do it. Trust yourself. You can do it.*

The dark-paneled cafeteria is crowded with thick, sturdy, old oak tables and imposing wooden chairs, like some gothic rathskeller. One giant fan labors futilely to cool the room. But the crowd is buzzing. For a one-day tournament — the first in Manhattan in two and a half years, since my virgin event at the Beverly Bridge Club — the turnout is huge, ninety-eight players, from Matt Graham and Joe Edley to Scrabblers as far afield as Boston and Philadelphia. Even a couple of parkies.

I'm seeded twenty-sixth of thirty-four players in the expert division, just where I need to be to make a big leap. An hour late, G.I. Joel takes a microphone and announces the pairings.

"Bob Felt versus Stefan Fatsis!"

An *ooooh!*, and a few laughs, circulate among the players, and I receive sympathetic claps on the back. "You've got to be kidding," I jokingly say to Joel, as I grab the scorecards from his hand. Felt, the one-time former national champion. Felt, the talkative word machine. Felt, who has a 1953 rating. Felt, the number-one seed in the tournament. (Felt, who has cleaned up his act since moving to New York recently and taking a new computer programming job; he has a smart wardrobe, tucks in his shirts, shaves regularly, and generally is more pleasant to be around.) But I don't shrug or whine. Hell, I've beaten Felt before (once in the ten or so times we've played). And what better time to do it again, when my rating can spike as a result.

I take a deep breath and open with a bingo. After a 36-point PFFT — an interjection expressing a sudden ending, but more important a delicious all-consonant word, like BRRR and CRWTH — I bingo again on turn six for a 110-point lead. Felt answers with a 69-point play. On turn eight, I miss the only bingo on my rack. Felt bingos to go ahead, 314–279. But I bingo back: 345–314. I can taste the win. Then, on turn eleven, I make a conservative blocking play instead of an offensive, higher-scoring one. It's a game-losing move caused by fear and nervousness — and a lack of confidence in my ability to close him out. *Trust yourself.* Felt has the tiles and outscores me the rest of the way. I'm 0–1.

I play Game 2 against eighteen-year-old Daniel Goldman. Danny started playing in tournaments at age ten, cracked 1600 at age fourteen, 1700 at fifteen, and 1800 at sixteen. He was touted as the next Brian Cappelletto and sent by the NSA to play Scrabble on TV with Regis and Kathie Lee. Danny is a smart, energetic, well-rounded kid who dresses in T-shirts, basketball shorts, and high-tops, and who has just been accepted at Columbia. To his credit, he has studied for school more than for Scrabble, so he's yet to become an elite player.

Danny also is an Orthodox Jew, and it's the Sabbath, so he has to modify the normal Scrabble conventions to play. There has been debate among Orthodox Jews over whether playing Scrabble is permissible at all on Shabbat, when, according to the Torah, work is forbidden, as are writing, measuring, and touch that may result in forbidden labor. When he studied at an ultra-Orthodox yeshiva, Sam Orbaum, a newspaper columnist who runs the Jerusalem Scrabble club, asked different rabbis for their interpretations of playing on the

Sabbath. "The responses I got were incredibly hairsplitting, because they were basically theoretical, but that's the nature of Talmudic interpretation," he says.

Generally, playing Scrabble is considered an intellectual pursuit, and therefore Sabbath-acceptable. *How* you play is the issue. One school of thought holds that using a deluxe board is permissible because the tiles are separated by ridges. That separation means the practice of forming words is not like writing, and it also means the letters aren't contiguous, so the game can be disassembled without breaking anything (breaking and separating are prohibited on the Sabbath). But an opposite interpretation holds that the letters on a deluxe board are fixed in place, so it *is* like writing; a flat board, on the other hand, offers no permanence to what is being set down, and is therefore permissible. Orbaum, who is nonreligious now and plays with a clean conscience on the Sabbath, was told that mixing the tiles isn't allowed, but that one could play if they were laid upside down on the table rather than placed in the bag. I once saw an Orthodox player use an assistant to draw tiles and hit the clock for him.

Danny plays with a deluxe board and without an assistant. But he uses a wind-up chess clock — electronic devices can't be used on the Sabbath — and even that, Danny says, is questionable because a clock is considered by some to involve measuring. After the game, Danny asks his opponent to pick up the tiles, so he doesn't do any breaking up, and to fill out the score sheets. Also to avoid writing, Danny keeps score and tracks tiles by using washers and nuts. On a sheet listing the numbers 1 to 600 and the tile frequency, Danny places nuts on the number indicating his score and washers on his opponent's score and on the tiles played.

Nuts, washers, whatever. I play ITEMIzER for 60 points late in the game. Danny challenges, it stays on the board, and I eke out a 380–346 come-from-behind victory. I take Game 3 when my opponent, Audrey Tumbarello, eats the Q. But when I drop Game 4, to 1900-rated Lynn Cushman, falling to 2–2, I figure the dream is dead.

I bingo late to win Game 5. I play a solid Game 6 against another strong player: PASHA yields 45 points thanks to three parallel hooks, SOILURe builds a lead, and a tactically sound ICE for 36 locks it up. When I drop down BLOVIATE (to talk or write verbosely or windily) on the second turn of Game 7, and then cruise to victory, despite not seeing a blank, I realize I've gone 5–2 against a strong field. Maybe I do still have a shot at 1700.

I finish in eighth place overall — ahead of a 4–3 Edley and a 3–4 Graham — and take home $125 for having the second-best record of players in the bottom half of the expert division. Joel shakes my hand heartily. I think he's proud of me. Edley, meanwhile, is grumpy, especially after an uncharacteristic error that cost him the last game. When I tell him my record, wait for his usual sincere congratulations, and suggest to him that I may reach 1700, he snaps, "You're not going to make it. No, you're not going to make it."

Danny isn't so sure, and eagerly volunteers to calculate an estimate. He still can't write because the sun hasn't set yet, so I record the numbers he tells me to while he performs a mental calculus, an amazing feat on its own. Danny mumbles, I scribble, and he totals the figures in his head.

"Oh, God," Danny says. "It's like 1696 or 1697. You're just going to miss. Let's hope I'm off by a few points in the right direction. But I don't think I am. That sucks. I can't believe it. That really sucks."

Any one game in the last month could have gone my way had I not overlooked some (in hindsight) obvious move, or had my fingers, pawing the bottom of a tile bag, clutched a blank instead of a W, an S rather than a U, or had my opponent done the opposite. The few points don't make me a better or worse player, don't mean I could be expected to perform better or worse in the top division of the Nationals.

So maybe, I muse, I'll ask for an author's exemption. I had begun this Plimptonian journey as a bottom-dwelling novice, playing (and losing) to the blue-hairs and other assorted stamp collectors. I would end it playing the greatest who had ever shuffled a rack, Edley and G.I. Joel and Cappelletto and Graham and Tiekert and Felt. I would prove that I belong. And I would end the tale on the biggest stage yet: the 2000 Nationals, the largest Scrabble tournament ever in North America.

Edley confirms the worst: 1697. Three measly points. "I'm sorry," he says.

Edley is a stickler for procedure, so I turn for my exemption to John Williams. I make a proposal: The annual twenty-game Fourth of July tournament in Albany — one of the best events on the circuit because of its length, strong field, and equitable pairing system — is the following weekend. Extend the July 1 deadline, I suggest. If I crack 1700 there, let me play Division 1.

John says he'll discuss it with Edley. But he reminds me how far I've come from the day we first played in a Manhattan hotel room and I pulled everything and won. John hasn't entered a tournament in two years, but he still considers himself a decent player. I've kidded him as I passed his current rating of 1350 and then his peak rating of 1550. And I've beaten him consistently of late, even racking up my first 600-point game.

"It's astonishing what you've achieved," Williams tells me. "You've come far so fast. And you're probably better than your rating, though it pains me to say that."

Go over 1700 at Albany, he tells me, and we'll talk.

Albany will be my fourth tournament in as many weeks, my sixth in nine weeks in four states and two time zones. I feel as if I'm running for president. My Scrabble dreams are becoming more frequent and intense: the floating words, the unsolvable games, the opponent phonies that stay on the board. I try to exercise daily between events, to clear my head of the most recent games and get stronger for the next, but lack the energy. I read more word lists instead.

Like any addict, I take pains to hide my addiction. I complain about the exhaustion, but privately can't wait for the next tournament. The flimsiest excuse is all I needed to register for Albany, and, happily, I have one. I tell a non-Scrabble pal that, after two months of nonstop tournaments, I'm completely Scrabbled out. But I *have* to play Albany, have to get to 1700, have to make it to Division 1. "For the book," I say.

"Yeah," he replies, honey-thick with sarcasm. "For the book."

Fine. I'll say it: for me. After almost a year as a full-time Scrabble player, I'm close to achieving something. It isn't just the number and the recognition that goes with it. When I mention to Ron Tiekert that I want to play Division 1 in Providence, he says, "I hope we don't meet up there given how you've played against me." Ron Tiekert! A former national champ! I'd been fortunate the last couple of times we've played — once he couldn't stop me from bingoing out with SANGRIA to win, 496–455 — and while I was nowhere near his caliber, and never would be, I finally was *accepted*, as a player.

Outside Albany, at the Marriott in suburban Colonie, along a highway lined with strip malls and corporate parks, in a top division of thirty-two, I split my first two games and face Ron in Game 3. He wins by 198 points.

In Game 5, I lose to Matt, 470–430, on a blunder; so accustomed am I to his playing phonies when he's down, I challenge SPAViET, which turns out to be the adjectival form of SPAVIN, a disease of horses. Had I not challenged, we determine, I could have won. I lose to another 1900-rated player, Randy Greenspan, when I thoughtlessly forfeit a turn on a word that I almost surely know to be, and is, phony. But I win the games I should. The opposition is all strong, and I'm intense, in the zone. After one game, I look down to see blood on one of my tiles; I cut my finger and didn't notice.

In Game 10, I meet up with Danny Goldman again. After playing ACIDURIa (a condition of having excessive acid in the urine) and then blocking the most fruitful bingo line, Danny has a 318–267 lead. The board looks like this:

Focus, I tell myself. Play like the expert you allegedly are. The letters on my rack are AABORST. The words ABATORS (which I see) and RABATOS (which I do not) don't fit anywhere on the board. On to Plan B. There are five tiles left in the bag, plus the seven on Danny's rack. Together, the unseen letters from my perspective are ADDEFLNORVW?. I write them down on my score sheet. Next, I conclude that I almost certainly must bingo to win. As it stands, there is but one place to bingo: down from the M at position O8. I examine my rack and determine that if I had a D instead of a B, I could play MATADORS.

My heart beats faster because this isn't too long a shot: There are two D's plus a blank unseen to me. So, if I were to play off the B, I would have a 3 in 12 chance of drawing what I need.

The problem is that in order to have a shot at MATADORS, I have to use the B to create a second place to play a bingo. Otherwise, Danny will simply kill the triple-word column below the M, effectively ending the game. I realize that if I place the B at position M2, making the word BO, I can hook it to form ABO (an Australian shorthand, usually disparaging, for "aborigine") as part of a triple-word-score bingo.

I place my bet on the 4-to-1 pony. Down goes the B. Into the bag goes my hand. Out comes a D.

Olé!

Danny blocks the Row 1 bingo line by playing VAT vertically to the T in OOT, taking a 338–271 lead. Both of our clocks have ticked below a minute.

My eyes as big as poker chips, I hurriedly deposit MATADORS onto the board. "Ninety-one!" I shriek. "Oh, shit!" Danny mutters. Danny is energetic and enthusiastic to begin with; whenever he draws tiles, he roots around the bag violently, as if there's a snake in there that needs strangling. Now, he's shaking with worry and excitement. I've surged ahead, 362–338.

There are two tiles left in the bag, but before I can extricate them Danny stuns me with FaVE at 1L through his V for 42 points and a 380–362 lead; VAT was a setup designed to counter a possible bingo by me. I shout "Hold!" — I can't remember whether it's FAVE or FAB that's unacceptable; I know one of them is no good. My two tiles are LW, and instantly I know I'm dead.

	A	B	C	D	E	F	G	H	I	J	K	L	M	N	O
1												F	a	V	E
2													B	A	
3			Z									O	O	T	
4		F	E	U					E	L	K				
5		E	P	I	C			A	M	I	A				
6					H	O	O	T							
7				J	I	N						Q			
8	G		B	O	D	E	G	A				E	X	A	M
9	R	P	I	E	S			W	O	N		T			A
10	I	R						E	H						T
11	E		Y	U	L	E	S								A
12	V	I	N	Y		A									D
13	E	T			A	C	I	D	U	R	I	a			O
14	R						N								R
15	S					L	U	N	G	E					S

If FaVE is good, there is nowhere for me to make up enough points to win; the most I can score is 5 points, with LaW at M12, to go out, absorbing 10 points from Danny's rack, and losing by 3, 380–377. If I had drawn an O to go with the W, I could have played OW at 14E (forming AWL) for 27 points and victory. The clock ticks. With no other apparent way to win, I challenge FaVE. It's good. (FAB* isn't.) Danny wins, 396–376.

We exhale simultaneously.

"Wow!" Danny says with hyperbolic teen excitement. "That was amazing!"

"What an incredible endgame," I say, still staring at the board.

"You made a brilliant play," he says, meaning my 4-point play of BO.

"I don't know about brilliant," I reply. "Anyway, you made an even better one."

It is my most satisfying Scrabble sequence yet. I did everything right: I considered how I could still win (by bingoing); I calculated the odds of a particular occurrence (4 to 1 for drawing a D or blank); I figured out the best way to make that happen — dumping the B — while simultaneously opening another spot to bingo; I willed a D out of the bag (that's what Edley would say); I played the bingo; and I challenged his play when I wasn't 100 percent sure. And I did it all under severe time pressure.

Danny and I reconstruct the sequence to check for blunders, but we can't find any. His 20-point VAT was the great move; he could have played FaVE right away, but that would have emptied the bag and I would have bingoed out with MATADORS. Danny needed to leave at least one tile in the bag; he left two.

A crowd gathers, as it does whenever it's clear a compelling end-game has transpired. I'm exhilarated — by the attention, and by Danny's effusive praise for the calculated fish that led to MATA-DORS, but more by the just-completed game itself. As the sequence unfolded over the board, nothing else mattered. The score didn't matter. Winning and losing didn't matter. My rating didn't matter. Playing Division 1 in Providence didn't matter. All that mattered was exploiting the new synaptic connections in my brain, understanding the puzzle and solving it — in short, thinking like a pro. And I did all of those things. I displayed calm, smarts, and sophistication. I did what true board-game experts do: assess the environment, see all of the possibilities, calculate the probability, and maximize the chance of winning. The tiles didn't fall my way, but that didn't matter either.

It's an epiphanic moment. I got it. I finally got it. I played the total game.

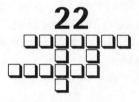

1697

MY BRAVURA PERFORMANCE is quickly upstaged by Ron Tiekert. Later in the tournament, playing Bob Felt, Ron holds a rack of EENRSU?. Through an existing A, B, and G, he plays all of his tiles, making the blank an I.

A *real* crowd gathers.

"AUBERGiNES! Jesus Christ! Jesus Christ!" Matt Laufer exclaims. "That's it. The ultimate has been reached."

People are clutching their heads, mouths are agape, eyes are bugging out. The buzz spreads through the expert division and players rush over. *Ron played AUBERGiNES! Through three disconnected letters!*

"That's better than STOREWIDE," Matt Graham says, citing one of his personal bests. "That's better than NEPHRITIC," he says, citing another.

"Through the A, the B, and the G!" Jan Dixon blares. "That's incredible!"

Ron stands over the board, bent slightly at the waist, the same position as when he walks; Ron's center of gravity seems to be in his eyeglasses. He is dressed in shorts, a short-sleeved dress shirt, and white sneakers. Thin, black dress socks stretch over his calves. He is massaging his gums with one of his ever-present dental picks. He pushes his eyeglasses back up on his nose and explains how it happened.

"I had seen it as something possible, something that was in the bag," Ron says. Which is even more incredible, because that means he had determined, based on the unplayed tiles, that AUBERGiNES was a possibility. And then the tiles fell into place.

"I saw it," Ron demurs. "What can I tell you?"

I won't make 1700 and I know it as soon as Albany ends. My "brilliant" sequence against Danny doesn't stop me from losing seven of the last ten games to finish with an 8–12 record. Danny does the math, but he doesn't need to. I'm cooked.

Yet there's no disappointment. Somehow, that one game, that carefully orchestrated sequence of moves, is enough to compensate for the lost opportunity, and it's oddly comforting. At least until my official rating arrives a few days later: 1691, a 6-point drop. And then I hear voices. How did I miss KOS to win in Game 14? How did I lose by just 7 points in Game 20? My mind drifts back. Choking against Felt in Game 1 in New York . . . those four easy wins at Milford that slipped away . . . the missed out play against Mike Baron in his backyard . . . hell, playing YER* at Danbury long ago when YE would have meant a 12–3 record and a road to a sure victory . . . *any one game that could have gone the other way.*

The Albany tournament, because of its length, is rated in two chunks of ten games each. After my 5–5 first half, the cross-table that arrives from NSA headquarters informs, my rating climbed to 1713. But midtournament ratings don't count for tournament qualifying. So I broke 1700, but I didn't. A tree fell in the forest, but no one heard it.

Everyone likes to complain about the ratings system. Some elite players moan that ratings at the top have deflated by 50 to 100 points in the last decade because there are more good players and because of a mathematical bias against the higher-rated. Simply put, the percentage of games experts must win against lower-rated opponents in order simply to sustain their ratings is greater than the percentage of games they do actually win. At the other end, lower-rated players complain that it's too hard to *gain* ratings points; with so many similarly skilled players, moving up can be a long, hard slog.

Both are right, and the mathematicians agree the system needs tweaking (someone even wrote a doctoral dissertation on Scrabble ratings). In a broader sense, though, it works uncannily well. I belly-ached as my rating flatlined. *I'm underrated!* I whined. *I should be winning more than I am! It's not fair that I have to play the blue-hairs when I know I'm better!* But I wasn't! My results — and my rating — said so. It wasn't until I began understanding *how* to win, when the teachings of Joe Edley took root, that my rating rose. Winning became a byproduct of good play, and my rating went up. I won when I deserved to, and lost when I didn't, and my rating was an accurate barometer of my skill level.

So when I fail to crack 1700, I conclude, it's because I don't deserve to crack 1700. Not in some cosmic, deterministic sense, but in a rigidly mathematical one. In Albany, seven of my eight victories were against players rated below or near me (1615–1734), while all twelve of my losses were against substantially higher-rated opponents (1746–1892). I won when I was expected to and lost when I was expected to and barely budged in the end.

Still, I'm faced with a dilemma. The angel on my left shoulder says I should accept the Albany results as a true gauge of my ability and play in Division 2. The devil on my right says I should still ask for that exemption to play in Division 1. Mike Baron wants me to play up to cap my Horatio Alger story. He even dashes off a sample letter to send to John Williams requesting the exemption.

"You have nothing to lose by asking, *sí*?" Mike writes me.

"Except my pride," I reply.

I decide to play in Division 2. While I have come far, I haven't come far enough. I didn't make it, fair and square. No bogus exemption for me. I won't be squaring off against G.I. Joel or Tiekert or Edley or Cappelletto, the *Rocky* theme echoing in my head as I topple former champions like dominoes en route to the greatest underdog win in sports history. But I won't be playing any blue-hairs, either.

I'm sitting on the sofa in my living room. I lift my eyes from the word list I happen to be studying and think about what I've accomplished. The previous six months have involved the most rigorous and disciplined course of study I've ever undertaken, college included. My Scrabble infatuation deepened with every new word learned, every game played, win or lose, every life-or-death blip in my rating. My appreciation for language and game strategy increased exponentially. And every time I reached a goal, I set another, higher one, and achieved all but the last.

Then I remember one more goal, Joe Edley's challenge from months earlier: Win Division 2. On to Providence.

In the month before the Nationals, I study at least an hour every day. I review the threes and fours. I study all of the fives that I don't know. On the subway, in the john, on the exercise bike at the gym, on the roof of my building. I plow through sevens (five thousand of them) and eights (twenty-five hundred) in order of probability, using my lime green and orange highlighters to mark off unfamiliar words. Mike Baron has posted to CGP the top hundred seven-letter stems, the eight-letter words they form by adding a letter to the stem, and an anamonic for each, and I even manage to commit many of those to memory: DETRAIN: CHOO-CHOO STOPS, I GET OUT; TOILERS: COULDN'T FLIP BUS; NUTSIER: BLAME IQ DIP ON TV; SIGNORE: ITALIAN WED BY CREEPS. Word lists cover my desk and coffee table and dining room table. Bingos starting with ANTI. Bingos ending in IZE. Q bingos. J, Q, X, and Z fives and sixes. Pages of sevens and eights. Score sheets from recent games waiting to be analyzed and reanalyzed. "Man, you serious," Marlon says when he visits. "Look at all this shit."

And I play. In the club, in the park, at Matt's apartment, where I drop five in a row in one session, forking over $25. I drive an hour to my friend Dominic Grillo's apartment in New Jersey. Another twenty-something expert, a biostatistician named Scott Appel, shows up. We play, and play, and play, until I'm exhausted and announce my departure, saying, "What time is it? Around eleven?" "Um, it's 1:00 A.M.," Dominic says, laughing. As I leave, they start another game.

More than twenty people show up in Washington Square Park one weekend afternoon — a record, the parkies say. G.I. Joel schedules extra club sessions to help people prepare for Providence; on a rainy Sunday, using a full set of tiles, Joel and a few others plow through all 1,501 words contained in Baron's stem list. I'm finding good stuff: ABDELOU through an N (UNDOABLE). The only bingo in CEEINR? that begins with a vowel (EIRENiC). AGIONST through an L (SOLATING). A triple-triple through a G with AEILLST in hand (LEGALIST). I play ZEROTH and OVERFAST against Bob Felt and UNIQUEsT through a Q against Danny Goldman and aNTE-FIXA through an X against Dominic. And when I miss plays, I try not to worry. The mental game, I tell myself, is as important as the actual moves made. Be Joe Edley. (Edley, by the way, doesn't study in the two weeks before the Nationals, focusing instead on rest and meditation. He is spending a week with his wife and daughter at the upstate retreat Chautauqua. Edley teaches a daily Scrabble class and then relaxes.)

I share my progress with Eric Chaikin out in Los Angeles. Eric was a word man long before I was — creating puzzles, poring through *Webster's Third,* studying linguistics at Brown — but mysteriously can't win consistently at Scrabble. Despite knowing hundreds more words than I do, Eric's rating is 1675, so we're both in Division 2 in Providence. Lately, though, he reports, he has made a breakthrough.

"I could tell from your recent reports that you've definitely gotten over the proverbial hump," Eric tells me in an e-mail. "Happily, I think I can finally say I've faced the demons and done the same." The previous week, Eric reports, he played twenty-one games — "against good people" — and won fourteen. He averaged 421 points per game, including scores of 561, 558, 507, and 501. He tallied forty-six bingos, including such obscure words as DIECIOUS, HEXADIC, and DEMESNES. He played oOTHECAE, TOkAMAkS, and WISE-ACRe. Eric's e-mail ends: "LET'S ROCK AT THE BIG DANCE!"

Strapped for money, Matt Graham considers playing in Division 2, where he figures he would be a mortal lock to take the $5,000 first prize. Matt's rating has slipped to 1877, so he has the choice of playing in the 1700–1900 group or where he belongs, in Division 1. But while ratings ebb and flow for many top players, no self-respecting high expert would play "down" with the likes of me and other low experts. But Matt needs the money. And he likes the intrigue. He genuinely believes that by spreading a rumor that he's playing Division 2, the top experts will issue a collective sigh of relief — and then he'll psyche everyone out by changing his mind at the last minute. People do talk about Matt's "decision." Not because they are relieved but because it's so absurd. As Marlon points out, "When you do stuff like that there's no way in the world you win."

Matt also believes he can win Division 1. He hasn't worked since his latest stint at the Conan O'Brien show ended two months ago, so all he's had to focus on is Scrabble. He pulled out flash cards he made to prepare for the 1996 Nationals. "I've probably added a thousand bingos," he tells me. Division 2? Please.

But in Albany, Matt is jittery. He seems to be taking more pills than ever. His hands shake noticeably. In the park one Sunday, Matt is playing a two-on-one money game, he and Richie Lund versus mild-mannered Ron Tiekert. In severe time trouble late in the game, Matt plays with both hands, laying down the tiles with one hand and simultaneously hitting the clock with the other, violating the spirit of the rules. It doesn't really matter, because Ron wins and Matt goes over by a second anyway, but Ron mentions that Matt was "holding and hitting." It's a sportsmanship issue, and Ron, acknowledged as the game's most ethical player, can't tolerate rules bending.

"Fuck you!" Matt screams, rising from the park bench. "Fuck you! I resent that!"

I watch in horror. Matt's cursing Ron! Gentleman Ron! Even worse, *Ron* apologizes for implying that Matt and his quivering hands were bending the rules. Of course, Ron knows Matt was bending the rules. But he also sees the rage and the red face and the shaking hands and figures the issue isn't worth pressing.

A couple of weeks later, Matt appears calm and centered. He says he has been getting up at 7:30 every morning to condition his body for the early starts in Providence. He has been working out at a gym a few blocks away (Matt sneaks in with a friend). He's excited, in what seems a healthy way. While studying, he tells me before a session at his apartment, he's been listening to a CD called *Tune Your Brain with Mozart*. The "alpha-wave" selections (including "Divertimento in B-flat Major, Fourth Movement, Adagio") supposedly help one concentrate and improve retention. Beta-wave cuts ("Sonata for Piano and Violin in B-flat Major, Third Movement, Allegretto") are designed for quick thinking and working at peak energy.

Then, just before we play, Matt dips his finger in a jar of Vicks and smears some under his nose. "Aside from all the fucking drugs I use," he says, "menthol helps your ability to recall." And he tells me he's thinking about renting a portable oxygen tank for the tournament; more oxygen in the bloodstream improves brain function, he says. "I'd look pretty kooky sitting there in the morning having coffee with the tubes in my nose," he says. "But effective is effective, right?"

As the tournament approaches, I begin to doubt Matt's potential. Sure, his anagramming skills are great, and his board vision is amazing. But he's just not emotionally centered enough to win. If it's just about the money — and for Matt, it actually might be — then I think he should drop down to Division 2. Because I don't think he can win Division 1.

After a session in the park in which he wins more than $200 — playing $50 games against his regular opponent, a bread deliveryman named Dave Lipschutz who is no better a player than I am but who loves to gamble — Matt contemplates an offer. Dave says he'll pay Matt $400 in exchange for a quarter of any winnings in Providence. Matt ponders the proposition. If he really believes he's going to win, a quarter of $25,000 is a lot more than $400. Matt turns it down.

Marlon, meanwhile, has been holed up in *his* room in Baltimore. "I'm living like that goofball," he says, meaning Matt. Marlon has stopped smoking cigarettes, and is watching his weight so as not to balloon with the nicotine deprivation. He has been writing his book, studying four to seven hours a day, and playing an occasional game with his mother, Hattie. (When I visited Marlon at home a few months earlier, Hattie insisted that we play. I won twice. "She embarrassing me!" Marlon bellowed. "He gonna sit up and beat my mother half to death! You ain't my mommy anymore!")

"I done went crazy studying extensions," he reports. "Every extension imaginable." Two-, three-, and four-letter front and back extensions to seven- and eight-letter words. He learned DONKEYWORK and TRAILERABLE and SAWTIMBER and NILPOTENT. He found DESPITEOUS, which he notes serves as an extension for both DESPITE and PITEOUS. "I don't want no surprises," he says. "That's why I've been doing everything."

Marlon comes to New York before the Nationals and stays over the night before we leave for Providence. We play a final ceremonial game in the morning. Marlon wins by a point. We drive to pick up

Matt and the visiting Jim Geary, who after winning the summer Reno tournament enters the Nationals rated above 2000, second to Brian Cappelletto. Matt isn't there when we arrive. After a few minutes, he strolls up the block carrying, among other things, a portable oxygen tank, which he has just bought for $130. "I figure it paid for itself yesterday in the park," he says.

Matt has typically, compulsively overpacked. A two-foot-long leather bag contains nothing but pills. He brings all of his clean laundry, still bagged. A white-noise machine. A basketball. His stuffed animals.

In the car, Matt is edgy. He pulls out some bingo flash cards, but he's slow in solving them while Geary is virtually automatic. (I beat them all to one: EFHIILST — TILEFISH.) After arriving in Providence, we go to a catered reception for players hosted by Hasbro and the NSA. Matt has a few beers, and I hear him carrying on about how well he's been playing and how Geary was making mistakes and deferring to him during warmup games.

A bunch of us walks over to a rock club a few blocks away owned by Rich Lupo, who introduced Eric Chaikin to the game when Eric was an undergraduate at Brown in the 1980s; Lupo has entered the tournament despite not having played competitively in more than a decade. At his club, Lupo has laid linoleum tiles on the dance floor in the form of a Scrabble board. Matt has a couple more beers, and becomes progressively more hostile and angry; I think he's mad because I dissed the oxygen tank; he accuses me of being anhedonic, that is, unable to experience pleasure.

Frankly, he's making me nervous. I had chosen to room with Matt, for journalistic reasons, but now I'm regretting the choice. I feel as if his presence is interfering with my preparation. Our room is better stocked than a nutrition store — smart drugs cover the bedroom and bathroom counters, fill two drawers, and spill onto the floor. I sleep badly; Matt snores, and I'm nervous about the tournament, and words are flying through my head like gnats at a picnic. I wake up at 5:00, toss until 7:00. When Matt leaves for his ritual two large cups of Dunkin Donuts coffee, I put on a classical music station. Maybe, I think, the music contains the alpha waves I'll need for the tournament. Or is it beta?

*   *   *

John Williams had boasted that the 2000 Nationals would be the most impressive yet, and it is. Playing in the Rhode Island Convention Center — a sleek, modern centerpiece of a downtown revival led by the city's ex-con mayor — and not a hotel ballroom makes it feel like a world-class sporting event. The NSA came to Providence to showcase Scrabble for Rhode Island–based Hasbro, which is spending about $500,000 on the event, including close to $90,000 in prize money. Hasbro Chairman Alan Hassenfeld is expected to make an appearance, which would be the first time a senior Hasbro executive has shown up at a Nationals.

The thirty-thousand-square-foot playing hall, nearly half a football field, is breathtaking. There are more than 150 tables — two games to a table — for the six divisions of competitors. The top three divisions are to the right as you enter, the bottom three to the left. The NSA persuaded Hasbro to print special boards for the event, replacing the dark, glary design made for the game's fiftieth anniversary which players consider unusable. (During the taping of an episode of her TV show devoted to Scrabble, which she loves, Martha Stewart off-camera called the old board "really ugly.") The center square of the special board — white background with the traditional red, pink, and blue premium squares — features a commemorative Providence logo. At the front of the hall, on a raised platform, data-entry workers record the results of every game on eight computers and a program spits out results and pairings. The NSA's Webmaster and an Internet reporter post continuous updates. The familiar giant Scrabble board bears the message HAVE A WORD WITH US.

Over the public-address system, Williams welcomes the throng and drops some stats. We'll play more than 9,000 games over the next five days and make more than 13,000 challenges. "And I expect 163,000 complaints about drawing bad tiles," he says.

"But the number we're focused on is six hundred players," Williams says. "Just for context, ten years ago at the national championships, we had two hundred forty players. Just amazing. One of the reasons we wanted to have this in Providence is to demonstrate that tournament Scrabble is dynamic, cool, fun, and exploding. I think we've done our job. Now let's play Scrabble."

* * *

Two years of playing, studying, and obsessing have come down to this moment. I want to do well, not only for myself, but for Edley and G.I. Joel and everyone else who has tutored and encouraged and taken me to school, as it were, over a board. I feel a debt to these people for whom Scrabble is life, who have helped to make Scrabble *my* life. They are like a pack of wolves raising a human baby: They took me in and taught me to hunt and gather and shielded me from the taunts of others. Now they're sending me out into the woods to fend for myself.

I high-five my buddies, Eric and Dominic and Scott and Marlon, who tells me to just do it. I'm focused, determined, pumped. Twenty-three wins in the thirty-one games should be enough to win the division — and I still believe I can do it, even though I'm seeded 49th out of 105. I'm determined, but also realistic, so twenty wins would make me happy. Twenty wins undoubtedly would place me in the Top 10. Twenty wins would send my rating skyward. I join the crowd around the bulletin board outside the playing room that lists the pairings. I scribble down the names of my first four opponents and their ratings: 1720, 1733, 1758, 1784.

Suddenly, a voice in my head says, *You could lose all four of these games.*

And then I do.

In Game 1, I call "hold" when my opponent, Ann Sanfedele of the New York club, lays down RANGLED*. I know this isn't good (DANGLER and GNARLED are the only words therein), but then I doubt myself, and I let it go. I lose by 11 points. In Game 2, I miss the easy bingo in AINOTT? on the second turn of the game (sTATION) and pass up the one I do see (ANTIpOT) because it slots the second T in the triple-word-score column. Then I miss the easy catch in BDEILLU (BULLIED) and lose by 92. In Game 3, a comeback falls short. In Game 4, I play perhaps my worst game of Scrabble ever, inexplicably opening with the phony YEY* (shades of YER*), challenging an acceptable three-letter word, falling behind by 160 points, and *still* managing to blow a chance to win, when both blanks materialize on my rack late in the game.

Eric Chaikin also starts 0–4. We are not rocking at the big dance.

In Game 5, after lunch, I manage a win, by 3 points, finding IN-

NArDS with my time dwindling. In Game 6, I miss another late-blank bingo that would win. And I wrap up the day from hell with a blank-less, S-less nightmare in which I lose by more points (239) than I score (218). Before it ends, I stare across the vast hall, just wishing it over. All the preparation. The lists, the games, the angst. For this? For a 1–6 record and a −546 spread? What happened to the confidence? The stoic demeanor over the board? The assiduous word study? Had I just been lucky? Could I really be this bad when it matters?

"Bet you twenty bucks you're not worse than me," Eric says afterward.

"No way," I say. "Well, I know you were oh and four. But you can't be worse. Okay. A dollar. I'm one and six."

"Oh and seven."

I hand him the dollar.

Joe Edley, who won all seven of *his* games, spots me looking suicidal and offers some advice. "Go work out, have a good meal, and get a good night's rest," he says. "And start over tomorrow."

Start over tomorrow. Easy for him to say. I have six losses. I'm out of it. And I'm incensed. I angrily hoist my bag and walk back to my hotel room. Matt Graham follows. I don't even ask how he did, because I do not care.

"I don't know why you and Eric are so upset when I'm the one with something on the line," he says, meaning he has no money and needs to win, he believes, in order to support himself.

That does it. I think, Fuck you, Matt. Just because you've chosen to stake your financial well-being on the remote possibility of winning a goddamn Scrabble tournament against the world's best players doesn't make your games more important than mine. "Why shouldn't it matter as much to us as it does to you?" I bark. "Are our losses any less meaningful than yours?"

Now I'm furious. I work out, have a good meal, and get a good night's rest. Tomorrow I will kick ass.

"Dude," Eric says the next morning as we peruse the standings and write down our pairings. "This is not us. We're better than this."

I'm in 101st place. Eric is in 104th.

"Yesterday," I say. "It's over."

"I'm looking forward to making up all of this ground," he says.

I'm still angry, but now I channel my anger. I quickly, confidently play a phony bingo on the second turn of Game 8, and it stays, and I romp. My record goes to 2–6. I draw great tiles in Game 9, get away with GOFERED*, and win 553–298. I'm 3–6. I stay mad in Game 10 and win by 30. Now I'm 4–6. In Game 11, I play superbly. I find DILATIVE from the D. PLEADING through the I. Off the board come two phony bingos attempted by my opponent, the second of which leads me to play HEY, creating a hook down the first column for the T that I possess and she doesn't. Boom. SHORTIA for 94, and a challenge (it's an herb). On the penultimate play of the game, I play two tiles — a blank and the Q, making SHORTIAs and sUQ across a triple-word score — for 63 points. Final score: 588–267. Record: 5–6. A perfect morning ends.

Another win after lunch, when I find BWANA in the endgame. And then I lose — my OVERsUP being too little, too late to overcome some early misplays. That makes me mad again, and in the day's final game I hoard the last two S's and the final U and pick the Q, as I'd planned, capitalizing on a deliberate, unstoppable setup that allows me to play SQUIBS for 63 points and a win. I finish the day with a 6–1 record and a spread of +819. I'm back to even and up to forty-fourth place. Thank you, Joe.

"That's great," says Edley, who is 11–3 and in second place in Division 1. "You did it. Wouldn't it be something if you won it after a 1–6 start?"

"One day at a time," I say.

Eric's comeback began that afternoon. He had plunged to 1–10, and then he, too, just decided to stop losing. Eric discovered that it helped to think bad thoughts about his opponents. *Really* bad thoughts. That they would be contracting fatal diseases or that their spouses would be leaving them. It wasn't quite like having a parapsychologist stare down opponents, the way Russian chess champion Anatoly Karpov used to do. But it worked. Eric won all three games.

The following day, after the morning session (me: 2–2; Eric: 3–1), we take a long walk up College Hill to the Brown campus, where Eric reminisces about his undergraduate days and tries to deduce why he (we) isn't (aren't) better at Scrabble. Eric says something just seems to happen when he's playing; he focuses so intensely on scouring a rack for bingos that he loses sight of the game's purpose: to make the best move.

Part of the problem, Eric reasons, is that he's always been infatuated with wordplay rather than competition. He demonstrates that devotion one night at the tournament, when he explains to other math-brained word lovers his concept of "supervocalics," a word he coined to describe words or phrases containing the letters A, E, I, O, and U once each (Julia Roberts is a supervocalic actress; Mozambique and Belorussia are the only two supervocalic countries; Hair Club for Men is a supervocalic . . . hair club). Eric is a patient, dedicated linguistic analyst, but over the board, in competition, something goes awry. "Maybe I'm just not good at games," he says.

So frustrated with his performance, Eric vowed to quit the game entirely when his record plunged to 1–10. His word obsession had eaten up too many hours of life. Studying wasn't paying off, so why bother? Now that he had rebounded to 7–11, he was less definitive.

And me? I still wanted to win twenty, as unlikely as that seemed with a 9–9 record. Regardless, we return to the playing room relaxed. Eric takes two out of three to improve to 9–12, and I play sharply. In Game 19, I catch a big break when, with the bag nearly empty, my opponent transposes the D and T in VELDT. His right hand is in the bag drawing fresh tiles when I spot the mistake, and I shout "Hold it!" before his hand emerges, and then "Challenge!" It's a game-saving play, because after I play QUEUE for 48 points in the same spot, there's dreck in the bag. Not only would I have eaten the Q but probably the K and a Y, too. I eke out another win in Game 20, helped by back-to-back bingos, LOCATORS and REFeRENT. And I prevail in a cat-and-mouse endgame in the next round when I calculate the odds of my opponent bingoing if I open a fresh line (for an eight-letter bingo ending in E, which I want to do because I have strong tiles). I determine that his only possible bingo is AcCURaTE, using both blanks, so I open the new line. It works out. I draw one of the blanks and play dISTANCE for 80 points with one tile in the bag.

I'm 12–9 and up to thirtieth place. Walking purposefully to the front of the hall to turn in the score sheet, I pump my fist like Tiger Woods and squeeze an angry "Yes!" through gritted teeth.

*   *   *

Brian Cappelletto was everyone's favorite to win it all. Joe Edley wasn't. But Edley had prepared for the event as only Edley could. He eliminated dairy from his diet. He began visiting an acupuncturist, who porcupined him regularly in the weeks before the tournament. "Twelve or thirteen needles," Edley tells me. "Four in my head, one in my neck, two in my chest. It did open me up." He maintained his qi gong, breathing, and meditation regimen. He studied and was confident in his word knowledge. "I felt like my body was opening up and I was able to get the energy in my head in a way it hasn't been for a while."

After Game 21, Edley has a 17–4 record and a one-game lead over Cappelletto, Adam Logan, and the Nigerian émigré Sammy Okasagah. After Game 25, Edley is 20–5, two games ahead of Logan and three ahead of six others, including Cappelletto, whom Joe has just defeated, 495–425, in what he called "the perfect game." And it nearly was. Brian played BLUNGERS and NOVERCAL and LACE-wOOD, while Edley found NEgATRON, MATTOIDS, TRAILSIDE (through the R and L), and, in a 68-point winning play, SHOWBIZ down from an existing S. A computer analysis later gave Joe an efficiency rating of 96.5 percent for the game and Brian 98.9. Remarkable.

"I feel like I'm the old guy," Edley says. "But when I feel good, I feel I can win."

He tells me this after dropping the last three games of that day, to fall to 20–8, in first place by just 44 spread points over David Wiegand, a quiet twenty-six-year-old mortgage underwriter from Portland, Oregon. Randy Hersom, a round, bearded forty-year-old computer programmer from Morganton, North Carolina, also has twenty wins, but is way behind on spread. Cappelletto has nineteen. There are three games left to play the following morning. "Ideally, I'd like to come in first, second, third, or fourth," Edley says. "If I can win two, I can win the tournament."

I ask Edley if he is motivated to prove that he's not over the hill, to stick it to his detractors who snipe behind his back. In truth, he hasn't played well of late, failing to win a tournament since Danbury more than two years earlier. There was the 0–11 run in Waltham, the detached retina, the lackluster performance in Australia. Other experts had proclaimed Edley washed up. "I would [think that] if I were them," Edley says. "But I don't feel like I needed to show anybody anything. I'm beyond that. I've won so much."

Of the forty people who bet on the tournament with Jim Geary, not one took Edley at 5 to 1 (including me, who squandered $20, split four ways, on Matt, Marlon, Lester Schonbrun, and Geary himself).

"I have goals that are reachable," Edley tells me. "It's a reachable goal for me to win it. If it doesn't happen, it doesn't happen." He goes off to eat dinner alone.

If you're not fatigued after twenty-eight games of Scrabble in four days, something is wrong; I caught even Edley napping in the hallway after lunch. I'm running on fumes. After lunch on day four — a win-loss-win-loss morning leaving me 14–11 — I sit on a park bench across from the convention center and watch the Scrabble players return to the building. They look like the zombies in *Night of the Living Dead*.

I continue the up-and-down routine in the afternoon, when Alan Hassenfeld of Hasbro does indeed show. He watches me slam down my pen and storm off after blowing Game 27, but I invite him to pull up a chair to watch me during Game 28 — after I've amassed a 170-point lead. I'm 16–12, and while I won't win twenty, it's about as good a showing as I could have hoped for after the dismal start. When I break it down, it looks okay: 1–6 followed by 15–6. Eric has his best day yet, winning six of seven to raise his record to 15–13. We've both been shying away from Matt, though his performance and mood actually have improved since day one. After a 7–7 start, Matt is 17–11, but with no chance to win significant lucre he doesn't much seem to care.

From thirtieth place, where I am again, I still have a chance to creep into the top fifteen in the division, and I'm determined to win the final three. But I also want to soak up the Scrabble scene. The after-hours games room buzzes. People sit on the floor playing because the dozen or so round tables in the room are filled. Others make and steal words in energetic games of Anagrams. There's a constant crowd around the bulletin boards where the standings and pairings are posted. I play speed Scrabble — five minutes per player, so frenetic you need someone else to keep score — and laugh and talk trash. G.I. Joel belts out Billy Joel's "I'm Moving Out" on the piano. Paul Epstein takes over with "Bésame Mucho." More Scrabble is played. Show tunes are sung. I stay out too late. But I love this place, and these people.

On the final morning of the 2000 National Scrabble Championship, Joe Edley rises at 4:30. For one hour, standing in the closet so as not to wake his wife, he meditates — knees bent slightly, arms spread to the sides like Steve Martin doing King Tut, eyes closed, and lungs modulating deep, steady breaths. Forty minutes of seated meditation follow. Then tai chi. Then a breakfast of organic sourdough bread and water.

For the final three rounds, the top forty players in each division (me included!) are paired in a king-of-the-hill format: first place versus second, third versus fourth, fifth versus sixth, and so on. The pairings are redone after each round. In Game 29, despite absent-mindedly playing EE* early on, Edley beats Wiegand by 64 points. Cappelletto bingos out with GEoTAXIS to defeat Hersom. In Game 30, Wiegand downs Edley by 84 points, while Brian beats Jim Kramer, the proofreader from Minnesota, who also has twenty wins. It sets up the closest finale in Nationals history. Heading into the last round, the standings look like this:

Edley	21–9	+1434
Wiegand	21–9	+1430
Cappelletto	21–9	+1279
Hersom	21–9	+227

Hersom can't win because his spread is too small. For Cappelletto to repeat as champion, he will need to blow out Hersom while Edley and Wiegand play a close match. Whatever happens, the 2000 champion will be decided not by who wins the most games but who has the best point differential. There is no playoff in the Nationals, as at the Worlds.

Cordoned off to give the finalists space, the top two tables are surrounded now: by cameras, by annotators recording every move, by players whose games end quickly. Edley's third straight game against

Wiegand finishes first, and a roar of applause and cheers erupts. Over at Table 19 in Division 2, where I sit, having lost both of my morning games, it's impossible to tell who's won. Then the word filters over: Edlcy. He finds CAPESKIN (a soft leather) to the N and hangs on for a 20-point victory.

Cappelletto and Hersom are still playing. The 1998 champion doesn't know it — in fact, he doesn't even know who won the other match — but now he needs to beat Hersom by 176 points. Brian is up by a bingo late in the game, and trying to find a spot for another one. Then he smiles knowingly: The Q has appeared on his rack and he realizes he will have to eat it. Edley cranes his neck to see the board, and someone whispers in his ear that Brian is winning, but not by enough. The game ends; Brian wins by 63 points. Edley wears his wry smile, the one that looks like a smirk. His wife hugs him and he quietly accepts congratulations from the onlookers. Zen to the end.

"Hard to believe," Edley says matter-of-factly. "Amazing."

And it is. Three players with a chance to win the $25,000 prize. The outcome decided by a total of 112 spread points. Over the tournament's thirty-one games, that's 3.6 points per game — a lucky draw here, a missed play there. I gave away more spread points in a single game.

Brian and Randy are still analyzing their game — neither seems to consider the idea of first congratulating Edley and then returning to complete the review — when a clutch of video and still photographers gathers around the champion at Table 1. John Williams, Edley's boss, pulls over a couple of standing tournament banners, grabs the giant check signed by Alfred M. Butts, and hands Edley a silver Tiffany bowl, in an impromptu awards ceremony for the video news release that will be sent out in time for the evening news. "It's draining after so many days," Edley says. "I'm not a kid anymore."

That's what makes his achievement so remarkable. Edley was the only two-time national champion, and now he's the only three-time winner. In a game dependent on memory, Edley has won the title in his thirties, forties, and fifties — in 1980, 1992, and now 2000, three different decades. His peers, so accustomed to griping about Edley, now are just stunned by him. "I can't believe the motherfucker won it again," says Marlon, who finished thirty-third with a 17–14 mark.

Eventually, most of the other experts offer congratulations, some of them no doubt grudging. Marlon does. Brian does. Hersom and Geary and Ron Tiekert do. Matt Graham, who finished twenty-fifth at 18–13, doesn't, but he does demonstrate the self-centered Scrabble behavior he so often mocks: As John Williams is getting ready to hand out the awards, Matt corners him with a rambling request concerning the tournament's so-called brilliancy prize for best strategic move.

To honor the winner, Eric Chaikin helps whip up a "Scrabblegram" — a message using all one hundred tiles. (This one also happens to be a limerick.) FOR FUN A CHAMPION EDLEY / KEPT VICTORIES GOING QUITE READILy / VERBOSE JOE IS / AN ANAGRAm WIZ / EXULTANT ABOUT HIS WORD MEDLEY. During the ceremony, Edley sits near the rear of the convention hall, at the same table as Cappelletto. G.I. Joel is a table away, upset over finishing fourteenth but happy his brother took fourth in my division. When another Division 2 player collects a prize, Rich Lupo, the Providence bar owner, leans over and whispers to me, "I saw that guy in the bathroom between rounds eating sardines."

After Brian accepts the $10,000 for second place, Edley walks past him to the front of the room, but they don't pause to shake hands or embrace, one champion to the next. "Many of you might know I've not done as well in tournaments the last couple of years," Edley tells the couple hundred players who have stuck around. He credits diet, exercise, and his acupuncturist. "If I can use being a three-time champion for any good," he says, "I'll use it for promoting Scrabble to the outside world."

To assess the role of luck in this game, I need only compare my 16–15 record and Edley's 22–9. You make your own luck, the cliché goes, and the best way to do that is to be innately talented, and to prepare.

Lacking innate talent leaves one possibility. It took me two years, capped by thirty-one games, to understand fully that intelligence and good fortune carry one only so far, and when I peruse the leader board and see Edley's name atop it — Edley, who will once again be rated over 2000, who will resume studying words the weekend after the tournament, who will return to NSA headquarters the fol-

lowing Monday and rate the tournament and create new board diagrams and continue to live a life of Scrabble — I'm not surprised
at all.

Does this make Edley the best Scrabble player of all time? Does it
mean that luck played no role in his third crown? Mike Baron, the
Edley detractor and Cappelletto booster, later points out that, as the
top seed, Brian played the toughest field statistically in the first
eleven games of the tourney, which were a round robin; Edley had
an easier go. Jim Geary, who finished eighteenth, praises Edley's
achievement; Jim is one top player who truly doesn't resent Joe's success. But he also cites a Scrabble truism: In the strongest overall field
in the world, the winner needs to be damn good *and* damn lucky. In
one four-round stretch, Geary notes, Edley posted the tournament's
high-scoring game three times.

"Does this make him some kind of supergenius?" Geary writes to
me afterward. "No, Scrabble doesn't work that way. You have to play
well, of course . . . but by and large those 550-point games are born
of having things go really, really well for one game. Additionally, in
those games, things are going pretty shitty for your opponent. The
other thing to note is that those games are remarkably easy on the
system. And [for Edley] they were between Rounds 21 and 24. What
fortune!

"In the long run," Geary says of luck,

> it's going to balance out, but thirty-one games isn't the long run. With
> ten other fantastic players in the field, you can't win the tourney with
> balanced luck. And you *really* can't with bad luck.
>
> I'm DEFINITELY NOT saying that Edley isn't a star, but I do say that
> people overstate the significance of small strings of statistical events
> based on their grouping. Granted this is the case in many, many com-
> petitive endeavors, but that doesn't mean that Joe Edley is the best
> player or that he was even the best player that week.
>
> I understand that that's just the way the game goes. If lightning
> should strike and I win the World Scrabble Championship, I won't kid
> myself too much about what it means.
>
> But I'll be happy.

*　　*　　*

I apply Geary's logic to my own game. Did I have bad luck or was I just bad? Or some combination of both? Or is it not really relevant once you leave the upper echelons of the game, because only with near-complete word knowledge is the game truly meaningful? Leaving aside the last, because, unlike Geary, I believe you can scale down the game to accommodate the incomplete vocabularies possessed by all but the top ten or twenty players, I had my share of fortune in Providence, including a 588-point game (the ninth-highest in the entire tournament) and a 553-point game. I saw more than half of the blanks (35 in the 31 games), and just under half of the S's (57 instead of 62). The average rating of my opponents was above mine. So I probably finished about where, logically and statistically, I should have.

Understanding that, and accepting the limitations imposed by lack of word knowledge, does not make it palatable. In other words, it's not just about the words. Take away the first and last days, I tell myself and anyone who will listen, and I would have been in the hunt. I went 1–9 on those two days and 15–6 in between. My pal Eric Chaikin was 0–10 and 15–6 in the same stretch. Eric the committed logophile and me the full-time Scrabble player. And we lost nineteen out of twenty games! You could line up the twenty highest-rated players in North America, never mind some of the Division 2 meatballs to whom we lost, and we wouldn't go 1–19. We could blame probability, those awful tiles, Matt's oxygen tank, the woman at the next table humming the *Jeopardy!* theme song. But we don't.

We blame ourselves. In games, as in life, you get what you deserve. I played like a blue-hair in at least four games. I can't explain why. And while both Eric and I made spirited comebacks, they ended with a thud. We sat next to each other at Tables 18 and 19 for a final, ignominious defeat, interrupted by the applause cascading from Division 1. Eric had the word SAXTUBA on his rack, which he shuffled around to form its anagram, SUBTAXA, but neither word fit on the board. My opponent, Alan Stern of Los Angeles, almost apologetically played STRiNGS three turns from the end of an undistinguished game to win. It had to end anticlimactically, I thought at that moment. It's what I deserved.

The players say their goodbyes, and the convention center empties.

I stagger around the cavernous space like a boxer who went fifteen rounds but can't remember any of them, saddened by my perceived failure, by another ho-hum result in an event on which I had placed so much import. Two years, I think, and for what? For 16–15? For mediocrity? *This* was my valedictory? Then I spot Edley, and I congratulate him again, and I tell him that he has been more influential than anyone in teaching me the game, and teaching me how to think, and how to win, even if I didn't here, and I thank him.

"*You* did the work," Joe tells me.

And maybe I did. No, *I did.* I came into this sport with a limited set of the requisite skills for becoming a real player — some math aptitude, some language facility, some competitive drive, a latent but untapped predisposition toward obsession. But I didn't possess the full range — the innate memory gift, the deep spatial perception, the monkish discipline. I just wasn't wired like the masters.

If I knew this before I started, why didn't I stop? What was I trying to prove? It was never entirely clear what attracted me to the game. A search for a quirky story — something to write about — was part of it. But I'd written hundreds of stories in my career, and I'd never wanted to do what my subjects did: sell junk bonds or prosecute white-collar criminals or negotiate athlete contracts or run minor-league baseball teams. Scrabble turned out to have a deeper connection. It recalled childhood snubs and competitive fears, the words of an editor who on a job interview lumped me favorably with the "insecure overachievers" the paper liked to hire (I got the job). Scrabble gave me a place to address my "issues" off of a therapist's couch. Recognition, expertise, validation — not to mention strategy, tactics, words, and winning — all turned out to matter more than I had imagined. And all turned out to be attainable. I might not ever find AUBERGiNES or WATERZOOI, but I could appreciate their intrinsic beauty, and create some of my own.

In the biggest tournament of my career, I finished 51st out of 105 players. But Edley's words — "You did the work" — make me feel as if I have achieved something important. I don't know why, but during my final three losses, I couldn't purge the *Rocky* theme from my head.

Flashback to the first morning of the tournament. I bump into Chris Cree in the hotel elevator. "I was thinking about you last night," he twangs. "I wanted to say this in front of more people." He stops talking and laughs, because he's not saying it in front of anyone but me, his wife, and a stranger. "But I wanted to tell you that I'm really impressed with what you've done in such a short time. You should be proud. It's like going down to a golf club never having played and becoming a five handicap. Really impressive."

We walk to the front of the convention center. I leave Chris and his wife there to smoke and I ride the escalator to the third floor, where we'll play. As I greet the other Scrabblers I wear a fat grin, like a celebrity at his own roast.

So what if I went on to lose six of seven games that day? Into this world of brilliant minds and misfits I waded à la Plimpton, ill-prepared to play at the highest levels. But I wasn't laughed at or humiliated by anyone but me. And I found that I shared more with the word freaks than I thought.

I probably won't ever see a 1900 or 2000 rating, and I won't be able to play the game, as Jim Geary told me, "the way it's meant to be played." But then I never imagined I'd get as far as I did. When G.I. Joel won the Worlds, he said it validated his existence, and I laughed. But now the number attached to my name, the one I wore for so long like a dunce cap, has finally come to validate mine. I think back to my initial 761 rating, which ranked me about two thousandth of twenty-three hundred in North America, and my sheet with the crossed-out two-letter words, and playing EXO* and YER*, and my snaillike advance, and the heart-pounding agony every time I tore open an envelope from the NSA bearing a new rating, and the usual subsequent humiliation at being linked to the number at the end of the row bearing my name.

After a four-hour journey back to New York, I drop off Matt and his oxygen tank on the East Side and Eric at a friend's in SoHo. When I return to Brooklyn, Marlon is waiting on the stoop of my building; he had taken a different ride to the city, but now he needs a place to crash. I head to bed, leaving him lying on the living room carpet, calculating our new ratings. At 7:00 the next morning, he's in the same spot, wrapped in a polka-dot sheet, pen, paper, and calculator discarded beside him.

"Well?" I ask him. "What is it?"

"Seventeen thirty-five, if I got it right," he says. "You there."

It's a number that intimidated me not long ago; *real* experts were rated 1735. It's a number of stature. A number that defines me as the 180th or so best Scrabble player in North America. A number that, at least for now, I can live with.

1735. I'm there.

Marlon holds out a fist for me to knock with mine. Which I do. I slowly nod and my mouth curls into a smile. I savor the feeling for a moment. And then we play a couple of games.

Epilogue

I DON'T SEE Matt Graham for several weeks after the Nationals. When I do, in Washington Square Park, the sight of him jars me. A red scar runs from one side of his neck to the other, just below his chin. Matt won't tell me what happened, but he says he's stopped drinking because of it.

In the months that follow, Matt rededicates himself to Scrabble. "There's too much I don't know anymore," he says. So he studies. Matt wins a tournament for the first time since 1998. In five events over seven months, he earns about $2,000 and his rating climbs from 1909 to 2024, the fourth highest in North America. That guarantees him a spot on the U.S. team at the next Worlds, scheduled for late 2001 in Las Vegas.

Despite his winnings, Matt is broke. He isn't optimistic about landing a possible full-time job at the Conan O'Brien show and hasn't looked for other work. The abstinence from alcohol is brief. "Life's anxieties stack up," he says.

Marlon Hill is still living in his childhood home, still studying words, still short on cash. "Nothing changes. Still the devil causing trouble with the righteous people," he says when I call one night and find him playing Scrabble with his mother. Marlon makes some money painting houses with his uncle and doing taxes for people in his neighborhood, but it doesn't last long. "I can't go nowhere," he says.

"It all dried up." But Marlon retains his equanimity. "I'm a do what I have to do," he says. "Whatever I have to do to survive, I do."

He does finish writing his book, which he titles *PanAfrikanist Rhapsody*, and starts another. When I ask if he'll try for a wild-card slot on the U.S. team at the Worlds — his 1852 rating is too low to qualify outright — Marlon says he may apply for Ghanaian citizenship and play for the West African nation instead. "I was going to do that aside from Scrabble," he says. Marlon already has settled on a Ghanaian name, Ampha Adom, meaning "blessings from God." When I ask why Ghana would give him citizenship, he says, "I'm a pan-Africanist. I got something to offer."

Joe Edley socks away his $25,000 prize money from the Nationals. In December, he has another medical drama: a kidney stone and an enlarged prostate, discovered just before he and his wife are to direct a ten-day Scrabble cruise along the Mexican Riviera. He goes anyway, wearing a catheter.

Edley, naturally, takes it all in stride. He practices new techniques to help his ailing body stay sharp; in one, he closes his eyes tightly and stares at the darkness, then opens them and focuses intensely. "Because of my peculiar biology, it seems to have a very strong effect," he says.

In February, for the third time in four years, Edley wins the Eastern Championships in Danbury, with an incredible 17–3 record. It pushes his rating to 2045, second only to Brian Cappelletto's 2072.

Lester Schonbrun's rating dips into the 1800s. He says he probably won't try to qualify for the Worlds; the prospect of relearning all of those British words is too daunting, the likelihood of success too small, and the threat to his *OWL* game too big. Lester is sixty-five, and feeling it. "I want to hang onto any prowess I have as long as I can," he says. "I'm looking at the Worlds as something that's potentially going to confuse me." In his spare time, he's compiling a leftist's dictionary of cultural and political terms, from abortion to the French Revolution to the labor theory of value to Vietnam. "To me, it's an anti-bullshit dictionary," he says.

*　　*　　*

G.I. Joel Sherman is, as he once put it, "the same": playing on-line word games incessantly, venturing from the Bronx rarely, climbing up on his chair at the club faithfully, looking after me paternalistically. "You played that endgame right," he says one night, nodding in approbation, just as he did three years ago when he wanted to know whether I was hooked. I find Joel's constancy a joy.

Joel, however, sees his anchor slipping away. In seven tournaments since the Nationals — from Bird-in-Hand to Atlanta to Phoenix — Joel says he has made but two memorable plays: QUARTERING through QUA and T (which he later extended to HEADQUAR-TERING) and INGUINAL through the first N. "I still have moments of brilliance, and an occasional good find," he tells me, "but I'm really feeling like my skills are eroding at an alarming pace, and it scares the hell out of me to contemplate my future if I can't be a prize-taking force in this game much longer."

And me? In calculating my rating after the Nationals, Marlon was off by 2 points. I actually wind up at 1733.

So content am I with my new number (and so overwhelmed with completing this book) that I don't study or play for several months. When I do finally enter a tournament — in November on Cape Cod — I feel liberated from the race to a goal; I even bring along my girl-friend. No pressure, no urgency, no panic, just pleasure in playing. But this also means I'm not focused on winning. I post a 5–7 record against the other experts and my rating slips to 1710.

Another three months go by — the book gets edited, I take a vaca-tion, I return to my time-sucking job at *The Wall Street Journal* — and still I haven't resumed studying. But it's February, and Danbury again, and my journey suddenly feels complete: I have risen from the fourth division to the third to the second and now to the first. In the opening round I am matched against none other than Joe Edley. It's teacher against pupil, and as we sit down to play I find myself mim-icking the master's calm. It doesn't help. Going first, Edley plucks — no, Edley wills — both blanks from the bag. I deduce this after he plays JOrAM for 42 points; he wouldn't have squandered a blank for so few points unless he had the other one. Two turns later, he plays FATIGUe to go up 151–20. Later, he finds DYSTOCIA and BALLONS, and I lose to my mentor, 495–317.

I don't play especially badly in Danbury, but I don't draw well; in one game, my opponent, Jan Dixon, gets both blanks and 11 of the 12 E's (not whining; just a fact). I do have one fabulous sequence: I open with QAID for 28, challenge off my opponent's phony bingo, lay down EIRENIC for 65, watch my opponent wrongly challenge it, and then triple-triple with SCOTcHES for 158 points and a 251–0 lead. But that game is one of just seven wins against thirteen losses, and my rating slips to 1694.

It's a number I can't live with. The next morning, on the subway to work, I whip out a list of five-letter words, and the cycle begins anew.

Brooklyn, New York
March 2001

APPENDIX

As I noted 370 pages ago, I wrote this book according to the rules of competitive Scrabble. Whenever I wondered whether a word was a word, I consulted the game's bibles: the *Official Tournament and Club Word List* and/or *Merriam-Webster's Collegiate Dictionary, Tenth Edition*. As a result, almost every two- through fifteen-letter word in the text that isn't capitalized, hyphenated, contracted, foreign, part of a multiword phrase, or marked with an asterisk is playable in Scrabble. Occasionally, however, I ran across words that weren't in either source or I took the liberty of creating new words. I wanted to neologize even more (in fact, I just did). But I usually bowed to the books; for instance, I wrote "wanna-be" with a hyphen, as *Merriam-Webster's* prescribes, when "wannabe" was what I wanted it to be. So, for the sake of accuracy and anality, and for the true word freaks out there, I offer the following list of words that appear in *Word Freak* but are unacceptable in Scrabble.

alphagram	industrywide	porcupined
anamonic	lemme	prefinals
antigram	logological	prematch
bingoed	logophile	pygeum
boardful	midmorning	pyroglutanic
bonusable	midtournament	rainman
brainiacs	midtwenties	schlumpy
coffeehousing	mistracked	staircasing
crackheads	moneyless	sublist
dammit	multiword	subluxury
decommercialize	muttonchopped	superexpert
detoxifier	neologize	supergenius
duh	neurolinguistic	superhustlers
est	newbie	supervocalics
expertdom	nonbingo	suphedrine
experthood	nondeclarative	tileheads
filterless	nonstudiers	unconflicted
flashcard	outbingoed	unenjoyable
flatlined	outsourced	unpleated
geekiness	overpacked	unspooling
gonna	palmful	wanna
gotta	parkies	windowless
homeys	picolinate	wordie
hydroxybutyrate	piercings	zitherlike

SOURCES

This is a work of nonfiction. No names have been changed. All of the dialogue is real.

Word Freak is based on my personal experiences over more than three years and thousands of hours of playing and watching competitive Scrabble. In addition to moving more tiles than Bill Gates's roofer, I spent hundreds of hours in formal interviews and informal conversation with dozens of current and former Scrabble players and others affiliated with this game and the games business. Everyone portrayed in these pages knew that I was writing a book in which they might be included. Any errors, however, are mine alone.

In the course of my research, I did rely on numerous printed sources. What follows is a list of books, manuscripts, newsletters, and magazine articles that were important to my work or that I would recommend for those interested in the many subjects I could only touch on. A few sources merit special mention. G. Wayne Miller's excellent *Toy Wars* supplied essential background on the history of Hasbro and Mattel. More than twenty-five years of back issues of what today is known as *Scrabble News* helped fill in blanks on the history of the competitive game. Joe Edley and John D. Williams, Jr.'s, *Everything Scrabble* is the best how-to manual in print. Joel Wapnick's CD-ROM "A Champion's Strategies," originally published in book form in 1986 as *The Champion's Strategy for Winning at Scrabble Brand Crossword Game,* was a strategic guide, while expert Darrell Day's monograph "Scrabble Tournament Success" offered indispensable practical advice. The three newsletters published in the early 1990s — Nick Ballard's *Medleys,* Jim Geary's *JG Newsletter,* and Brian Sheppard's *Rack Your Brain* — were endlessly informative, entertaining, and challenging. On words and wordplay, Dmitri Borgmann's *Language on Vacation,* Ross Eckler's *Making the Alphabet Dance,* and Chris Cole's *Wordplay* all make terrific bathroom reading.

Augarde, Tony. *The Oxford Guide to Word Games.* Oxford, England: Oxford University Press, 1984.

Ballard, Nick. *Medleys.* Seattle: Nick Ballard, January 1991–December 1993.

Baron, Mike, and Brian Sheppard. *The Complete Wordbook.* Corrales, N.M.: Wordbooks & Listmats, 1994.

———, and Jim Homan. *The Complete Blankbook.* Albuquerque, N.M.: Wordbooks & Listmats, 1992.

Bergerson, Howard W. *Palindromes and Anagrams.* New York: Dover Publications, 1973.

Bombaugh, C. C. *Oddities and Curiosities of Words and Literature.* New York: Dover Publications, 1961.

Borgmann, Dmitri A. *Beyond Language: Adventures in Word and Thought.* New York: Charles Scribner's Sons, 1967.

——. *Language on Vacation: An Olio of Orthographical Oddities.* New York: Charles Scribner's Sons, 1965.

The Chambers Dictionary. Edinburgh, Scotland: Chambers Harrap, 1998.

Chamish, Barry. "Masters of the Tiles." *The Atlantic Monthly,* June 1987.

Cockburn, Alexander. *Idle Passion: Chess and the Dance of Death.* New York: Village Voice/Simon and Schuster, 1974.

Cole, Chris. *Wordplay: A Curious Dictionary of Language Oddities.* New York: Sterling Publishing, 1999.

Conklin, Drue K., ed. *The Official Scrabble Players Handbook,* New York: Harmony Books, 1974.

Day, Darrell. "Scrabble Tournament Success." Plano, Tex.: Day Marketing Concepts, 1991.

Eckler, A. Ross. *Making the Alphabet Dance: Recreational Word Play.* New York: St. Martin's Griffin, 1996.

——, ed. *Word Ways: The Journal of Recreational Linguistics.* Morristown, N.J.: A. Ross Eckler, 1968–present.

Edley, Joe. *The Official Scrabble Puzzle Book.* New York: Pocket Books, 1997.

——, and Williams, John D., Jr. *Everything Scrabble.* New York: Pocket Books, 1994.

Ericsson, K. Anders, ed. *The Road to Excellence: The Acquisition of Expert Performance in the Arts and Sciences, Sports, and Games.* Mahwah, N.J.: Lawrence Erlbaum Associates, 1996.

Frank, Alan. "The Tournament Anagram Book: Volume 1: 2- to 8-Letter Words." Bowling Green Station, N.Y.: Matchups, 1998.

Geary, Jim. *JG Newsletter.* Phoenix: Jim Geary, February 1996–February 1997.

Goldman, Stu. *Confessions of a Compulsive Tile Pusher.* San Francisco: Stu Goldman Publications, 1992.

Grant, Annette. "Quiety Meets Rebanana in Brooklyn." *Harper's,* December 1974.

Harridge, Barry, Lesley Mack, and Geoff Wright, eds. *Redwood Scrabble International Edition.* Dingley, Australia: Hinkler Book Distributors, 1997.

Holden, Anthony. *Big Deal: One Year as a Professional Poker Player.* London: Bantam Press, 1990.

Kaye, Marvin. *The Story of Monopoly, Silly Putty, Bingo, Twister, Frisbee, Scrabble, Et Cetera.* Briarcliff Manor, N.Y.: Stein and Day, 1977.

Landau, Sidney I. *Dictionaries: The Art and Craft of Lexicography.* New York: Cambridge University Press, 1989.

Levy, David. *Chess and Computers.* Potomac, Md.: Computer Science Press, 1976.

Merriam-Webster's Collegiate Dictionary, Tenth Edition. Springfield, Mass.: Merriam-Webster, 1999.

Miller, G. Wayne. *Toy Wars: The Epic Struggle Between G.I. Joe, Barbie, and the Companies That Make Them.* New York: Times Books, 1998.

Morice, David. *Alphabet Avenue: Wordplay in the Fast Lane.* Chicago: Chicago Review Press, 1997.

Morton, Herbert C. *The Story of Webster's Third: Philip Gove's Controversial Dictionary and Its Critics.* New York: Cambridge University Press, 1994.

Murray, K. M. Elisabeth. *Caught in the Web of Words: James A. H. Murray and the Oxford English Dictionary.* New Haven, Conn.: Yale University Press, 1977.

Norton, Clark. "Wise to the Words." *San Jose Mercury News,* August 23, 1987.

The Official Scrabble Players Dictionary. Springfield, Mass.: Merriam-Webster, 1978.

The Official Scrabble Players Dictionary, Second Edition. Springfield, Mass.: Merriam-Webster, 1991.

The Official Scrabble Players Dictionary, Third Edition. Springfield, Mass.: Merriam-Webster, 1996.

Official Scrabble Words, Third Edition. Edinburgh, Scotland: Chambers Harrap, 1994.

Official Scrabble Words, Fourth Edition. Edinburgh, Scotland: Chambers Harrap, 1999.

Official Tournament and Club Word List. Springfield, Mass.: Merriam-Webster, 1997.

Orleans, Jacob. *The Scrabble Word Guide.* New York: Grosset & Dunlap, 1953.

———, and Edmund Jacobson. *How to Win at Scrabble.* New York: Grosset & Dunlap, 1953.

Pinker, Steven. *Words and Rules: The Ingredients of Language.* New York: Basic Books, 1999.

Plimpton, George. *Paper Lion.* New York: Harper & Row, 1965.

Pratt, Daniel L. "A Brief History of The Official Scrabble Players Dictionary," *Verbatim,* Winter 1999.

Price, S. L. "Your Words Against Mine." *Sports Illustrated,* December 12, 1995.

Rayment, Tim. "Irritable Vowel Syndrome." *Sunday Times of London,* January 11, 1998.

Scarne, John. *Scarne's Encyclopedia of Games.* New York: Harper & Row, 1973.

Sheppard, Brian. *Rack Your Brain.* Concord, Mass.: Sheppard Company, July 1993–September 1994.

Squire, Larry R., and Kandel, Eric R. *Memory: From Mind to Molecules.* New York: Scientific American Library, 1999.

Waitzkin, Fred. *Searching for Bobby Fischer: The Father of a Prodigy Observes the World of Chess.* New York: Penguin Books, 1988.

Wallace, Robert. "A Little Business in the Country." *Life,* December 14, 1953.

Wapnick, Joel. "A Champion's Strategies." Montreal: Joel Wapnick, 1999 (CD-ROM).

Watkins, Mark. *Wordgame.* El Dorado Hills, Calif.: Mark Watkins, February 2000–present.

Webster's Third New International Dictionary of the English Language, Unabridged. Springfield, Mass.: Merriam-Webster, 1961.

Winchester, Simon. *The Professor and the Madman: A Tale of Murder, Insanity, and the Making of the Oxford English Dictionary.* New York: HarperCollins, 1998.

ACKNOWLEDGMENTS

Matt Graham, Marlon Hill, Joe Edley, Joel Sherman, Lester Schonbrun, Ron Tiekert, Jim Geary, Mike Baron, and Eric Chaikin let me into their lives, welcomed me into their world, and taught me how to play. I couldn't have written this book without them.

I'm grateful to the members of Scrabble Club 56 in Manhattan, the Washington Square Parkies, and everyone else against whom I played a game of Scrabble, especially the losers. Space permits me to mention only a large handful of devotees by name, but I would like to recognize the following:

Scott Appel, Phil Appleby, Paul Avrin, David Boys, Sheree Bykofsky, Brian Cappelletto, Charlie Carroll, James Cherry, John Chew, Chris and Kathy Cree, Lynn Cushman, Steve Dennis, Pamina Deutsch, Mark DiBattista, Jan Dixon, Bob Ellickson, Robert Felt, Diane Firstman, Gregg Foster, David Gibson, Daniel Goldman, Dominic Grillo, Roz Grossman, Matt Hopkins, Merrill Kaitz, Laura Klein, Mark Landsberg, Matthew Laufer, Joseph Leonard, David Lipschutz, Adam Logan, Ben Loiterstein, Richie Lund, Andrea Carla Michaels, Ann Mirabito, Joan Mocine, Rita Norr, Mark Nyman, Lisa Odom, Sam Orbaum, Steve Pellinen, the late Roy Peshkin, Steve Pfeiffer, Sal Piro, Nigel Richards, Sherrie Saint John, Ann Sanfedele, Brian Sheppard, Larry Sherman, Hilda Siegel, Martin Smith, Susi Tiekert, Audrey Tumbarello, Joel Wapnick, Mark Watkins, David Webb, Ginger White, Margaret Bauer Williams, Steve Williams, and Trey Wright.

Though he rarely wins a game against me these days, John D. Williams, Jr., was unflinchingly supportive of this book and my quest for Scrabble greatness. His dedication to and love for the game have helped the competitive scene flourish. I'd also like to thank Jane Ratsey Williams, Kathy Hummel, and Yvonne Gillispie at the National Scrabble Association for catering patiently to my journalistic needs. At Hasbro, I'm grateful to Alan Hassenfeld, Dave Wilson, Wayne Charness, and Mark Morris for providing insight and access. Thanks also to Philip Nelkon and Ian Anderson of Mattel.

I am indebted to Robert Butts for allowing me, on several visits to his home and office, to pore through his uncle Alfred's personal papers. John Nason's files and reminiscences aided my writing about Selchow & Righter. Beryl Harrison at the Booth Library in Newtown, Connecticut, tracked down material about the game's manufacturing roots. Language maven Paul Dickson shared his copious files. Thanks to them all.

Paul Steiger and Daniel Hertzberg of *The Wall Street Journal* generously granted me a leave of absence to go play a board game, no doubt a first in the annals of journalism. I'd also like to thank *Journal* editors Stephen J. Adler,

Joanne Lipman, Jonathan Dahl, Laura Landro, and Jeffrey Trachtenberg, and the newspaper's toy-industry reporters, Lisa Bannon and Joseph Pereira.

Jonathan and Lynn Hock were unflagging boosters, even if they now claim my obsession ruined the game for them. Adam Sexton enthusiastically endorsed the idea for this book when I wasn't so sure, and his comments greatly improved the manuscript. Thanks to Lampros Fatsis and Dan Margolies for their long-ago infatuation with Scrabble, Andrew Lenney for our high school games, and Mariann Caprino for unleashing the Scrabble monster within. My friends Melissa Block, Charles Heaphy, Alex Reyes, Bob Rifkin and Jane Levin, Amy Stevens, and David Stone and Robin Aronson put me up during my travels or just put up with me.

The advice, wisdom, and good sense of my agent, Robert Shepard, and my editor, Eamon Dolan, inform every page of this book. I've been fortunate to work with two such talented professionals. Thanks also to Emily Little, Jayne Yaffe Kemp, Martha Kennedy, and Walter Vatter at Houghton Mifflin, and to Leslie Goldman.

Finally, as G.I. Joel Sherman did after winning the 1997 World Scrabble Championship, I'd like to thank the late Alfred Mosher Butts for inventing this great American game. I don't know where I'd be without it either.